Green Salad Seasons

THEODORE CLYMER

Ginn and Company

Acknowledgments

Grateful acknowledgment is made to the following publishers, authors, and agents for permission to use and adapt copyrighted materials:

Atheneum Publishers, Inc., for "The Long Way Around" by Jean McCord. Adapted from "The Long Way Around" (pp. 55-67) from *Deep Where the Octopi Lie* by Jean McCord with the permission of Atheneum Publishers. Copyright © 1968 by Jean McCord.

Curtis Brown, Ltd., for "I Like Skunks," adapted from *We Took to the Woods* by Louise Dickinson Rich. Reprinted by permission of Curtis Brown, Ltd. Copyright © 1942 by Louise Dickinson Rich. Also for "The Baobab Tree" from *When the Stones Were Soft* by Eleanor B. Heady. Reprinted by permission of Curtis Brown, Ltd. Copyright © 1968 by Eleanor Heady.

Doubleday & Company, Inc., for "Someday," copyright © 1956 by Royal Publications from the book *Earth Is Room Enough* by Isaac Asimov. Reprinted by permission of Doubleday & Company, Inc. Also for "The Way Through the Woods," copyright 1910 by Rudyard Kipling from *Rudyard Kipling's Verse: Definitive Edition.* Reprinted by permission of the National Trust and Doubleday & Company, Inc.

Elsevier-Dutton Publishing Company, Inc., for the poem "Lacy Clouds Drift By" from *Wind, Sand and Sky* by Rebecca Caudill. Copyright © 1976 by Rebecca Caudill. Reprinted by permission of the publisher, E. P. Dutton. Also for the poem "The Flower-Fed Buffaloes" by Vachel Lindsay. Reprinted by permission of Hawthorn Properties (Elsevier-Dutton Publishing Co., Inc.). From the book *Going to the Stars* by Vachel Lindsay. Copyright © 1926, 1954, Vachel Lindsay.

Elsevier/Nelson Books for the adaptation "Saved from a Subterranean Pit" by Vincent H. Gaddis. Reprinted by permission of Elsevier/Nelson Books. From the book *Courage in Crisis* by Vincent H. Gaddis. Copyright © 1973 by Vincent H. Gaddis.

Farrar, Straus and Giroux, Inc., for *The Eyes of the Amaryllis* by Natalie Babbitt. Copyright © 1977 by Natalie Babbitt. Reprinted by permission of Farrar, Straus and Giroux, Inc.

Harcourt Brace Jovanovich, Inc., for "Karen Pryor and the Creative Porpoise" by Margery Facklam. Abridged and adapted from *Wild Animals, Gentle Women,* copyright © 1978 by Margery Facklam. Reprinted by permission of Harcourt Brace Jovanovich, Inc. Also for the poem "Yarns" by Carl Sandburg, abridged from selection #45 in *The People, Yes* by Carl Sandburg, copyright 1936 by Harcourt Brace Jovanovich, Inc.; copyright 1964 by Carl Sandburg. Reprinted by permission of the publisher.

Contents

A Generation

In our families and in many other areas of our lives, each of us comes into contact with people of other generations—with people who are much older or much younger than we are. The following stories show what it means to be "a generation away."

You will discover how the generations can learn from each other. You will see a very old person protecting the rights of the very young. You will read how a young golfer, Nancy Lopez, is supported and encouraged in her career by her parents. Finally, you will see how conflicts between the generations can lead to understanding and growth.

Will you see yourself in any of these stories? Start finding out by turning the page.

way

Your World

Georgia Douglas Johnson

Your world is as big as you make it.
I know, for I used to abide
In the narrowest nest in a corner,
My wings pressing close to my side.

But I sighted the distant horizon
Where the sky line encircled the sea
And I throbbed with a burning desire
To travel this immensity.

I battered the cordons around me
And cradled my wings on the breeze
Then soared to the uttermost reaches
With rapture, with power, with ease!

Spelling Bee

Laurene Chambers Chinn

It takes courage to make changes in
our lives and to accept new things.
How do Ellen and her mother both show
this kind of courage in the next story?

With the closing of the door, Ellen left one of her lives behind
and entered upon the other. She moved slowly down the long
flight of stairs that flanked the restaurant, and turned left
toward the hotel.

"No use eating dinner there," Mama had protested. "You
can eat at home and go later."

"We are supposed to have dinner at the hotel, Mama. Ellen
spoke the word "Mama" in the Cantonese[1] way, as if it were
two words, with a quick, light stress on the second half.
"When you are American, you do as Americans do."

"No harm being Chinese," Mama said.

Mama wasn't going to the high school with her tonight.

[1]Cantonese (kan'tə nēz'): of Canton, a city in China, of its people or their
speech

Mama never went with her. On the street, Ellen shut out the world of home. This is easy when you speak Cantonese in one world and American in the other. Still, when you have won the county spelling bee, you can't help wanting your mother to watch you in the regional match. . . .

A big bus carried the thirty-five county champions from the dinner at the hotel to the high school. At eight o'clock the curtains parted revealing the audience to the boys and girls on stage. Thirty-five boys and girls on stage, thought Ellen, feeling a little bit sad, and thirty-four mothers in the audience. Henry was there, with his girl friend, Dorothy. Now that Father was gone, Henry was head of the family. It ought to be enough that her brother was in the audience.

The teacher said, "Botany," and smiled at Ellen. They had finished with the sixth-grade spelling books and were starting on the seventh. Twenty-eight girls and boys were still on stage.

"Physician," said the teacher. Henry was a physician. Less than a year ago he had been an intern. He worked hard. It isn't easy to establish confidence when you wear an alien face.

"Intense," Miss Kinsman said. If Mama had learned to speak English, maybe she wouldn't be so intensely shy. Mama had wrapped herself in her black sateen Chinese coat and trousers, wrapped herself also in her cloak of language, and refused to leave her kitchen even to buy groceries or a hat. Did Mama own a hat? Yes, Henry had bought one for her to wear at Father's funeral.

"Tragedy," said Miss Kinsman. They were in eighth-grade spelling now, and nineteen contestants remained.

"Tragedy," said Ellen, smiling at Miss Kinsman. "T-r-a-g-e-d-y."

Mrs. Dillard had begun helping her after school when she became school champion, and they redoubled their labor after she won the county spelling bee. Mrs. Dillard had said, "Barring accidents, you might even win and represent our region at the national spelling bee in Washington."

Now, after an hour in the eighth-grade speller, with fewer than a dozen champions still on stage, Ellen was beginning to think Mrs. Dillard might be right. Ellen might win. Only a nitwit would want not to win. Well, then, she was a nitwit.

One of the judges rose. "Perhaps it is time to go into the old Blueback," he suggested.

A sigh rippled up among the contestants. Mrs. Dillard had taken Ellen all the way through the Blueback. "Trust your hunches," Mrs. Dillard had said, and her eyes had grown dreamy. "My goodness, I'd be proud to see a pupil of mine win the national spelling bee!"

But Ellen didn't want to go to Washington!

The teacher was smiling at Ellen. "Deign."

The girl next to Ellen had just spelled "reign." Ellen recalled the section, a group of words with silent g's. Ellen spelled, "D-a-n-e." She turned blindly to leave the stage. She had betrayed her talent for spelling, and she had betrayed Mrs. Dillard, and she had betrayed Henry.

"Just a minute," said Miss Kinsman. "I wanted you to spell d-e-i-g-n, meaning *condescend*, but you have correctly spelled its homonym, and capital letters aren't necessary by the rules of the contest."

"O-o-o-h," wailed Ellen. It's a fine thing when you try to miss a word and can't. "Could I—could I have a drink, please?" she gulped.

The judge said, "We will have intermission until the bell rings."

With a whoop the champions scattered. Ellen hurried down the aisle toward Henry and Dorothy. Dorothy hugged her. "I had no idea you were so smart, little genius."

Henry said, "I'd be very proud to see you win, Ellen."

"I don't want to win." Suddenly she knew why. She put the knowledge into a rush of words, speaking in Cantonese. "To go to Washington without my mother would advertise she is old-fashioned and very shy and goes nowhere—not even here—with me."

Henry's face paled. His eyes turned from Ellen's and met Dorothy's. Ellen rushed into the hall. She wished the tears would quit coming in her eyes. She knew what she would do. She wouldn't win, but she would stay as long as she could without winning.

After three rounds in the Blueback, six contestants remained. Miss Kinsman turned to the "Words Difficult to Spell" section at the back. "Abeyance," she said.

Acerbity. Ache. Acquiesce. Amateur. Queer spellings remind you of other peoples in other times who have used these words in other ways. Language is a highway, linking all peoples and all ages. Mama was wrong to use language as a wall.

Caprice. Carouse. Catastrophe. . . .

Three contestants remained. Miss Kinsman turned to a page of words of seven and eight syllables. Henry was alone at the back now. Maybe Dorothy had got bored and gone home. Ellen thought of her mother. Thirty-four mothers had driven in from thirty-four neighboring counties, and Mama hadn't come six blocks to see the contest.

"Incomprehensibility," said Miss Kinsman. It was a lonely word. Things build up inside a person that other people don't comprehend. And people can't comprehend the shyness of a foreign-born mother unless they've had a foreign-born mother.

"Indestructibility," said Miss Kinsman. Ellen had risen, but she wasn't listening. Two people had come in at the back. One was Dorothy. The other was completely familiar, yet, in the hat and dress, completely strange. They went to sit beside Henry, and Mama was smiling at Ellen on the stage. Ellen had lived all her life with that loving smile.

"I'm sorry. I didn't hear the word." Turning to Miss Kinsman, Ellen raised her voice for the proud announcement, "My mother just came in."

"Indestructibility," said Miss Kinsman.

Ellen spelled the word clearly. Mama wouldn't understand, but this was a beginning. Mama had found the courage to come. Mama would find future courage—enough to become American. She had to win, now, and take Mama with her to the nation's capital. She and Mama would look at the buildings and the statues. After such a trip, Mama would never hide away again.

If Mama could do what she had done tonight, Ellen could keep her wits about her for as long as it might take to be winner.

Focus

1. What two worlds did Ellen live in?
2. Why do you think Ellen's mother stayed away from the spelling bee?
3. Explain what Ellen meant when she said that her mother used language as a wall.
4. What was Ellen's plan for getting through the spelling bee? Did she want to win?
5. How do you know Ellen cared about her mother? How do you know Ellen's mother cared about her?
6. Why do you think it might have been easier for Ellen and Henry to learn American ways than for their mother?
7. How is this story an example of the theme that the love between family members can help people to make difficult changes?
8. Do you think that Ellen won the spelling bee? Explain the reasons for your prediction.

In Writing

Write a journal entry that Ellen might have written the night after the spelling bee. The entry should include whether or not Ellen won and what her feelings were about the night. Write another entry from either Ellen's mother or Henry's point of view.

Vocabulary

On a piece of paper, write the numbers *1* to *5*. Then look at the words in the first column and find a definition for each word in the second column. Next to each number on your paper, write the letter of the correct definition for each word.

1. flanked	A. a satinlike fabric
2. sateen	B. an assisting doctor
3. redoubled	C. was at the side of
4. intern	D. made fun of
5. alien	E. different; foreign
	F. increased greatly

Fathers' Day

Nathaniel Benchley

In this story, a father gets an
unexpected glimpse into his son's
feelings about him.

George Adams finished his coffee and stood up. "I'm off," he
said to his wife as he went to the coat closet. "See you around
six."

"Don't forget Bobby's school," she said.

Adams stopped, and looked at her. "What about it?" he asked.

"They're having Fathers' Day," she said. "Remember?"

Adams paused, then said hurriedly, "I can't make it. It's out of
the question."

"You've got to," she said. "You missed it last year, and he was
terribly hurt. Just go for a few minutes, but you've *got* to do it. I
promised him I'd remind you."

Adams drew a deep breath and said nothing.

"Bobby said you could just come for English class," Eleanor
went on. "Between twelve twenty and one. Please don't let him
down again."

"Well, I'll try," Adams said. "I'll make it if I can."

"It won't hurt you to do it. All the other fathers do."

"I'm sure they do," Adams said. He put on his hat and went out
and rang for the elevator.

Eleanor came to the front door. "No excuses, now!" she said.

"I said I'd do it if I could," Adams replied. "That's all I can
promise you."

Adams arrived at the school about twelve thirty, and an attendant at the door reached out to take his hat. "No, thanks," Adams said, clutching it firmly. "I'm just going to be a few minutes." He looked around and saw the cloakroom, piled high with hats and topcoats, and beyond that the auditorium, in which a number of men and boys were already having lunch. Maybe I'm too late, he thought hopefully. Maybe the classes are already over. To the attendant, he said, "Do you know where I'd find the seventh grade now? They're having English, I think."

"The office'll tell you," the attendant said. "Second floor."

Adams ascended a steel-and-concrete stairway to the second floor and, through the closed doors around him, heard the high, expressionless voices of reciting boys and the lower, precise voices of the teachers. As he passed the open door of an empty room, he caught the smell of old wood and chalk dust and library paste. He found the office, and a woman there directed him to a room on the floor above. He went up and stood outside the door for a moment, listening. He could hear a teacher's voice, and the teacher was talking about the direct object and the main verb and the predicate adjective.

After hesitating a few seconds, Adams turned the knob and quietly opened the door. The first face he saw was that of his son, in the front row, and Bobby winked at him. Then Adams looked at the thin, dark-haired teacher, who seemed a surprisingly young man. He obviously had noticed Bobby's wink, and he smiled and said, "Mr. Adams." Adams tiptoed to the back of the room and joined about six other fathers, who were sitting in various attitudes of discomfort on a row of folding chairs. He recognized none of them, but they looked at him in a friendly way and he smiled at them, acknowledging the bond of uneasiness that held them together.

The teacher was diagramming a sentence on the chalkboard, breaking it down into its parts by means of straight and oblique lines. Adams, looking at the diagram, realized that, if called upon, he would be hard put to it to separate the subject from the predicate, and he prayed that the teacher wouldn't suffer a fit of whimsy and call on the fathers. As it turned out, the students were well able to handle the problem, and Adams was gratified to hear his son give correct answers to two questions that were put to him. Well, I'll be, Adams thought. I never got the impression he knew all that.

Then the problem was completed, and the teacher glanced at the clock and said, "All right. Now we'll hear the compositions." He walked to the back of the room, sat down, and then looked around at a field of suddenly upraised hands and said, "Go ahead, Getsinger. You go first."

A thin boy with wild blond hair and a red bow tie popped out of his seat and, carrying a sheet of paper, went to the front of the room and, in a fast, singsong voice, read, "He's So Understanding. I like my Dad because he's so understanding." Several of the boys turned in their seats and looked at one of the fathers and grinned as Getsinger went on, "When I ask Dad for a dime he says he'll settle for a nickel, and I say you can't get anything for a nickel any more and he says then he'll settle for six cents. Then pretty soon Mom calls and says that supper is ready, and the fight goes on in the dining room. After a while Dad says he'll make it seven cents, and before supper is over I have my dime. That's why I say he's understanding."

Adams smiled in sympathy for Mr. Getsinger. When the next boy got up and started off "Why I Like My Father," Adams realized with horror that all the compositions were going to be on the same subject. He saw that his own son had a piece of paper on his desk and was waiting eagerly for his turn to read. The palms of Adams's hands became moist. He looked at the clock, hoping that the time would run out before Bobby got a chance to recite. There was a great deal of laughter during the second boy's reading of his composition, and after he sat down, Adams looked at the clock again and saw that there were seven minutes left. Then the teacher looked around again. Five or six hands shot up, including Bobby's, and the teacher said, "All right—let's have Satterlee next," and Bobby took his hand down slowly, and Adams breathed more easily and kept his eyes riveted on the clock.

Satterlee, goaded by the laughter the previous student had received, read his composition with an attempt to be comical. He told how his father was unable to get any peace around the house, with his sister practicing the violin. It occurred to Adams that the

compositions were nothing more than the children's impressions of their own home life, and the squirming and the nervous laughter from the fathers indicated that the observations were more acute than flattering. Adams tried to think what Bobby might say. He could remember only things like the time he had stopped Bobby's allowance for two weeks, for some offense he couldn't now recall, and the way he sometimes shouted at Bobby when he got too noisy around the apartment. He remembered the time Bobby had threatened to leave home because he had been forbidden to go to a vaudeville[1] show—and the time he *had* left home because of a punishment Adams had given him. Adams thought also of the

---

[1]vaudeville (vôd'vil): theatrical entertainment featuring many different acts

night he and Eleanor had had an argument, and how, the next day, Bobby had asked what "self-centered" meant, in reply to which Adams had told him it was none of his business.

Satterlee finished. The clock showed two minutes to one, and Adams wiped his hands on his trouser legs and gripped his hat, which was getting soft around the brim. Then Bobby's hand went up again, almost plaintively now, and the teacher said, "All right, Adams, you're on," and Bobby bobbed up and went to the front of the room.

Several of the boys turned and looked at Adams as Bobby began to read, but Adams was oblivious of everything except the stocky figure in front of the blackboard, whose tweed jacket looked too small for him and who was reading fast because the bell was about to ring. What Bobby read was a list of things that Adams had completely forgotten, or that had seemed of no great importance at the time. Bobby related things like being allowed to stay up late to watch a show, and being given an old fencing mask when there was no occasion for a gift (Adams had simply found it in a second-hand store and thought Bobby might like it), and having a model airplane made for him when he couldn't do it himself, and the time his father had retrieved the ring from the subway grating. By the time Bobby concluded with "That's why he's O.K. in *my* book," Adams had recovered from his surprise and was beginning to feel embarrassed. Then the bell rang and class was dismissed, and Adams and the other fathers followed the boys out of the room.

Bobby was waiting for him in the corridor outside. "Hi," Bobby said. "You going now?"

"Yes," said Adams. "I'm afraid I've got to."

"O.K." Bobby turned and started away.

"Just a minute," Adams said, and Bobby stopped and looked back. Adams walked over to him and then hesitated a moment. "That was—ah—a good speech," he said.

"Thanks," said Bobby.

Adams started to say something else, but could think of nothing. "See you later," he finished, and quickly put on his hat and hurried down the stairs.

Focus

1. Give details from the story that show that Mr. Adams was a rather impatient person.
2. What was happening in Bobby's classroom?
3. As Mr. Adams sat in the classroom, what kinds of moments with his son did he recall? What kinds of incidents did Bobby tell about? Compare the characteristics of their remembrances.
4. What do you think these different memories suggest about family life?
5. What do you think Mr. Adams learned about Bobby from his son's composition? What do you think he learned about himself?
6. How do you know that Mr. Adams cared about his son? How do you know that Bobby cared about his father?
7. Mr. Adams did not want to visit Bobby's school. In "Spelling Bee" Ellen's mother did not want to go to Ellen's school. Compare the reasons for the two parents' reluctance. Why do you think each parent finally did visit the school?

In Writing

Write a brief sequel to the story, beginning with the following:

That evening Mr. Adams returned home and sat down on the sofa, next to his wife. "Bobby has gone to the store," she said. "He told me you made it to Fathers' Day. How did it go?"

Vocabulary

On a piece of paper, write the numbers 1 to 5. Then look at the words in the first column and find a synonym for each word in the second column. Next to each number on your paper, write the letter of the synonym for each word.

1. oblique	A. fanciful humor
2. oblivious	B. helpfully
3. plaintively	C. slanting
4. acute	D. unaware
5. whimsy	E. sharp
	F. sadly

STUDY SKILL: Time on a Line

A time line is a useful way to organize information. It presents important events in the order in which they happened. It also shows the amount of time between those events. Look at the time lines on this and the next page.

A time line can be drawn horizontally (left to right) or vertically (up and down). On the horizontal line, the earliest event is on the left. The most recent event is on the right. On a vertical time line, the earliest event is on the bottom; the most recent event is on the top. Notice that the lengths of the line segments differ between events. The longer the line segment, the greater the amount of time.

The vertical time line shown here records some of the important events in the life of Franklin Delano Roosevelt, the thirty-second president of the United States. As a young man, his legs were permanently paralyzed by polio. He successfully coped with his handicap and was elected president for four terms of office. Use the information in the vertical time line to answer these questions.

1. Is Roosevelt's birth recorded at the top or bottom of the time line?

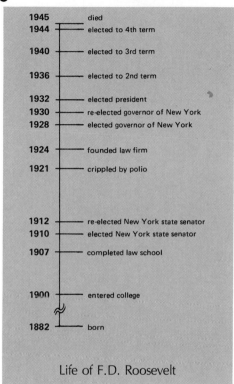

1945	died
1944	elected to 4th term
1940	elected to 3rd term
1936	elected to 2nd term
1932	elected president
1930	re-elected governor of New York
1928	elected governor of New York
1924	founded law firm
1921	crippled by polio
1912	re-elected New York state senator
1910	elected New York state senator
1907	completed law school
1900	entered college
1882	born

Life of F.D. Roosevelt

2. How many times was he elected as state senator of New York?

3. How old was Roosevelt when he was crippled by polio?

4. The United States entered World War II shortly after the attack on Pearl Harbor in 1941. In which term of Roosevelt's presidency did this happen?

5. How many years did Roosevelt serve as president?

6. When did Roosevelt establish a law firm?

Now read the passage called *Great Salt Lake.*

Great Salt Lake

One of the most interesting natural phenomena in the United States is the Great Salt Lake in Utah. It covers approximately 1700 square miles. Great Salt Lake began during the Ice Age. At that time, most of Utah and parts of Nevada and Idaho were covered by Lake Bonneville. After the Ice Age, Lake Bonneville gradually receded. The remains of this ancient lake are now Great Salt Lake.

Because the lake has no outlets, it is very salty. The streams that supply water to the lake carry minerals from the nearby mountains. No water flows out. Therefore, the minerals remain in the lake and accumulate at the estimated rate of two million tons yearly.

Historical records on the lake were begun in 1847. Records show that the depth of the lake changes considerably. The water level was at its highest in 1882 and at its lowest in 1963. The water level depends on the balance between amount of inflowing water and the amount of water that evaporates.

Great Salt Lake was discovered in 1824 by Jim Bridger. Although many people visited the lake after its discovery, John C. Fremont and Kit Carson made the first accurate map of the lake in 1843. The lake then became the site of a wide variety of recreational activities. It was very popular from 1870 to 1940. Elegant resort hotels were built. The most elegant of these was built in 1893. However, in 1935 the lake receded and left this hotel far from the water's edge.

In addition to providing recreational facilities, the lake is a source of many natural resources. It is a major source of brine shrimp. It also supplies minerals, such as salt, lithium, magnesium, and potash. In 1978 a search for gas and oil was begun.

7. Copy the time line shown here. Next to every date marked on the line, write the important event that occurred at this time. Reread the article to find the events.

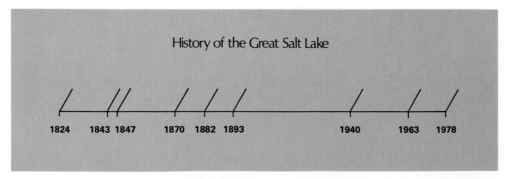

History of the Great Salt Lake

1824 1843 1847 1870 1882 1893 1940 1963 1978

Gentleman of Río en Medio

Juan A. A. Sedillo

Records of a family's history can come in a variety of forms. How do Don Anselmo's unusual records affect the sale of his property?

It took months of negotiation to come to an understanding with the old man. He was in no hurry. What he had the most of was time. He lived up in Río en Medio, where his people had been for hundreds of years. He tilled the same land they had tilled. His house was small and wretched, but quaint. The little creek ran through his land. His orchard was gnarled and beautiful.

The day of the sale he came into the office. His coat was old, green and faded. I thought of Senator Catron, who had been such a power with these people up there in the mountains. Perhaps it was one of his old Prince Alberts. He also wore gloves. They were old and torn and his fingertips showed through them. He carried a cane, but it was only the skeleton of a worn-out umbrella. Behind him walked one of his kin—a dark young man with eyes like a gazelle.

The old man bowed to all of us in the room. Then he removed his hat and gloves, slowly and carefully. Chaplin once did that in a picture. Then he handed his things to the boy, who stood obediently behind the old man's chair.

There was a great deal of conversation, about rain and about his family. He was very proud of his family. Finally we got down to business. Yes, he would sell, as he had agreed, for twelve hundred dollars, in cash. We would buy, and the money was ready. "Don Anselmo," I said to him in Spanish, "we have made a discovery. You remember that we sent that surveyor, that engineer, up there to survey your land so as to make the deed. Well, he finds that you own more than eight acres. He tells us that your land extends across the river and that you own almost twice as much as you thought." He didn't know that. "And now, Don Anselmo," I added, "these Americans are *buena gente,* they are good people, and they are willing to pay you for the additional land as well, at the same rate per acre, so that instead of twelve hundred dollars you will get almost twice as much, and the money is here for you."

The old man hung his head for a moment in thought. Then he stood up and stared at me. "Friend," he said, "I do not like to have you speak to me in that manner." I kept still and let him have his say. "I know these Americans are good people, and that is why I have agreed to sell to them. But I do not care to be insulted. I have agreed to sell my house and land for twelve hundred dollars and that is the price."

I argued with him but it was useless. Finally he signed the deed and took the money but refused to take more than the amount agreed upon. Then he shook hands all around, put on his ragged gloves, took his stick and walked out with the boy behind him.

A month later my friends had moved into Río en Medio. They had replastered the old adobe house, pruned the trees, patched the fence, and moved in for the summer. One day they came back to the office to complain. The children of the village were overrunning their property. They came every day and played under the trees, built little play fences around them, and took blossoms. When they were spoken to they only laughed and talked back good-naturedly in Spanish.

I sent a messenger up to the mountain for Don Anselmo. It took a week to arrange another meeting. When he arrived he repeated his previous preliminary performance. He wore the same faded cutaway, carried the same stick and was accompanied by the boy again. He shook hands all around, sat down with the boy behind his chair, and talked about the weather. Finally I broached the subject. "Don Anselmo, about the ranch you sold to these people. They are good people and want to be your friends and neighbors always. When you sold to them you signed a document, a deed, and in that deed you agreed to several things. One thing was that they were to have the complete possession of the property. Now, Don Anselmo, it seems that every day the children of the village overrun the orchard and spend most of their time there. We would like to know if you, as the most respected man in the village, could not stop them from doing so in order that these people may enjoy their new home more in peace."

Don Anselmo stood up. "We have all learned to love these Americans," he said, "because they are good people and good neighbors. I sold them my property because I knew they were good people, but I did not sell them the trees in the orchard."

This was bad. "Don Anselmo," I pleaded, "when one signs a deed and sells real property one sells also everything that grows on the land, and those trees, every one of them, are on the land and inside the boundaries of what you sold."

"Yes, I admit that," he said. "You know," he added, "I am the oldest man in the village. Almost everyone there is my relative and all the children of Río en Medio are my *sobrinos* and *nietos,* my descendants. Every time a child has been born in Río en Medio since I took possession of that house from my mother I have planted a tree for that child. The trees in that orchard are not mine, Señor, they belong to the children of the village. Every person in Río en Medio born since the railroad came to Santa Fe owns a tree in that orchard. I did not sell the trees because I could not. They are not mine."

There was nothing we could do. Legally we owned the trees but the old man had been so generous, refusing what amounted to a fortune for him. It took most of the following winter to buy the trees, individually, from the descendants of Don Anselmo in the valley of Río en Medio.

Focus

1. Explain the two complications in the sale of Don Anselmo's property. How were these complications settled?
2. Compare the attitudes of the narrator and Don Anselmo toward business. How were their approaches to business deals different?
3. Why were the trees important to Don Anselmo? What did this tell you about him?
4. What event in the story showed that the new owners understood Don Anselmo's reasoning?

In Writing

Different families have different ways of recording important events. Think of one way you might record the important events in your family. Write a paragraph explaining what events you would record and how you would do this.

Vocabulary

On a piece of paper, write the numbers 1 to 5. Then read the sentences below and select the word from the list that best fits each sentence. Next to each number on your paper, write the correct word for the sentence.

negotiation	obediently	preliminary
quaint	deed	broached
pruned	adobe	

1. Juan ___ the idea carefully, unsure how his friends would react.
2. The tourist from America thought that the old German village was ___.
3. The dog followed its owner's commands ___; that is, it did whatever it was told.
4. The ___ report, made before the project had gotten very far, stated that there would not be enough money to complete the project.
5. The ___ was signed and legal, so the property changed hands.

Dream Dust

Langston Hughes

Gather out of star-dust
   Earth-dust,
   Cloud-dust,
   Storm-dust,
And splinters of hail,
One handful of dream-dust
   Not for sale.

My Appalachia

Rebecca Caudill

In this story, Rebecca Caudill remembers the place where she grew up and one event in particular that helped her to grow. What part did her family play in the incident?

The Appalachia that was mine as a child was a narrow valley in Harlan County. Through the valley ran the Poor Fork of the Cumberland River. High mountains walled the valley, Pine Mountain to the north of us, Big Black to the south. The house in which I lived formed the hub of my world, and the other parts that I knew intimately radiated from the hub like spokes in a wheel.

In whatever season, the mountains that towered over us were glorious and majestic, and continually full of surprises. Spring came to them shyly and tenuously. In the beginning appeared the whitish flowers of the maples that the unknowing could easily mistake for young and tender leaves. Let the earth be treated to a few days of warm sunshine, and the mountainsides unfurled in every shade of green.

Before leaves appeared on the trees, starting even before water from the melting snows had run down the steep mountainsides to swell the rivers, wild flowers had begun their seasonal procession across the mountains. In early March, if the winter had not been too long and cold, we could climb

34

Broomsedge Hill and find spring beauties and blue-eyed grass, fragile and dainty, coming out of the woods and running down the mountain to meet us. In our joy at finding them, we knelt and cupped them lovingly in our hands, and buried our noses in them.

Each April, on a Sunday afternoon, our family went up into the mountains in a picnic mood to observe a springtime ritual. Whenever my father decided the proper day had arrived, he shouldered an ax, my mother gave to each of us children a teaspoon, and off we went, up the mountain to a spot where grew a grove of black birch trees. Father looked over the grove carefully, chose a sapling for the sacrifice, and chopped it down. Then, with his ax, he pried off the smooth bark in squares and gave a square to each of us. We sat about on stumps or on fallen tree trunks, and with our spoons scraped the inside of the bark for the sap that was both sweet and spicy, like wintergreen. This was the best of all spring days.

When the season of riotous blooming was over, came the season of fruiting. In the woods we gathered buckets full of wild huckleberries, and along fencerows even greater quantities of large and luscious blackberries. In the fall, there were pawpaws to pick and, after frost, juicy persimmons.

In September, though the days were sometimes sultry, the nights grew chill. Quietly, almost imperceptibly, the mountains changed. Here a leaf on a sour gum tree turned red, there a leaf on a poplar turned gold, harbingers of glory to come. Then, October flamed across the steep mountainsides and deep into every hollow. There was the glory of the scarlet oak, the bronzy beech, and the sweet gum, its star-shaped leaves a riot of color from pale gold to purple. This was outdone only by the saucy sassafras sprout which might boast no more than a dozen leaves, but each a different vivid hue.

As we had our springtime ritual, so we had also our autumn ritual. This always took place on a Saturday afternoon after the first hard frost, when all the children living along the river followed my father to the woods. Each of us carried a basket or a bucket, or wore an apron that could be gathered up for carrying things. We were going chestnut-hunting, and the

mood was gay, the chatter lively. When we arrived at a chestnut tree, my father climbed it and shook the branches one by one. Down peppered the rich brown chestnuts, freed by the frost from their prickly burrs, while underneath the tree we greedily gathered them up for the winter.

The fall I was three, when the older children were getting ready to go to school one morning, Father, who for some reason was going across the mountain with them, said, "Get Becky ready, too."

"What for?" chorused my brother and sisters.

"She can go to school today," said Father.

Getting me ready became a family project. While Mother scrubbed my face and neck and ears, Cappie brought my other dress (as children we had only two dresses in a season), Stella combed my hair, and Will tied my shoes. Off we set, skirting Broomsedge Hill and crossing the mountain to the schoolhouse that stood on the other side of Clover Lick Creek. On the way, other children joined us, all of them sharing generously the excitement of my going to school.

There was one obstacle on the path to school about which I knew nothing. Encountering it, I was plunged into fear. A swinging bridge, built of barrel staves woven together with wire, spanned Clover Lick Creek, and it had to be crossed to reach the schoolhouse. Stout ropes, stretched on either side of the bridge and fastened securely to trees, served as guard rails. Short lengths of saplings nailed side by side to stringers formed a long ramp at each end of the bridge.

As the other children started up the ramp in long striding steps, I hung back in fear. I wanted to ask my father to carry me across. But pride at being allowed to go to school kept me from it. I must walk like the other children, like Clara, I told myself.

My father took my hand in his, and up the ramp we started. Our progress was slow, for I had to step on every sapling crosspiece, not with one foot only, but with both.

"We're getting there," encouraged my father.

I was high enough on the ramp so that when I looked down I could see, beneath me, bushes and saplings waving in the wind.

"Keep your eyes on the bridge," said Father.

Finally we arrived at the bridge, but keeping my footing while the bridge bounced and swayed under the footsteps of the other children was more difficult than climbing the first ramp. And, after the bridge, there was the other ramp to go down.

Finally we made it to the ground and continued the short distance to the schoolhouse. There my father deposited me, with or without the approval of the teacher, I don't know. Then he went on his way.

In the schoolhouse, Stella and her deskmate, Zerah Cornett, took charge of me. Seated between them, I was highly entertained all day by making marks and drawing pictures on Stella's slate, and looking at pictures in a geography book. When the first grade children were called to the front of the room, Stella sent me with them, to sit on the hard recitation bench, and to look and listen. A big chart standing in the front of the room was the "book" from which the children learned their lesson. The page serving as the lesson that day had on it the picture of a cat. Underneath the picture were bold black marks—c-a-t—that, according to the teacher, said *cat*. I sensed there was something important about those marks. A cat could be three different kinds of creature, I thought: a cat, the picture of a cat, and c-a-t.

The reading classes were called to the recitation bench by turns the first periods of the morning. I sat quietly and with prickles on my arms as I listened to wonderful stories and fables and fairy tales and poetry. The prickles grew larger as I listened to Stella read *Robert of Lincoln*. Stella was never one to do anything halfheartedly. When she stood up straight before the class and read:

Bob-o-*link*! Bob-o-*link*!

Spink! Spank! Spink!

I forgot for a moment that I wasn't hearing real bobolinks calling and calling across the tall windblown grass on Broomsedge Hill.

I made one other discovery that day—as important as divining that printed symbols were a way of communication. All day, hidden as deeply as I could bury it, was the knowledge that the bridge had to be crossed on the way home, and that my father would not be along to hold my hand.

When school was out, most of the boys and girls made for the bridge with a whoop. Cappie, seeing my hesitation, took me by the hand and led me. When we reached the ascending ramp, Clara pranced by and started up the ramp, showing no fear whatever. For a minute I watched her as I clung to Cappie's hand. Then, quite ungratefully, I jerked my hand free and started up the ramp alone, stepping on every crosspiece, first with one foot, then with the other, but making progress.

At the bridge Cappie again offered aid, and again I spurned it. Clinging tightly to one of the guide ropes, I finally crossed the bridge and descended the ramp on the opposite side, backwards, as I would have climbed down a ladder, stepping on every crosspiece, first with one foot, then with the other. All the other children were a long way ahead of me when finally my feet touched safe earth. But what did that matter? In the act of crossing the bridge alone, I had become Somebody, Myself, I. Through the woods I ran till I caught up with the others. Proudly I walked along with them, now one of them.

Focus

1. Describe the two "rituals" that the author's family participated in each year. What do these suggest to you about her family life?
2. Name three incidents in the story that showed that the family members cared about each other.
3. Do you think that the author's age influenced the degree of fear she felt about crossing the bridge? Explain your answer.
4. How did the author's family try to help her overcome this fear?
5. People sometimes use the phrase *cross that bridge* to mean "overcome some difficulty." Rebecca crossed two kinds of bridges that day at school. Explain what they were.

In Writing

Write a paragraph describing something you did for the first time when you were younger. Describe how things looked and sounded and how you felt. If you cannot recall such an incident, make one up.

Vocabulary

On a piece of paper, write the numbers *1* to *5*. Then look at the words in the first column and find an antonym for each word in the second column. Next to each number on your paper, write the letter of the antonym for each word.

1. tenuously	A. edge
2. sultry	B. obviously
3. ritual	C. not routine
4. imperceptibly	D. cool and dry
5. hub	E. strongly
	F. unbelievably

STUDY SKILL: Tables of Contents

Suppose you need to locate some specific information. You have found a book on the general topic, but you know that it is not necessary to read the entire book. What will you do? The table of contents is the best place to start. By looking at the unit and chapter titles, you can decide which unit or chapter is most likely to contain the information you need. The table of contents also tells you on what page each chapter begins.

On the next page are the tables of contents from two books about American history. Look at these tables now. You will notice that both books span the same time period in history—from the discovery of America to the Revolutionary War. However, the books organize this information differently.

The unit and chapter titles summarize the information presented in each section. To gather information efficiently from these books, scan the tables and look for key words that signal your topic. For example, if your topic is "The Causes of the American Revolution," which chapters would you read from each book? Scan the table of contents for *American History for Today*. You will notice that

Unit Four is titled "The Colonies Win Freedom." Within this unit, Chapter Three—"Steps toward War"—would be a good place to begin reading. You might also wish to skim other chapters in this unit for additional material.

Next, look at the table of contents for *This Is America's Story*. In this book, Unit Three—"New Nations Are Born as the New World Shakes Off European Rule"—covers your topic. Which chapter in this unit would you read first? Chapter Eight covers your topic; however, you might also wish to skim other chapters.

The following list of questions focuses on this period in American history. What will you read to answer these questions? Be sure to tell: the name of the books; the units and/or chapters in the books; the pages you will read.

1. Where were most of the Spanish colonies?

2. How did people support themselves in the colonies?

3. What were the major battles of the War of Independence?

4. Who was the first European to reach the Pacific Ocean?

5. What role did France play in the New World?

American History for Today

THIS IS AMERICA'S STORY

Contents

Whistles and Shaving Bristles

Frank B. Gilbreth, Jr., and
Ernestine Gilbreth Carey

How do you train twelve people to come running when you whistle?

Dad was a tall man, with a large head and jowls. He was no longer slim. He had passed the two-hundred-pound mark during his early thirties, and left it so far behind that there were times when he had to use railway baggage scales to learn his displacement. But he carried himself with the self-assurance of a successful gentleman who was proud of his family and proud of his business accomplishments.

Dad had enough gall to be divided into three parts, and the ability and poise to back up the front he placed before the world. He'd walk into a factory like the Zeiss works in Germany or the

Pierce Arrow plant in this country and announce that he could speed up production by one-fourth. He'd do it, too.

One reason he had so many children—there were twelve of us—was that he was convinced anything he and Mother teamed up on was sure to be a success.

Dad always practiced what he preached, and it was just about impossible to tell where his scientific management company ended and his family life began. His office was always full of children, and he often took two or three of us, and sometimes all twelve, on business trips. Frequently, we'd tag along at his side, pencils and notebooks in our hands, when Dad toured a factory which had hired him as an efficiency expert.

On the other hand, our house at Montclair, New Jersey, was a sort of school for scientific management and the elimination of wasted motions—"motion study," as Dad and Mother named it.

Dad took moving pictures of us children washing dishes, so that he could figure out how we could reduce our motions and thus hurry through the task. Irregular jobs, such as painting the back porch or removing a stump from the front lawn, were awarded on a low-bid basis. Each child who wanted extra pocket money submitted a sealed bid saying what he would do the job for. The lowest bidder got the contract.

Dad installed process and work charts in the bathrooms. All children old enough to write—and Dad expected his offspring to start writing at a tender age—were required to initial the charts in the morning after they had brushed their teeth, taken their baths, combed their hair, and made their beds. At night, the children had to weigh themselves, plot the figures on a graph, and initial the process charts again after they had done their homework, washed their hands and faces, and brushed their teeth. Mother wanted to have a place on the charts for saying prayers, but Dad said as far as he was concerned prayers were voluntary.

It was regimentation, all right. But bear in mind the trouble most parents have in getting just one child off to school, and multiply it by twelve. Some regimentation was necessary to prevent bedlam. Of course there were times when a child would initial the charts without actually having fulfilled the requirements.

However, Dad had a shrewd eye and a terrible swift sword. The combined effect was that truth usually went marching on.

Yes, at home or on the job, Dad was always the efficiency expert. He buttoned his vest from the bottom up, instead of from the top down, because the bottom-to-top process took him only three seconds, while the top-to-bottom took seven. He even used two shaving brushes to lather his face, because he found that by so doing he could cut seventeen seconds off his shaving time. For a while he tried shaving with two razors, but he finally gave that up.

"I can save forty-four seconds," he grumbled, "but I wasted two minutes this morning putting this bandage on my throat."

It wasn't the slashed throat that really bothered him. It was the two minutes.

Some people used to say that Dad had so many children he couldn't keep track of them. Dad himself used to tell a story about one time when Mother went off to fill a lecture engagement and left him in charge at home. When Mother returned, she asked him if everything had run smoothly.

"Didn't have any trouble except with that one over there," he replied. "But a spanking brought him into line."

Mother could handle any crisis without losing her composure.

"That's not one of ours, dear," she said. "He belongs next door."

None of us remembers it, and maybe it never happened. Dad wasn't above stretching the truth, because there was nothing he liked better than a joke, particularly if it were on him and even more particularly if it were on Mother. This much is certain, though. There were two red-haired children who lived next door, and the Gilbreths all are blondes or red heads.

Dad was happiest in a crowd, especially a crowd of kids. Wherever he was, you'd see a string of them trailing him—and the ones with plenty of freckles were pretty sure to be Gilbreths.

He had a way with children and knew how to keep them on their toes. He had a respect for them, too, and didn't mind showing it.

He believed that most adults stopped thinking the day they left school—and some even before that. "A child, on the other hand, stays impressionable and eager to learn. Catch one young enough," Dad insisted, "and there's no limit to what you can teach."

Really, it was love of children more than anything else that made him want a pack of his own. Even with a dozen, he wasn't fully satisfied. Sometimes he'd look us over and say to Mother:

"Never you mind, Lillie. You did the best you could."

We children used to suspect, though, that one reason he had wanted a large family was to assure himself of an appreciative audience, even within the confines of the home. With us around, he could always be sure of a full house, packed to the galleries.

Whenever Dad returned from a trip—even if he had been gone only a day—he whistled the family "assembly call" as he turned in at the sidewalk of our large, brown home in Montclair. The call was a tune he had composed. He whistled it, loud and shrill, by doubling his tongue behind his front teeth. It took considerable effort and Dad, who never exercised if he could help it, usually ended up puffing with exhaustion.

The call was important. It meant drop everything and come running—or risk dire consequences. At the first note, Gilbreth children came dashing from all corners of the house and yard. Neighborhood dogs, barking like crazy, converged for blocks around. Heads popped out of the windows of near-by houses.

Dad gave the whistle often. He gave it when he had an important family announcement that he wanted to be sure everyone would hear. He gave it when he was bored and wanted some excitement. He gave it when he had invited a friend home and wanted both to introduce the friend to the whole family and to show the friend how quickly the family could assemble. On such occasions, Dad would click a stopwatch, which he always carried in his vest pocket.

Like most of Dad's ideas, the assembly call, while something more than a nuisance, made sense. This was demonstrated in particular one day when a bonfire of leaves in the driveway got out of control and spread to the side of the house. Dad whistled, and the house was evacuated in fourteen seconds—eight seconds off the all-time record. That occasion also was memorable because of the remarks of a frank neighbor, who watched the blaze from his yard. During the height of the excitement, the neighbor's wife came to the front door and called to her husband:

"What's going on?"

"The Gilbreths' house is on fire," he replied, "great!"

"Shall I call the fire department?" she shouted.

"What's the matter, are you crazy?" the husband answered incredulously.

Anyway, the fire was put out quickly and there was no need to ask the fire department for help.

Dad whistled assembly when he wanted to find out who had been using his razors or who had spilled ink on his desk. He whistled it when he had special jobs to assign or errands to be run. Mostly, though, he sounded the assembly call when he was about to distribute some wonderful surprises, with the biggest and best going to the one who reached him first.

So when we heard him whistle, we never knew whether to expect good news or bad, rags or riches. But we did know for sure we'd better get there in a hurry.

Sometimes, as we all came running to the front door, he'd start by being stern.

"Let me see your nails, all of you," he'd grunt, with his face screwed up in a terrible frown. "Are they clean? Have you been biting them? Do they need trimming?"

Then out would come leather manicure sets and pocket knives. How we loved him then, when his frown wrinkles reversed their field and became a wide grin.

"Let's see, what time is it?" he asked once. Out came wrist watches for all—even the six-week-old baby.

Focus

1. Give examples of some efficiency plans Mr. Gilbreth organized for his children.
2. Why do you think efficiency was important in the Gilbreth family?
3. When was the assembly whistle used? How did this relate to efficiency plans?
4. Explain the humor in the authors' account of their father shaving with two razors.
5. How do you think the authors feel about their father? Give reasons for your opinion.
6. Compare the author in "My Appalachia" with the authors in this story. How are they similar? How are they different?

In Writing

This story is part of an autobiography. Write a brief true story about your own family. Use one person (parent, sister, brother, aunt, uncle, grandparent) as the most important person to the story. In three or four paragraphs, write your views about this person. It may be a humorous or serious story.

Vocabulary

Read the word list and paragraph below. Decide which word makes the best sense in each blank space. Then write the numbers 1 to 6 on a piece of paper and write the correct word next to each number.

elimination	evacuate	composure
submitted	jowls	impressionable
shrewd	converge	installed

When we had to __(1)__ the shopping mall because of a fire, my friends and I decided to __(2)__ on the baseball field for an afternoon game. Even though I disliked the responsibility, I __(3)__ to my friends' request that I be the pitcher. I kept my __(4)__, however, and walked over to the pitcher's mound as though I did this all the time. Once __(5)__ on the mound, I felt like I was really at the center of things. With a __(6)__ expression on my face, planning my throw, I released a fast ball and heard "Strike one!"

NANCY LOPEZ

Wendy B. Murphy

When professional golfer Nancy Lopez decided to make golf her career, she received much support from her family. What effect did this support and, later, the admiration of her fans have on her?

Around the pro circuit, Nancy Lopez has been viewed with a combination of envy and affection. Nothing like her dazzling performance had ever been seen in the world of competitive women's golf. In her first year as a professional, in 1977, she won $190,000 in prize money. She won both the "Rookie of the Year" and "Player of the Year" titles from the Ladies Professional Golf Association, and she gathered a fan club second to none in loyalty and enthusiasm.

For any golfer, such achievements would be remarkable, something for the record books. But for a young Mexican American, raised in modest circumstances and in a community that had little interest in professional golfing, such sudden and total success was unprecedented. Nancy Lopez's career vividly demonstrates the old saying that where there's a will—and a good measure of natural talent—there is, indeed, a way.

Nancy Lopez was born on January 6, 1957, in Torrance, California, the second daughter of Marina and Domingo Lopez. Shortly after her birth, the Lopez family moved to Roswell, New Mexico, a railroad center in the southeastern part of the state. There were many Mexican Americans living there, and Domingo, an auto mechanic by trade, opened a body shop to support the family.

When she was just seven years old, Nancy had her first experience with the sport that would make her famous. On Sunday afternoons she would trail along behind her parents as they played Roswell's nine-hole public golf course. Her father gave her a sawed-off "four wood," one of the sizes of clubs used by golfers, and told her to hurry along, that there were others impatient to play behind them.

Domingo Lopez was a late-comer to golf, and he played in the unorthodox manner of those who are self-taught. However, he proved a wonderfully supportive teacher. Technique, he told her repeatedly, would come in time. The important thing was to enjoy the sport. "Play happy," Nancy remembers hearing again and again. "Don't be afraid. If you're behind, just give them another good round. Hit the ball and let it fly. If you botch one hole, forget it and go on to another. You can't bring the hole back. Remember, it's a game."

By the time Nancy was nine, she was playing so well that when she entered a peewee tournament she came home the winner by a resounding 110 strokes! At eleven, she was regularly beating her father. At twelve, Nancy—with no formal training and no backers but her family—won the New Mexico Women's Amateur championship, competing against a field of experienced adults.

Domingo Lopez was convinced by now that the family had a champion under their roof, so they saw to it that Nancy had the time and energy to give her talents a chance. Nancy was excused from most household chores in order to practice her game. And, to finance the cost of equipping her and sending her to tournaments around the Southwest, the rest of the family went without the better house they had hoped to buy.

In Nancy's high school years, she picked up a host of regional and national junior girls' titles, and she led an otherwise all-male team to a state championship. She says that between tours, she tried to be "just a normal person," active in basketball, track, gymnastics, swimming, Girl Scouts, and a group of friends who called themselves "The Chums."

She went from Roswell High School into the University of Tulsa, Oklahoma, on an athletic scholarship. There, she won a string of intercollegiate titles, and in both her freshman and sophomore

years was voted The Most Valuable Player and Female Athlete of the Year.

With her career taking shape so fast, there was little time for studies, and she needed money to relieve her family of some of the financial burden they had carried so long. At the end of her second year of college, Nancy decided to leave college and to become a professional golfer. She made her debut as a professional in July of 1977 by finishing second in the U.S. Open Tournament. She followed this triumph by taking runner-up spots in the Colgate European Open and in the Long Island Charity Classic.

Then, personal tragedy struck. Marina Lopez, who had given so generously to her daughter over the years and was now on the brink of sharing her successes, died suddenly in late September, due to complications after an appendectomy.[1]

The tragedy proved pivotal in Nancy's career. "I don't know what my mother's death did to me," the golf star said, "except that somehow it made me more powerful mentally, more ready to win." Golfing friends of Nancy noted a difference in her game strategy in the months that followed. Before, she had played a strong but safe game, taking few chances. When she began to use

---

[1]appendectomy (ap'ən dek' tə mē): removal of the appendix by surgery

her new ability to concentrate, she could take the risks that made her game catch fire.

On February 27, 1978, in Sarasota, Florida, the new Nancy showed what she could do. Leading her nearest rival by only one stroke as she approached the last hole, she recalls, "I had to fight back from breaking down and crying. All I kept thinking about was my mother. After I won, I just cried and cried." Nancy went on that spring to win six of the next seven tournaments. Now she knew who and what she could be—the first-class champion that her father had predicted—and she was ready to go after this goal.

If Domingo Lopez was delighted with Nancy's performance, so was the Ladies Professional Golf Association. "She's electrifying," said the LPGA's commissioner, Ray Volpe. "There seems to be a different personality to all the tournaments she's in and more excitement, a special glow of interest. The practices seem to be more fun. Everyone seems to be happier." Nancy's relaxed and modest way with fans and sports writers, and her infectious enthusiasm for the game, quickly earned her a huge following. Young people, who have often viewed golf as a middle-aged sport, were turning out in noisy numbers, wearing "Nancy's Navy" buttons on their tee shirts, to cheer their favorite on. Largely because of Nancy's popularity, prize money and tournament attendance tripled in a few years after her entry into adult golf competition.

A friend of Nancy is Lee Trevino, another professional golfer. The story is told that Domingo Lopez once asked Lee to help Nancy with her swing, which Domingo thought was awkward. After seeing her hit the ball, Lee advised Domingo to bring Nancy back to him " . . . when she started hitting the ball bad."

Living as a celebrity is a mixed blessing, Nancy has readily admitted. Because she will never forget being one of the outsiders looking in, she is always ready to give an autograph or a smile to a well-wisher. But there are times when she wishes for anonymity. Keeping a private, "normal" side to her life with so much time spent on the pro circuit is difficult. But Nancy wouldn't change a thing that has happened to her as a golfer. What matters most, she has said, is that her success might give others the will to try against the odds.

Focus

1. How did the Lopez family provide Nancy with practical support? With emotional support?
2. How did her mother's death affect Nancy Lopez's attitude toward her career?
3. Why has Nancy Lopez's career been a special achievement?
4. Why do you think many young people are enthusiastic about Nancy Lopez?
5. Do you think Nancy Lopez would have become a champion if her family had not supported her? Give reasons for your opinion.

In Writing

Do you think that Lopez's decision to drop out of college was a good one? Write a paragraph that supports your conclusion with specific reasons.

Vocabulary

On a piece of paper, write the numbers 1 to 5. Then look at the words in the first column and find a definition for each word in the second column. Next to each number on your paper, write the letter of the correct definition for each word.

1. host
2. vividly
3. pivotal
4. modest
5. unorthodox

A. not speaking highly of oneself
B. likely or normally
C. not generally done
D. strongly or clearly
E. a large number
F. central

LIFE SKILL: Interesting Savings

It's fine to use a piggy bank to accumulate small sums of money and to keep that money handy. However, piggy banks don't help you to increase your savings. Savings banks do. A savings account will pay you for keeping your money in the bank. The money you earn on your account is called the *interest*.

How can a bank afford to pay its customers for saving? The bank "borrows" some of the money you are saving and uses it to make loans to other customers. The bank charges a fee to the people who borrow money. Then it uses some of that fee to pay interest to you for saving there.

Different Accounts Pay Different Amounts

Before you open a savings account, you will have some decisions to make. The bank will give you an informational brochure on the types of savings accounts it offers. Look at the portion of a typical brochure shown below.

This bank offers three kinds of savings accounts. Each account earns interest at a different rate. The rate is shown as a percentage, telling you what part of your money you will "earn again" in a year. For example, suppose you put $100 in an account that pays 5½% interest. After one year, the bank will have added $5.50 to your account. The same amount saved in an account that pays a 5% interest rate earns only $5.00. So, the higher the interest rate, the more you earn.

Why, then, would someone choose an account that pays a lower interest rate? Another part of the bank's brochure explains the terms of each account. Study that part now (top of next page).

Did you notice that the description of the Regular Passbook Account

CSB CENTRALPORT SAVINGS BANK	
TYPE OF ACCOUNT	*ANNUAL RATE OF INTEREST*
REGULAR PASSBOOK ACCOUNT	**5½ %**
COMBINATION ACCOUNT	**5 %**
SPECIAL NOTICE ACCOUNT	**5¾ %**

says that your money is readily available? That means that you can withdraw it anytime the bank is open. The Special Notice Account is very different in this feature. Read the terms of the Special Notice Account again.

There are only four days in the year that you may withdraw your money without written notice and still keep the interest. Otherwise, you must write to the bank 90 days before you withdraw money, telling them of your intention. If you take the money out without giving the 90-day notice, you lose interest. You have to plan ahead to take advantage of the higher interest rate on the Special Notice Account.

The Combination Account is both a checking and a savings account. That means that you can write checks on the account, and you can withdraw cash anytime the bank is open. At the same time, you are earning interest on the money left in the bank.

To choose the right savings plan, you need to think about your savings habits and how you plan to use the money you save.

1. Which account has the highest interest rate? The lowest?

2. Which two accounts allow you to withdraw money at any time in the year?

3. If you were saving your money to go away next July, which account would be best? Give two reasons for your choice.

4. Suppose you want to have money handy for emergencies, but you don't need a checking account. Which account would you choose? Why?

5. If you are going to be visiting relatives in different cities across the country, would the Combination Account or the Passbook Account be more useful? Why?

6. If you are starting to save for college, which account would be best? Why?

The Long Way Around

Jean McCord

Stepchildren and stepparents need time to accept each other. How does Patty feel about her stepmother? How do you think her stepmother feels about Patty?

I hadn't spoken to my stepmother in three days. I was absorbed by an inner grief and anger because she had given away my mother's dresses to the Salvation Army.

I could still feel my mother around the house. Sometimes I'd come bursting in from school with some important piece of news that I wanted to share immediately. Coming through the door, I'd shout, "Mother, I'm home. Where are you?" and instantly, before the echo had died, I'd remember, too late.

My stepmother had answered once, the first time, coming out from her bedroom with a smile on her face, thinking I was calling her. "Yes, Patty, what is it?" But my face was set in a frozen scowl, and I was standing there rigid, unyielding and furious at myself for such a mistake. She understood and turning away without pressing me any further, she went back into her room and closed her door.

My mother had died two years

before when I was twelve, and even though I knew better, sometimes in the middle of the night, I'd awake in a terrible fear. To comfort myself back to sleep I'd whisper into the pillow, "She's only gone away on a trip. And she'll be back." In the morning I had to face my own lie.

My father had married again last year and though my two little brothers, Jason and Scott, called this new woman "Mother," my father had told me I didn't have to do so. I called her Alice even though sometimes it felt strange to call a grown woman by her first name. This Alice wasn't anything at all like my own mother. For one thing, she couldn't cook. My mother had been the best cook in the whole neighborhood. Even the other mothers around us used to say that and would come over for coffee and butter scones[1] and things that my mother would just whip up on a moment's notice. This Alice . . . well, sometimes our whole supper ended up in the garbage can, and my father would take us out to a restaurant. I thought it was pretty stupid and expensive, but of course Jason and Scott loved it.

To make things even worse, so it seemed to me, my father had taken a new job, and we had moved away. We left the town and the neighborhood where I'd spent my whole life with kids I knew and had grown up with and gone to school with and graduated with.

Now I was in Jr. High with a whole new batch of kids and I didn't like any of them. They didn't like me, either. I kept my distance and when school was over, I walked home alone, carrying my books with my head down and hurrying by the groups of girls laughing over some private joke. I could feel them looking at my back and the talk always hushed a little until I was by, then they'd break out into stifled snickers when I was down the street a ways.

Actually I hated them all. I hated the teachers and the new school and my new stepmother and my father who seemed a new person too. Even my little brothers seemed to deserve a good slap for the way they had forgotten and called this Alice "Mother" as if they had never had a mother of their own.

The only one who hadn't changed, who was still the way he had always been, was Rufus, our old Samoyed. Rufus is as old as I am, and in his way he understood. After my mother died, he'd lain on his braided rag rug and refused to move for over two weeks. He wouldn't eat because he was used to my mother fixing him up a

---

[1]scones (skōnz): thick, flat, round cakes cooked on a griddle or in an oven

strange mixture of dog food with raw egg and bacon drippings, and nobody else seemed to know just how to do it. Finally I tried and after a while he ate while looking at me from the corner of his eyes and seeming to apologize for it. I sat down beside him and cried into his neck, and he stopped eating long enough to lick my face which only made me cry harder.

Now the only reason I had for getting up in the morning was to greet Rufus and give him an egg. After school the only reason I came home was to take Rufus for a walk and together we had covered most of this new town. The only trouble was that the town stayed new. Somehow no matter how often we walked down the same streets, the houses always seemed strange. Rufus would plod along at my side, his head just at the reach of my hand. He stumbled once in a while over a curb, but that was because his eyesight wasn't too good any more. My own eyesight seemed slightly affected too because there was a gray film between me and everything I looked at.

We walked all over town after school, my feet just leading the two of us. Finally I knew we had tromped over every square inch of all the streets, but still nothing looked familiar. Sometimes returning home, I wouldn't even know

we had reached the end of the walk until Rufus turned off the sidewalk and went up our front steps.

One Saturday morning I woke up very early. This was about a month ago, I think, or maybe two months. I had lain awake a long time that night watching the shadow patterns change on the ceiling when the wind tossed the big snowball bush outside my window. It seemed like the night was trying to tell me something, but I couldn't quite make out what it was. Out in the kitchen I could hear that Rufus was awake too, because every time he left his rug and walked across the floor, his toenails clicked on the linoleum. He seemed to be pacing the floor as if he wanted to go out into the night. Maybe he sensed something waiting out there for him. If my mother had been here, she'd know . . . she would have known . . .

Somewhere there in the middle of the night, I must have made up my mind what I was going to do. When the dawn came, I just rose and dressed and without even consciously thinking about it, I packed my small overnight case. I put in my parents' wedding picture which I had retrieved from a trunk in the attic, all the socks I had, two books from the library which were due in three days, and

one book of my own. I rolled up my printed-rose quilt and tied it in several places with my belts. Then in blue jeans and a ski jacket I tiptoed out to the kitchen with my belongings and looked down at Rufus who thumped his tail hard against the floor and got up. He stood with his chin over his dish waiting for me to break his egg into it. I saw then that I couldn't leave him behind so while he slurped his egg I rolled his rug around the outside of my quilt. Now it was a big sloppy bundle but I didn't care.

Just as I was easing open the kitchen door I remembered I had no money, so I had to carefully put everything down and return to my bedroom. I had three dollars put away for a long time because there was nothing I wanted to spend it on. Outside in the snowball bush the birds were beginning to cheep and call with a tremendous clatter. They were so noisy I wondered how anyone could sleep through that, and I knew I had to get away quickly.

Rufus was waiting with his head leaning against the kitchen door. He knew we were going for a walk. I wanted to take his dish, but didn't see how I could carry everything. We'd manage somehow. I stepped out into the cool grayness with those birds still clattering and the eastern sky beginning to flag out in streaks of red. It was going to be a warm day, and I knew I wouldn't need the ski jacket. Still, I thought . . . at night . . .

Rufus and I headed towards what I hoped was south. This was vaguely the direction where our old town and old friends were. I had looked at it often enough on the map, but I wasn't sure of just what road to go along. And besides I wanted to stay off the roads. I could picture my father driving along looking for us soon enough, right about breakfast time, I thought, when they would first miss me. But they wouldn't know anything for sure, I told myself, until I remembered I was carrying Rufus's rug.

"That was very stupid of you," I told Rufus severely, "to let me take your old rug when you knew it would give us away."

I walked a few swift steps ahead of him.

"Just for that, I ought to make you go back alone. Without me. Serve you right."

I was very angry. Rufus was hanging his head. The tone of my voice told him he'd done something really bad, but I finally had to forgive him. After all, it had been my own idea.

We used the road only far enough to get us out of town, then I decided we'd better strike across country even though it would be harder traveling, and we would have to climb a lot of fences. It would be safer that way. I soon found out I was right about one thing; it was a lot harder going. We walked through pasture where the ground was spongy and wet and my shoes became waterlogged. We fought our way through brush that kept trying to tear my bundles away from me, and by this time, they really felt heavy. I gave Rufus a sour look, wishing he could carry his own rug at least. We puffed up hills that gave me a stitch in the side, and I noticed that Rufus wasn't holding up too well. He was panting and beginning to lag behind.

By the time the sun was high, I was starving to death. Rufus, at least, had eaten an egg for breakfast, but I hadn't had a bite. And of course by now, I had lost my sense of direction completely. I had no idea which way was south although I had been keeping my eyes open looking for the moss that is supposed to grow on the north side of trees. I hadn't found any.

Every once in a while we would come close to a farmhouse and there was always trouble. Farmers must keep the meanest dogs in the world. At each place a big shrieking dog would come bounding out at us, and try to pick a fight with Rufus just because we were walking nearby. Rufus would say, "Urrgghh," and show all his teeth with his black lips drawn so far back he looked like a snarling wolf and the farm dogs would back off towards home, but never shut up. I was afraid the farmers might call the police, so we would hurry on.

It was a long time before I saw a country road which I figured was safe enough to walk on. In a couple of miles we came up to a crossroads and a store with one red gas pump squatting to one side and looking like it never had any customers.

I dropped my bundles outside and went into darkness and unfamiliar smells. There was this old farmer-type man dressed in striped overalls sitting on a sack of something. I didn't know what I wanted to buy, but anything would do. I bought some cheese and crackers. I decided that canned dog food would keep the best for Rufus, so I got seven cans which took all the rest of my money.

"Stranger round here, aren't you, Miss?" the storekeeper said.

I mumbled something and waved backwards, because my mouth was full of stale-tasting crackers. He put the cans in a sack and I left, but he followed me to the door and watched very slyly as I had to pick up my suitcase and rolled quilt which left me no way to carry the dog food. I struggled to force it under my arm, but the sack broke and the cans rolled all over the ground. In desperation I knelt and shoved them into my suitcase

and Rufus and I marched down the road with the striped overalls watching us all the way.

I could just almost hear him on the telephone, if he had such a thing, saying, "Sheriff, there's a strange gal going down the road with a big old dog and a suitcase full of dog food. Looks mighty suspicious to me." So there was no choice; we had to leave the road and go back to the pastures and farmhouses.

In the middle of the day I knew I couldn't carry that terribly heavy suitcase any farther, so I said to Rufus, "You are going to carry some of your own food inside of you."

We sat down in the shade of some bushes, and I opened the suitcase to get out a couple of the cans. Then I broke into a sheer rage. I had forgotten to bring along a can opener.

Rufus looked at me sadly, laying his heavy head on my knee, and banging his tail, which was full of burrs and briars, against the stony ground.

My vaguely formed idea when we first started out was that we'd make our way back to our old town and maybe one of the old neighbors or even my favorite teacher, Miss Virginia Townsend, would take us in and keep us both if I worked for our board and room. Now I saw clearly that we weren't going to make it. It was over two

hundred miles back there, and
without even a can opener,
well. . . .

We rested for an hour or so
while I talked it over with Rufus
who was a good listener and always agreed with me.

"You knew it was a long ways
when you started out with me,
didn't you?"

He thumped his tail once. I
guess he was too tired to argue.

"I always understood that dogs
knew their own way back to their
old homes. Why didn't you lead?"

He looked away down the hill as
if he was searching for the right
direction.

"If we go back, you know what it
means, don't you? They'll all be
against us, and you'll certainly
have to mind your P's and Q's
from here on in!"

He hung his head in shame, but
how can you ask a fourteen-year-
old dog to walk two hundred miles

when he was all worn out from
doing about ten?

We stood up and looked out
over a valley that faded into a blue
haze in the far distance. I picked
up the luggage, and we went back
down the hill towards the country
store. By the time we got there
Rufus was limping.

I went into that dim interior
again, and the man was back on
his sack, just resting and waiting
with his legs crossed.

"Thought you'd be back," he
said with a snort of choked laughter.

"Could I please use your telephone?" I asked with great dignity.

"In the back there. Ask the
Missus." He jerked his head.

I had to go into their living
quarters. It seems they lived right
there surrounded by all those groceries and hardware and chicken
feed and medicine for cows and

horses. His Missus was a pleasant, stumpy woman with square glasses, and after I'd called home, she gave me a glass of lemonade. I had to ask her where we were, and she took the telephone to give my father directions. He was really boiling mad and hollered over the phone at me, "Swanson's Corner! Where is that?"

I went outside to call Rufus, and she let him come into the kitchen for a drink of cold water. While we waited for my father, I tried to think how to explain all those cans of dog food and the quilt and Rufus's rug, but there didn't seem to be any way. When my father drove up we climbed in and rode all the way home in guilty silence. My stepmother, Alice, must have told him not to say a word.

When we got home my little brothers looked at me fearfully and my father said with a glint in his eye, "Go to your room and stay there. I'll deal with you later."

Nothing more ever came of it which surprised me no end because I waited all week for punishment.

So now it was a month later, or maybe more.

I still kept to myself at school and if a person talked to me, I just turned away because I had nothing to say to any of them.

On the 5th of November it was my birthday. I woke up with poison in my heart and an ache in my throat and I had to keep swallowing. I was remembering my twelfth birthday when my mother had made a dress for me and also bought me *Tales of Robin Hood* which I don't read anymore, but it was the book I had taken with me when Rufus and I ran away.

Breakfast seemed strangely quiet, all the more so because nobody said a thing, not even "Happy Birthday." I knew they had forgotten.

At school, like always, I answered if I was called on, but not otherwise. I ate my lunch by myself and passed most of the day thinking of how many birthdays I would have to live through before Rufus and I could leave again for good. About four more, I decided, then knew with a deep sorrow that Rufus wouldn't last to be eighteen.

When school was out, I turned in the wrong direction from home and headed for a park up on a high bluff. It was pleasant and empty. The trees were dropping their leaves in little piles and a couple of squirrels chased each other around tree trunks like they were on a merry-go-round. I wanted to stay there forever. I wanted the leaves to cover me like little Hansel and Gretel when they were lost in the woods. I wondered if they had had a stepmother who drove them off, and then I said aloud, "No, that isn't fair. You know it isn't Alice's fault. I don't know whose fault it is for feeling so left out of things."

I looked again at the fallen leaves

and thought that my family was like the strong tree that would survive the winter, but I was probably one of the lost leaves.

"I didn't expect them to give me any presents," I kicked at the leaves. I propped my chin on my knees and sat for a long time, thinking and because it was getting late, I read my next day's history lesson. Finally it was too hard to read and looking up, I saw it was almost dark and it was a long way home.

I walked home like I always walked, neither slow nor hurrying. It was just too bad if I was late for supper. I didn't want any anyhow.

When I opened the door the house felt strange. My father was sitting in the front room behind his paper which he put aside for a moment, looked at me and said, "Humph!"

Jason came dancing up to me and grabbed me by the hand pulling me into the dining room.

"Where you been, Patty?" he said. "Everybody waited and waited."

Rufus rushed out from the kitchen to greet me as always, but he was wearing a silly little paper hat tied under his chin. I stood in the brightly lighted room and looked around confused. There had obviously been a party. Used paper plates lay all over and the remains of a big frosted cake was crumpled in the center of the table which had a good linen cloth on it. A pile of wrapped presents lay on the sideboard.[2] In the kitchen I could hear Scott chattering to Alice like a little parakeet and Jason, still clutching my hand, was trying to tell me something.

"All your classmates, Patty," he was saying. "All of them. When you didn't come home, we had to have the party without you. Your presents are here."

He tried to drag me towards them, but I shook him off and rushed to my room.

I was pretty shamefaced when Alice came in to see if I wanted supper. She sat beside me on the bed and patted me on the back.

"It was my fault," she said. "I shouldn't have tried to surprise you. Anyway, come on out and feed Rufus. I think he's going to be sick from all that cake he was given."

So that's how matters stand now.

Nothing is going to change very much. I don't feel quite so mad at the whole world, and I notice my actions towards Alice are a lot friendlier. It doesn't bother me anymore when the boys call her "Mother." Maybe, sometime, a long time from now, I might start calling her that myself. Maybe, by spring or so, I might start growing myself back on that family tree.

---

[2]sideboard: a low cabinet with drawers and shelves

Focus

1. List some reasons Patty gave for resenting her stepmother, Alice. Do you think Patty really believed that Alice was to blame for Patty's problems? Explain your answer.
2. How did Patty's behavior isolate her from her family? From her classmates? Give examples from the story to support your answers.
3. How do you think Alice felt about Patty? Cite evidence from the story to support your opinion.
4. Did Patty change by the end of the story? Give reasons for your opinion.
5. Patty tells the story from her own point of view. Explain how this point of view is as important to the story as the actual events are.
6. How does this story illustrate the theme that family members need to be understanding and patient with each other?

In Writing

Pretend that you are Patty and that you keep a journal. In one paragraph, write an entry for November 5 (your birthday). Explain what your feelings are on that day. Then pretend you are Alice, and write an entry for the same day.

Vocabulary

On a piece of paper, write the numbers 1 to 5. Then read the sentences below. Next to each number on your paper, write the word from the list that best completes each analogy.

shamefaced	scowl	angry
severely	waterlogged	stifled
vague	stitch	unyielding

1. Cramp is to leg as ___ is to side.
2. Bore is to electrify as ___ is to clear.
3. Wink is to flirt as ___ is to disapproval.
4. Dampened is to spirit as ___ is to laughter.
5. Nuisance is to pest as ___ is to stubborn.

Acknowledgement

Dilys Laing

Thank you for your silence,
for saying nothing at all
when the moment was too big,
the heart too small.

CHECKPOINT

Read the word list and paragraph below. Decide which word makes the best sense in each blank space. Then write the numbers *1* to *6* on a piece of paper and write the correct word next to each number.

Vocabulary: Word Identification

shrewd   sateen   acute
stifled   shamefaced   unorthodox
pried   gratified   broached
quaint   anonymity

He sat on a bench and waited for his uncle. His __(1)__ expression revealed the confusion and embarrassment that he felt. He came from a __(2)__ village in the mountains, and his arrival in the city was an __(3)__ shock. The bus trip had taken him from a village where he was known by everyone to a city where his __(4)__ was complete. His village clothing gave him an __(5)__ appearance in this modern city. He realized that he would need to be __(6)__ in these surroundings if he was to be of help to his uncle's business.

Comprehension: Supporting Details

7. In the third paragraph on page 23, what details suggest that Mr. Adams was nervous?
8. In the last paragraph on page 38 (ending on page 39), what details suggest that Becky's school was very different from most schools today?

Comprehension: Main Idea

9. Reread the last paragraph on page 39. Write a sentence stating the main idea of that paragraph.
10. Reread the first two paragraphs on page 50. Write a sentence stating the main idea that they present.

Study Skills: Graphic Information (Time Lines)

11. Reread the short biography of Nancy Lopez on pages 49 to 52. Make a time line of the important events in her life. Review the sample time line on page 27 to use as a model for your time line.

Wat

Beyond our houses and apartments, beyond the limits we often put on our civilized lives, there exists a world of oceans, rivers, shrubs, and creatures. Come along on a safari, and explore the territory of nature.

You will learn that, in the sea, there are highly intelligent animals that have befriended humans. You will also see how the wild world can be hostile and make us struggle for survival. You will see nature in some lighthearted moods when you "follow the scent" of a pet skunk and when you meet Herb Greene, who gives lie-detector tests to plants.

Are you ready for this expedition? Then check your gear and begin your exploration.

Wood, and Wildlife

ter,

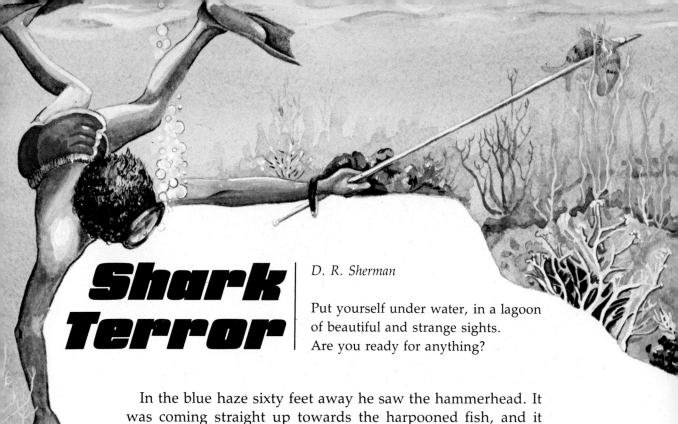

Shark Terror

D. R. *Sherman*

Put yourself under water, in a lagoon
of beautiful and strange sights.
Are you ready for anything?

In the blue haze sixty feet away he saw the hammerhead. It
was coming straight up towards the harpooned fish, and it
came from the deep water on the other side of the reef. The big
shark closed the distance rapidly, and its dorsal fin stuck
straight up in the water.

Fear gripped the boy. As the shark came in closer he
measured its length with his eye, and the cold around his heart
bit a little deeper. It was all of nine feet long, but it was not its
size alone which was so terrifying. What chilled him was the
impression of dormant power and indestructibility that the
sleek gray body conveyed as he followed its pitiless and
unhurried approach.

If only I had a knife, he thought, but at the back of his mind
he knew that even a knife would be of little use against such a
fish. Their skins were unbelievably rough and thick, and he
had seen a smaller shark than this one with an axe buried deep
in its brain, thrashing and snapping as it bit and struck and
splintered the planking of a big boat.

He remembered the harpoon he had been hauling in, and
which he had forgotten about when he first saw the shark. He
knew it was not much, but it would be better than a pair of

70

empty hands. The minute he started hauling in the line the shark accelerated toward the fish on the end of the harpoon. The lazy rhythm of its waving tail did not change, but he knew without a doubt that it was moving faster. He wondered fearfully how fast it could move in the water.

With a last furious heave on the line he got the harpoon into his hands. The hammerhead came on unhesitantly. He snatched a quick breath and dived to confront it. He was not brave: he did it without thinking, because he could think of nothing else to do.

The shark closed to within six feet of him and then veered off suddenly as he went down to meet it. It began to circle him in the water. He turned with it, so that he could keep it in sight. He saw the strange-looking eyes on either side of the awful hammer. They focused on him, one at a time, cold and strange and like something made from stone.

He began to feel dizzy as he turned endlessly round and round to keep the circling shark in sight. That wasn't too bad, but his chest began to feel as if it were going to explode. He thrashed out suddenly for the surface four feet above him and snatched a breath of air.

He dived instantly after that, choking on the water he had swallowed. It was not a second too soon. The shark was already closing in on him. It veered off the moment he faced it, and it began to circle him once more.

A minute later he ran out of air. He went up for a breath, and his stomach turned over as he lost sight of the shark. In that instant his terror was so great that he thought he felt a compression wave in the water and he imagined the shark arrowing in towards his belly.

He dived again. For a second he did not see the shark. He spun round wildly, half hoping that it had gone. But it hadn't gone, and his heart lurched violently as he saw it coming up through the water toward him. He drew his legs up into his body protectively, and then in a moment of sudden fury, without thinking of what he was doing or of the possible consequences, he lunged out at the shark with the harpoon, thrashing angrily after it. As he tumbled awkwardly he realized it had been a futile and very foolish gesture. To his astonishment the shark darted away. It began its circling once again, but farther out than it had been before.

He felt a moment of unspeakable relief, and then he felt a little flutter of hope within his breast. He began to wonder if the shark might not also be afraid of him. He did not really believe it, but the possibility sent his hopes soaring. If he could keep it at bay by poking it with the harpoon and frightening it off, he might just be able to work his way back to the safety of the canoe. It never occurred to him to get rid of the porgy on the harpoon which had attracted the shark in the first place.

He went up again and gulped another mouthful of air. Already he was beginning to feel tired. He did not think he would be able to go on much longer, not like this, snatching a little air and then having to hold it till his lungs were almost bursting. He dived quickly, and the momentary elation he had felt drained away.

The shark was again closing on him rapidly. He felt a sudden spurt of rage at its behavior. He stabbed out at it with the harpoon. The shark veered off instantly. It began to circle him again, but not as far out as it had been before.

72

The boy stayed down till his breath ran out. When he could hold it no longer he struck out for the surface. He took two quick breaths and then slipped under the water again.

The shark had closed the distance between them. It was right on him. He struck out at it desperately. The harpoon point glanced off its blunt head, and it shot off six feet and then began its endless circling once again.

The boy knew then that it *was* afraid of him, but he knew also that it was a thing which did not matter at all. The shark was tireless, and it could go on forever, and soon he would be too tired to move and frighten it away. He realized then with a numbing certainty that it was hopeless.

He felt the beat of his frantic heart begin to slow, and as he turned slowly in the water to keep the shark in sight he felt a spell of terrible dizziness. He began to think that he was going to lose his balance and fall, and he wondered if the shark was waiting for that. It was funny to think of falling when he was already under the water. It was a foolish thing to imagine, but any second now he knew it was going to happen just the same. He spread his arms wide in the water to steady himself as the silent green world round him began to spin wildly.

I have done this before, he thought, and he remembered turning round and round as a child till he lost all equilibrium, and then laughing and screaming as the spinning world far below him came closer and closer till finally it came up close enough to knock the breath out of him, and then he knew it was he who had fallen as he lay giggling and gasping on the grass, waiting for the earth and sky to separate.

He saw the shark sweeping in towards him. The shape of it was vague and blurred. He steadied his reeling senses with a great effort of will. He felt a sudden calmness then, and the dreadful knot in the pit of his stomach untied itself. He knew it was the end, and because he understood it so perfectly he no longer felt afraid. The fingers of his left hand clamped lovingly round the slim shaft of the harpoon.

I will hurt *you* also, his mind screamed at the shark.

He tensed himself to strike, but he realized without any consternation that he would not hurt it at all.

Under the water his face twisted in a silent shudder. The shark was almost upon him when he saw the dark shape of another great fish. It swept in furiously from the murky water which stretched away to his right in deepening shades of blue. He thought it was a shark, and though he had never heard of such a thing before, for one wild moment he wondered whether it might have come to attack the hammerhead. If they fought over the right to eat him, he might be able to skip away while they tore each other to pieces.

He felt a spurt of hope which was so intense it sickened him. It entered him so suddenly and violently that he felt its entry as a physical assault on his body. He sagged limply in the water for a moment, and then a fresh current of fear shot through his nerves and electrified him.

The great fish closed the distance between them at an astonishing speed. He saw with another wild surge of hope that it was heading directly for the shark in front of him. The pointed snout of the great fish slammed into the gill-slits of the shark. The battering impact rocked the shark in the water. It turned over on its side and then righted itself slowly, and then in a state of shock and fright the big hammerhead darted away. It vanished into the dark blue shadows on the other side of the reef.

The boy felt the return of a terrible despair. In the still silence of his mind he cursed the cowardly hammerhead with monotonous repetition. His words went through his mind and passed without leaving a trace of meaning or understanding. If only the hammerhead had stayed to fight, he thought.

He forced his arms and legs to start moving. He kicked himself wearily to the surface. He drew a sobbing breath and went under again, and he wondered what kind of a shark it was that could frighten a hammerhead off with a single blow from its pointed snout. He searched for it, twisting and turning frantically as he scanned the water. He did not see it anywhere, and he began to wonder if it might not have followed the hammerhead out to sea in pursuit. He began to hope again. Just then the great fish swam up from below him.

He recoiled in terror, but in that instant he saw clearly for the first time the protruding beak with the undershot jaw which seemed to set the mouth in a fixed smile of secret satisfaction.

Porpoise, he thought, and his heart gave a great shout of joy.

He had seen porpoises before, far out to sea, and once when he had been fishing with his father he had seen a great school of them which looked a mile long and a mile wide in the blue sea. And as he watched the black shapes coming up out of the water to breathe and then sliding back into the sea together in a slow smooth roll he was glad for once that the school was far away, because it did not seem right to him that any of them should die. In all the times they had caught the black-backed fishes he had never really appreciated their swift grace and beauty till then, and it saddened him a little to think that such a beautiful fish should lose its freedom and then die with a harpoon in its heart.

The big fish swam past the boy just below the surface of the water and then it turned and swam back towards him. He had never heard any fishers tell of a porpoise harming a person, but he eyed it warily just the same. It was a big fish, and the fear of the shark was still in him, and he feared it because of its great size which was equal to that of the shark.

He went up for a breath of air, and the fish went up with him. He saw a fine spray of water shoot from the crescent-shaped blowhole at the top of its head. The instant it stopped spouting he heard a noise which was like the sound of a quickly drawn breath and then the blowhole shot off with a soft plop.

The big fish swam in closer to the boy, and he was astonished to hear the faint whistles and squeaks which came from its blowhole as it swam past him in the water with its head held high and its swept-back dorsal fin sticking up in the air and looking like a piece of slippery wet rubber.

The black-colored back, which had a purplish tint, slipped past him two feet away. The boy paddled himself round so that he could keep an eye on it, because he was still unsure of the great fish. He saw it turn and start back towards him, and he saw the startling whiteness of its belly as it rolled over onto its side just before it turned.

It swam past him again, and he realized then that the big fish was not a porpoise. It did resemble the porpoises he had seen, but he saw that it was only a surface resemblance. It had a definite beak, and the undershot jaw sticking out like a chin turned the mouth upwards and fixed it in a smile, whereas the mouth of the porpoise was simply an opening in a blunt-shaped head which no amount of imagination could transform into a beak. He thought the big fish must be a kind of porpoise, but he was not certain.

He knew it was not a fish in the true sense of the word. He had listened in the past to someone explain that a porpoise was a mammal and not a fish. But it came from the sea and it lived in the sea, and that was why he preferred to think of it as a fish.

He studied the big fish. It was longer and heavier than any porpoise he had ever seen. He knew then without a doubt that the fish swimming in the water beside him was certainly not a porpoise as he knew it.

It was a bottle-nosed dolphin, a close relative of the porpoise, but even if he had known this it would not have eased his mounting nervousness: to him it was a fish he had never seen before, an unknown quantity, and because he was without any knowledge of it he felt afraid. He knew only that it had driven off a hammerhead shark with one blow from its powerful-looking beak.

As the dolphin slid past him in the water that was the thought which was uppermost in his mind, and he wondered whether it was going to attack him on its next pass. The great head of the fish half turned to keep him in view as it glided past: it actually turned, and to his astonishment he found himself looking straight into one enormous eye. In that instant all his fear vanished, because the eye that regarded him was like the eye of a human. It did not stare at him with a cold glassy badness as the eye of the shark had done. The eyeball itself was almost two inches in diameter, and in the huge black pupil he saw an expression of friendly curiosity that was almost human.

Ten feet away from him the dolphin made a wide sweeping turn and then plunged its beak into the water and its glistening back seemed to roll forward slowly like a wheel as it followed the head below the surface of the sea in a continuation of the same fluid movement. The last thing he saw was the black tip of the raked-back dorsal fin and then that too slid smoothly under the water.

He saw the big fish come curving in towards him at a depth of five feet. It looked dark and threatening, but he felt no fear because the memory of the big friendly eye was still fresh in his mind. He stopped treading water and allowed himself to sink till the faceplate of his mask was just below the refractive surface film which blurred his vision.

He did not see the fish. He was wondering whether it had already gone past him when he felt a sudden gentle jolt. His heart skipped a beat and he felt a moment of breathtaking terror. He felt the body of the great fish come pressing up between his legs and then he felt himself being lifted up on its back till his head and shoulders were right out of the water. The fish started to swim off with him, heading towards the open sea. He was facing backwards as they moved off, and it was a terrifying sensation.

He kicked out wildly, trying to get free of the fish. But he did not get free, and the fish only increased its speed. In desperation the boy threw his whole body to the right. He toppled off

77

the back of the fish, with the harpoon and the speargun lashing out wildly. He felt the smooth rubbery skin on the flank of the fish sliding and rubbing against the inside of his thigh and then finally all contact between them was broken as it swam on past him.

He came up to the surface choking and gasping. He transferred the harpoon to his right hand, holding it together with the speargun. He struck out for the canoe. The hot panic left him and he felt a great bursting relief. But it lasted only a moment, because he had not taken three strokes when he felt the fish coming up beneath him once more.

It came up from behind him, and it lifted him up so quickly that he had no time to struggle and escape it. He felt himself come surging up through the water and then he slid along the wet back of the fish till the dorsal fin brought him up short. The fish accelerated suddenly, and he saw that they were heading directly towards the distant canoe.

He threw his arms round the neck of the big fish to keep himself from falling off, at the same time gripping its body with his knees and his thighs. He bent his right wrist backwards, so that the harpoon and speargun did not touch the fish: he acted not out of consideration, but because he was still a little bit afraid of the fish and he did not like to think of what might happen if he prodded it accidentally with the sharp point of the harpoon.

He lay crouched forward over the back of the fish as they sped through the water and he felt the drag of the sea against his body as it tugged at him and tried to tear him from the slippery back of the fish. The water sprayed round his shoulders and face. In a moment of sudden wild exuberation he started to laugh and shout and cheer.

The fish began to rise even higher, and the top of its head broke the surface of the water. The boy fell quiet, and in the abrupt silence which followed he heard the startlingly loud *whoosh* as the fish spouted, and his nostrils twitched at the warm fishy smell of its breath which came straight up into his face. He heard the soft moan of air being drawn into the blowhole. It snapped shut with a wet plop an instant later and

he felt the back of the great fish arching smoothly beneath him.

The boy began to cheer wildly again. His joyful cries were cut short a second later as the dolphin dived. He barely had the time to snatch a hurried breath before the water closed over his head. Panic shot through him. What if the fish dived right to the bottom of the sea and stayed down there with him for longer then he could hold his breath? He felt a little foolish when he realized that all he had to do was let go and make his own way up to the surface whenever he wanted.

The dolphin leveled out at three fathoms. The boy felt his breath running out. He wondered whether he should abandon the fish and strike out for the surface or hang on in the hope that it would go up itself within the next few seconds. He decided to stay with the fish for as long as he could. If he jumped off now he knew he might never see it again, and for some reason or the other the thought of being parted from the great fish filled him with a deep sense of loss.

He stayed with it a while longer. He lay almost flat along its back and he rode it like a racehorse as it slipped noiselessly through the silent blue water. He glanced at the seabed which sped by two and a half fathoms below him. The coral pattern looked familiar. He was not quite sure about it though, but then he recognized the spreading antlers of a large elkhorn coral and he knew that they were not far from the deep channel which ran between the mainland and Ile aux Cerf.

His head began to hurt and his chest felt on fire. He knew he did not have a moment to spare, but at the same time he could not bring himself to part company with the great fish that was carrying him through the water with such effortless ease.

He hung on a little longer, punishing his body heedlessly. With each second of suffocating agony that passed he prayed that the fish would start swimming up towards the surface so that he would not have to leave it. But his prayer was not answered.

The big fish swam on tirelessly at the same depth. The boy felt a sudden dizziness sweep over him. He shook his head to clear it and hung on grimly. Black spots began to dance in front of his eyes. He knew it would be madness to stay down any longer. He threw himself sideways and off the back of the great fish.

He turned end over end through the water. When he got his bearings he struck out for the surface. The air inside his bursting lungs began to bubble from his mouth. Out of the corner of his eye he saw the big fish swimming away on its side with the bow-shaped flukes of its tail pointing straight up and down in the water.

The boy surfaced with a last frantic kick. He turned over onto his back and lay gasping and blowing. He barely managed to summon the strength to keep his legs moving and stay afloat. After a while his breathing returned to normal.

He flipped over onto his belly suddenly, remembering the big fish. He pushed his face down under the water and searched for it anxiously. He did not see it anywhere. He lifted his head and began to tread water. He felt a moment of utter desolation as he stared round the empty sea.

He started swimming towards the canoe. His arms and legs felt heavy and tired as he splashed through the water, and his heart was full of despair.

When he got back to the canoe he reached up over the gunwale and dropped the speargun and the harpoon into the boat. The striped porgy was still on the end of the harpoon. It was quite dead now, and its cold fish eyes looked like pebbles of colored glass.

He swam round to the stern of the boat and dragged himself aboard. The effort took the last of his remaining strength. He sat down on the planking and peeled the mask off his head. He stared out across the sea, but it was quite empty. He felt a hurting disappointment.

If only it would show itself to me again, he thought.

He did not know what he would do if he saw the big fish again, but he knew that it would make him very happy. He felt an aching emptiness as he thought about the dolphin.

It was a fine fish, he told himself admiringly, and I think that it truly saved my life from that terrible shark with the ugly flat face.

He searched the sea again, but there was nothing to be seen. He scuffed despondently at the planking of the boat with his bare toes. The porgy on the harpoon caught his attention. He stared at it. It was dead, and it looked dead, and the brilliant fires which had flamed in yellow and black beneath its scales had all gone out. He reached out listlessly for the harpoon, and just then the surface of the sea burst open fifteen feet away to his right. He saw it out of the corner of his eye, and he was so startled and surprised for an instant that he was unable to move.

It seemed to him that there was a big black hole in the water with a tunnel going down into the sea, and then as he straightened up and swung to face it he realized that it was not a tunnel or a hole but the body of some great fish coming up through the water.

He saw the blunt domed head of the dolphin break through the surface and then the rest of its body followed dripping and black and wet from the hole in the water. For a second it appeared to be standing on its tail, and then with a final lazy wriggle of its flukes it cleared the water completely. It went up with an agonizing slowness, but then suddenly it gained momentum and it lifted higher and higher till finally it seemed that it was hanging in the air ten feet above him. He saw the great white expanse of its belly, and then a second later it turned its head and he saw the friendliness in the big brown eye which watched him. It seemed to hang in the air a moment longer and then it rolled gracefully and hurtled down. It entered the sea with a splash that sent a burst of spray all over him and the boiling water which shot back to the surface made the canoe rock and heave.

Focus

1. Summarize the boy's efforts to defend himself against the shark.
2. Explain why the boy could not win the battle against the shark.
3. What happened when the shark was about to strike the boy? Describe the changes in mood that the boy experienced at this time.
4. What factual details about dolphins did the author include?
5. Summarize the two ways in which the dolphin helped the boy.
6. At what point did the mood of the story change? Compare the boy's experiences before and after this point.

In Writing

Imagine that the boy saw the dolphin the next time he went fishing. Write a paragraph describing what happened.

Vocabulary

Make two columns on your paper. Label the first column *Positive* and the second column *Negative*. Then look at the words in the list below. Decide whether each word has a positive or negative connotation. Write the word in the correct column. Then write a sentence using each word.

futile   despondently   monotonous
exuberation   indestructibility   desolation

KAREN PRYOR
and the
Creative Porpoise

Margery Facklam

Some sea animals can be friends to people. Read here
about the training of porpoises, wild animals with unusual brains.

The porpoise shows at the Ocean Science Theater at Sea Life Park in Makapuu Point, Waimanalo, Hawaii, had been going smoothly for some time—so smoothly that Karen Pryor, the curator of mammals at the park, decided that they were not exciting any more. So she and one of the trainers thought it might be fun to show the audiences the first steps in training a porpoise by reinforcing, or rewarding, the animal with a piece of fish when it performed correctly. They wanted to show how trainers waited for the animal to do something spontaneously and then let the animal know they wanted it to do it again. That is called conditioning.

The first time it was easy. Malia, the small porpoise, was swimming around the tank, waiting for a cue or signal that would tell her what she was supposed to do. But the trainer did nothing. There was no cue. The porpoise became impatient after a minute or two and slapped her tail on the water, which is porpoise language for annoyance. The trainer immediately blew her whistle and tossed Malia a piece of fish.

Karen said, "That was enough for Malia. She got the message and slapped, ate her fish, slapped, ate, slapped repeatedly. In less than three minutes she was motorboating around the tank pounding her tail on the water, and the audience burst into applause."

That was exactly what they wanted to show the audience—the animal as a real being and not just a robot doing what it is told.

But when it was time for the next show and they wanted to show the next audience something new, they couldn't very well reward Malia for slapping her tail on the water. They had to wait for her to do something new. Malia grew more and more angry. Finally she threw her whole body into the air and came down sidewise, slapping the water with a huge splat. The trainer blew the whistle right away and threw Malia a fish. And Malia immediately began doing it over and over, pleased to have discovered what the trainer wanted and pleased to have her fish.

The trainers continued this routine for a couple of days, waiting at each performance for the animal to do something different so they could reward her and explain to the audience what had happened. Of course, there is more to training than waiting for an animal to do something, but in this case they wanted to show the first steps in training, those moments when the animal and the trainer are thinking together.

This procedure became more and more difficult, however, and there were one or two embarrassing shows when Malia went splashing around the tank doing all the things she knew, but nothing new that the trainers could reinforce and reward.

Then Malia solved the problem. "On the last show of the third day we let her out of the holding tank, and she swam around waiting for a cue. When she got no cues, instead of launching herself into a series of repetitions of old behavior, she suddenly got up a good head of steam, rolled over on her back, stuck her tail in the air, and coasted about fifteen feet with her tail out: "Look, Ma, no hands!"

After that, Malia seemed to be delighted with herself. She continued, show after show, to produce new and astonishing things to do. She spun in the air, swam upside down, revolved like a corkscrew.

"She thought of things we never could have imagined," said Karen.

The porpoise had obviously learned that the trainer was only rewarding things that had never been rewarded before. She was deliberately coming up with something new. "Sometimes she was very excited when she saw us in the mornings. . . . I had the unscientific feeling that she sat in her holding tank all night thinking up stuff and rushed into the first show with an air of "Wait till you see *this* one."

The animal had shown an example of first-order learning. Karen said, "Originality. Rare, but real, in animals. Almost never observable in a laboratory situation."

After the thrill of seeing Malia improvise, the trainers worked on another animal, and finally they began the long, exacting task of proving scientifically that the animals involved in the sessions were really creating, really "thinking."

Karen never meant to be a porpoise trainer, but she could hardly avoid the swimming pool in her yard, full of porpoises fresh from the ocean. These beautiful marine mammals were wild but friendly, as porpoises usually are, and they had already stumped the first team of trainers who tried to get them ready for the opening of Sea Life Park.

It really all began when Karen's husband, Tap, was a graduate student studying sharks. He needed a place to do his research—a place that would help support the research and allow him to be near his wife and three children. So he built a combination oceanarium-research station where he could learn and where people would pay to be entertained.

Things were going fairly well until three months before the scheduled opening, when everyone had just about given up trying to train the porpoises. The animals were intelligent and healthy, but the trainers were new at the job. "In fact," said Karen, "the porpoises had trained the trainers to give them fish for nothing."

When her husband suggested that she herself give it a try, Karen thought she might be able to handle it. She had trained a pony and a dog, and she kept thinking how nice it would be to have a job just four hours a day right near home.

"I had no idea I was about to be caught up in one of the major efforts of my life."

Being curator of mammals at Sea Life Park included scrubbing and hosing tanks, cutting up fish, and training trainers as well as animals.

Karen had majored in English literature at Cornell University, but she had done graduate work in biology at the University of Hawaii. She was not entirely new to the science of animals.

The porpoises, however, were new both to Karen and to the life they were going to lead. At Sea Life Park, the animals were called porpoises, although in many places the same species are called dolphins. They are small whales, and they all belong to a group of mammals called cetaceans[1]. They breathe air, their young are born alive, and the babies are nursed for eighteen months to two years.

The porpoise, or dolphin, breathes through a blowhole on top of its head and it emits a series of whistles, clicks, and rusty-hinge noises through this hole, too. Porpoises have no

---

[1]cetaceans (si tā′shənz)

vocal cords, but they can also send out a series of signals from air pockets in the nasal (nose) passages. These sounds work like a sonar system. (Sonar is an abbreviation for **so**und **na**vigation **r**anging.) Humans use sound waves bounced from equipment in a submarine, for example, to let them know what is around. They got the idea from bats and porpoises. Underwater, where the sea is dark, the cetaceans can send out a series of sounds, sometimes at frequencies too high for humans to hear, and these sounds bounce back from objects they hit, like an echo. A porpoise can tell the difference between two similar fish by this system, even if it is blindfolded.

The porpoise's skin is smooth and firm. It feels like a peeled hard-boiled egg. A porpoise can live out of water, but its skin must be kept wet to keep it from cracking and to keep the animal from overheating through its thick layer of blubber.

Before aquariums began to exhibit these marine mammals, many porpoises were killed for shark bait as they gracefully leaped and played in the bays off the Florida and California coasts. But today more arguments are raging among scientists over the porpoise than almost any other animal. Some say that a porpoise is no smarter than a dog; others say the porpoise's brain—a brain more complex than the human's—is capable of language.

Karen stands somewhere in the middle, admiring the porpoise for what it is—a beautiful marine mammal living in an entirely different kind of world from ours. She is a scientist-trainer, and she approached her new job with a combination of scientific doubt and practical ideas.

87

One of the first things Karen had to do was teach herself to be a trainer. She read what she could find, but there was very little available on the subject in 1963. Taming is one thing; training is another. There are some basic scientific rules for training. Karen had ninety days before the opening of the show in which to train the animals, and she said, "About nine-tenths of what I now know about training I would learn in the next three months."

First, the animal has to be conditioned. There are different kinds of conditioning. Pavlov was a Russian scientist who showed that animals and people can be conditioned by an unconscious process. He rang a bell whenever he fed his dogs. In time, the dogs' mouths would water whenever they heard the bell, even if no food appeared.

Operant conditioning, which is used to train the porpoises, is a different process. In this kind of training, the animal makes something happen. The animal starts it; the animal is the operator. When it does something, a reward appears. It is the same sort of training you use when you ask a dog to sit up and speak and reward it with a snack.

Karen says, "Animals seem to enjoy this. I think they like to be able to make things happen for themselves."

The first thing that must be done is to teach the animals a signal that means that food or another reward is coming. You have to have some way to let the animal know what it is doing right. Karen decided on a whistle because the porpoises could hear it above or below the water and would not confuse it with other sounds. And it was a sound the trainer could make much more quickly than the pressing of a buzzer, for example. It didn't take long to whistle-condition the porpoises.

Once an animal "understood" what the whistle meant, that sound could be used to change what it was doing a little at a time. That is called shaping. By blowing the whistle every time the animal turns to its right, for example, you can have the animal swimming in a tight circle to its right in just a few minutes. And with a little patience, and by using the whistle exactly at the right moment, you can have an animal do things it might never have done otherwise—like standing on its head and waving its tail in the air.

Every animal trainer has secret "recipes" for shaping the animals to do different things. Karen says there are probably as many ways to shape a single behavior as there are trainers to do it. It takes imagination and hard work.

"Shaping is fun," Karen wrote. "It is, however, only half of the training procedure. The other half is to set up cues or signals that let the animal know what you want and when you want it. This is called 'bringing the animal under stimulus control.' It is a tricky business. When you have good stimulus control, you have, in effect, a sort of language between yourself and the animal and not entirely a one-way language. Your actions and its reactions begin to add up to mutual communication."

Karen found it exciting when an animal caught on to an idea. Sometimes, when an animal is on the wrong track, or is refusing to do what you ask, or is doing something that might be dangerous—like playing with a toy it could swallow—there has to be a punishment. You can't very well spank a porpoise. So the punishment becomes a "time out." The trainer picks up the pail of fish and just walks away. No fish, no reward. In all porpoise shows, the animals are trained to retrieve things that might be tossed or dropped into the pool, such as cameras, toys, and money, and part of the training is this "time out." If the porpoise does not bring the camera or coin to the trainer in return for a fish, the trainer calls a time out. It doesn't take long for the animal to learn what it must do to keep the fish coming.

Sometimes teaching a new behavior is a matter of waiting for the porpoise to do something you can reward and shape. You can't very well show a porpoise how to do a tail walk or a leap in the air. But when the porpoise does it on its own, you can blow the whistle and throw it a fish to say that you liked what it did. But, said Karen, "It meant walking around all day with your whistle in your teeth and a fish in your pocket."

Then the new behavior can be broken down into small steps so that the animal is shaped very gradually, one step at a time. Horse trainers, sports coaches, and symphony conductors use this shaping, which Karen believes is a mixture of science and art.

When the shows were going smoothly at Sea Life Park, and

other trainers were handling most of the problems, Karen turned to other things when she had the time. The Navy was interested in how fast porpoises could swim. By their calculations, it was estimated that a porpoise ought to be able to do about twenty miles per hour. But there were so many reports of porpoises keeping up with huge destroyers and other ships that the Navy wondered if their calculations could be correct.

Karen whistle-conditioned a teenage porpoise named Keiki. The plan was to take the animal into the open ocean for tests. "At that time nobody had ever taken a tame porpoise deliberately out to sea, with the idea of getting it back," she said.

Keiki enjoyed it. He liked chasing the boat, the way some dogs love chasing cars. But when all the test results were in, the Navy calculations were right. The porpoise swims at a top speed of twenty miles per hour. It can stay with fast ships by riding the wake, like a surfer rides a wave—in fact, it seems to be a worldwide porpoise sport, even older than the invention of boats. Humpback whales, speeding along the surface, have been seen with porpoises playing in their bow wake, hitching a ride.

Several porpoises trained at Sea Life Park took part in Navy research projects, some finding lost airplane parts on the ocean bottom, others carrying tools and messages to divers. Kai was a porpoise trained to wear a harness for tests to determine the depth a porpoise could dive. He had to dive through a hoop that broke a light beam to signal the depth and then return for his fish. He had done many days of dives, but the Navy needed just one more day of tests. Karen took off his harness that last day and put a soft nylon collar around his neck.

Kai worked hard. When he came up from a dive, he circled next to the boat, breathing repeatedly, resting before he obeyed the signal that told him to return to his cage to wait for the next dive. That day he suddenly circled around the boat, looked at the hoop and cage and Karen and the others in the boat. Then he took off. They watched as he leaped and chased the flying fish ahead of him, a wild animal that had suddenly chosen to go back to the wild. "Kai had earned his freedom," Karen wrote.

Focus

1. What useful experiences did Karen Pryor bring to her job as a porpoise trainer?
2. What are cetaceans? List some of their physical characteristics.
3. Explain the steps in training a porpoise by operant conditioning.
4. How is operant conditioning different from the conditioning Pavlov used with dogs?
5. Name two ways, other than entertainment, that trained porpoises have been helpful to people.
6. What qualities do you think someone would need in order to train porpoises well?

In Writing

You read that teaching an animal to do something is often accomplished by "shaping." Write a brief description of how you could use shaping to train a horse to turn in a full circle counterclockwise.

Vocabulary

On a piece of paper, write the numbers *1* to *5.* Then look at the words in the first column and find a definition for each word in the second column. Next to each number on your paper, write the letter of the correct definition for each word.

1. spontaneously
2. routine
3. deliberately
4. improvise
5. exacting

A. to pretend to be someone else
B. carefully or on purpose
C. requiring much effort and care
D. a fixed way of doing something
E. without planning ahead of time; on impulse
F. to make up on the spur of the moment

River Madness

David Sumner

A rubber raft in roaring
river rapids runs rampant
if not restrained!

A dusty road runs beside the main stem of Idaho's legendary Salmon River for 46 miles west of the tiny mountain town of North Fork. As I drove along that winding route one clear summer day, I had an overpowering sense of my surroundings. Above me, the dark canyon walls angled up sharply to block out the sun. Below me, the wide river surged and tossed between jagged banks of granite boulders. I strained for a better look at the water, and my hands tensed on the wheel. I was about to raft through the wildest stretch of the Salmon. It would be my first real test at running such rough rapids and I was worried.

When I met up with the other nine members of my party at the end of the road, our leader, Verne Huser, allayed my doubts. A 20-year veteran of western rafting, Huser had six Salmon trips behind him, and he liked the way the river looked now. It was high, and Verne said that would make our passage easier by covering many of the large boulders and other obstacles. Early the next morning, we inflated our 13½-foot rubber rafts, loaded up and agreed on a plan. Verne's raft would move out first and mine would follow a safe distance behind. When necessary, he would hand signal back to me. Before we hit the major rapids, we would pull ashore and scout them out.

We pushed off long before the July sun had reached the canyon floor. Verne's boat immediately caught the current and sped away. Then we accelerated too, feeling the wonderful tug that is the joy of river running. Moving water: for the next five days and 80 miles, this is the way we would go. Little did I realize, though, what lay ahead.

My first river trip had taken place in 1972 on this same stretch of the Salmon. Like most beginners, I went as part of a group

with a commercial outfitter. The intensity of that experience was so overwhelming that I was instantly hooked on the sport. Two years ago, I bought my own raft. I also had to buy oars, life jackets, a pump, rope, watertight bags, a repair kit, tools, buckets and a rowing frame.

Equipment alone doesn't make a boater, however, and I quickly learned that the only way to get proficient at river running is to do it. I did it cautiously at first and with an experienced boater along as coach. Being an old friend, Verne joined me on my first major run down the Green River in Colorado's Dinosaur National Monument. He talked me through the lesser rapids and took the oars on the big ones as I watched and learned.

As my confidence grew, I set my sights on a return trip down the Salmon. This river has presented a stiff challenge to boaters ever since it was first navigated in the 1890s. At that time, to get their supplies downriver, miners, hunters and homesteaders used 40-foot, flat-bottomed boats. Those cumbersome crafts were then either used for their lumber or left ashore at the end of each trip. Since there was no going back, the Salmon soon became known as the "River of No Return."

Our party of ten included Verne's three teenaged children and a nephew. One of his business friends also joined us. My crew consisted of two friends from Idaho, Janet Goodnoe and Les Freeman, and Jane Lamb, a visitor from England.

From the moment we took off, the river began working its magic on us. Drifting through its mile-high gorge—second deepest in North America—we were dazzled by the ever-changing landscape. There were angular lines and long shadows cast by Ponderosa pines and Douglas-fir growing high above us.

Working the oars, I was getting acquainted with the Salmon as I never did during my earlier trip. Rowing a river is like life itself. With some notable exceptions, the way to go is with the flow. Most beginning boaters tend to push and jerk a raft down a river, wasting tremendous amounts of energy. The better the boaters, the fewer the strokes they take. Yet they almost always end up in the right place at the right time, letting the river do the work.

Initially, the Salmon's whitewater came at regular intervals and it was deceptively gentle. So much so that by the end of the first day, my confidence was brimming. When we took off the next day, I felt prepared for any challenge. The first one came very quickly.

After we had drifted through a relatively quiet stretch, Verne raised his hands and rowed hard for the right bank, where he made fast. As the sound of a large rapid boiled up ahead, I followed him. This was Salmon Falls, and we all got out to look at it. The drop was about five feet and flowed through three open slots into a froth of bright standing waves. We decided to run the slot on the far right, which proved to be a quick, bouncy shot for both rafts. First a long, slow glide across the still water above the falls, then the sharp drop of the bow over the brink and into the hole, the jolt and rise of the raft as it bucked the standing wave, and finally the speedy outrun. We were in Salmon Falls for all of ten seconds.

Late that afternoon, we stopped again before approaching a series of five major rapids: Bailey, Split Rock, Big Mallard, Elkhorn and Growler. "Bailey is only big waves," said Verne. "Just take them straight." He said nothing about Split Rock but insisted on pulling ashore to scout Big Mallard.

Bailey was great! Dipping and surging, we felt like we were on a roller coaster. At Split Rock, the river swings to the right against a low cliff in a line of heavy waves. Verne pulled far to the left before sneaking around a point and shooting on through. I followed ten feet to the right of his course.

One second we were cruising along buoyantly. The next, we had dropped three feet and were surrounded by water. Then, everything turned upside down. It happened that fast. We had plunged into a huge hole—and flipped.

I bobbed up under the front compartment of the overturned raft, into a calm, green space. This, I immediately realized, was no place to be. There was nothing to hold onto and it was impossible to see where I was going. I ducked out from under the boat into a chaos of whitewater. I gasped for air and lunged at the safety rope on the side of the raft. The whole river seemed to be washing over me. I was on the verge of panic.

Going hand-over-hand on the safety rope, I worked my way around the raft as it continued to barrel downriver. Everyone else had managed to hold on, too, except for Jane. Where had she gone? We spotted her in an eddy 30 yards away, floating calmly toward shore in her orange life jacket.

Verne, too, had moved into an eddy downriver. Having seen the entire flip, his crew began rowing back into the current to intercept us as we approached. When their raft maneuvered to within 30 feet, they heaved a coiled line. We caught it and attached it to our raft, all the while trying to keep our heads above the icy water. Then Verne began straining to row toward shore. It didn't work. My raft hung in the racing current like an anchor and dragged Verne's back out.

Split Rock Rapids has three sections and as we accelerated into the second one, all we could do was hang onto the overturned raft. We ran through a shallow, choppy passageway. Underwater rocks bumped and scraped against my legs. By this time, we had been in the water for several minutes and my teeth were chattering uncontrollably. Next to me, Les was glassy eyed with fatigue.

As we continued downriver, Verne finally managed to pull Janet, Les and me into his raft. Then, we swept into the third part of the rapids—two rafts in tandem and out of control. Finally, we hit calm water and Verne rowed us all to shore. My friends and I had been floundering around in the Salmon River for ten harrowing minutes, and during that time we had traveled about 1½ miles. A short while later, another boating party showed up with Jane aboard. She had reached shore and was hiking downriver when they picked her up.

Later, we floated to a campsite and beached for the night. But our travels were far from over. Immediately below the campground was Big Mallard Rapid, the most difficult passage on the Salmon. We hiked down to it and scouted the run from several different angles. Then, back around the campfire, Verne led a step-by-step review of our flip and its aftermath. "No one wants to flip," he said, "but if you run rivers much, chances are you will." I slept uneasily that night, troubled both by the memory of Split Rock and the anticipation of what lay ahead.

Boaters respect Big Mallard more than any other rapid on the main stem of the Salmon. The only safe run is just off the left bank through a 12-foot-wide slot that goes between two boulders. The art of running Big Mallard lies in exact alignment—what boaters call "setting up"—above the slot. Missing by more than 18 inches either way means trouble. Below the two rocks are deep churning holes. Falling into one of them would be like jumping into a washing machine.

After we took to the river that morning, I carefully followed Verne and maneuvered my boat tensely into position. The slow water that dammed behind Big Mallard gave me plenty of time. A few boat lengths above the slot, the current picked up; then we flew between the two boulders, down the drop past the holes and through the choppy outwash below. It was over in seconds. We had licked Big Mallard.

We spent two more days on the Salmon, both of which had their share of majestic scenery and challenging whitewater. As our trip came to an end, I was already thinking ahead to the next challenge. The flow of a river, the magic of moving water, is habit-forming. The end of one run brings on dreams of another.

Focus

1. What training made Verne Huser a qualified leader for the trip? What training did the narrator have before this trip?
2. What is the purpose of scouting rapids on foot before rafting through them?
3. List the events in the order they happened when the rafts went through the three sections of Split Rock Rapids.
4. Why do you think the narrator's raft flipped over?
5. How does a first-hand account help to convey the excitement of a sport? Support your answer with examples from the story.
6. Why do you think river running can be habit-forming?

In Writing

What is your favorite sport that you participate in? Think about what parts of the experience are exciting or exhilarating. Write down phrases that describe the way you feel then—how those moments feel, sound, look. Using these phrases, create a brief poem about your favorite sport.

Vocabulary

Read the word list and paragraph below. Decide which word makes the best sense in each blank space. Then write the numbers *1* to *6* on a piece of paper and write the correct word next to each number.

allayed	harrowing	floundering
chaos	proficient	tandem
verge	cumbersome	aftermath

Maria and Sue are both lifeguards. Well trained and athletic, they are __(1)__ at what they do. When they saw the boy __(2)__ helplessly in the water, they knew exactly what to do. Working in __(3)__ —together—they pushed the heavy, __(4)__ boat into the water. When they reached the boy, he was on the __(5)__ of drowning. They were able to pull him aboard, however, and save him. It was a very __(6)__ experience for all three.

There are rivers
that I know,
born of ice
and melting snow,
white with rapids,
swift to roar,
with no farms
along their shore,
with no cattle
come to drink
at a staid
and welcoming brink,
with no millwheel,
ever turning,
in that cold
relentless churning.

Only deer
and bear and mink
at those shallows
come to drink,
only paddles,
swift and light,
flick that current
in their flight.

I have felt
my heart beat high,
watching
with exultant eye,
those pure rivers
which have known
no will, no purpose
but their own.

Wilderness Rivers

Elizabeth Coatsworth

98

TEXTBOOK READING: What's It All About?

Have you ever felt lost in a jungle of words? Sometimes, it is hard to understand what you read. There are two helpful ways to approach reading. The quick way is to *skim*. The slower way is to *read carefully*.

Take a first look. Skim a whole chapter or section page by page, before you read it. This quick look will give you an idea of what the material is about. It can tell you whether it is fact or fiction, or if the topic is new to you. If there are pictures, they tell more about a report. Read the main heading, or title, and any subheadings. Also look for key words, which tell what main ideas to think about.

The last step is to read carefully. Give special attention to the first sentence in each paragraph. This "introduction" can be a summary for the rest of the paragraph.

Try out these two techniques on the story *Listen to the Silent Sea*. Then answer the questions that follow.

Listen to the Silent Sea

Do you think the sea is a quiet place? You may know something of icebergs colliding. You may have read of underwater volcanoes erupting. You may have heard waves crashing. But what of the marine life beneath the calm surface waters? Are fish, water mammals, and crustaceans (animals with jointed shells) silent?

A Quiet Loudness

On a peaceful day, the deep ocean can seem quiet. However, if you put your special listening ears into the water, you might hear a commotion. A lot of noise vibrates from the ocean depths. Some of it is beyond human hearing.

An Ocean Orchestra

Certain sea creatures can communicate through sound. A beluga whale can bark, chirp, and whistle. This mammal produces sounds within air-filled pouches around the blowholes at the top of its head. A spiny lobster can screech like a piece of chalk scratching a board. This crustacean makes music by rubbing its sensitive antennae against its hard body shell. A drumfish strums by moving cordlike muscles against its air sac like a musician tuning up.

Hearing with a Different Ear

Can this symphony of the sea also hear? Yes! Most marine life has sharp hearing. In fact, sound moves better in water than in air. As well as traveling faster, sound can be much clearer in the sea—clearer to aquatic animals, that is. People have trouble hearing under water because air gets trapped in their external (outer) ears. Humans have to use special listening devices called *hydrophones* to hear sea sounds. These are microphones that can be used in water.

Most aquatic creatures have internal (inside) ears. Some water mammals and fish collect sound waves right through the skin and bones of their heads. Some crustaceans pick up sound waves through their antennae. Then the sounds are sent into their brains.

Can Aquatic Animals Help Humans?

Maybe! It is said that goldfish can hear the rumble of a storm before humans notice a cloudy sky. But, then, goldfish can't hear a high-C note. Whether or not you want to ask a goldfish about the weather is up to you.

Ancient peoples knew of aquatic communication. It helped them to fish better. The sea sounds led fishers to the best spot to drop their nets. This is how they could make good catches with the least amount of work.

What all the sea sounds mean has yet to be determined. Some possibilities are close to the same reasons that people communicate through sound. Aquatic life may want to attract friends by making their location known. They may want to announce approaching danger. They may want to threaten other marine life to keep away from their territory. They may feel good and just want to "sing."

People really don't know. What we do know is that human beings have a lot to learn about sea sounds. Careful listening has just begun.

1. Is *Listen to the Silent Sea* fact or fiction? How do you know?

2. How can people listen to a silent sea? Which paragraph told you?

3. The first subheading, "A Quiet Loudness," seems mysterious. Did you discover if something can be both quiet and loud? Explain your answer.

4. What is meant by the subheading "An Ocean Orchestra"?

5. How does a spiny lobster sound? How does it make "music"?

6. How does the first sentence under "An Ocean Orchestra" summarize the entire paragraph?

7. Is sound clearer and faster in air or in water? Under which subheading did you find the answer?

Three Set Out

Sheila Burnford

An unusual cooperation forms as three housepets embark on an incredible journey of hundreds of miles towards home.

They had kept a fairly steady pace for the first hour or so, falling into an order which was not to vary for many miles or days; the Labrador[1] ran always by the left shoulder of the old dog, for the bull terrier[2] was very nearly blind in the left eye, and they jogged along fairly steadily together—the bull terrier with his odd, rolling, sailorlike gait, and the Labrador in a slow lope. Some ten yards behind came the cat, whose attention was frequently distracted, when he would stop for a few minutes and then catch up again. But, in between these halts, he ran swiftly and steadily, his long slim body and tail low to the ground.

When it was obvious that the old dog was flagging, the Labrador turned off the quiet, graveled road and into the shade of a pinewood beside a clear, fast-running creek. The old dog drank deeply, standing up to his chest in the cold water; the cat picked his way delicately to the edge of an overhanging rock. Afterwards they rested in the deep pine needles under the trees, the terrier panting heavily with his eyes half closed, and the cat busy with his eternal washing. They lay there for nearly an hour, until the sun struck through the branches above them. The young dog rose and stretched, then walked towards the road. The old dog rose too, stiff-legged, his head low. He walked toward the waiting Labrador, limping slightly and wagging his tail at the cat, who suddenly danced into a patch of sunlight, struck at a drifting leaf, then ran straight at the dogs, swerving at the last moment, and as suddenly sitting down again.

They trotted steadily on, all that afternoon—mostly traveling on the grassy verge at the side of the quiet country road; sometimes in the low overgrown ditch that ran alongside, if the acute hearing of the young dog warned them of an approaching car.

By the time the afternoon sun lay in long, barred shadows across the road, the cat was still traveling in smooth, swift bursts, and the young dog was comparatively fresh. But the old dog was very weary, and his pace had dropped to a limping walk. They turned off the road into the bush at the side, and walked slowly through a clearing in the trees, pushing their way through the tangled undergrowth at the far end. They came out upon a small open place where a giant spruce had crashed to the ground and left a hollow where the roots had been, filled now with drifted dry leaves and spruce needles.

The late afternoon sun slanted through the branches overhead, and it looked invitingly snug and

---

[1]Labrador (lab'rə dər): a type of retriever dog

[2]bull terrier: a type of dog formerly used to chase prey into its burrow

secure. The old dog stood for a minute, his heavy head hanging, and his tired body swaying slightly, then lay down on his side in the hollow. The cat, after a good deal of careful observation, made a little hollow among the spruce needles and curled around in it, purring softly. The young dog disappeared into the undergrowth and reappeared presently, his smooth coat dripping water, to lie down a little away, apart from the others.

The old dog continued to pant exhaustedly for a long time, one hind leg shaking badly, until his eyes closed at last, the labored breaths came further and further apart, and he was sleeping—still, save for an occasional long shudder.

Later on, when darkness fell, the young dog moved over and stretched out closely at his side and the cat stalked over to lie between his paws; and so, warmed and comforted by their closeness, the old dog slept, momentarily unconscious of his aching, tired body or his hunger.

In the nearby hills a timber wolf howled mournfully; owls called and answered and glided silently by with great outspread wings; and there were faint whispers of movement and small rustling noises around all through the night. Once an eerie wail like a baby's crying woke the old dog and brought him shivering and whining to his feet; but it was only a porcupine, who scrambled noisily and clumsily down a nearby tree trunk and waddled away, still crying softly. When he lay down again the cat was gone from his side—another small night hunter slipping through the unquiet shadows that froze to stillness at his passing.

The young dog slept in fitful, uneasy starts, his muscles twitching, constantly lifting his head and growling softly. Once he sprang to his feet with a full-throated roar which brought a sudden splash in the distance, then silence—and who knows what else unknown, unseen or unheard passed through his mind to disturb him further? Only one thing was clear and certain--that at all costs he was going home, home to his own beloved master. Home lay to the west, his instinct told him; but he could not leave the other two—so somehow he must take them with him, all the way.

In the cold hour before dawn, the bull terrier woke, then staggered painfully to his feet. He was trembling with cold and was extremely hungry and thirsty. He walked stiffly in the direction of the pool nearby, passing on his way the cat, who was crouched over something held between his paws. The terrier heard a crunching sound as the cat's jaws moved, and, wagging his tail in interest, moved over to investigate. The cat regarded him distantly, then stalked away, leaving the carcass; but to the terrier it was a disappointing mess of feathers only. He drank long and deeply at the pool and on his return tried the feathers again, for he was ravenous but they stuck in his throat and he retched them out. He nibbled at some stalks of grass, then, delicately, his lips rolled back over his teeth, picked a few overripe raspberries from a low bush. He had always liked to eat domestic raspberries this way, and although the taste was reassuringly familiar, it did nothing to ease his hunger. He was pleased to see the young dog appear presently; he wagged his tail and licked the other's face, then followed resignedly when a move was made towards the direction of the road. They were followed a few moments later by the cat, who was still licking his lips after his feathery breakfast.

In the gray light of dawn the trio continued down the side of the road until they reached a point where it took a right-angled turn. Here they hesitated before a disused logging trail that led westward from the side of the road, its entrance almost concealed by overhanging branches. The leader lifted his head and appeared almost as though he were searching for the scent of something, some reassurance; and apparently he found it, for he led his companions up the trail between the overhanging trees. The going here was softer; the middle was overgrown with grass and the ruts on either side were full of dead leaves. The close-growing trees which almost met overhead would afford more shade when the sun rose higher. These were all considerations that the old dog needed, for he had been tired today even before he started, and his pace was already considerably slower.

Both dogs were very hungry and watched enviously when the cat caught and killed a chipmunk while they were resting by a stream in the middle of the day. But when the old dog advanced with a hopeful wag of his tail, the cat, growling, retreated into the bushes with his prey. Puzzled and disappointed, the terrier sat listening to the crunching sounds inside the bushes, saliva running from his mouth.

A few minutes later the cat emerged and sat down, daintily cleaning his whiskers. The old dog licked the black Siamese face with his panting tongue and was affectionately patted on the nose in return. Restless with hunger, he wandered up the banks of the creek, investigating every rock and hollow, pushing his hopeful nose through tunnels of withered sedge[3] and into the yielding earth

---

[3]sedge (sej): a grasslike plant

of molehills. Sadly he lay down by an unrewarding blueberry bush, drew his paws down tightly over his blackened face, then licked the dirt off them.

The young dog, too, was hungry; but he would have to be on the verge of starvation before the barriers of deep-rooted Labrador heredity would be broken down. For generations his ancestors had been bred to retrieve without harming, and there was nothing of the hunter in his make-up; as yet, any killing was abhorrent to him. He drank deeply at the stream and urged his companions on.

The trail ran high over the crest of this hilly, wooded country, and the surrounding countryside below was filled with an overwhelming beauty of color; the reds of the occasional maples; pale birch, and yellow poplar, and here and there the scarlet clusters of mountain ash berries against a rich dark-green background of spruce and pine and cedar.

Several times they passed log ramps built into the side of the hill, picking their way across the deep ruts left by the timber sleighs below; and sometimes they passed derelict buildings in rank, overgrown clearings, old stables for the bush horses and living quarters for the men who had worked there a generation ago. The windows were broken and sagging and weeds were growing up between the floorboards, and even one old rusted cookstove had fireweed springing from the firebox. The animals, strangely enough, did not like these evidences of human occupation and skirted them as far as possible, hair raised along their backs.

Late in the afternoon the old dog's pace had slowed down to a stumbling walk, and it seemed as if only sheer determination were keeping him on his feet at all. He was dizzy and swaying, and his heart was pounding. The cat must have sensed this general failing, for he now walked steadily beside the dogs, very close to his tottering old friend, and uttered plaintive worried bleats. Finally, the old dog came to a standstill by a deep rut half-filled with muddy water. He stood there as if he had not even the strength to step around it; his head sagged, and his whole body was trembling. Then, as he tried to lap the water, his legs seemed to crumple under him and he collapsed, half in and half out of the rut. His eyes were closed, and his body moved only to the long, shallow, shuddering breaths that came at widening intervals. Soon he lay completely limp and still. The young dog became frantic now: he whined, as he scratched at the edge of the rut, then nudged and pushed with his nose, doing everything in his power to rouse the huddled, unresponsive body. Again and again he barked, and the cat growled softly and continuously, walking back and forth and rubbing his whole length against the dirty, muddied head. There was no response to their attention. The old dog lay unconscious and remote.

The two animals grew silent, and sat by his side, disturbed and uneasy; until at last they turned and left him, neither looking back—the Labrador disappearing into the bushes where the crack of broken branches marked his progress farther and farther away; the cat stalking a partridge which had appeared at the side of the trail some hundred yards away and was pecking unconcernedly at the sandy dirt. But at the shrill warning of a squirrel, it flew off across the trail with a sudden whirr into the trees, while the cat was still some distance away. Undaunted, still licking his lips in anticipation, the cat continued around a bend in the trail in search of another, and was lost to sight.

The shadows lengthened across the deserted track, and the evening wind sighed down it to sweep a flurry of whispering leaves across the rut, their brown brittleness light as a blessing as they drifted across the unheeding white form. The curious squirrel peered in bright-eyed wonder from a nearby tree, clucking softly to itself. A shrew[4] ran halfway across, paused and ran back; and there was a soft sound of wings as a whiskey-jack[5] landed and swayed to and fro on a birch branch, tilting his head to one side as he looked down and called to his mate to come and join him. The wind died away—a sudden hush descended.

Suddenly, there was a sound of a heavy body pushing through the undergrowth, accompanied by a sharp cracking of branches, and the spell was broken. Chattering shrilly in alarm and excitement, the squirrel ran up the trunk of the tree and the whisky-jacks flew off. Now onto the trail on all fours scampered a half-grown bear cub, round furry ears pricked and small deep-set eyes alight with curiosity in the sharp little face as he beheld the old dog. There was a grunting snuffling sound in the bush behind the cub: his mother was investigating a rotten tree stump. The cub stood for a moment and then hesitantly advanced toward the rut where the terrier lay. He sniffed around, wrinkling his facile nose at the unfamiliar smell, then reached out a long curved black paw and tapped the white head. For a moment the mists of unconsciousness cleared and the old dog opened his eyes, aware of danger. The cub sprang back in alarm and watched from a safe distance. Seeing that

[4]shrew: a mouselike mammal with a long snout
[5]whiskey-jack: a type of bird, a Canada jay

there was no further movement, he loped back and cuffed again with his paw, this time harder, and watched for a response. Only enough strength was left in the old dog for a valiant baring of his teeth. He snarled faintly with pain and hatred when his shoulder was raked by the wicked claws of the excited cub, and made an attempt to struggle to his feet. The smell of the drawn blood excited the cub further; he straddled the dog's body and started to play with the long white tail, nibbling at the end like a child with a new toy. But there was no response: all conscious effort drained, the old dog no longer felt any pain or indignity. He lay as though asleep, his eyes veiled and unseeing, his lip still curled in a snarl.

Around the bend in the trail, dragging a large dead partridge by the wing, came the cat. The wing sprang back softly from his mouth as he gazed transfixed at the scene before him. In one split second a terrible transformation took place; his blue eyes glittered hugely and evilly in the black masked face, and every hair on the wheat-colored body stood upright so that he appeared twice his real size; even the chocolate-colored tail puffed up as it switched from side to side. He crouched low to the ground, tensed and ready, and uttered a high, ear-splitting scream; and, as the startled cub turned, the cat sprang.

He landed on the back of the dark furred neck, clinging with his monkeylike hind legs while he raked his claws across the cub's eyes. Again and again he raked with the terrible claws, hissing and spitting in murderous devilry until the cub was screaming in pain and fear, blinded with blood, making ineffectual brushing movements with his paws to dislodge the unseen horror on his back. His screams were answered by a thunderous roar as the huge black she-bear crashed through the bushes and rushed to the cub. She swiped at the clinging cat with a tremendous paw; but the cat was too quick for her and with a hiss of fury leaped to the ground and disappeared behind a tree. The unfortunate cub's head received the full force of the blow and he was sent spinning across the track into the bushes. In a blind, frustrated rage, maddened by the cries of her cub, the mother turned for something on which to vent her fury, and saw the still figure of the old dog. Even as she lumbered snarling towards him the cat distracted her attention with a sudden leap to the side of the track. The bear halted, then reared up to full height for attack, red eyes glinting savagely, neck upstretched and head weaving from side to side in a menacing, snakelike way. The cat uttered another banshee scream and stepped forward with a stiff-legged, sideways movement, his

squinting, terrible eyes fixed on his enormous adversary. Something like fear or indecision crept into the bear's eyes as the cat advanced; she shuffled back a step with lowered head. Slow, deliberate, purposeful, the cat came on—again the bear retreated, bewildered by the tactics of this terrible small animal, distraught by her cub's whimpering, slowly falling back before the relentless inch-by-inch advance. Now the cat stopped and crouched low, lashing his tail from side to side—the bear stopped too, shifting her weight uneasily before the spring that must follow, longing to decamp but afraid to turn her back. A sudden crackle of undergrowth turned the huge animal into a statue, rigid with apprehension—and when a great dog sprang out of the bush and stood beside the cat, teeth bared and snarling, every hair on his back erect, she dropped to all fours, turned swiftly and fled towards her cub. There was a last growl of desperate bravado from the bush and a whimpering cry; then the sounds of the bears' escape receded in the distance. Finally all was quiet again; the curious squirrel leaped from his ringside seat and scrambled farther down the trunk of the tree.

The cat shrank back to his normal size. His eyes regained their usual cool, detached look. He shook each paw distastefully in turn, glanced briefly at the limp, muddied bundle by his feet, blood

109

oozing from four deep parallel gashes on the shoulder, then turned and sauntered slowly down the track towards his partridge.

The young dog nosed his friend all over, his lips wrinkling at the rank bear smell, then attempted to stop the bleeding with his rough tongue. He scratched fresh leaves over the bloodstained wounds, then barked by the old dog's head; but there was no response, and at last he lay down panting on the grass. His eyes were uneasy and watchful, the hairs still stood upright in a ridge on his back, and from time to time he whined in perplexity. He watched the cat drag a large gray bird almost up to the nose of the unconscious dog, then slowly and deliberately begin to tear at the bird's flesh. He growled softly, but the cat ignored him and continued his tearing and eating. Presently, the enticing smell of raw, warm meat filtered through into the old dog's senses. He opened one eye and gave an appreciative sniff. The effect was galvanizing: his muddied half-chewed tail stirred and he raised his shoulders, then his forelegs, with a convulsive effort, like an old work horse getting up after a fall.

He was a pitiful sight—the half of his body that had lain in the rut was black and soaking, while the other was streaked and stained with blood. He looked like some grotesque clown. He trembled violently and uncontrollably through-out the length of his body, but in the sunken depths of the slanted black eyes there was a faint gleam of interest—which increased as he pushed his nose into the still-warm bundle of soft gray feathers. This time there was no growling rebuff over the prey: instead, the cat sat down a few yards away, studiedly aloof and indifferent, then painstakingly washed down the length of his tail. When the end twitched he pinned it down with a paw.

The old dog ate, crunching the bones ravenously with his blunt teeth. Even as his companions watched him, a miraculous strength slowly seeped back into his body. He dozed for a while, a feather hanging from his mouth, then woke again to finish the last morsel. By nightfall he was able to walk over to the soft grass at the side of the track, where he lay down and blinked happily at his companions, wagging his pitiful tail. The Labrador lay down beside him, and licked the wounded shoulder.

An hour or two later the purring cat joined them, carelessly dropping another juicy morsel by his old friend's nose. This was a deer mouse, a little creature with big eyes and long hind legs like a miniature kangaroo. It was swallowed with a satisfying gulp, and soon the old dog slept.

But the cat purring against his chest and the young dog curled at his back were wakeful and alert most of the remaining night; neither moved from his side.

Hunger was now the ruling instinct in the Labrador and it drove him out to forage in the early dawn. He was desperate enough to try some deer droppings, but spat them out immediately in disgust. While he was drinking from a marsh pool still covered with lily pads, he saw a frog staring at him with goggle eyes from a small stone: measuring the distance carefully, he sprang and caught it in the air as it leaped to safety. It disappeared down his throat in one crunch and he looked around happily for more. But an hour's patient search rewarded him with only two, so he returned to his companions. They had apparently eaten, for there were feathers and fur scattered around and both were licking their lips. But something warned him not to urge his old companion on. The terrier was still utterly exhausted, and in addition had lost a lot of blood from the gashes suffered at the cub's claws the day before. These were stiff and black with blood, and had a tendency to open and bleed slightly with any movement, so all that day he lay peacefully in the warm fall sunshine on the grass sleeping, eating what the cat provided, and wagging his tail whenever one of the others came near.

The young dog spent most of the day still occupied with his ceaseless foraging for food. By evening he was desperate, but his luck turned when a rabbit, already changing to its white winter coat, suddenly started up from the long grass and swerved across his path. Head down, tail flying, the young dog gave chase, swerving and turning in pursuit, but always the rabbit was just out of reach of his hungry jaws. At last, he put all his strength into one violent lunge and felt the warm pulsating prize in his mouth. The generations fell away, and the years of training never to sink teeth into feathers or fur; for a moment the Labrador looked almost wolflike as he tore at the warm flesh and bolted it down in ravenous gulps.

They slept in the same place that night and most of the following day, and the weather mercifully continued warm and sunny. By the third day the old dog seemed almost recovered and the wounds were closed. He had spent most of the day ambling around and sleeping, so that by now he seemed almost frisky and quite eager to walk a little.

So, in the late afternoon, they left the place which had been their home for three days and trotted slowly along the track together again. By the time the moon rose they had traveled several miles, and they had come to the edge of a small lake which the track skirted.

A moose was standing in the water among the lily pads on the

far shore, his great antlered head and humped neck silhouetted clearly against the pale moon. He took no notice of the strange animals across the water but thrust his head again and again under the water, raising it high in the air after each immersion, and arching his neck. Two or three water hens swam out from the reeds, a little crested grebe[6] popped up like a jack-in-the-box, in the water beside them, and the spreading ripples of their wake caught the light of the moon. As the three sat, ears pricked, they watched the moose squelch slowly out of the muddy water, shake himself, and turn, cantering up the bank out of sight.

The young dog turned his head suddenly, his nose twitching, for his keen scent had caught a distant whiff of wood smoke, and of something else—something

---

[6]grebe (grēb): a diving bird somewhat like a duck

unidentifiable. . . . Seconds later, the old dog caught the scent too, and started to his feet, snuffing and questioning with his nose. His thin whippy tail began to sweep to and fro and a bright gleam appeared in the slanted black-currant eyes. Somewhere, not too far away, were human beings—his world: he could not mistake their message—or refuse their invitation—they were undoubtedly cooking something. He trotted off determinedly in the direction of the tantalizing smell. The young dog followed somewhat reluctantly, and for once the cat passed

them both; a little moon-mad perhaps, for he lay in wait to dart and strike, then streaked back into the shadows, only to reappear a second later in an elaborate stalk of their tails. Both dogs ignored him.

The scent on the evening breeze was a fragrant mixture of roasting rice, wild-duck stew and wood smoke. When the animals looked down from a hill, tantalized and hungry, they saw six or seven fires in the clearing below—their flames lighting up a semicircle of tents and conical birch-bark shelters against a dark background of trees; flickering over the canoes drawn

up on the edge of a wild rice marsh and dying redly in the black waters beyond; and throwing into ruddy relief the high, flat planes of brown Ojibway[7] faces gathered around the centers of warmth and brightness.

The men were a colorful lot in jeans and bright plaid shirts, but the women were dressed in somber colors. Two young boys, the only children there, were going from fire to fire shaking grain in shallow pans and stirring it with paddles as it cooked. One man in long soft moccasins stood in a shallow pit trampling husks, half his weight supported on a log frame. Some of the band lay back from the fires, smoking and watching idly, talking softly among themselves; while others still ate, scooping the fragrant contents of a black iron pot onto tin plates. Every now and then one of them would throw a bone back over a shoulder into the bush, and the watching animals gazed hungrily after. A woman stood at the edge of the clearing pouring grain from one bark platter to another, and the loose chaff drifted off on the slight wind like smoke.

The old dog saw nothing of this, but his ears and nose supplied all that he needed to know: he could contain himself no longer and picked his way carefully down the hillside, for his shoulder still pained him. Halfway down he sneezed violently in a swirl of chaff. One of the boys by the fire looked up at the sound, his hand closing on a stone, but the woman nearby spoke sharply, and he waited, watching intently.

The old dog limped out of the shadows and into the ring of firelight, confident, friendly, and sure of his welcome; his tail wagging his whole stern ingratiatingly, ears and lips laid back in his nightmarish grimace. There was a stunned silence—broken by a wail of terror from the smaller boy, who flung himself at his mother—and then a quick excited chatter from the Indians. The old dog was rather offended and uncertain for a moment, but he made hopefully for the nearest boy, who retreated, nervously clutching his stone. But again the woman rebuked her son, and at the sharpness of her tone the old dog stopped, crestfallen. She laid down her basket then, and walked quickly across the ring of firelight, stooping down to look more closely. She spoke some soft words of reassurance, then patted his head gently and smiled at him. The old dog leaned against her and whipped his tail against her black stockings, happy to be in contact with a human being again. She crouched down beside him to run

---

[7]Ojibway (ō jib'wā): a tribe of American Indians formerly living around Lake Superior

114

her fingers lightly over his ears and back, and when he licked her face appreciatively, she laughed. At this, the two little boys drew nearer to the dog and the rest of the band gathered around. Soon the old dog was where he most loved to be—the center of attention among some human beings. He made the most of it and played to an appreciative audience; when one of the men tossed him a chunk of meat he sat up painfully on his hindquarters and begged for more, waving one paw in the air. This sent the Indians into paroxysms of laughter, and he had to repeat his performance time and time again, until he was tired and lay down, panting but happy.

The Indian woman stroked him gently in reward, then scooped some of the meat from the pot onto the grass. The old dog limped towards it; but before he ate he looked up in the direction of the hillside where he had left his two companions.

A small stone rebounded from rock to rock, then rolled into the sudden silence that followed.

When a long-legged, blue-eyed cat appeared out of the darkness, paused, then filled the clearing with a strident plaintive voice before walking up to the dog and calmly taking a piece of meat from him, the Indians laughed until they were speechless and hiccupping. The two little boys rolled on the ground, kicking their heels in

an abandonment of mirth, while the cat chewed his meat unmoved; but this was the kind of behavior the bull terrier understood, and he joined in the fun. But he rolled so enthusiastically that the wounds reopened: when he got to his feet again his white coat was stained with blood.

All this time the young dog crouched on the hillside, motionless and watchful, although every driving, urgent nerve in his body fretted and strained at the delay. He watched the cat, well-fed and content, curl himself on the lap of one of the sleepy children by the fire; he heard the faint note of derision in some of the Indians' voices as a little, bent, ancient crone addressed them in earnest and impassioned tones before hobbling over to the dog to examine his shoulder as he lay peacefully before the fire. She threw some cattail roots into a boiling pot of water, soaked some moss in the liquid, and pressed it against the dark gashes. The old dog did not move; only his tail beat slowly. When she had finished, she scooped some more meat onto a piece of birch bark and set it on the grass before the dog; and the silent watcher above licked his lips and sat up, but still he did not move from his place.

But when the fires began to burn low and the Indians made preparations for the night, and still his companions showed no signs of

115

moving, the young dog grew restless. He skirted the camp, moving like a shadow through the trees on the hill behind, until he came out upon the lake's shore a quarter of a mile upwind of the camp. Then he barked sharply and demandingly several times.

The effect was like an alarm bell on the other two. The cat sprang from the arms of the sleepy little Indian boy and ran towards the old dog, who was already on his feet, blinking and peering around rather confusedly. The cat gave a throaty yowl, then deliberately ran ahead, looking back as he paused beyond the range of firelight. The old dog shook himself resignedly and walked slowly after—reluctant to leave the warmth of the fire. The Indians watched impassively and silently and made no move to stop him. Only the woman who had first befriended him called out softly, in the tongue of her people, a farewell to the traveler.

The dog halted at the treeline beside the cat and looked back, but the commanding, summoning bark was heard again, and together the two passed out of sight and into the blackness of the night.

Focus

1. Describe the three animals that traveled together in this story.
2. Which animal was "in charge" of the journey? How did the author tell you this?
3. Which animal was most fitted for survival on its own? Explain why that animal was more fitted than each of the other two.
4. How did the Labrador change during the story?
5. What is the story's setting? Name three events that could not have happened if the story had been set in a city.

In Writing

Suppose you were one of the Ojibways in the group visited by the animals that night. Describe your impressions when the animals first entered the camp. Also describe your thoughts when they left.

Vocabulary

On a piece of paper, write the numbers 1 to 5. Then look at the words in the first column and find a synonym for each word in the second column. Next to each number on your paper, write the letter of the synonym for each word.

1. derelict		A. intending
2. receded		B. confused
3. strident		C. harsh
4. enticing		D. tempting
5. distraught		E. abandoned
		F. withdrew

Tracking and Trailing

Ernest Thompson Seton

Do you live among wild animals? You may change your answer after reading this.

Of all the feats common to hunting life and woodcraft, none seems to me half so wondrous as tracking and trailing. As practiced by humans, tracking is wonderful enough. But far more marvelous is the power by which a dog or a fox can follow its prey at full speed, guided only by scent without erring or being led astray.

To us the word "scent" has but little meaning. It is the name of a power with which the human is, comparatively, almost unendowed. We go into the woods and see nothing but a leaf-strewn ground, thinly scattered over with herbs and thickly planted with trees. We see no quadruped, and find no sign of any, perhaps, save the faraway chatter of a squirrel. But our dog, merrily careening about, is possessed of a superior power. At every moment of his course he is gathering facts and reading a wonderful record of the past, the present, and even of the future. "Here," says his unseen guide, "is where a deer passed a minute ago" or "an hour ago." "This was the course of a fox a week ago." "That was the direction in which a rabbit flew by a few minutes ago, and, oho! there was a weasel after him!" "This track of a woodchuck leading away to yonder hole; there he lies still, and with the help of your master, you will take him home with you."

Such is the curious record of scent, revealed to the dog but hidden to us, and even unexplainable to us. Though we have some knowledge of the subject, it is too imperfect to make us fully understand that each individual animal has its own scent. Thus the dog can tell the difference between not only the bucks, does, and fawns of the deer tribe, but can pick out of a dozen the track of the particular buck that he is following, and never leave it or lose it. Moreover, he can tell by the scent which way the animal is going, and he is never known to run backward on a trail. Now, when we compare this wonderful power with our own feeble sense of smell, we will be ready to admit that it is a faculty of which humans, comparatively, have little.

It is a remarkable fact that there are always more wild animals about than any but the experts has an idea of. For example, there are, within twenty miles of New York City, full fifty different kinds—not counting birds, reptiles, or fishes—one quarter of which at least are abundant. Or, more particularly, within the limits of Greater New York there are at least a dozen species of wild beasts, half of which are quite common.

"Then how is it we never see any?" is the first question of the incredulous. The answer is: long ago the beasts learned the dire lesson—humans are your worst enemy; shun them at any price. And the simplest way to do this is to come out only at night. Humans are daytime creatures; they are blind in the soft half-light that most beasts prefer.

While many animals have always limited their activity to the hours of twilight and gloom, there are not a few that were diurnal, but have given up that portion of their working day in order to avoid their archenemy.

Thus they came to flourish under our noses and eat at our tables, without our knowledge or consent. They come and go at will, and the world knows nothing of them. Their presence long ago goes unsuspected but for one thing, well known to the hunter, the trapper, and the naturalist: wherever the wild fourfoot goes, it leaves behind it a record of its visit, its name, the direction whence it came, the time, the things it did or tried to do, with the time and direction of departure. These it puts down in the ancient script of tracks in the mud, dust, or snow. Each of these dotted lines called a trail is a wonderful unfinished record of the creature's life during the time it made the same, and it needs only the patient work of the naturalist to figure out that record and from it learn much about the animal that made it, without that animal ever having been seen.

The ideal time for tracking, and almost the only time for most folk, is when the ground is white. After the first snow the student walks forth and begins at once to realize the wonders of the trail. A score of creatures whose existence, maybe, the student did not know of, are now revealed, and the reading of their autographs becomes easy.

It is when snow is on the ground, indeed, that we take the fourfoot census of the woods. How often we learn with surprise from the telltale white that a fox was around our henhouse last night, a mink is living even now under the woodpile, and a deer—yes! there is no mistaking its sharp-pointed, unsheeplike footprint—has wandered into our woods from the farther wilds.

Never lose the chance of the first snow if you wish to become a trailer. Nevertheless, remember that the first morning after a night snowfall is not so good as the second. Most creatures "lie up" during the storm. The snow hides the tracks of those that do go forth, and some actually go into a "cold sleep" for a day or two after a heavy downfall. But a calm, mild night following a storm is sure to offer abundant and ideal opportunity for beginning the study of the trail.

Here are some important facts to keep in view when you set forth to master the basics.

First: No two animals leave the same trail. Not only each kind, but each individual and at each stage of its life, leaves a trail as distinctive as the creature's appearance. And it is obvious that, in that, they differ among themselves just as we do, because the young know their mothers, the mothers know their young, and the old ones know their mates, when scent is clearly out of the question.

Another simple evidence of this is the well-known fact that no two human beings have the same thumb mark. All living creatures have corresponding peculiarities, and all use these parts in making a trail.

Second: The trail was begun at the birthplace of that creature and ends only at its death. It may be recorded in visible track or peculiar odor. It may last a few hours, and may be too faint even for an expert with present equipment to follow, but evidently the trail is made, wherever the creature journeys afoot.

120

Third: It varies with every important change of impulse, action, or emotion.

Fourth: When we find a trail we may rest assured that, if living, the creature that made it is at the other end. And if one can follow, it is only a question of time before coming up with that animal. And be sure of its direction before setting out; many a novice has lost much time by going backward on the trail.

Fifth: In studying trails, one must always keep probabilities in mind. Sometimes one kind of track looks much like another; then the question is, which is the likeliest in this place?

If I saw a jaguar track in India I should know it was made by a leopard. If I found a leopard trail in Colorado I should be sure I had found the mark of a cougar or a mountain lion. A wolf track on Broadway would doubtless be the doing of a large dog. And a St. Bernard's footmark in the Rockies, twenty miles from anywhere, would most likely turn out to be the imprint of a gray wolf's foot. To be sure of the marks, then, one should know all the animals that belong to the neighborhood.

In the winter of 1900, I was standing with my brother, a businessman, on Goat Island, Niagara, when he remarked, "How is it? You and I have been in the same parts of America for twenty years, yet I never see any of the curious sides of animal life that you are continually coming across."

"Largely because you do not study tracks," was my reply. "Look at your feet now. There is a whole history to be read."

"I see some marks," he replied, "that might have been made by some animal."

"That is the track of a cottontail," was the answer. "Now let us read this chapter of its life. See, it went in a general straight course as though making for some well-known haunt. Its easy pace, with eight or ten inches between each set of tracks, shows unalarm. But see here, joining on is something else."

"So there is. Another cottontail."

"Not at all. This new track is smaller, the forefeet are more or less paired, showing that the creature can climb a tree. There is a suggestion of toe pads and there is a mark telling evidently of a long tail. These things combined with the size and the place identify it clearly. This is the trail of a mink. See! he also found the

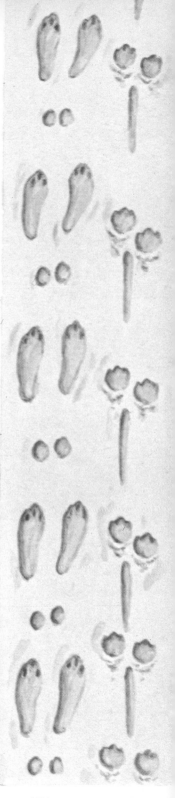

rabbit track, and finding it fresh, he followed it. His bounds are lengthening now, but the rabbit's are not, showing that the latter was unconscious of the pursuit."

After 100 yards the double trail led us to a great pile of wood, and into this both went. Having followed his game into dense cover, the trailer's first business is to make sure that it did not go out the other side. We went carefully around the pile; there were no tracks leading out.

"Now," I said, "if you will take the trouble to move that woodpile you will find in it the remains of the rabbit half-devoured, and the mink himself, at this moment, is no doubt curled up asleep."

As the pile was large and the conclusion more or less self-evident, my brother was content to accept my reading of the events.

Although so much is to be read in the winter white, we cannot now make a full account of all the woodland fourfoots, for there are some kinds that do not come out in the snow. They sleep more or less all winter.

Thus one rarely sees the track of chipmunk or woodchuck in truly wintry weather. And never, as far as I know, have the trails of jumping mouse or mud turtle been seen in the snow. These we can track only in the mud or dust. Such trails cannot be followed as far as those in snow, simply because the mud and dust do not cover the whole country, but they are usually as clear and in some respects more easy to record.

It is a most fascinating amusement to learn some creature's way of life by following its fresh track for hours in good snow. I never miss such a chance. If I cannot find a fresh track I take a stale one, knowing that it is fresher at every step, and from practical experiences that it always brings one to some track that is fresh.

How often I have wished for a perfect means of transferring these wild-life tales to paper or otherwise making a permanent collection. My earliest attempts were in freehand drawing, which answered, but has a great disadvantage—it is a translation, a record discolored by an intervening personality, and the value of the result is likely to be limited by one's own knowledge at the time.

Casting in plaster was another means attempted; but not one track in 10,000 is fit to cast. Nearly all are blemished and imperfect in some way, and the most abundant—those in the snow—cannot be cast at all.

Then I tried spreading plastic wax where the beasts would walk on it, in pathways or before dens. How they did scoff! The simplest ground squirrel knew too much to step on my waxen snare: around it or, if hemmed in, over it, with a mighty bound, but never a track did I get.

Photography naturally suggested itself, but the difficulties proved as great as unexpected, almost as great as in casting. Not one track in 1,000 is fit to photograph: the essential details are almost always left out. You must have open sunlight, and even when the weather is perfect there are practically but two times each day when it is possible. Those are in mid-morning and mid-afternoon, when the sun is high enough for clear photographs and low enough to cast a shadow in the faint track.

Then a new method was suggested in an unexpected way. A friend of mine had a pet raccoon which he kept in a cage in his apartment uptown. One day, during my friend's absence, the raccoon got loose and set about a series of long-deferred exploring expeditions, beginning with the bedroom. The first promising object was a writing desk. Mounting by a chair, the raccoon examined several uninteresting books and papers, and then noticed higher up a large stone bottle. He had several times found pleasurable stuff in bottles, so he went for it. The cork was lightly in and easily removed, but the smell was far from inviting, for it was a quart of ink. Determined to leave no stone unturned, however, the raccoon upset the ink to taste and try. Alas! it tasted even worse than it smelled; it was an utter failure as a beverage.

And the raccoon, pushing it contemptuously away, turned to a pile of fine handmade notepaper—the pride of my friend's heart. And when he raised his inky little paws there were left on the paper some beautiful black prints.

This was a new idea; the raccoon tried it again and again. But the ink held out longer than the paper, so the fur-clad printer worked over assorted books and the adjoining walls, while the ink, dribbling over everything, formed a great pool below the

desk. Something attracted the artist's attention, causing him to jump down. He landed in the pool of ink, making it splash in all directions; some of the black splotches reached the white counterpane[1] on the bed. Another happy idea! The raccoon now leaped on the bed racing around as long as the ink on his feet gave results. As he paused to rest, or perhaps to see if any place had been neglected, the door opened, and in came the landlady. The scene which followed was too painful for description; no one present enjoyed it. My friend was sent for to come take his raccoon out of there forever. He came and took him away. I suppose "forever." He had only one other place for him—his office—and there it was I made the animal's acquaintance and heard of his exploits: an ink-and-paper if not a literary affair.

This gave me the hint I needed, a plan to make authentic records of animal tracks. Armed with printer's ink and paper rolls, I set about gathering a dictionary collection of imprints.

After many failures and much experiment, better methods

----
[1]counterpane: bedspread

124

were devised. A number of improvements were made by my wife; one was the substitution of black paint for printer's ink, as the latter dries too quickly. Another was the padding of the paper, which should be light and soft for very light animals, and stronger and harder for the heavy. Printing from a mouse, for example, is much like printing a delicate etching. The ink, paper, dampness, etc., must be exactly right, and furthermore you have this handicap—you cannot regulate the pressure. This is, of course, strictly a zoo method; all attempts to secure black prints from wild animals have been total failures. The paper, the smell of paint, etc., are enough to keep the wild things away.

In the zoo we spread the black pad and white paper in a narrow, temporary lane. Then one by one we drove, or tried to drive, the captives over them, securing a series of tracks that are life-sized, properly spaced, absolutely authentic, and capable of yielding more facts as the observer learns more about the subject.

As related here, all this sounds quite easy. But you have no idea how cross-crooked and contrary a creature can be until you wish it to repeat for you some ordinary thing that it has already done hourly. Some of them balked at the paint, some at the paper, some made a leap to clear all, and thereby wrecked the entire apparatus. Some would begin very well, but rush back when halfway over so as to destroy the print already made, and in most cases the calmest, steadiest, tamest of beasts become unmanageable when approached with "trackological" intent.

Even tame animals are difficult. A cat that was highly trained to do anything a cat could do, was selected as promising for a black track study, and her owner's two boys volunteered to get all the tracks I needed. They put down a long roll of paper in a hall, painted the cat's feet black, and proceeded to chase her up and down. Her docility vanished under the strain. She raced madly about, leaving long, useless splashes of black. Then, leaping to a fanlight,[2] she escaped upstairs to take refuge among the snowy draperies. After which the boys' troubles began.

These, however, are mere by-incidents and illustrate the

---

[2]fanlight: a semicircular window with radiating bars, often over a door

many practical difficulties. After these had been conquered with patience and ingenuity, there could be no doubt of the value of the prints. They are the best of records for size, spacing, and detail, but fail in giving *incidents of wild life* or the landscape surroundings. The drawings are best for a long series and for faint features. In fact, the drawing alone can give *everything you can perceive*; but it fails in authentic size and detail.

Photography has this great advantage—it gives the essential surroundings, the essential landscape and setting and, therefore, the local reason for many changes of action on the part of the animal. Also the esthetic beauties of its records are unique and will help to keep the methods in high place.

Thus each of the three means may be successful in a different way, and the best, most nearly perfect alphabet of the woods would include all three, and consist of a drawing, a pedoscript,[3] and a photograph of each track, i.e., a simple footprint and the long series of each animal.

My practice has been to use all whenever I could, but still I find freehand drawing is the one most practical application. When I get a photograph I treasure it as an adjunct to the sketch.

There is another feature of trail study that gives it exceptional value—it is an account of the creature *pursuing its ordinary life*. If you succeed in getting a glimpse of a fox or hare in the woods, the chances are a hundred to one that it was aware of your presence first. They are much cleverer than we at this sort of thing, and if they do not actually sight or scent you, they observe, and are warned by, the action of some creature that *did* sense you, and so cease their occupations to steal away or hide. But the snow story will tell of the life that the animal ordinarily leads—its method of searching for food, its kind of food, the help it gets from its friends, or sometimes from its rivals—and thus offers an insight into its home ways that is scarcely to be gained in any other way. The tracker has the key to a new storehouse of nature's secrets. It is like the rolling away of fogs from a mountain view, and the tracker comes closer than others to the heart of the woods.

---

[3]pedoscript (pēd′ə skript): a footprint

Focus

1. When is the ideal time for tracking animals? Why? Name one disadvantage of tracking at this time.
2. Why do we see so few wild animals around us, even when many are there?
3. Describe three of the methods the author has used in his attempt to record animal tracks.
4. Why is it important to record a sample of an animal's stride as well as its footprint?
5. Why does the author say that studying tracks will give a more accurate picture of an animal's ordinary life than actually seeing the animal itself?
6. What qualities do you think a person would need in order to enjoy tracking animals?

In Writing

Research one kind of wild animal that lives in your area. Find information about its living habits and the kind of tracks it makes. Write a brief report and include drawings of sample tracks.

Vocabulary

On a piece of paper, write the numbers *1* to *5*. Then read the sentences below and select the word from the list that best fits each sentence. Next to each number on your paper, write the correct word for the sentence.

novice	haunt	translation
astray	diurnal	devised
careening	balk	docility

1. The ___ made several mistakes, but the expert made none.
2. The ___ of the speech from English to Spanish did not take long and was appreciated by the Spanish-speaking audience.
3. Lisa had ___ a plan that made it possible for everyone to leave early.
4. The sudden flash of lightning made the horse ___ at entering the stable.
5. The cars were ___ along the track at very high speeds.

The Way through the Woods

Rudyard Kipling

They shut the road through the woods
Seventy years ago.
Weather and rain have undone it again,
And now you would never know
There was once a road through the woods
Before they planted the trees.
It is underneath the coppice and heath
And the thin anemones.
Only the keeper sees
That, where the ring-dove broods,
And the badgers roll at ease,
There was once a road through the woods.

Yet, if you enter the woods
Of a summer evening late,
When the night-air cools on the trout-ringed pools
Where the otter whistles his mate,
(They fear not men in the woods,
Because they see so few.)
You will hear the beat of a horse's feet,
And the swish of a skirt in the dew,
Steadily cantering through
The misty solitudes,
As though they perfectly knew
The old lost road through the woods. . . .

But there is no road through the woods.

STUDY SKILL: Using Information on Maps

If you planned to spend your summer vacation hiking in Vermont, you would want to look at the maps shown here. These could help you to plan the best places to go.

Although the maps show the state of Vermont, they look very different. Do you know why?

The first map is called a *physical map*. It shows different land and water forms such as the hills, plains, mountains, rivers, and lakes. The other map is called a *political map*. It shows the political divisions of the area. Cities, towns, and counties are all political divisions.

Look at the Key on the map of a portion of Vermont. Find the symbol for "mountains." Every time you see that symbol on the map, it indicates a mountain. Next to each of these symbols you will find the name and the height of that mountain. Can you find the highest mountain? What is its height?

If you compared the heights of the different mountains shown, you found that Mt. Mansfield is the highest mountain. It is 4,393 feet high.

Now that you have looked at some of the highest mountains in the state, you decide to do a little research on them. Someone sug-

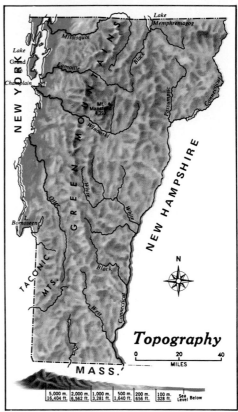

Map copyright of
Hammond Incorporated, Maplewood, N. J.
Physical Map

gests that you might browse through the records kept at the state capital or in the county courthouses in each county seat. Look again at the Key on the political map. Find the symbols for the state capital and the county seats. Each colored section on this map is a separate county.

130

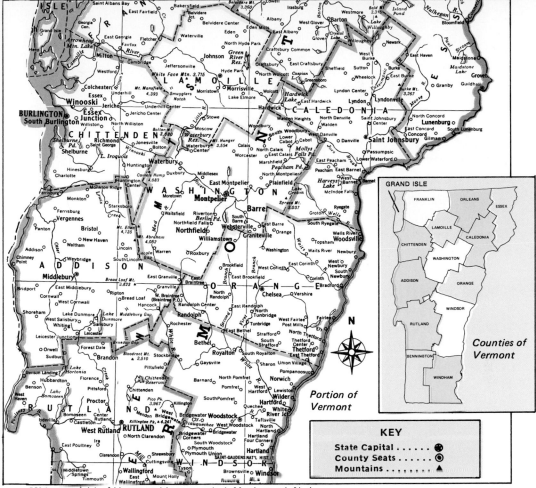

Map copyright of Hammond Incorporated, Maplewood, N. J.

Political Map

Use the political map to answer the following questions.

1. Into how many counties is Vermont divided?

2. In which county is Mt. Mansfield (NE of Burlington)?

3. If you planned to climb Mt. Mansfield, in which town might you stay?

4. Name four other mountains that are shown north of Burlington.

5. In which counties are these mountains located?

6. What is the state capital of Vermont? In which county is it?

7. What is the county seat of Chittenden?

8. Suppose you wanted to do some research on the historical records of the area around Killington. Where would you go for this information?

I Like Skunks

Louise Dickinson Rich

If a skunk became a member of your family,
what changes do you think
would occur?

We don't believe in confining wild animals; so, feeling as we do, we never try to make pets of the wild life around us. Just once we made an exception, but that was none of our seeking. This is the way it happened. I had ordered three lemons, so when Ralph, my husband, came home with the mail and handed me a little paper bag I thought I knew what was in it. I tipped it up, and dumped the contents out on the kitchen workbench.

"Take that thing away from here," I shrieked. My lemons had changed into a two or three days old skunk.

When I recovered my composure enough to look the thing over, I had to admit it was cute. It was about three inches long, with an equally long tail and about half-inch legs, and it was striped black and white like any other skunk. Ralph had seen it in the road when he went up to get the mail, and when he came back, over an hour later, it was still there. By then it had fallen into a deep rut and was unable to get out. He stopped the car to help it, and discovered that it was almost too weak to stand. We discovered later that, the day before, a mother skunk accompanied by her new and numerous babies had had a skirmish there with a dog. In the fracas, this little fellow, whom we named Rollo, got lost.

132

You can't go off and leave a young thing to die of starvation, naturally, so Ralph picked it up and brought it home. He put it in the lemon bag so that he could hold it without hurting it while he drove with one hand. He thought he could probably figure out some way to feed it after he got it home.

Cookie, Kyak's mother and the best dog we ever had, was our dog of the moment. Not to put too strong a point on it, she was the best dog anybody ever had, bar none. Kyak and the other pups were a couple of weeks old, and we were still keeping them in a pen in the corner of the kitchen, where they'd be warm and where Cookie could reach them easily. While we were debating the skunk question, she came in to dispense the evening meal to her family. That seemed to be the answer. We found an unoccupied nipple, told Cookie everything was under control, and added Rollo to the group. She looked a little startled, but, being the dog she was, took our word for it that it was all right. That's the kind of good dog she was.

Cookie was willing, and Rollo had the right idea, but a husky is built on a somewhat grander scale than a skunk, so it wouldn't work. Then we thought of a medicine dropper, and that did work. Poor little Rollo went at it, clutching the dropper frenziedly with both front paws, and never stopped drinking the warmed canned milk and water until his little stomach was as round and hard—and about as large as a golf ball. By this time Cookie's four pups were gorged and asleep, so we dumped Rollo in with them. Cookie looked at us, smelled of him, and looked at us again, trying to understand what was expected of her. She understood that we meant that she was to take care of this odd-looking addition to her family. So she rolled him over with her nose and, despite his struggles, lapped Rollo thoroughly from stem to stern, just as she washed her own children. After that Rollo belonged. Nobody was going to accuse her of favoritism; and from that day on, Rollo was just another husky puppy, as far as she was concerned.

I think he, himself, thought he was a dog. Certainly the other pups treated him like one of themselves. The whole lot of them played together as puppies do, roughhousing and mock-fighting, chewing each other's tails and ears, and attempting mayhem in any form. At first we used to try to rescue Rollo. The pups were almost ten times as big as he was, and I was afraid he'd get killed. But he didn't thank me at all for my concern. When I put him down again at a safe distance from the fray, he'd stamp his hind legs in a towering rage—the skunk method of expressing extreme irritation, and the last step before the gas attack—and rush back to fling himself into the battle.

I still don't understand why he didn't get completely ruined. I've often seen one dog grab him by the scruff of the neck while another grabbed his tail, pulling him in opposite directions with all their might, growling and shaking him as puppies will do with a piece of rope. It made my stomach ache to watch, but he apparently loved it, for when they released him he'd always rush in for more. It's my opinion that the twenty-four hours of being lost in the wilderness so early in life left a bad scar on his subconscious, so that he valued any attention as preferable to no attention. He'd never let himself be left alone for a moment, if he could help it, and when the pups slept he was never content to sleep on the edge of the heap. He'd always burrow down into the center, completely out of sight.

He used to follow me around like a shadow as I did my housework. He'd be at full gallop never more than six inches behind my heels, and if I reversed my field he'd sidestep and fall right in again. It was lucky he was so fast on his feet. Half the time I'd never know he was there, and if I'd ever stepped on him, there wouldn't have been even a grease spot left. He was so tiny he could easily curl up in one of my shoes and have plenty of room left.

It made him simply furious to have me go upstairs. The steps were much too high for him to negotiate, and I'd come back down to find him stamping back and forth in a fit of anger below the first step. That stamping never failed to amuse me. He'd not only be mad—he'd be good and mad! And yet, though he obviously wanted to make a noise like thunder and stamp the house down, the best he could make was a little pattering sound on the floor. If you've ever gone out of a room

in a fury and slammed the door behind you with what was supposed to be a shattering crash, only to find it was equipped with a pneumatic check[1] and so eased soundlessly into place, you can appreciate how he probably felt.

Still, despite his rages, he never in all the time he was with us made the slightest smell in the house. We thought some of having him operated on, but the vet in Rumford said frankly he had never done such an operation, so we let it go. We are glad

---

[1]pneumatic (nü mat'ik) check: a device that prevents a door from closing quickly

now that we didn't find someone who could do it. He was cleaner around the house than any cat we ever had and he never, even in his infancy, made a single error.

Only once that we know of did he ever make a smell, and we couldn't blame him for that; in fact, Ralph applauded him. We had at that time a cat named Jane. She and Rollo had always hated each other, for no good reason that we could ever see, for they always left each other strictly alone. One evening I had made a chocolate malted milk for Rollo—that was his favorite food—and set it out. Rollo was just starting in on it when Jane appeared around the corner. Rollo stamped violently but Jane continued to approach and sniffed at the saucer. She wasn't going to touch the contents, I'm sure; she was just curious. But he had warned her and she had paid no attention. Faster than the eye could follow, he turned end for end, arched his tail over his back, and—whisht! smack into Jane's face at a range of less than a foot. She rolled right over backward, scrambled to her feet, and went off like a bullet. She never came back. Presently she made her home at the nearest lumber camp.

We had been afraid that after the pups and the skunk reached the age where they could eat solid food, Rollo would starve unless we fed him separately. He could never hold his own, we thought, against that gang of ruffians. We might as well have spared ourselves the worry. He was quite capable of looking out for himself. When the crush around the pan of puppy biscuit and milk became too great, he would wade right into the middle of the dish, forcing the pups to eat along the edges while he stuffed himself practically into a coma.

Rollo became really a terribly spoiled brat before the summer had advanced very far. We gave him too much attention, and so did the dogs, and so did the tourists who kept on coming in increasing numbers as the news of our pet skunk spread. I never thought to have my social career sponsored by a skunk, but that is what it amounted to. I met more new people during that summer than I ever have before or since in the same length of time. Perfect strangers, they'd come drifting into the yard, say "Good morning," and then come to the point: "We heard you've got a pet skunk."

The result was always the same: Would it be all right for them to have their pictures taken holding Rollo? Rollo became as camera-conscious as a child movie star, and as objectionable. He'd look bored and sulky, but he'd never miss the chance to have his picture taken. His complete composure served as an excellent foil, I might add, to the nervous apprehension on the faces of his picture companions. Nobody ever seemed to take our word for it that he was perfectly safe.

Skunks are a horribly maligned animal. Everyone shuns them. Everyone accuses them, and without finding out the facts, of various crimes, such as hen killing. Actually they don't do so much damage; on the contrary, they are the natural enemies of vermin of all sorts and are among the human's best friends in the country. They are naturally gentle and easily tamed. A skunk will never attack until it is sure its person is in danger, or unless it is startled. I wish more people would bother to be nice to skunks. We were, and it paid. Rollo, in spite of being spoiled, made a perfect house pet.

We never made any effort to confine him, so it couldn't last forever. He was always free to come and go as he pleased. We even untacked a corner of the screen in the kitchen door so that he could get in and out at will. As he grew older, he began to return to nature, and the skunk nature is nocturnal. He slept more days, and roamed about nights. When we went out to the woodshed in the early, dewy morning to get kindling to start the breakfast fire, we would more and more often meet him, just coming home from a night's outing. Then for a while he wouldn't come home for two or three days at a time, and finally he didn't come home at all. We'd meet him sometimes a mile or more down the road, and he'd run up to us and we'd pick him up. He never forgot us, and we never forgot him.

Finally we stopped seeing him altogether. I don't know what eventually did happen to him—whether he wandered away, or whether he met with an accident. Very few wild animals die of old age. One thing we were glad of then: that if he did meet with death in any of the common swift wilderness forms, at least he was able to go down fighting. We hadn't made him defenseless.

Focus

1. How was Rollo's strength and endurance tested by a litter of husky pups? How did he measure up to this test?
2. Why did the family decide not to have Rollo de-scented? Did they regret this later? Why or why not?
3. A well-intentioned rescue of a wild animal can sometimes lead to harm. What harm could have come to Rollo?
4. How are skunks helpful to people?
5. Why do you think skunks are often so disliked by people? Is this reaction justified? Explain your answer.

In Writing

People's dislike for many animals stems from lack of knowledge about the animals. Many people, for example, think that:

- Hogs are dirty and stupid.
- Bats fly into people's hair.
- Snakes are slimy and sneaky.
- Buzzards kill animals and then eat them.

Select one of these animals, or another maligned animal you know of, and write a defense of the animal based on the facts. Answer such questions as these: Does this animal help people? What are the facts about its living habits? Why do so many people dislike this animal?

Vocabulary

On a piece of paper, write the numbers 1 to 5. Then read the sentences below. Next to each number on your paper, write the word from the list that best completes each analogy.

dispense	mayhem	maligned
favoritism	foil	vermin
frenziedly	ruffians	subconscious

1. Upset is to distraught as ____ is to distribute.
2. Passive is to active as ____ is to encourage.
3. Slandered is to people as ____ is to animals.
4. Strident is to harsh as ____ is to pests.
5. Ravenous is to full as ____ is to calmly.

LUCAS AND JAKE

What makes you judge an animal to be ferocious or gentle? The lion in this story has lived as both.

Paul Darcy Boles

It was the time when he could relax a little, letting go in all the clean sun that showered down on this part of the zoo.

So Lucas, who would be sixty-five next Tuesday, July six-teenth, was sitting on a box beside Jake's cage down on one of the side paths where not many sightseers came. He was eating a winesap apple, a fine specimen of its kind. He took distinct pleasure in biting into it with teeth that were largely his own.

All morning he'd been thinking back to when he'd been a boy and, on a day like this, would have been footloose and free as a big bird. He'd always liked zoo work, even if it didn't give you much status with friends and fellow workers. Yet a person needed somebody to look up to him. An admirer, maybe a relative. Lucas didn't have one ring-tailed relative, admiring or not, on earth.

He finished his apple, flipped its core into a trash can and leaned back, hugging his knees and cutting an eye at Jake.

Jake lay quiet, cinnamon-colored body shadowed, just a few flecks of sunlight picking out bits of his mane, one splash of light in his left eye. The eye, large and golden, resembled some strange pirate coin. Jake possessed awful patience. He could watch an inconsequential bug on the cage floor hours on end, not even his tail twitching, its very tuft motionless.

Lucas sat up as two boys came around the lilac bush and moved toward Jake's cage. And Lucas's moustache bristled a bit. His eyes got the stern cool look of a TV Westerner's—a town marshal, summing up transients.

The older boy, about twelve, padded along on sneakers soundless as a brace of leopards. The younger, eight or nine, with a head of sheep-doggish hair, was fiddling with a Yo-Yo. It reeled out smartly enough, but when he tried to flip it back it nearly banged his nose.

Both stopped at the cage and looked in at Jake. Lucas waited for their first bit of smart talk. But the bigger boy's voice sounded thoughtful, not smart talking at all. "Wonder how come they keep him here, Paddy? Not back with all the others?"

The smaller boy shrugged. He went on making his Yo-Yo climb up and roll down. "Maybe he *likes* it here."

That was as good an answer as Lucas had ever heard from someone who couldn't know anything solid about lions. Most people thought they were lion experts.

The bigger boy's eyes widened toward Lucas. "Sir, how come he's here? Not messing around with the other lions up at the moat?"

Paddy let his Yo-Yo spin to a stop. He wanted to know too.

Lucas cleared his throat. But before he could say word one, information fountained out of the taller boy: "My name's Ridefield Tarrant. This is Patrick McGoll. Call him Paddy, sir. We came out on the bus. We each had 75 cents for Saturday. I didn't like the baboons, they make me nervous barking. But I sure like the lions and the tigers. Especially lions." He drew fresh breath. "We could have gone seen a movie, but it felt like a better day for animals."

When he was sure Ridefield had finished, Lucas nodded. "You can't miss, with animals." He waited: the word coast still seemed clear. "You asked about this lion. His name's Jake. They keep Jake all by himself for"—Jake coughed—"for certain secret reasons."

Ridefield's face lighted all over. He was polite, but in a flash

Lucas could tell nobody was ever going to break his inquiring spirit. The knowledge made Lucas happy about something in the universe no one ever really had a name for: glory, ecstasy; he wouldn't know.

With a glance at his own bronzed knuckles, hard as oak roots soaking up sunlight, Lucas nodded again. "Going to tell you boys the secret. Because you look like you want to know. Listen real close."

Ridefield Tarrant was leaning toward Lucas like an arrow set on the bowstring, and the mouth of Paddy McGoll had come a trifle open like that of a young bird expecting food.

Lucas narrowed his eyes. "Ever hear of a Cape lion?"

Their heads shook.

"Well"—Lucas shook his head—"only the kings of the whole lion breed. That's all they are, gents. Never in your life see a Cape lion doing push-ups on a barrel in a circus. No, sir! Wouldn't catch him dead in such a place." Almost casually, Lucas added, "Jake's a Cape lion."

"Yike," murmured Ridefield.

Lucas folded his arms. "Yep. Took from his mother when he

was a young brave. Fought all the way. Killed . . . more'n you could count. Notice the bars of this here now cage." He pointed. "Put Jake in a cage with *lighter* bars, why, he'd be right out among you with a baseball bat. Put him up at the moat with the rest, he'd eat 'em like cornflakes. Cornflakes." Lucas touched his moustache reflectively. "He's my sole and particular charge. Jake's my special talent."

At this moment Jake twitched his left ear to discourage a bluebottle fly. Paddy McGoll stiffened like a little post with hair all over the top of it. Ridges and valleys leaped into the leather of Lucas's forehead. They vanished into the tufts of white hair which made him resemble a Santa Claus. "Now, I hope I did right to tell you, gents. Most people, you tell 'em about Jake, they'd write to editors about him, stir up trouble. I'd hate for the zoo to have to shoot him."

Ridefield said, "I won't say a thing! Neither will Paddy."

Paddy nodded. "I don't write so good, anyhow. In penmanship I use my fingers instead of my wrists. I wouldn't *tell* anybody."

"Good." Lucas stood. He felt his joints creak, but the looseness of the sun was warming him too. "Well, I got to be going. I won't be far off—but I hate to leave you here alone with him—"

Ridefield spoke rather swiftly. "We'll be going, we haven't seen the birds yet."

Lucas snorted. "Birds. They're all right, but a lion like Jake— now, he teaches you something. Well, c'mon."

The three started off. Lucas noted that Ridefield and Paddy were walking backward, taking one last look.

And it was just then that Paddy did the foolish thing. It happened because his Yo-Yo finger was too small for the string's loop. Suddenly, there went the whole Yo-Yo, string and all, sailing between the cage bars and coming to rest with a clack eight inches in front of Jake's nose.

"*Yike,*" breathed Ridefield.

Lucas could feel all the radiance of the day pour itself into his veins as though he himself were young again, tough as nails, but desperately searching for a key to the whole world and all the whirling planets. Low-voiced, he said, "Don't move an inch."

Ridefield's nostrils were white. Paddy stood as if whacked to the spot with spikes. Lucas walked back to Jake's cage.

He could hear the soda water fizz of Jake's breath through great nostrils. The gold coins of the eyes—sometimes pale green, at other times so full of sun they, too, were like suns—were tightly covered. Jake's chin lay on the backs of his paws.

Lucas put his right arm between the bars. The arm moved very slowly. Then his fingers were touching the Yo-Yo, his arm actually brushing Jake's whiskers. Lucas drew his arm out, stepped back to the boys, said, "Here y'ar," and put the Yo-Yo in Paddy's fingers.

Ridefield tried to speak, and couldn't. He stuck his right hand up to Lucas, and Lucas shook it. Then Paddy, dropping the Yo-Yo into a pocket, stuck his hand out, and he and Lucas shook. Then Ridefield and Paddy moved off. It was as if they held something so tremendous they might burst. Strength and wonder and greatness, all understood, all there . . .

They were out of sight around the lilac bush before Lucas smiled. It was the smile of a man who'd earned something: more than status. And after a moment Lucas strolled back to Jake's cage. He thrust his arm in, took hold of the mane, which felt like rope fibers and gave it a minor tug.

All at once Jake came awake, the eyes staring at Lucas with green-gold enigmatic quiet. Jake was no Cape lion. But he might have been. *All* animals of this kind were brave and glorious. If they got old and preferred to sleep, if they couldn't really be terrible any longer, or even roar much, that was their business. In some definite way Lucas felt he'd done something for Jake today; for the whole kingdom of lions.

He couldn't have put a finger on it. He tousled the dark mane, felt of the veined surface behind the left ear—soft as a velvet mouse—and drew his arm back out of the cage. He turned away; there was plenty to do, and he didn't want to get chewed out for not doing it. He walked off.

Behind him, alone again to sleep out his years quietly, Jake kept his eyes open for a few more seconds. Then the eyelids trembled. The eyes shut. The body lay unmoving, powerful, in the huge green afternoon.

Focus

1. Describe the setting of this story.
2. Why was Jake separated from the rest of the lions? What reason did Lucas give Ridefield and Paddy?
3. How were Lucas and Jake alike? How did the story Lucas told about Jake give them both dignity?
4. What did Jake do throughout the story? Compare Jake's actions with the story told about him.
5. What did Lucas feel he had done "for the whole kingdom of lions"?

In Writing

Imagine that you are Ridefield and you are writing to a friend about your experience at the zoo. Describe your impressions of Lucas.

Vocabulary

On a piece of paper, write the numbers *1* to *5.* Then look at the words in the first column and find an antonym for each word in the second column. Next to each number on your paper, write the letter of the antonym for each word.

1. transients	A. unthinkingly
2. tousled	B. orderly
3. inconsequential	C. understandable
4. reflectively	D. homebodies
5. enigmatic	E. important
	F. intentionally

CRYING WILLOW

Edward Rager

Do willows weep?
Why would they, and would
we hear them if they did?

When I tell people I head a plant protection agency they usually figure I'm in industrial security. The truth is I'm with LEAF, the League to Eliminate the Abuse of Flora. The agency is charged with seeing that our green friends aren't wantonly destroyed or abused. We take on any job which seems to fall within our jurisdiction, including regulating and setting standards for the use of herbicides, coordinating the activities of forest rangers, and setting and enforcing laws against picking flowers.

Our newest, and strangest, operative is a different breed altogether. His name's Herb Greene and he's trying to communicate with plants both electronically and psychically. There's no need to tell you what I think about his psychic hogwash, but I must admit that some of his electronic equipment is

145

certainly impressive. He attaches lie detector probes to the leaves to measure a plant's psychogalvanic reflexes—whatever they are. Says changes in the lines on the chart correspond to the plant's reactions to thoughts and actions from the outside. He's trying to use this to verify his attempts at communication. He's even got kids believing they're making beans grow faster by thinking good thoughts about them.

He must be some kind of a crackpot, but I'm stuck with him. The regional director told me to give him a free hand. Anyway, he gets us a lot of publicity and the visitors all go away impressed. I'll have to take the time someday to find out exactly what he's doing.

A few days ago Greene came to the office to tell me that there was a tree in agony somewhere in the city. I almost dropped my pipe. "What's that?" I managed.

"I've received an impression from a tree about two or three miles northeast of here," he said. "The signal corresponds to a tree's equivalent of pain, though I'm not sure whether it feels anything or not. It just responds as if it does. The graphs indicate that it's been happening several times a day since yesterday morning."

"Well, what do you think we should do about it?" I said, trying to humor him.

"I can home in on it by attaching the polygraph to one of the bean plants in the mobile unit. The plant will pick up the tree's distress signals and the polygraph will record its sympathetic response. The intensity will increase as we get closer."

We? He must mean his old buddy the bean plant. Seems to me he'd get along better with a nut.

"Sounds good," I said, "but I'd like to give it a little more thought. Run some more tests and see me in the morning." What was I going to do? I was supposed to give Greene a free hand, but I couldn't go out on a limb by having him knocking on someone's door and telling them they had a tree in pain.

Right after lunch, however, I got a call from the police department. It seems a woman had complained that a tree in her neighbor's yard was crying and bothering her. The police had understandably refused to investigate when she further told them she thought it was a weeping willow. The captain turned the case over to us, and not without a trace of mirth in his voice.

"Julius," I said to myself, "here's a perfect job for Greene." Even if he hadn't come to me with a similar case, it was right up his alley. One crackpot helping another.

I put him on it right away. He took his log book and some equipment and left in the mobile unit.

I was just locking up my office when Greene returned in a highly agitated condition. I hadn't seen

146

anyone in the department that upset since the time Dr. Pollard spilled the beans about the graft in the conifer branch.

"The man's a maniac! He should be committed," Greene said, waving a lie detector chart in my face. All I could make out was a long, jagged line with some high plateaus.

"Can't it wait, Greene? I'm just going home."

"But look at the graph! He's torturing that poor tree! We've got to stop him!"

"Well, come in and we'll talk it over," I said, thinking what the trip home would be like if I didn't get out before the rush-hour traffic.

"His name's Marcus D. Shade," Greene said, before I could even hang my coat up. "I remember him from a group that toured my lab a few weeks ago. He asked me questions for fifteen minutes; mostly about how to measure the psychogalvanic reflexes and what they indicate. Now he's using that information to satisfy his sick tendencies at the expense of that poor willow."

I wasn't even going to ask Greene if it was a weeping willow.

He held the chart up again. "I made this by recording the sympathetic responses of an iris plant in his neighbor's yard. These sharp rises in the curve show where he applied his tortures. In the few hours I was there, Shade scraped the outer layers off several leaves, dipped some others in boiling water, and burned the trunk with a soldering iron. He's crazy!"

"What about the woman?" I asked. "She said it was crying."

"It's that monster Shade! He's attached electrodes to the leaves like I do, only they're connected to a sound system instead of a polygraph. He's adjusted the output so that the signals sound like human cries when the tree is disturbed. It adds to his sick pleasure."

"Well, it does sound like we're dealing with a crackpot here," I said. Another crackpot. "Maybe we could get an injunction or impound his tree."

"No! I checked. There's no law

protecting willow trees from any kind of abuse as long as they belong to the abuser. He's not breaking any laws, except maybe disturbing the peace."

"Suppose he wore earphones," I offered.

"That wouldn't help the tree."

"You're absolutely right," I said. "This looks like a job for the boys in PR."

"Plant Rescue might take too long to decide what to do. I've got a plan ready for tomorrow morning if I can stay over tonight to work out the details."

"Go right ahead," I said, grabbing my coat. "The sooner you get started the better."

I didn't see Greene until early the next afternoon. He was all smiles as he lumbered into my office and draped his long limbs over a chair. I had reason to be happy, too, because of a call I'd just received from the police department. I gave him my news before he could speak.

"Well, Greene, our crackpot finally flipped his lid. He went crying to the police that his tree was out to get him. Said it threatened him verbally and demanded to be left alone. The captain is holding him for a psychiatric exam. Our troubles are over."

"Yes, Mr. Cedar, but not the way you think. You see, last night I ran some tests to determine exactly what frequency Shade would have

to be using to receive the tree's responses in that particular timbre. I fixed up a small transmitter to broadcast in that range. This morning, just as he was about to release a jar of caterpillars onto the tree, I spoke into my rig. The output was adjusted to the same pitch as the tree's screams and I threatened him with everything from falling branches to Dutch elm disease. It would have scared anyone."

"Of course." Is the man a crackpot or a genius? "I don't suppose there was any chance that the tree could really have harmed him?"

"No, sir. I'm afraid its bark is worse than its blight. Plants have no central control systems as in animals' brains. Individual cells can transmit to other cells and receive, but they can't think or act."

"One thing I've been curious about," I said. "You seemed to know about the willow's problem before the police report. How did you find out?

"You see, sir, plants do broadcast their fears to other plants, but usually only those in the immediate vicinity can pick much of it up. However, an antenna can be made by allowing a vining plant with broad leaves to grow along a specially shaped trellis. I have such a system."

"That's what enabled you to pick up the willow's distress signals?"

"Yes, sir. I heard it through the grapevine."

148

Focus

1. What did "LEAF" stand for? What was its job?
2. List some of the people's names in the story. How did these add to the humor of the story? Use a dictionary if you need help.
3. What was the narrator's attitude toward Greene? Give evidence from the story to support your opinion.
4. In what ways is this story similar to a typical police story that might appear on TV? Consider the events, the characters, and the way the story was told to the reader.
5. Explain the two meanings of the last sentence of the story.

In Writing

There are many puns in "Crying Willow" made from homophones and words with more than one meaning. Write a humorous description or story about a dog or other animal. Use homophones (such as paws—pause, fur—fir, etc.) or words with multiple meanings (such as bark, pants, shepherd) for the names of your characters and their actions.

Vocabulary

On a piece of paper, write the numbers *1* to *5*. Then look at the words in the first column and find a definition for each word in the second column. Next to each number on your paper, write the letter of the correct definition for each word.

1. wanton
2. injunction
3. abuse
4. blight
5. impounded

A. an order from a court of law
B. confined
C. weighed carefully
D. done in a reckless, meaningless way
E. to mistreat
F. a disease in plants

To the Wayfarer

Anonymous

**A Poem Fastened to Trees
in the Portuguese Forests**

Ye who pass by and would raise your hand
against me, hearken ere you harm me.

I am the heat of your hearth on the cold winter
nights, the friendly shade screening you
from summer sun, and my fruits are refreshing draughts, quenching your thirst as you
journey on.

I am the beam that holds your house, the board
of your table, the bed on which you lie, the
timber that builds your boat.

I am the handle of your hoe, the door of your
homestead, the wood of your cradle, and the
shell of your coffin.

I am the bread of kindness and the flower of
beauty.
Ye who pass by, listen to my prayer: harm me
not.

LIFE SKILL: Choosing a Campsite

Is there a camping trip in your future? You can find just the right campsite if you use a regional map. This is a local map with a table of information on parks and camps. A table arranges information in rows and columns. The following table lists some of the state parks in Ohio. It also tells what kinds of facilities are available.

Look at the top line of the table. This describes the type of information contained in the table. The first column gives you the name of the park. Look down the first column and see if you can find Ash Cave State Park. The second column gives you the coordinates (map location) for each park. This helps you to find the park on the map. What are the coordinates for Ash Cave? Did you find I-13? Look in the next column, titled "Nearest City." What city is Ash Cave nearest? Find

Ohio State Parks	Map Location	Nearest City	Camp Areas	Cabins	Lodges	Boating	Fishing	Hiking Trails	Nature Programs	Bridle Trails	Shelters	Swimming	Scuba Permitted	Beach Concession	Food Service
Adams Lake	F - 16	West Union				•	•	•			•		•		
Alum Creek	G - 9	Delaware	•			•	•	•		•		•	•		
Barkcamp	N 10	Belmont	•			•	•	•	•	•	•	•	•	•	
Beaver Creek	P - 7	E. Liverpool	•				•	•	•	•					
Blue Rock	K 11	Philo	•			•	•	•			•	•	•	•	
Buck Creek	E - 11	Springfield				•	•	•			•	•	•	•	
Buckeye Lake	I - 11	Hebron				•	•				•	•			
Buss Oak	K - 12	Glouster	•	•	•	•	•	•	•		•	•	•	•	•
Catawba Island	H - 4	Port Clinton				•	•				•				
Cowan Lake	D - 13	Wilmington	•	•		•	•	•	•			•		•	
Crane Creek	G - 3	Oak Harbor				•	•	•				•		•	
Deer Creek	G - 12	Williamsport	•			•	•	•	•			•		•	•
Delaware	G - 9	Delaware	•			•	•	•	•			•		•	
Dillon	J - 10	Zanesville	•	•		•	•	•	•	•	•	•	•	•	•
East Fork	D - 15	Batavia	•			•	•	•		•		•	•		
East Harbor	H - 4	Port Clinton	•			•	•	•	•		•	•	•	•	•
Findley	J - 6	Wellington	•			•	•	•	•		•	•	•	•	•
Forked Run	L - 14	Reedsville	•			•	•	•	•		•	•	•	•	•
Geneva	N - 2	Geneva-on-the-Lake		•		•	•				•	•			
Guilford Lake	O - 7	Lisbon	•			•	•				•	•	•		
Hocking Hills	I - 13	Logan						•	•					
Ash Cave	I - 13	Logan						•			•			
Cantwell Cliffs	I - 12	Logan						•						
Cedar Falls	I - 13	Logan						•						
Conkles Hollow	I - 13	Logan						•						
Old Man's Cave	I - 13	Logan	•	•		•	•	•			•	•			•
Rock House	I - 13	Logan						•			•			
Hueston Woods	A - 12	College Corner	•	•	•	•	•	•	•	•	•	•	•	•	•
Independence Dam	C - 5	Defiance	•			•	•	•			•			
Jefferson Lake	O - 8	Richmond	•			•	•	•			•	•	•	
Kelleys Island	H - 3	Port Clinton	•			•	•	•	•		•	•		
Lake Alma	I - 14	Wellston	•			•	•	•			•	•		
Lake Hope	J - 13	Zaleski	•	•		•	•	•	•		•	•	•	•	•
Lake White	G - 14	Waverly	•			•	•				•	•	•	•
Madison Lake	F - 11	London				•	•				•	•	•	•
Malabar Farm	I - 8	Lucas					•	•	•	•				•

another park near the city of Logan.

All the remaining columns tell the kinds of facilities available at each park. Which facilities would be your first three choices if you were choosing a campsite? Run one finger across the Ash Cave row. Run another finger down each column of facilities. When your two fingers meet, see if there is a dot. If so, Ash Cave has that facility. What facilities does Ash Cave have? Are you surprised that it has only hiking trails and shelters?

Find two Ohio parks that offer many facilities. You can tell by running a finger across the row for a park and seeing if there is a dot in nearly every column.

Here is a table of parks and camps for the northwest section of Oregon.

Oregon State Parks

	Map Location	Nearest City	Camp Areas	Cabins	Lodges	Boating	Fishing	Hiking Trails	Nature Programs	Bridle Trails	Shelters	Swimming	Scuba Permitted	Beach Concession	Food Service
Fort Stevens	A - 1	Astoria				●	●	●	●			●			●
Cullaby Lake	F - 3	Seaside					●	●	●	●		●			
Kloochy Creek	B - 2	Seaside							●						
Ecola	D - 4	Cannon Beach					●	●	●	●		●	●		
Saddle Mountain	A - 6	Necanicum Jct.	●				●	●	●						
Spruce Run	C - 1	Elsie	●				●	●	●			●			
Hug Point	D - 3	Cannon Beach					●					●		●	
Barview	B - 5	Garibaldi	●				●					●	●	●	●
Jones Creek	G - 2	Tillamook	●				●			●					
Trask River	G - 3	Tillamook					●								
Cape Lookout	G - 4	Tillamook	●			●	●	●	●			●			●
Sand Beach	C - 3	Pacific City					●					●	●	●	
Whalen Island	C - 2	Pacific City	●				●					●		●	
Keenig Creek	G - 5	Tillamook	●				●								
Diamond Mill	G - 6	Tillamook	●												
Arcadia Beach	D - 2	Cannon Beach					●					●	●	●	●
Rockaway Wayside	A - 5	Rockaway					●					●		●	●
Oceanside	B - 4	Oceanside										●		●	

Use both park tables to answer these questions.

1. If you wanted to camp near Williamsport, Ohio, which park would you choose? What are the map coordinates for this park?

2. Name three parks near Cannon Beach, Oregon. Do any of them have camping areas?

3. Which park near Tillamook, Oregon, has the most facilities? Can you go scuba diving there?

4. If you wanted to find a park in Oregon that had nature programs only, where would you go? What are the map coordinates?

5. In Oregon, name the parks where you can camp and study nature.

6. Where can you camp in Ohio if you also want to ride horseback and to scuba dive?

7. Which city in Ohio has the most parks near it? How many of those parks have camp areas?

8. Name six Ohio parks with shelters, but no camp areas.

152

CHECKPOINT

Read the word list and paragraph below. Decide which word makes the best sense in each blank space. Then write the numbers 1 to 6 on a piece of paper and write the correct word next to each number.

Vocabulary: Word Identification

undaunted	allay	curator
cumbersome	proficient	abuse
balked	diurnal	maligned
inconsequential	blight	wanton

He explained his plan to the entire staff of the zoo. As the new __(1)__ of the zoo, he was going to make it the best in the country. He was able to __(2)__ the fears of those keepers who had __(3)__ at his ideas when they were first introduced. As he outlined the details of his plan, the keepers realized he was a __(4)__ manager. They regretted their conversations in which they had __(5)__ his efforts. Soon their concerns seemed __(6)__ , and they realized that his leadership was just what their zoo needed.

7. Reread pages 146 and 147. Write the following events in the order in which they actually happened: Green reports tree in agony; Shade visits lab; narrator learns woman complained about crying tree.

Comprehension: Sequence

8. Reread pages 88 and 89. Write the steps used to train a porpoise through operant conditioning.

9. Reread the paragraph that begins at the bottom of page 121. Name the four things the author was referring to when he said, "These things. . . ."

Comprehension: Referents

10. Reread the first three paragraphs on page 122. What is the conclusion that the author calls "more or less self-evident"?

11. On another piece of paper, make a five-column chart. List the names of ten classmates on one side. At the top of the columns, write the following headings: *Skating, Basketball, Swimming, Bicycling, Other*. Ask each of the ten people which activities he or she enjoys. Put an X in the appropriate space for each activity.

Life Skills: Consumer Information (Charts)

American Vi

A vista is a wide view, sometimes stretching over time as well as space. As you will learn in the following selections, the vista of today's America comes from different cultures and from a blending of the past into the present.

You will go with young people on swift, dangerous journeys—to warn of an attack, to escape from slavery into freedom. You will learn how the written language of the Cherokee people was developed. You will discover the work of a Mississippi riverboat pilot and then the lonely beauty of a sheepherder's job. Finally, pick over the offerings of a modern-day garage sale and get angry at a modern-day machine.

The American scene is rich and varied. Enjoy just a sample of its variety in this unit.

sta

Burning in the Night

Thomas Wolfe

Go seeker, if you will, throughout the land
And you will find us burning in the night.

There where the hackles of the Rocky Mountains
Blaze in the blank and naked radiance of the moon,
Go—
Make your resting-stool upon the highest peak.
Can you not see us now?

The continental wall juts sheer and flat,
Its huge black shadow on the plain,
And the plain sweeps out against the East,
Two thousand miles away.
The great snake that you see there
Is the Mississippi River.

Behold
The gem-strung towns and cities
Of the good, green East,
Flung like star-dust through the field of night.
That spreading constellation to the north
Is called Chicago,
And that giant wink that blazes in the moon
Is the pendant lake that it is built upon.
Beyond, close-set and dense as a clenched fist,
Are all the jeweled cities of the eastern seaboard.
There's Boston,
Ringed with the bracelet of its shining little towns,
And all the lights that sparkle
On the rocky indentations of New England.
Here, southward and a little to the west,
And yet still coasted to the sea,
Is our intensest ray,
The splintered firmament of the towered island
Of Manhattan.
Round about her, sown thick as grain,
Is the glitter of a hundred towns and cities.
The long chain of lights there
Is the necklace of Long Island and the Jersey shore.
Southward and inland, by a foot or two,
Behold the duller glare of Philadelphia.
Southward farther still,
The twin constellations—Baltimore and Washington.

Westward, but still within the borders
Of the good, green East,
That nighttime glow and smolder of steel-fire
Is Pittsburgh.
Here, St. Louis, hot and humid
In the cornfield belly of the land,
And bedded on the mid-length coil and fringes
Of the snake.
There at the snake's mouth,
Southward six hundred miles or so,
You see the jeweled crescent of old New Orleans,
Here, west and south again,
You see the gemmy glitter
Of the cities on the Texas border.

Turn now, seeker,
On your resting-stool atop the Rocky Mountains,
And look another thousand miles or so
Across moon-blazing fiend-worlds of the Painted Desert
And beyond Sierra's ridge.
That magic congeries of lights
There to the west,
Ringed like a studded belt
Around the magic setting of its lovely harbor,
Is the fabled town of San Francisco.
Below it, Los Angeles
And all the cities of the California shore.
A thousand miles to north and west,
The sparkling towns of Oregon and Washington.

Observe the whole of it,
Survey it as you might survey a field.
Make it your garden, seeker,
Or your backyard patch.
Be at ease in it.
It's your oyster—yours to open if you will.
Don't be frightened,
It's not so big now,
When your footstool is the Rocky Mountains.
Reach out
And dip a hatful of cold water
From Lake Michigan.
Drink it—we've tried it—
You'll not find it bad.
Take your shoes off
And work your toes down in the river oozes
Of the Mississippi bottom—
It's very refreshing
On a hot night in the summertime.

Help yourself to a bunch of Concord grapes
Up there in northern New York State—
They're getting good now.
Or raid that watermelon patch
Down there in Georgia.
Or, if you like, you can try the Rockyfords
Here at your elbow, in Colorado.
Just make yourself at home,
Refresh yourself, get the feel of things,
Adjust your sights, and get the scale.
It's your pasture now, and it's not so big—
Only three thousand miles from east to west,
Only two thousand miles from north to south—
But all between,
Where ten thousand points of light
Pick out the cities, towns, and villages,
There, seeker,
You will find us burning in the night.

A Race with Time

Frances Duncombe

Sometimes, your place in history can make demands that require unusual courage. Hannah Mills is in such a place. Will she be able to do what needs to be done?

During the American Revolution, towns and even families were often divided. There were those who remained loyal to King George, and there were those who wanted independence. In this story, the Mills and the Isaacs families support the cause of independence. The Halstead family is divided. The father and brother are loyal to the British king. But Tamar Halstead has decided that she supports the Americans.

In this episode, Mr. Isaacs and his son Jacob are driving cattle to the American camp near Peekskill, New York. Tamar has overheard a plot to steal the cattle for the British. She tells Hannah Mills about it. They had been best friends before the war started, but now Hannah is not sure that she can trust Tamar.

Suddenly Tamar had Hannah by the shoulders. For a girl so fragile-looking she had a strength that always took Hannah by surprise.

"No, I won't go away. And you have to listen. Unless you want De Lancey to steal the cattle the Isaacses are driving to the Hudson today."

Anger got in the way of clear thinking. Hannah stared at Tamar, unable to make sense of what she was saying. Tamar went on. "A man came to our house very late last night. He pounded on the door and waked us all. He had listened behind a rock to Mr. Isaacs and Jacob talking. He told us the cattle are collected in that hollow behind the Raymonds' barn. He told us how many head there are and the route they are taking to Peekskill."

Tamar paused for breath and then continued. "I came as soon as I could slip out, but there isn't much time. My brother rode off to give Uncle Roger the news for Colonel De Lancey. The Isaacses left as soon as it was light this morning. I saw them pass our house."

"Tamar, it's not true!"

"It is true, Hannah. And I'm telling you because the Isaacses have been kind. There is another reason, though. One you wouldn't believe." She paused, looking at Hannah straight. "I want those cattle to get to the American army."

There was antagonism in the eyes of both girls as they stood facing each other. Then slowly the expression in Hannah's eyes changed. Tamar was telling the truth.

"I do believe you, Tamar. Everything you said. The Isaacses must be warned."

"Yes," Tamar said, her expression also changing. "Only I can't help anymore. Except to lend you my horse. I don't dare. Our family is divided. My father is still loyal to the king. He wants that drove of cattle to reach the British, not the American army. My mother and I are against the king, but we don't dare cross Father."

Hannah put out a hand and touched her arm. "I wish I'd known, Tamar. I wouldn't have been so mean." It was something she had to say, though Tamar was impatient to finish.

"I have to go now. I'll be waiting on the top of Indian Hill as soon as I saddle my horse."

"Tamar, I saw you ride the other day. You were riding sidesaddle. I don't know how."

"I have no other now. You will have to ride without."

"It's the way Pa taught us," Hannah replied.

"I'll tell you how to go when we meet on Indian Hill. I can't stay here any longer. I mustn't be seen with you."

Tamar climbed up the cliff, dislodging some pebbles. Hannah ran down the road to the village.

Tamar was waiting in the field on top of Indian Hill. She was holding her little brown mare by the length of the reins so she could nibble on grass.

"You have ridden Queenie before, so you know her ways," she said.

"Yes," Hannah replied, putting a hand out to stroke the horse's shoulder. When they'd still been friends, Tamar had let her ride Queenie once in a while. She had never been used for farmwork. Raised for pleasure riding, she was easy-gaited and well mannered. Hannah knew how much Tamar loved the little animal.

"I'll try to be careful of her," she promised, and then suddenly hopeful, she added, "And maybe I won't have far to ride. Maybe the Isaacses aren't actually moving the cattle till dark for safety and I'll find them still at the Raymonds' just getting things ready."

Tamar shook her head. "Cowboys robbed a farm west of Guard Hill night before last. Mr. Isaacs was more worried about meeting up with outlaws on the road at night than he was of traveling in the daytime."

She led Queenie over to a rock so Hannah could get on more easily. When Hannah was mounted, Tamar gave her the reins but still kept a hand on one, up near the bit.

"If the Isaacses haven't already started, they will soon," she said. "Ride Queenie as hard as you need, to warn them. Those cattle mustn't be taken. And besides, who knows what De Lancey's men might do to the Isaacses if they put up a fight?"

Hannah's stomach jumped. Jacob would fight. She knew that. Mr. Isaacs, too. They wouldn't give up the cattle without a struggle.

Tamar went on giving directions. "Mr. Isaacs is driving up over Guard Hill. At the bottom, go right until you come to the house of the old Quaker woman. Do you know where that is?"

Hannah nodded. "Yes, but I've never been any farther."

"Listen, then. You turn left there and go downhill. You won't pass any more houses. It's mostly woods. In about a mile you will ford a brook. Pine's Bridge crosses the Croton River a mile beyond that."

Queenie was getting restless, but Tamar still held onto her.

"Another road comes up from North Castle Church to Pine's Bridge. That's the one De Lancey's party will take. If they don't see the cattle tracks at the bridge, they will ride up the road toward the Quaker woman's and wait for the Isaacses behind a turn."

"Tamar, how do you know?"

"I heard the instructions Father gave my brother for Uncle Roger. I know this, too. De Lancey's men are below Tarrytown, but they will ride as fast as they can to catch the Isaacses on this side of the Croton. They won't want to cross the bridge unless they have to because there's a house on the other side sometimes used as an American outpost."

"Tamar, I'm scared," Hannah said. "I haven't ridden in over a year, except on Lieutenant Smith's Dandy once or twice in back of the barn. What if I can't make Queenie go fast enough? What if I fall off and can't catch her again?"

"I wish I dared go myself, Hannah, but if I'm not home for dinner at noon, Father will want to know why. He mustn't ever guess I had anything to do with warning the Isaacses. He'd lock me up in my room for days, and he'd never believe Mother wasn't in on the plan."

Briefly Tamar turned away, thinking about her parents. Then, with a little shake of her shoulders, she turned back to Hannah.

"You will be all right, Hannah. You can depend on Queenie. Now you had better go. Here, tie my kerchief over your hair. There is no one at the north end of the village right now to see you on Queenie, but if you should meet anyone, duck your head so all they will see is the kerchief. When you get back, leave Queenie's bridle on the ground where the meetinghouse shed stood. Turn her loose there, and she'll come home. She's my friend." Tamar gave a bitter little laugh. "About my only one, I guess."

She took her hand off Queenie's rein, but Hannah held the horse in a moment longer.

"I want to be your friend again, if you will let me, Tamar," she said a little awkwardly. "Please do."

Tamar nodded, but she didn't speak, and Hannah turned the mare north down the long sloping field to the Salem road. Once there she touched Queenie's side with her heel and gave her her head. They went fast through the crossroads and didn't meet anyone who would recognize either the horse or herself. In spite of her recent misgivings, Hannah found herself as comfortable on Queenie as though she'd been riding her every day. The little mare had a smooth gallop and was willing to do what she asked.

It hadn't rained in two weeks. Dust coated the weeds growing along the sides of the road, but the dust raised by Queenie's hooves was always behind them. The sun was behind them, too, as they rode west. Later it might be hot, but now it was only pleasantly warm on Hannah's back and shoulders.

Until she reached the Raymonds' farm, Hannah let herself hope the Isaacses had made a late start and she could stop them there from going on. But when she came to an opening in the wall, she saw the cattle had already passed through it. The dusty road was pock-marked with cloven hoofprints.

Hannah put Queenie into a gallop again, hoping as she topped each rise and rounded each turn, to see cattle ahead of her. But she didn't, and when she came to the very top of the road, she pulled up and let Queenie rest, while her eyes searched the country ahead for a moving cloud of dust. Suddenly she felt Queenie's muscles tighten. She didn't shy, but her ears went forward, and her head swung to the left. A moment later some bushes parted and a man of about sixty came out onto the road. From the direction he'd come Hannah guessed he was one of the

men over militia age who stationed themselves by turn as sentinels on the high ridge south of the road.

From there you could see for miles. Once Hannah had ridden up there with Pa. He had shown her Tarrytown on the Hudson River, thirteen miles away, and much nearer, near enough to make out some of the buildings, even, the little village called North Castle Church. It was the way De Lancey's party would come to get to Pine's Bridge.

The man stopped beside Hannah and smiled. "Josiah Mills's girl, aren't you? Nice little mare you have there. Want to sell her?"

"No," Hannah replied and added a "thank you" before she asked, "Did you see some cattle pass while you were up there?"

"Sure did. Fifty or sixty head going west. Soon after sunrise and traveling slow as though they had a long way to go."

Sunrise! And it must be close to eight-thirty now. Even going slow like the man said, that meant the cattle were miles ahead of her. If Tamar's brother had found his uncle right away where he expected and if De Lancey's men had ridden up fast, there mightn't be time to catch up with the Isaacses before it was too late.

"Did you see anything down by North Castle Church that looked like a troop of horses?" Hannah's heart was in her throat as she asked the question.

"Not me. If I'd seen as much as a handful of dust or a pinpoint of sun on metal, I'd be running to give an alarm right now, not walking home for breakfast."

So there was still time, but maybe not much. Hannah dug her heels in Queenie's sides and slapped her shoulder with the end of the reins. Surprised, the little mare took off at a gallop that lengthened and flattened into a run.

"Don't stumble, Queenie, please don't." Hannah begged as they raced downhill. Near the bottom there was a place as steep as a shed roof. Hannah made Queenie walk there, but when they were down she urged her on again. She forgot she'd ever been scared she couldn't make Queenie move fast enough. She forgot about falling off, though by now the mare's back and sides were slippery with sweat. When she felt herself sliding she'd grab at Queenie's mane. The miles flew by under Queenie's hooves. Hannah tried to remember the directions Tamar had given her, but it didn't really matter. She had only to follow the hoofmarks in the churned-up, dusty road.

They passed the Quaker woman's house and turned sharp left downhill. Somewhere soon they should come to the brook Tamar had told her about. Hannah couldn't see very far ahead because of the woods on each side and the curves in the road. She was going too fast to hear anything but the pound of Queenie's hooves.

Suddenly Queenie propped her legs under her and came to an abrupt stop. Hannah went over her head. She wasn't hurt, but it took a moment to gather her wits. She seemed to be sitting in about three inches of water with a couple of young steers, who were backing away from her in alarm.

166

"Hannah?" It was Jacob's voice.

Yes, she was sitting in shallow water and surrounded by cattle. They'd been drinking. Their mouths were still dribbling, and they looked surprised and rather reproachful. Both up and down stream were more cattle.

"Hannah, oh, Hannah!" Jacob looked as surprised as the steers, but he wasn't as polite. He was laughing. *Laughing!*

Hannah got up and squeezed water out of her skirts. "So you think it's funny," she said furiously. "You think it's funny to see a girl spilled when she's ridden hard all the way from Bedford to catch up with you. To tell you De Lancey's men aim to make off with your cattle. That you don't have much time to do anything about it."

"Hannah, what is this all about?" Mr. Isaacs had ridden up. He had a gun in front of his saddle and Queenie's reins looped over one arm.

"It's this, sir," Hannah said, turning her back on Jacob. "De Lancey was sent word last night about your taking cattle to Peekskill by way of Pine's Bridge."

"Who told you that?" Mr. Isaacs sounded impatient. He wasn't wasting any time laughing at her. And his hand touched his gun.

"I can't tell you, sir, I promised not to."

"Hannah, I have to know if I'm to believe it."

"I know who it was, sir," Jacob took Queenie's reins from his father. "But if Hannah promised not to tell, I can't either. Believing won't hurt us any, though. And not believing could cost us the cattle."

He turned to Hannah, and he wasn't laughing now either. "How much time do we have, Hannah?"

"The man on Guard Hill hadn't seen any sign of mounted troops when I rode by. That's all I know. Except I rode faster than I've ever done before."

Jacob faced his father again. "If we run the cattle, there may still be time to get them across the bridge and take up the planks."

Mr. Isaacs pulled at his beard and thought. In less than a minute he'd made up his mind.

"Jon! Sam!" he called, and two men Hannah hadn't seen before answered. One was upstream and one down, behind the drinking cattle.

"Get the cattle out of the water and on the road," Mr. Isaacs shouted. "And get them running. Jacob, you stay here, and don't let them turn back toward Bedford."

Mr. Isaacs spurred his horse into the stream. Whips cracked, cattle bawled, and water splashed.

Jacob lifted Hannah up on Queenie and then mounted his own horse. "I'm sorry I laughed," he apologized. "It was the critters more than you. They looked so surprised."

"It's all right, Jacob," Hannah said. Maybe when there was time, she'd laugh about it, too.

As the cattle came out of the water, Jacob turned the ones that tried to head back. Hannah broke a sapling branch and made herself a switch.

"Go on home, Hannah," Jacob said once, but after that he

168

seemed glad of her help. Queenie was handy, and whenever an animal left the road for the woods, Hannah rode after it. Then, when the strays were back in the water and headed the right way, she and Jacob went splashing into the stream, too. When the water came up to the horses' knees. Queenie put her head down to drink.

"Don't let her. She'll founder," Jacob called back as he splashed on ahead. Hannah pulled Queenie's head up and kicked her. In a minute she was following Jacob's horse up the west bank.

The cattle that hadn't strayed were some distance on, running with tails and rumps high and heads low, kicking up a storm of dust. Hannah heard Jon and Sam shouting, but she couldn't see them on account of the dust. She could hardly see Mr. Isaacs, who was just in front of her. She choked, and Jacob came up beside her and grabbed Tamar's kerchief from her head. "Tie it over your nose," he shouted. If it hadn't been already tied, Hannah couldn't have done it, but she managed to slip it into position without losing either reins or switch. Now that she could breathe again she was enjoying the run so much she almost forgot why they were running. Then through the dust straight ahead, over the backs of the cattle she saw a broad curve of water. The Croton! As they neared it, the woods fell away, and she could see the bridge and the road leading toward it from North Castle Church.

There were two small figures on the road close to the bridge. Men on horses. Even through the dust she could see that. Hannah was too excited to feel immediate fear, but then it came flooding through her. The men could be scouts for De Lancey, and the other men close behind. They'd take the cattle. Maybe they'd kill Jacob. She and Queenie hadn't done any good in coming.

Then she heard Mr. Isaacs say, "I'll go help Jon and Sam. Let the animals slow down if they will, Jacob." He rode to the left of the cattle, spurring his horse until he passed them.

"Whoaup," Jacob sang out, "whoaup, you critters."

It took a moment for Hannah to understand and pull Queenie in. The two horsemen were Mr. Isaacs's helpers. They had gone to block the road from North Castle Church and steer the cattle onto the bridge.

Gradually the cattle slowed to a lope, their rumps moving up and down and their necks held higher so she could see their horns. At first they didn't want to go over the bridge. They tried to scatter, and it took fast riding by Jon and Sam to keep them together and moving in the right direction. One or two tried to bolt into the river, but Mr. Isaacs was ready for them.

"If they turn, get out of the way fast," Jacob told Hannah, but the cattle didn't turn. With Jacob and Hannah behind them they moved steadily forward.

"Look!" Jacob pointed to the bridge. "That's the heifer we belled because she acted the leader while the cattle were fenced up back of the Raymonds'. There won't be any more trouble. Now she's on the bridge the others will follow."

They watched some others set foot on the bridge, too. Then Jacob said, "Good-bye, Hannah. You have helped more than there's time to say. Now go back. I don't want you around when De Lancey's men find the bridge is taken up."

"Jacob, when will I know that you got the cattle safe to Peekskill? That you are safe?"

"Don't worry if we're not back for a while. We will lay up for a day in a safe place my father knows about. And then we'll take a roundabout route instead of the usual one. It will take longer."

Jacob rode over the bridge behind the last of the cattle. The men dismounted and took up the planks one by one and carried them to the far shore.

Hannah waved good-bye to Jacob, and he waved back. At first in a friendly way and then gesturing as though he were impatient. Of course, it was too far to be sure, but it looked like that. She turned Queenie and rode slowly away. When they passed the first turn, she slipped from the horse's back.

"Oh, Queenie, you were good, real good!" she said, stroking the lathered neck. "We are going to walk all the way home to Bedford, and I'll lead you as far as the brook. If you're not cool enough when we come to it, we'll wait until you are, so you can have a nice long drink."

Focus

1. What did Tamar tell Hannah about the Isaacses' cattle? How did Tamar learn this news? What were her two reasons for telling Hannah?
2. What was Hannah's "race with time"?
3. What do you think would have happened if De Lancey's party had found the cattle before Hannah did?
4. Do you think the cattle were finally delivered to the Americans? Give reasons for your prediction.
5. Tamar and Hannah had been friends once. What do you think caused the break in their friendship? Do you think they will become friends again? Why or why not?

In Writing

What do you think will happen the next time Tamar and Hannah meet? Write their conversation in dialogue form.

Vocabulary

On a piece of paper, write the numbers *1* to *5.* Then look at the words in the first column and find a synonym for each word in the second column. Next to each number on your paper, write the letter of the synonym for each word.

1. fragile
2. founder
3. misgivings
4. antagonism
5. sentinels

A. stumble
B. hostility
C. guards
D. cross
E. doubts
F. delicate

The Miracle of the Talking Leaves

C. Fayne Porter

Great achievements grow out of great beliefs in ideals.
Sequoyah accomplished a task that has never been equaled
in history. Why were the "talking leaves" so important to him?

In a small Georgia village called New Echota, a four-page newspaper, damp and smelling of printer's ink, made its first press run on February 21, 1828. There would seem to be nothing very startling in this simple fact, but there was—something very startling indeed. That newspaper was the *Cherokee Phoenix*, and its run marked the publication of the first Indian paper in a native tongue to be printed anywhere.

It marked a giant step forward in the progress of a very intelligent and a very alert people. And it marked an almost impossible personal triumph for an illiterate, uneducated Cherokee genius named Sequoyah. Not a fighter in the usual sense, he was the dogged foe of ignorance wherever he encountered it, and his struggle against age-old tradition was contested not with weapons but in the minds of people. His is one of the most inspiring of all stories of human-kind's slow and painful climb out of darkness toward light.

As a youth Sequoyah showed a marked ability to work with his hands. He was a gifted silversmith, with infinite patience and attention to detail. His coin-silver bracelets and earrings, his silverware and buttons and buckles—every piece he made—bore the stamp of a superb artisan.

An injury to one of his legs while he was yet a boy made him destined to walk with a slight limp. The name Sequoyah is sometimes translated as The Lame One. The exact nature of the injury is a mystery to us. Some sources say that it came as the result of a hunting accident, others that it was due to a sickness.

The handicap did not keep him from enlisting, along with his Cherokee friends, on the side of the United States in the War of 1812. If the truth were known, the Cherokees chose to fight not because of any love for the United States but rather because their enemies, the Creeks, had already allied themselves with the British.

Before he went off to war, Sequoyah had married and had become the father of a number of boys, probably four, and of a daughter, Ah-yoka. He had supported the family well. His house had been kept neat and orderly, his vegetable garden carefully tended and productive. But when he returned from fighting in Georgia, his habits and his whole way of life changed. He came home listening to the voices of the talking leaves.

When had the wonderful talking leaves first whispered to him? What was the spark that lighted in the mind of a lonesome, crippled Cherokee boy? No one knows.

Perhaps he had first seen the white people talk with paper as a child and had accepted it as more of the powerful medicine like the magic of guns. As he matured and learned to use and to understand the white people's tools, perhaps the nagging thought persisted at the back of his mind. Perhaps there was another tool, more important than all the others—a tool by which people could talk across the miles, and by which the old knowledge could be set down. What did the white people do when a problem arose about which they knew little? They went to the talking leaves that others had

made, and there they found answers. What a glorious gift this would be for his Cherokees! What doors it would unlock for them!

Available evidence indicates that Sequoyah had a growing awareness of this for about three years prior to his going away to war. Thrown in service into closer contact with whites than he had been before, he must have watched them closely. He must have seen the soldiers, huddled around the campfires at night, carefully making the strange dark marks on that thin stuff no thicker than a leaf, which would whirl away in the wind just as a leaf does, and which the whites called paper. But the white leaves went away and talked the men's minds—the minds of homesick husbands and fathers.

Then other leaves came back, and Sequoyah watched the faces of the soldiers as they read the letters, with news of wives and children and home. For himself, there was no news—not one word in two long years, because none of the Cherokees knew the secret of the talking leaves.

So Sequoyah came to his great task. Of course the task was impossible—any linguist could have told him that. How many thousands of years did it take to produce and refine the alphabet with which this page is written? Intelligent and well-trained people had already tried to set the Cherokee tongue into a pattern of letters, but with no success.

In Sequoyah's ignorance lay his strength. He had no preconceived ideas to overcome, since these were lines upon which no Indian had ever thought before. He could neither read, write, nor speak English. But he knew that he had to succeed. Factions were rising among his people. Already the Creeks to the south were badly split, and more and more the Cherokees were being pushed hard by the white surge from the east. Indian families were breaking up, some of them starting to wander westward into Arkansas. Once an Indian left his family and was torn from the kinship system which

meant so much to him, he became nothing. A way must be found to keep the Cherokees together. It must be done, or the Principal People, as they called themselves, would scatter and drift and die.

In the beginning, Sequoyah set about developing a form of picture-writing. Before, he had worked long hours in the garden and had kept his small house in good repair and had busied himself over his silversmith's tools. Now he sat in the sunshine with charcoal and sycamore[1] bark, making the intricate designs on the bark and stacking the pieces together and sorting and re-sorting them according to their forms and sounds.

When a friend would stop by to talk, Sequoyah would listen avidly. And when a word would be used that Sequoyah could not immediately call to mind, he would interrupt the conversation, dive into the piles of bark, and search for the mark which stood for that word. If the search was successful he would return to hear more words. But if a careful review showed the word not to be in his collection, Sequoyah would seize his charcoal and bit of bark and lose himself in the contemplation of how best to represent the idea behind that word. Small wonder, then, that his old friends looked questioningly at him. And small wonder that it

---

[1]sycamore (sik′ə môr): a shade tree with bark that breaks or peels off in tiny scales

174

started to be whispered that Sequoyah was making strong medicine and bad medicine.

As The Lame One became more and more obsessed with his work, the neat house of which he had once been so proud fell into disrepair. The rows of corn and beans were taken over by weeds. His sons were not old enough to take on the task of managing the home and the small plot of land. And one day while he was absent his wife, in high rage, collected his hundreds of bits of sycamore bark and pitched them into the great open fireplace.

When Sequoyah returned, he had no need to ask what had happened. His wife's face told him that. Laughed at by his friends, scorned and humiliated by his wife, he called his young daughter Ah-yoka to him. Gathering her up in his arms, he turned to the path that led away into the woods and set out. He never went back.

Several miles away stood an old, tumble-down cabin that had been abandoned for years. There Sequoyah and his daughter, now about six years old, established their home. And there Sequoyah started again on the long and tedious task of making the leaves talk in Cherokee.

Then a wonderful stroke of good fortune befell him. As he and Ah-yoka were walking along the path one day, her quick eyes were the first to see it. There it lay, half-hidden in the grass—a strange, flat thing which the little girl did not recognize. She picked it up and brought it to her father questioningly. It was a book—it was the talking leaves of the whites.

Like someone in a dream, Sequoyah took it back to the cabin and placed it on the table. He examined it carefully—the strange black lines which marched so evenly across the paper, but which were broken up in ways he did not understand. He looked again at the countless letters, but of course he could not call them letters in his mind, since they were a new concept to him. But he saw that some of the marks were repeated. Ah, was that it? A sign for a sound?

He worked now with great care, identifying the marks, checking them, counting them. Yes, that was right. Twenty-six. The whole book was made up of twenty-six signs, repeated over and over again. What did it mean? What could the leaves say to him who was seeing them closely for the first time?

They told him one vital thing—that all English words were made up of a relatively few combinations of sounds. No need to have a different picture for every word. Identify the sounds in Cherokee, make a symbol for each sound, and the task would be done. Sequoyah, with Ah-yoka sitting quietly by his side and wondering at this strange transport of her father's, must have sat in his cabin that afternoon and felt within himself that pure pleasure which great minds know when they chance upon an elemental and universal truth. Now he could do it, he knew. He saw the plan, the scheme, the pattern. Now he could capture the words of his people and set them down forever on that fragile stuff called paper!

The work started again from the beginning, but with a new direction. This time it was easier—much, much easier. His method again marked with exacting care, Sequoyah identified two hundred sounds—syllables, really—in the Cherokee tongue. Using the letters from the white people's book for some of his characters (there were nine variations on the letter J in his completed work) and making up others of his own, a Cherokee syllabary[2] began to emerge. With it he could set down his thoughts, and Ah-yoka, quick of mind and eager to learn, could trace a childish finger over the characters[3] and read back to her father what he had written. The system worked. He had succeeded.

Still the dark talk ran through his tribe that Sequoyah was in with the

---

[2]syllabary (sil′ə ber′ē): a table or listing of syllables

[3]characters: individual letters or symbols

spirits of evil. The great and humble man, now probably in his mid-forties, reflected on all this and came to a grave decision. He needed time to think, to get away from this place where he was scorned and rejected. His wife had married again, and now that his work was almost done there was nothing to hold him any longer. Perhaps the Cherokees who had gone west would listen to him. Perhaps Arkansas was the place to get his fresh start.

With his precious symbols drawn on a piece of deerskin and with a few silversmith's tools to support the pair as they went, the two inseparable companions made their way slowly out of the Smokies toward the Mississippi. When they reached the mouth of the Arkansas River, they fell in with other Cherokees moving westward. Among them was a widowed woman and her eight-year-old son. By the time the group reached Fort Smith, Arkansas, Sequoyah was again a husband. With his new wife, Sally, he found the companionship, the compassion, and the understanding of his work which he had never known with his first wife.

The next three years were spent in making a home for his new family in a new land and in refining his syllabary. Ah-yoka, who had grown up with her father's work, was almost as quick in its use as was its inventor. His step-son and his new wife also picked it up easily, and the family used to spend their evenings in testing it and working with it. Many of what Sequoyah had at first identified as separate syllables he now recognized as combinations of simpler syllable unions. So one at a time, he weeded the combinations out. When he had cut the language down to its essentials, he emerged with a final syllabary of eighty-six characters.

With these finishing touches put on his talking leaves, Sequoyah knew that the time was ripe to present his work to the Principal People. Many of his friends in Arkansas had shown interest in this new device. But the Cherokee Nation of the West, as it was called, still looked eastward to the homeland for guidance. So Sequoyah knew that if his syllabary were to be accepted, it would have to be accepted by those who had laughed at him and scorned him and who had openly blamed his obsession for the dark days which had come to the Cherokees.

Leaving his wife and her son to care for their new holdings, The Lame One and his daughter retraced the long road that led to the east and to home. Here Sequoyah sought out his old friend and now one of the head men of the Cherokees and chairman of the tribal council, John Ross. Ross himself had an excellent education in the white people's schools. He was said to be able to read and write in English, French, Spanish, Latin, and Greek—and, of course, could speak in Cherokee. He would know, reasoned Sequoyah, something about languages.

John Ross was anything but enthusiastic at first. He remembered the old talk about Sequoyah, and he knew that there were many who understood nothing of what he was trying to do. But Sequoyah was persuasive, and so Ross agreed that The Lame One might present his work at a meeting of the tribal council.

The day about which Sequoyah had long dreamed was finally at hand. Twelve years of his life had gone into this work, and now he faced his personal moment of truth. Soon he would know.

The tribal council gathered, solemn and impassive. He recognized in the group some old friends—and some old enemies. Ah-yoka, now about ten years old and almost as skillful as her father in the use of the syllabary, was to set down on paper the words which the council would say to her. Sequoyah would then read back from her writing.

The slim little girl sat at a great table, the white paper and a slender pencil before her. Sequoyah looked at the bronzed faces with their eyes riveted on the girl, laid a gentle hand briefly on his daughter's shoulder, and left the room. The test had begun.

What went through the Cherokee's mind can only be guessed, but now his whole life depended upon a sheet of paper, a sliver of lead, and the quick mind of a ten-year-old girl. Would she be able to set down the message of the council? Knowing how much it meant to him, would she panic? Would the strange setting and the strange faces and the thick tension in the room drive from her young head the memory of those characters they had worked on so long together? Ah, he would know soon—very, very soon.

The door opened, a hand beckoned, and Sequoyah re-entered the room. Ah-yoka sat with her eyes downcast, the pencil and paper in the same place on the table before her. Quiet hung heavy in the air. Sequoyah breathed a prayer to the gods of the Principal People and walked slowly to the table. His eyes were fixed first on his daughter's face, but he could read nothing there. Then he looked down at the paper—and what had before been a blank sheet was now filled with the markings that had been born in the mind of Sequoyah.

He picked it up, and saw the neat and precise hand of Ah-yoka. The characters perhaps swam for a moment before his eyes, and then he started to read. And he read it all. The words given to the girl by the council and set down on the talking leaves came back to them as if by magic. Cherokee words! The

178

work was done and proved—the leaves could be made to speak in Cherokee!

The tribal council was stunned and silent. Then the silence broke, slowly at first, and the excitement grew until there was a babble of sound in the room. Reserved men became like children with new toys, crowding around Sequoyah and the girl and looking at the strange marks on the paper and demanding to know how to set down marks that would say their names and the names of their families and loved ones.

The tide that started to swell in that gathering of the tribal council rose until it swept over the whole Cherokee Nation. The Principal People were electrified as the news spread. Sequoyah was asked by the council to stay in the east so that he could teach those who wanted to learn. Cherokee youths came to The Lame One as students, and they went out to teach others. The marks of the syllabary appeared everywhere—written on paper, scratched on the sides of houses and on fences and on trees, drawn with eager fingers in the dust of the roadside.

And the Cherokees learned. They learned how to read and write and they became a literate people in a shorter span of time than any other group, any place in the world. Soon letters were shuttling back and forth between the

Eastern Cherokees and those in Arkansas and Oklahoma. Within a year, observers said, these people had passed from a state of having no written language at all to a high degree of literacy.

In the long view of history, what had Sequoyah accomplished? He had done something which no one before him had done and which no one following him has done. He is the only person in the entire history of the world to invent, completely by himself, a simple and usable alphabet or syllabary. It was a beautifully uncomplicated tool, capable of expressing the complete language and thought of the Cherokees. It was unquestionably the work of pure genius.

And for its inventor, sudden fame. The Cherokee Nation awarded him an income of $500 a year, one of the few purely literary pensions ever granted within the boundaries of the United States. The council of 1824 awarded him a handsome medal, and in a letter stated " . . . the great good designed by the author of human existence in directing your genius in this happy discovery, cannot be fully estimated . . . it is incalculable."

From his invention came the type, cast into his eighty-six characters, with which the *Cherokee Phoenix* was printed. Magazines and a system of schools using the new method followed shortly after the first newspaper appeared.

The spirit and the work and the memory of Sequoyah live on. Today the old Cherokees still read with his syllabary—fewer and fewer of them now, but the system is still alive after a century and a half. And as long as the sun wheels across the sky and the grass grows green, his name will be remembered. There is a mountain on the North Carolina-Tennessee border named after him, and a statue in Georgia, and a marker which fixes the place where the print shop stood in New Echota on that day in 1828 when the *Cherokee Phoenix* was first printed. And there is a county which bears his name in Oklahoma, and the state itself was very nearly called Sequoyah. Following its admission to the Union in 1907, the first statue which Oklahoma placed in Statuary Hall in the nation's capital at Washington was a likeness of the Cherokee. In the Congressional Library are representations of the faces of people who, throughout history, have done the most to perfect written language, and among them is Sequoyah.

But perhaps the most enduring of his honors is this: those inspiring trees of California, the Big Trees (*Sequoiadendron giganteum*) and the Redwoods (*Sequoia sempervirens*), which are among the most nearly immortal and which reach closest to heaven of all the living things on earth, bear his name. And it is fitting.

180

Focus

1. Describe Sequoyah's first efforts to record the Cherokee language. What happened to change the direction of his efforts?
2. What did the people of his tribe think of Sequoyah's efforts? How did their attitude change when he proved the success of his syllabary?
3. Explain Sequoyah's method of recording the Cherokee language in written form.
4. What was especially unusual about Sequoyah's accomplishment?

In Writing

The letters of the alphabet are symbols for individual sounds. Sequoyah wrote symbols for *syllables* of sound. As an experiment, make a list of common syllables that, when combined, will form words. Then create one symbol for each syllable. Now, try to write words using your syllable symbols.

Vocabulary

Read the word list and paragraph below. Decide which word makes the best sense in each blank space. Then write the numbers *1* to *6* on a piece of paper and write the correct word next to each number.

illiterate	literary	factions
riveted	artisan	reserved
preconceived	perfect	avidly

There are some topics that many people have no opinion about. Few people are __(1)__ , however, when the subject of modern art comes up. Some have a __(2)__ idea that they do not like modern art even before they have seen any. Those people form a group on one side of the argument. People who form the opposite __(3)__ support modern art __(4)__ , with eagerness. Both groups contain people who are __(5)__ as well as people who are well read, __(6)__ types.

STUDY SKILL: Using Information from a Graph

A graph is a clear way to arrange information. Graphs are made in many shapes. Bar graphs and circle graphs are two types of graphs that are frequently used. You see them in science texts and in other information-type books.

A bar graph is made of barlike shapes placed side by side. This kind of graph uses either vertical (up-and-down) lines or horizontal (left-to-right) lines. Each bar represents a quantity, which tells "how much." A bar graph is an easy way to compare different quantities. All you have to do is compare the length of the bars.

The bar graph provided here shows the length of the first four ships that anchored in Scavenger Harbor (a fictitious, chilly place) after the icebergs broke apart last spring. Compare the lengths of the ships *Icicle* and *Flying Eagle*. First, find the bar marked "Icicle." The length of *Icicle* is represented by the bar that starts at the ship's name. It runs left to right (horizontally) across the graph. Run your finger along the bar for *Icicle*. Now move your finger straight down to the bottom line of the graph. Your finger should be on 30'. The caption under the row of numbers says "Length in Feet." So, this means that *Icicle* is 30 feet long. (The metric equivalent lengths are shown in parentheses.)

Now soar toward the bar for "Flying Eagle." Again, run your finger from the name of the ship across to the right end of the bar. Drop straight down from that point to the number at the bottom of the graph. You have discovered that *Flying Eagle* is 90 feet long. This comparison tells you that *Flying Eagle* is 60 feet longer than *Icicle*. (Subtract the 30-foot long *Icicle* from the 90-foot long *Flying Eagle*. The answer shows a 60-foot difference in size.)

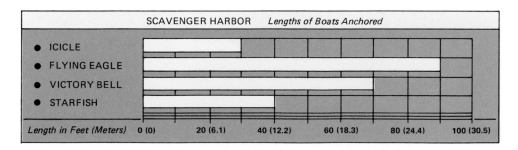

SCAVENGER HARBOR   *Lengths of Boats Anchored*

- ICICLE
- FLYING EAGLE
- VICTORY BELL
- STARFISH

Length in Feet (Meters) 0 (0)   20 (6.1)   40 (12.2)   60 (18.3)   80 (24.4)   100 (30.5)

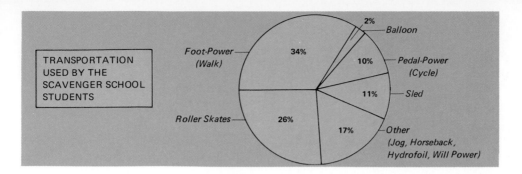

TRANSPORTATION USED BY THE SCAVENGER SCHOOL STUDENTS

Foot-Power (Walk) 34%
Balloon 2%
Pedal-Power (Cycle) 10%
Sled 11%
Other (Jog, Horseback, Hydrofoil, Will Power) 17%
Roller Skates 26%

A circle graph (sometimes called a "pie chart" because of its round shape) is an easy way to compare parts of a whole, like slicing up a pie. This round graph is used to show the parts, or percents, of a total amount. The circle graph provided here shows how students get to the Scavenger School. The numbers represent what percent of the students use each type of transportation. The percentage is written directly on each wedge section of the circle graph or is labeled with a leader line to the wedge.

Look at the labels for each of the wedge sections. The wedge labeled "Other" stands for all the other ways combined that students use to get to school. (This could include students who jog, ride horseback, skim over the water on a hydrofoil, and even those who use only will power.) What percent of students use "other means" to arrive at school?

Did you notice that when the percentages are added together, they total 100%? A circle graph accounts for each part of the whole. If there are no missing pieces, a circle graph can tell you how the pie was divided.

Now it's time for a graph "scavenger hunt" (a contest in which people are sent out to find something within a time limit).

1. What was the longest boat anchored in Scavenger Harbor?
2. Which boat is longer, *Starfish* or *Icicle?* Tell how much longer.
3. What is the combined (total) length of *Icicle* and *Starfish?* How did you get the answer?
4. Compare the lengths of *Victory Bell* and *Starfish.* Which is shorter? By how much?
5. What percent of students get to the Scavenger School by sled?
6. What percent use foot-power to arrive at school?
7. Do balloons or do roller skates carry the larger percent of students to school?
8. Are more students getting to school using pedal-power or sled? How many more?
9. How much of the pie has been eaten? How did you find the answer?

183

A Glory over Everything

Ann Petry

People take great risks for their freedom. Harriet Tubman was responsible for helping more than three hundred people escape from slavery. How did she feel, alone, the first time?

One day, in 1849, when Harriet Tubman was working in the fields, near the edge of the road, a white woman wearing a faded sunbonnet went past, driving a wagon. She stopped the wagon, and watched Harriet for a few minutes. Then she spoke to her, asked her what her name was, and how she had acquired the deep scar on her forehead.

Harriet told her the story of the blow she had received when she was a girl. After that, whenever the woman saw her in the fields, she stopped to talk to her. She told Harriet that she lived on a farm. Then one day she said, not looking at Harriet, but looking instead at the overseer, far off at the edge of the fields, "If you ever need any help, Harriet, ever need any help, why you let me know."

That same year the young heir to the Brodas estate died. Harriet mentioned the fact of his death to the white woman in the faded sunbonnet, the next time she saw her. She told her of the panic-stricken talk in the quarter,[1] told her that the slaves were afraid that the master, Dr. Thompson, would start selling them. She said that Doc Thompson no longer permitted any of them to hire their time. The woman nodded her head, clucked to the horse, and drove off, murmuring, "If you ever need any help—"

The slaves were right about Dr. Thompson's intention. He began selling slaves almost immediately. Among the first ones sold were two of Harriet Tubman's sisters. They went with the chain gang on a Saturday.

---

[1]quarter: shacks where slaves were housed

When Harriet heard of the sale of her sisters, she knew that the time had finally come when she must leave the plantation. A few days later, a slave working beside Harriet in the fields motioned to her. She bent toward him, listening. He said the water boy had just brought news to the field hands, and it had been passed from one to the other until it reached him. The news was that Harriet and other members of her family had been sold to a slave trader, and that they were to be sent with the chain gang that very night.

Harriet went on working but she knew a moment of panic. She would have to escape. She would have to start as soon as it was dark. She could not go with the chain gang. She might die on the way, because of those inexplicable sleeping seizures, caused by that blow on her head. But then she—how could she run away? She might fall asleep in plain view along the road.

But even if she fell asleep, she thought, the Lord would take care of her. She murmured a prayer, "Lord, I'm going to hold steady onto You and You've got to see me through."

Afterward, she explained her decision to run the risk of going alone, in these words: "I had reasoned this out in my mind. There was one of two things I had a *right* to, liberty or death. If I could not have one, I would have the other; for no man should take me alive. I should fight for my liberty as long as my strength lasted, and when the time came for me to go, the Lord would let them take me."

At dusk, when the work in the fields was over, she started toward the Big House. She had to let someone know that she was going, someone she could trust. Her sister Mary worked in the Big House, and she planned to tell Mary that she was going to run away, so someone would know.

As she went toward the house, she saw the master, Doc Thompson, riding up the drive on his horse. She turned aside and went toward the quarter. A field hand had no legitimate reason for entering the kitchen of the Big House—and yet—there must be some way she could leave word so that afterward someone would think about it and know that she had left a message.

As she went toward the quarter she began to sing. Dr. Thompson reined in his horse, turned around and looked at her. It was not the beauty of her voice that made him turn and watch her, frowning, it was the words of the song that she was singing, and something defiant in her manner, that disturbed and puzzled him.

> *When that old chariot comes,*
> *I'm going to leave you,*
> *I'm bound for the promised land,*
> *Friends, I'm going to leave you.*
>
> *I'm sorry, friends, to leave you,*
> *Farewell! Oh, farewell!*
> *But I'll meet you in the morning,*
> *Farewell! Oh, farewell!*
>
> *I'll meet you in the morning,*
> *When I reach the promised land;*
> *On the other side of Jordan,*
> *For I'm bound for the promised land.*

That night when the fire had died down in the cabin, she took the ashcake that had been baked for breakfast, and a good-sized piece of salt herring, and tied them together in an old bandanna. By hoarding this small stock of food, she could make it last a long time, and with the berries and edible roots she could find in the woods, she wouldn't starve.

She decided that she would take the quilt with her, too. Her hands lingered over it. It felt soft and warm to her touch. Even in the dark, she thought she could tell one color from another, because she knew its pattern and design so well. She left the cabin quickly, carrying the quilt carefully folded under her arm.

Once she was off the plantation, she took to the woods, not following the North Star, not even looking for it, going instead toward town. She needed help. She was going to ask the white woman who had stopped to talk to her so often if she would help her. Perhaps she wouldn't. But she would soon find out.

When she came to the farmhouse where the woman lived, she approached it cautiously, circling around it. It was so quiet. There was no sound at all, not even a dog barking, or the sound of voices. Nothing.

She tapped on the door, gently. A voice said, "Who's there?" She answered, "Harriet, from Dr. Thompson's place."

When the woman opened the door she did not seem at all surprised to see her. She glanced at the little bundle that Harriet was carrying, at the quilt, and invited her in. Then she sat down at the kitchen table, and wrote two names on a slip of paper, and handed the paper to Harriet.

She said that those were the next places where it was safe for Harriet to stop. The first place was a farm where there was a gate with big white posts and round knobs on top of them. The people there would feed her and when they thought it was safe for her to go on, they would tell her how to get to the next house, or take her there. For these were the first two stops on the Underground Railroad.

Thus Harriet learned that the Underground Railroad was not a railroad at all. Neither did it run underground. It was composed of a loosely organized group of people who offered food and shelter, or a place of concealment, to fugitives who had set out on the long road to freedom.

Harriet wanted to pay this woman who had befriended her. But she had no money. She gave her the patchwork quilt, the only beautiful object she had ever owned.

That night she made her way through the woods, crouching in the underbrush whenever she heard the sound of horses' hooves, staying there until the riders passed. Each time she wondered if they were already hunting for her. It would be so easy to describe her, the deep scar on her forehead like a dent, the old scars on the back of her neck, the husky speaking voice, the lack of height, scarcely five feet tall. The master would say she was wearing rough clothes when she ran away, that she had a bandanna on her head, that she was muscular and strong.

She knew how accurately he would describe her. One of the slaves who could read used to tell the others what it said on those handbills that were nailed up on the trees, along the edge of the roads. It was easy to recognize the handbills that advertised runaways, because there was always a picture in one corner, a picture of a black man, a little running figure with a stick over his shoulder, and a bundle tied on the end of the stick.

Whenever she thought of the handbills, she walked faster. Sometimes she stumbled over old grapevines, gnarled and twisted, or became entangled in the tough, sinewy vine of the honeysuckle. But she kept going.

In the morning, she came to the house where her friend had said she was to stop. She showed the slip of paper that she carried to the woman who answered her knock at the back door of the farmhouse. The woman fed her, and then handed her a broom and told her to sweep the yard.

Harriet hesitated, suddenly suspicious. Then she decided that with a broom in her hand, working in the yard, she would look as though she belonged on the place, certainly no one would suspect that she was a runaway.

That night the woman's husband, a farmer, loaded a wagon with produce. Harriet climbed in. He threw some blankets over her, and the wagon started.

It was dark under the blankets, and not exactly comfortable. But Harriet decided that riding was better than walking. She was surprised at her own lack of fear, wondered how it was that she so readily trusted these strangers who might betray her. For all she knew, the man driving the wagon might be taking her straight back to the master.

She thought of those other rides in wagons, when she was a child, the same clop-clop of the horses' feet, creak of the wagon,

and the feeling of being lost because she did not know where she was going. She did not know her destination this time either, but she was not alarmed. By this time someone must have told the master that she was gone. Then she thought of the plantation and how the land rolled gently down toward the river, thought of her parents, Ben and Old Rit, and that Old Rit would be inconsolable because her favorite daughter was missing. "Lord," she prayed, "I'm going to hold steady onto You. You've got to see me through." Then she went to sleep.

The next morning when the stars were still visible in the sky, the farmer stopped the wagon. Harriet was instantly awake.

He told her to follow the river, to keep following it to reach the next place where people would take her in and feed her. He said that she must travel only at night, and she must stay off the roads because the patrol would be hunting for her. Harriet climbed out of the wagon. "Thank you," she said simply, thinking how amazing it was that there should be white people who were willing to go to such lengths to help a slave get to freedom.

When she finally arrived at the next stop, she had traveled roughly ninety miles. She had slept on the ground outdoors at night. She had been rowed for miles up the river by a man she had never seen before. She had been concealed in a haycock,[2] and had, at one point, spent a week hidden in a potato hole[3] in a cabin which belonged to a family of free Blacks. She had been hidden in the attic of the home of a Quaker. She had been befriended by stout German farmers, whose guttural speech surprised her and whose well-kept farms astonished her. She had never before seen barns and fences, farmhouses and outbuildings, so carefully painted. The cattle and horses were so clean they looked as though they had been scrubbed.

When she crossed the line into the free state of Pennsylvania, the sun was coming up. She said, "I looked at my hands to see if I was the same person now I was free. There was such a glory over everything, the sun came like gold through the trees, and over the fields, and I felt like I was in heaven."

---

[2]haycock: a small cone-shaped pile of hay in a field
[3]potato hole: a pit used for the storage of potatoes

Focus

1. What was the Underground Railroad? How did it work?
2. Why do you think the woman in the sunbonnet kept looking at the overseer while she was talking to Harriet?
3. What events led to Harriet's decision to escape from the plantation?
4. How do you know that Harriet Tubman was determined to gain her freedom?
5. Why do you think Harriet trusted the strangers who helped her?
6. What hardships, physical and emotional, did Harriet endure to gain her freedom?

In Writing

Harriet Tubman was a heroic woman. Think about the costs of personal courage. In one or two paragraphs, tell how you might feel and react if you were trapped alone in enemy territory. Are you brave and determined to be free? What are you willing to risk?

Vocabulary

On a piece of paper, write the numbers *1* to *5*. Then look at the words in the first column and find a definition for each word in the second column. Next to each number on your paper, write the letter of the correct definition for each word.

1. produce
2. concealment
3. acquired
4. inexplicable
5. pinion

A. farm products
B. not rightful or lawful
C. bind the arms of
D. not able to be explained
E. the hiding of something
F. came to have; obtained

Runagate Runagate

Robert Hayden

Runs falls rises stumbles on from darkness into darkness
and the darkness thicketed with shapes of terror
and the hunters pursuing and the hounds pursuing
and the night cold and the night long and the river
to cross and the jack-muh-lanterns beckoning beckoning
and blackness ahead and when shall I reach that somewhere
morning and keep on going and never turn back and
    keep on going
        Runagate
          Runagate
          Runagate
Many thousands rise and go
many thousands crossing over

Alacrán

J. Frank Dobie

In the days when wild mustangs roamed the West, capturing and taming one was a great achievement. Such a horse did not allow just anyone to ride it.

About the time the Civil War was ending in the United States, vaqueros were mustanging on the plains of Coahuila[1] some fifty miles south of Eagle Pass, Texas. They captured a dappled-gray, two-year-old stallion. The stallion was led farther south by his owner and kept from escaping by a hair rope that tied a front foot to the limb of a tree. This stallion was very strong for his age and proved to be a fierce bucker. He tried to bite anyone coming near him, and his owner tossed from a distance what hay or fodder he fed him. This owner disliked him and sold him at a bargain to Don Miguel Guajardo.

Tied up short to a hayrack, the young horse tried to bite and kick his new owner whenever he brought hay and corn. Don Miguel scolded him and calmly let him go hungry until he accepted food as a favor. Soon he was caressing and currying him and bathing him at the waterhole. He put a saddle on him, without drawing the cinch tight, and left it all day. Next he tied a piece of rawhide to his tail and left it there until the horse ceased to fear it and to twist and kick at it. The hairs growing out of the end of his tail were sparse, and when he raised it, it resembled the tail of a scorpion. Thus he received a name— Alacrán, or Scorpion.

Soon Alacrán was a different horse from the starved, abused animal that Don Miguel bought. Fat and sleek, as alert and ready as a wild gobbler, he carried himself haughtily. After saddling him one day, Don Miguel told a vaquero to mount him. A few jumps and Alacrán was riderless. Don Miguel tied a bundle of hay on either side of the saddle and left him until he was used to the burden. The next day he mounted the horse

---

[1]Coahuila (kō'ä wē'lä)

himself, rode him gently, and began teaching him to rein. Thereafter, no one else tried to ride him; he became Don Miguel's most trusted mount.

About this time cotton was bringing high prices. Many wagons of it were freighted out of northern Mexico to Eagle Pass, thence to San Antonio and on to a Gulf port to be shipped to England. When Alacrán was five years old, his owner rode him to conduct a train of cotton wagons. On the route a cow-buyer headed for the Rio Grande joined the train. Danger from bandits made company desirable. One afternoon the freighters camped on a creek north of the Rio Sabinas—in the very range where Alacrán had been captured as a mustang. Don Miguel staked him on the prairie by digging a hole in the ground with his knife, tying a double-knot in the end of the rope, putting the knot well down in the hole, and packing the earth back on top of it. A well-buried knot can be pulled up vertically, but it cannot be pulled up by a horse setting back or running on his rope.

The cow-buyer had come to admire Alacrán so much that during the evening he offered two hundred pesos for him—a very high price at the time—and was refused. That night during a rainstorm Alacrán broke the rope, near his neck, and left. When daylight came, though visibility was very poor on account of low, heavy clouds, Don Miguel climbed on top of a load of cotton to look. In the distance he made out a moving object that he took to be Alacrán. He shelled corn into a *morral* (a fiber nose bag), wrapped himself in his blue cape, and started off afoot.

"You had better ride one of the mules, Don Miguel," advised a driver. "Your horse is far off and the grass is very wet."

"If I ride, Alacrán will mistrust me," Don Miguel replied. "This is his country. He remembers how riders raced and caught him here."

Don Miguel walked on through the thick, wet grass and in time neared the grazing runaway. At sight of the man, Alacrán snorted and turned as if to flee. Don Miguel stopped, rattled the corn in the *morral,* and called the horse's name loudly in accustomed tones. The mustang snorted, took two steps forward, snorted again, then walked to put his nose in the *morral,* not without a final puff. Don Miguel unloosed his belt and used it to lead Alacrán.

As he walked into camp, the cow-buyer said, "Don Miguel, yesterday I offered you two hundred pesos for that horse. Today I offer you three hundred."

"I do not wish to sell the horse at any price," Don Miguel replied, "but I shall have need of the money in San Antonio. I accept your offer. Before I deliver the horse to you, however, I must tell you something of his peculiarities, even defects."

"Nothing you could tell me would alter my estimate of the horse," the cow-buyer quickly interposed. "I too am a man of the camps. Let us count the money. The horse is mine."

The silver pesos were counted out of the owner's saddle-bags. Despite the buyer's indifference to information, Don Miguel gave him these warnings: "Before mounting Alacrán you will do well to look him in the eyes. If they are inflamed and red, calm him and wait until the wild look subsides before stepping into the stirrup. You had better uncoil the rope attached to Alacrán's neck and hold it in your hand before dismounting. He always knows whether or not he is loose. Until he becomes used to you, you had better hobble as well as stake him at night. I present you with this pair of hobbles."

The buyer rode on north, ahead of the wagon train, leaving the horse he had been riding to be delivered at the Rio Grande. It was known that he carried five hundred silver pesos, wrapped in paper, in his saddlebags.

Over the rain-soaked ground the wagons made slow progress. While the train was resting next day, the cow-buyer dragged into camp afoot. He had been out all night and was famished. After reviving on coffee, frijoles and tortillas, he made explanation.

"Yesterday about dark," he said, "I rode up to the camp of a goatherder who was cooking supper in front of a well-thatched shed. He gladly gave me permission to spend the night. Like a fool, I started to dismount without taking down the rope as you advised. Just as my right foot was out of the stirrup, a dog rushed up barking. Alacrán reared back, throwing me to the ground, and ran off—with saddle and the five hundred pesos. The last I saw of him he was coming down the road in this direction. I have hunted for him all morning without seeing him or even his tracks. Don Miguel, will you help me find him?"

"I will help you hunt for him," replied Don Miguel, "but I cannot assure you of success. Was the saddle cinched tight or loose?"

"Tight," the cow-buyer replied. "There is no danger of his getting rid of it."

"It is not that," observed Don Miguel. "If the saddle is tight, the horse will not travel far without stopping. How far from here did Alacrán break away?"

"About three leagues."

The two men saddled horses and rode forth immediately. The cow-buyer wanted to search the country on both sides of the road. Don Miguel said, "If I am to help you, you must follow me. We will ride up the road until we strike Alacrán's tracks turning out of it. Then I will trail him."

They found where Alacrán had turned out of the road not a great distance south of the goatherder's camp.

"Was he sweaty when he broke away?" Don Miguel asked.

"The heavy ground had made sweat drip from him," the cow-buyer replied.

"Good!" exclaimed Don Miguel. "That means less travel."

After the general course of the runaway was evident, Don Miguel rode in wide circles, scanning in all directions. About sundown he spied Alacrán at the foot of a range of low hills. The two rode in a roundabout way so as to approach without being seen. When they were fairly near, Don Miguel dismounted, wrapped himself in his blue cape, told the other man to remain out of sight, and started walking. He could see mud on the saddle, from the horse's having rolled on it. On account of the stinging sweat on his back and the pinching girth, Alacrán was switching his tail nervously. He was in the act of lying down to roll again when Don Miguel called his name. He pitched his head up, whinnied for pleasure, and ran to his old friend, rubbing his neck against him.

Don Miguel loosed the cinch, took the rope down from the saddle horn, and led him to where the cow-buyer was waiting. "I have left the saddle for you to remove," he said.

The cow-buyer appeared to be more concerned over his silver than over his horse. Examining the saddlebags, he found only eighty or ninety pesos left. "Somebody has robbed me," he cried.

"Impossible," said Don Miguel. "No human being on earth

but myself could have approached this horse near enough to touch the saddle without either roping or shooting him. Any robber who got his hands on the silver would have taken all. It is my belief that Alacrán while wallowing broke the wrappings about the pesos and spilled them on the ground. ·

"Listen, my friend. To show this intelligent horse that you understand him and to win his gratitude, remove the saddle and blanket at once and then with handfuls of dry grass rub the caked mud and sweat from his sensitive skin. Later, when we arrive in camp, we will bathe him and he can rest refreshed."

It was now too late to hunt for the pesos. That night Alacrán was washed and well fed. In the morning Don Miguel mounted him and, followed by the cow-buyer, rode to the spot where he had left the wagon road. Alacrán seemed disinclined to follow his old tracks, but Don Miguel knew that he, like many other range horses, was expert at trailing himself, either forward or backward. As he was gently made to understand what was desired, he began to step in the very tracks he had made two nights and one day preceding.

"Watch for wallowing places," advised Don Miguel.

For hours the trailers rode at a walk. Frequently Alacrán put his nose to the well-turfed ground to smell. In many places the grass pressed down by his hooves had sprung back erect, leaving no visible trail. The trailers wound in and out and around. About midday they came to a spot where Alacrán had lain down but had not wallowed to any extent. An hour later they came to a waterhole where he had drunk and then wallowed energetically. Pesos were shining in the sand. By dusk most of the missing money had been recovered from a half dozen or so wallowing places. Then Alacrán forsook the trail he had so patiently followed and made for camp. He had done his duty. It was unsaddling time.

The cow-buyer's education in the management of an intelligent horse had been greatly advanced. That night, he insisted, without success, on Don Miguel's accepting half of the recovered money. When he rode off the next morning, he was more than owner of Alacrán. He was his understanding friend and partner.

Focus

1. List the steps involved in taming the mustang Alacrán.
2. How did Don Miguel view Alacrán? How did the cow-buyer view Alacrán?
3. What clues did Don Miguel use to track Alacrán?
4. In the end, the author said that the cow-buyer had become Alacrán's "understanding friend and partner." How do you think this change affected the cow-buyer's daily work with Alacrán?

In Writing

Imagine that you own an animal that is lost. Write an advertisement for the lost-and-found section of your local newspaper, describing the animal in great detail. (This particular newspaper prints any length of lost-and-found ad for free, so money is no object!)

Vocabulary

Make two columns on your paper. Label the first column *Positive* and the second column *Negative*. Then look at the words in the list below. Decide whether each word has a positive or negative connotation. Write the word in the correct column. Then write a sentence using each word.

wallowing   haughtily   inflamed
defects   energetically

The Flower-Fed Buffaloes

Vachel Lindsay

The flower-fed buffaloes of the spring
In the days of long ago,
Ranged where the locomotives sing
And the prairie flowers lie low:—
The tossing, blooming, perfumed grass
Is swept away by the wheat,
Wheels and wheels and wheels spin by
In the spring that still is sweet.
But the flower-fed buffaloes of the spring
Left us, long ago.
They gore no more, they bellow no more,
They trundle around the hills no more:—
With the Blackfeet, lying low,
With the Pawnees, lying low,
Lying low.

STUDY SKILL: Multiple Dictionary Entries

Sometimes, words that look the same are really quite different. Look at the dictionary sample on the next page. Find the dictionary entries for *fritter*. Each entry has a small raised number after it. The raised number signals that this spelling of the word has more than one definition. *Fritter* is an example of a multiple dictionary entry. "Fritter[1]" means to waste something valuable without getting anything in return.

> Sometimes, I fritter my time away doing nothing. I call those wasted times my "ho-hum hours."

"Fritter[2]" means some small bit of food dipped in batter and lightly fried.

> Yesterday, we had a fritter festival. There were delicious apple, meat, and fish fritters.

The two fritter examples point out the need to be aware when you use the dictionary. A word may have more than one entry. When you see the raised number signal, check all the separate entries for that particular word. This awareness will help you to find the definition you want. Also, look for clue words in sentences. Clue words tell which definition to choose. If you're frittering time, you're wasting it. This is "fritter[1]." If your fritter is delicious, you're eating it. This is "fritter[2]."

Frizzle is another word that is a multiple dictionary entry. Find *frizzle* in the sample. How many multiple entries for *frizzle* does the dictionary show? (Remember, don't give up with the first entry. Look for the raised number that signals a multiple dictionary entry.)

fringe (frinj), **1** border or trimming made of threads, cords, etc., either loose or tied together in small bunches. **2** anything like this; border: *A fringe of hair hung over her forehead.* **3** make a fringe for. **4** be a fringe for: *Bushes fringed the road.* 1,2 *n.*, 3,4 *v.*, **fringed, fring ing.**

Fris bee (friz′bē), trademark for a saucer-shaped disk of colored plastic for skimming back and forth in play. *n.*

frisk (frisk), **1** run and jump about playfully; dance and skip joyously: *Our lively puppy frisks all over the house.* **2** search for concealed weapons or stolen goods by running a hand quickly over a person's clothes. *v.* —**frisk′er,** *n.*

frisk i ly (fris′kə lē), in a frisky manner; briskly. *adv.*

frisk i ness (fris′kē nis), a frisky quality or condition; briskness. *n.*

frisk y (fris′kē), playful; lively. *adj.*, **frisk i er, frisk i est.**

frit ter[1] (frit′ər), waste little by little: *fritter away a day watching TV.* *v.*

frit ter[2] (frit′ər), sliced fruit, vegetables, meat, or fish covered with batter and fried. *n.* —**frit′ter er,** *n.*

fri vol i ty (fri vol′ə tē), **1** a being frivolous; silly behavior; trifling. **2** a silly thing; frivolous act. *n.*, *pl.* **fri vol i ties.**

friv o lous (friv′ə ləs), **1** lacking in seriousness or sense; silly: *Frivolous behavior is out of place in a courtroom.* **2** of little worth or importance; trivial: *Don't waste time on frivolous matters.* *adj.* —**friv′o lous ly,** *adv.*

frizz or **friz** (friz), **1** form into small, crisp curls; curl. **2** hair curled in small, crisp curls or a very close crimp. 1 *v.*, **frizzed, friz zing;** 2 *n.*, *pl.* **friz zes.**

friz zle[1] (friz′əl), **1** curl (hair) in small, crisp curls. **2** a small, crisp curl. 1 *v.*, **friz zled, friz zling;** 2 *n.*

friz zle[2] (friz′əl), **1** make a hissing, sputtering noise when cooking; sizzle: *The ham frizzled in the frying pan.* **2** a hissing, sputtering noise; sizzle. 1 *v.*, **friz zled, friz zling;** 2 *n.*

friz zly (friz′lē), full of small, crisp curls; curly. *adj.*, **friz zli er, friz zli est.**

friz zy (friz′ē), frizzly. *adj.* **friz zi er, friz zi est.**

fro (frō). **to and fro,** first one way and then back again; back and forth: *A rocking chair goes to and fro.* *adv.*

frock (frok), **1** a woman's or girl's dress; gown. **2** robe worn by a member of the clergy. *n.*

For each of the following statements, tell which definition of *fritter* or *frizzle* fits the sentence. Show the word and the raised number that signals the correct definition. Then tell what clue words in the sentence helped you to decide.

1. That family frittered away a fortune on useless clothes.

2. Those silly frizzles are tickling my eyelids!

3. I realized the frying pan was hot when the eggs started to frizzle loudly.

4. Apple fritters are a special treat.

5. I frittered my allowance away on junk this week.

6. My scalp is overwhelmed with frizzles!

7. The recipe for hamburg fritters looks easy.

LIFE ON THE MISSISSIPPI

Mark Twain

Every era has its superstars. For Mark Twain, they were the pilots of the Mississippi riverboats. What surprises were in store for him when he trained to be a pilot?

When I was a boy, there was but one permanent ambition among my friends in our village[1] on the west bank of the Mississippi River. That was, to be a steamboatman. We had transient ambitions of other sorts, but they were only transient. When a circus came and went, it left us all burning to become clowns. The first musical show that ever came to our section left us all suffering to try that kind of life. Now and then we had a hope that, if we lived and were good, Fate would permit us to be pirates. These ambitions faded out, each in its turn; but the ambition to be a steamboatman always remained.

Boy after boy managed to get on the river. The minister's son became an engineer. The doctor's and the postmaster's sons became "mud clerks"; four sons of the chief merchant, and two sons of the country judge, became pilots. Pilot was the grandest position of all. The pilot, even in those days of small wages, had a princely salary—from a hundred and fifty to two hundred and fifty dollars a month, and no board to pay. Two months of his wages would pay a preacher's salary for a year. Now some of us were left disconsolate. We could not get on the river—at least our parents would not let us.

So, by and by, I ran away. I said I would never come home again till I was a pilot and could come in glory. But somehow I could not manage it. I went meekly aboard a few of the boats that lay packed together like sardines at the long St. Louis wharf, and humbly inquired for the pilots, but got only a cold shoulder and short words from mates and clerks. I had to make

---

[1]Hannibal, Missouri

the best of this sort of treatment for the time being, but I had comforting daydreams of a future when I should be a great and honored pilot.

Months afterward the hope within me struggled to a reluctant death, and I found myself without an ambition. But I was ashamed to go home. I was in Cincinnati, and I set to work to map out a new career. I had been reading about the recent exploration of the river Amazon by an expedition sent out by our government. It was said that the expedition, owing to difficulties, had not thoroughly explored a part of the country lying about the headwaters, some four thousand miles from the mouth of the river. It was only about fifteen hundred miles from Cincinnati to New Orleans, where I could doubtless get a ship. I had thirty dollars left; I would go and complete the exploration of the Amazon. This was all the thought I gave to the subject. I never was great in matters of detail. I packed my valise, and took passage on an ancient tub called the *Paul Jones*, for New Orleans. For the sum of sixteen dollars I had the

scarred and tarnished splendors of "her" main saloon principally to myself, for she was not a creature to attract the eye of wiser travelers.

When we presently got underway and went poking down the broad Ohio, I became a new being, and the subject of my own admiration. I was a traveler! A word never had tasted so good in my mouth before. I had a joyous sense of being bound for mysterious lands and distant climes which I never have felt in so uplifting a degree since. I was in such a glorified condition that all ignoble feelings departed out of me, and I was able to look down and pity the untraveled with a compassion that had hardly a trace of contempt in it. Still, when we stopped at villages and wood-yards, I could not help lolling carelessly upon the railings of the deck to enjoy the envy of the country boys and girls on the bank. If they did not seem to discover me, I presently sneezed to attract their attention, or moved to a position where they could not help seeing me. And as soon as I knew they saw me I gaped and stretched, and gave other signs of being mightily bored with traveling.

I kept my hat off all the time, and stayed where the wind and the sun could strike me, because I wanted to get the bronzed and weather-beaten look of an old traveler. Before the second day was half gone I experienced a joy which filled me with the purest gratitude; for I saw that the skin had begun to blister and peel off my face and neck. I wished that the boys and girls at home could see me now.

We reached Louisville in time—at least the neighborhood of it. We stuck hard and fast on the rocks in the middle of the river, and lay there four days. I was now beginning to feel a strong sense of being a part of the boat's family, a sort of infant son to the captain and younger brother to the officers.

What with lying on the rocks four days at Louisville, and some other delays, the poor old *Paul Jones* fooled away about two weeks in making the voyage from Cincinnati to New Orleans. This gave me a chance to get acquainted with one of the pilots, and he taught me how to steer the boat, and thus made the fascination of river life more potent than ever for me.

It also gave me a chance to get acquainted with a youth who had taken deck passage[2]—more's the pity; for he easily borrowed six dollars of me on a promise to return to the boat and pay it back to me the day after we should arrive. But he probably died or forgot for he never came. It was doubtless the former, since he had said his parents were wealthy, and he only traveled deck passage because it was cooler.

I soon discovered two things. One was that a ship would not be likely to sail for the mouth of the Amazon under ten or twelve years. And the other was that the nine or ten dollars still left in my pocket would not be enough for so impossible an exploration as I had planned, even if I could afford to wait for a ship. Therefore it followed that I must come up with a new career. The *Paul Jones* was now bound for St. Louis. I planned a siege against my pilot, and at the end of three hard days he surrendered. He agreed to teach me the Mississippi River from New Orleans to St. Louis for five hundred dollars, payable out

---

[2]deck passage: less expensive than other fares

of the first wages I should receive after graduating. I entered upon the small business of "learning" twelve or thirteen hundred miles of the great Mississippi River with the easy confidence of my time of life. If I had really known what I was about to require of my faculties, I should not have had the courage to begin. I supposed that all a pilot had to do was to keep his boat in the river, and I did not consider that that could be much of a trick, since it was so wide.

The boat backed out from New Orleans at four in the afternoon, and it was "our watch" until eight. Mr. Bixby, my chief, "straightened her up," plowed her along past the sterns of the other boats that lay at the Levee, and then said, "Here, take her; shave those steamships as close as you'd peel an apple." I took the wheel, and my heartbeat fluttered up into the hundreds; for it seemed to me that we were about to scrape the side off every ship in the line, we were so close. I held my breath and began to claw the boat away from the danger. And I had my own opinion of the pilot who had known no better than to get us into such trouble, but I was too wise to express it. In half a minute I had a wide margin of safety between the *Paul Jones* and the ships. And within ten seconds more I was set aside in disgrace, and Mr. Bixby was going into danger again and flaying me alive with abuse of my cowardice. I was stung, but I was obliged to admire the easy confidence with which my chief loafed from side to side of his wheel, and trimmed the ships so closely that disaster seemed ceaselessly imminent. When he had cooled a little he told me that the easy water was close ashore and the current outside, and therefore we must hug the bank, up-stream, to get the benefit of the former, and stay well out, down-stream, to take advantage of the latter. In my own mind I resolved to be a down-stream pilot and leave the up-streaming to people dead to prudence.

Now and then Mr. Bixby called my attention to certain things. Said he, "This is Six-Mile Point." I assented. It was pleasant enough information, but I could not see the importance of it. I was not conscious that it was a matter of any interest to me. Another time he said, "This is Nine-Mile Point." Later he said, "This is Twelve-Mile Point." They were all about level with the water's edge; they all looked about alike to me; they were monotonously unpicturesque. I hoped Mr. Bixby would change the subject. But no; he would crowd up around a point, hugging the shore with affection, and then say: "The slack water ends here, abreast this bunch of China trees; now we cross over." So he crossed over. He gave me the wheel once or twice, but I had no luck. I either came near chipping off the edge of a sugar-plantation, or I went too far from shore, and so dropped back into disgrace again and got abused.

The watch was ended at last, and we took supper and went to bed. At midnight the glare of a lantern shone in my eyes, and the night watchman said:

"Come, turn out!"

And then he left. I could not understand this extraordinary procedure; so I presently gave up trying to, and dozed off to sleep. Pretty soon the watchman was back again, and this time he was gruff. I was annoyed. I said:

"What do you want to come bothering around here in the middle of the night for? Now, as like as not, I'll not get to sleep again tonight."

The watchman said:

"Well, if this ain't good, I'm blessed."

The "off-watch" was just turning in, and I heard some cruel laughter from them, and such remarks as "Hello, watchman! ain't the new cub turned out yet? He's delicate, likely. Give him some sugar in a rag, and send for someone to sing 'Rock-a-by Baby' to him."

About this time Mr. Bixby appeared on the scene. Something like a minute later I was climbing the pilot-house steps with some of my clothes on and the rest in my arms. Mr. Bixby was close behind, commenting. Here was something fresh—this thing of getting up in the middle of the night to go to work. It was a detail in piloting that had never occurred to me at all. I knew that boats ran all night, but somehow I had never happened to reflect that somebody had to get up out of a warm bed to run them. I began to fear that piloting was not quite so romantic as I had imagined it was; there was something very real and worklike about this new phase of it.

It was a rather gray night, although a fair number of stars were out. The big mate was at the wheel, and he had the old tub pointed at a star and was holding her straight up the middle of the river. The shores on either hand were not much more than half a mile apart, but they seemed wonderfully far away and ever so vague and indistinct. The mate said:

"We've got to land at Jones's plantation, sir."

The vengeful spirit in me cheered. I said to myself, "I wish you joy of your job, Mr. Bixby. You'll have a good time finding Mr. Jones's plantation such a night as this. And I hope you never *will* find it as long as you live."

Mr. Bixby said to the mate:

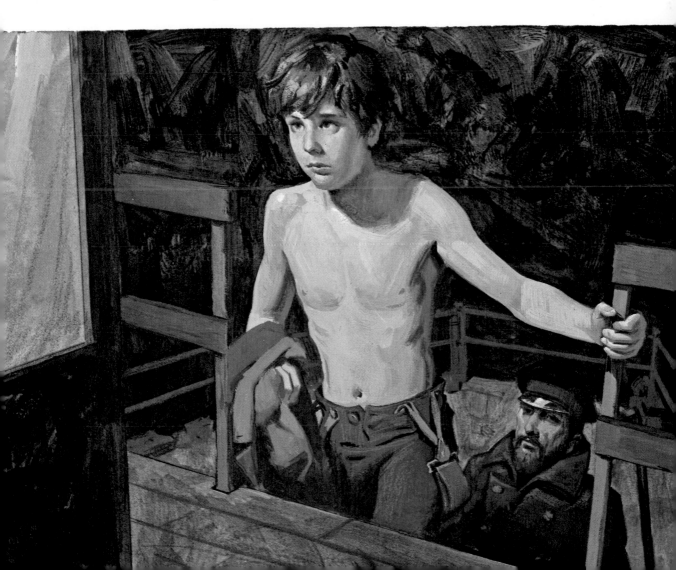

"Upper end of the plantation, or the lower?"

"Upper."

"I can't do it. The stumps there are out of water at this stage. It's no great distance to the lower, and you'll have to get along with that."

"All right, sir. If Jones don't like it, he'll have to lump it, I reckon."

And then the mate left. My cheering began to cool and my wonder to come up. Here was a man who not only proposed to find this plantation on such a night, but to find either end of it you preferred. I dreadfully wanted to ask a question, but I was carrying about as many short answers as my cargo-room would admit of, so I held my peace. All I desired to ask Mr. Bixby was the simple question whether he was fool enough to really imagine he was going to find that plantation on a night when all plantations were exactly alike and all of the same color. But I held in. I used to have fine inspirations of prudence in those days.

Mr. Bixby made for the shore and soon was scraping it, just the same as if it had been daylight. And not only that, but singing. It seemed to me that I had put my life in the keeping of a peculiarly reckless outcast. Presently he turned on me and said:

"What's the name of the first point above New Orleans?"

I was gratified to be able to answer promptly, and I did. I said I didn't know.

"Don't *know?*"

This manner jolted me. I was down at the foot again, in a moment. But I had to say just what I had said before.

"Well, you're a smart one!" said Mr. Bixby. "What's the name of the *next* point?"

Once more I didn't know.

"Well, this beats anything. Tell me the name of *any* point or place I told you."

I studied awhile and decided that I couldn't.

"Look here! What do you start out from, above Twelve-Mile Point, to cross over?"

"I—I—don't know."

"You—you—don't know?" mimicking my drawling manner of speech. "What *do* you know?"

"I—I—nothing, for certain."

"By the great Caesar's ghost, I believe you! You're the stupidest dunderhead I ever saw or ever heard of, so help me Moses! The idea of *you* being a pilot—*you!* Why, you don't know enough to pilot a cow down a lane."

Oh, but his wrath was up! He was a nervous man, and he shuffled from one side of his wheel to the other as if the floor was hot. He would boil awhile to himself, and then overflow and scald me again.

"Look here! What do you suppose I told you the names of those points for?"

I tremblingly considered a moment, and then the devil of temptation provoked me to say:

"Well to—to—be entertaining, I thought."

This was a red rag to the bull. He raged and stormed so (he was crossing the river at the time) that I judged it made him blind, because he ran over the steering-oar of a trading-scow. Of course the traders sent up a volley of red-hot language. Never was a man so grateful as Mr. Bixby was; because he was brimful, and here were subjects who could *talk back*. He threw open a window, thrust his head out, and such an irruption followed as I never had heard before. The fainter and farther away the scowmen's curses drifted, the higher Mr. Bixby lifted his voice and the weightier his adjectives grew. When he closed the window he was empty. You could have drawn a fine net through his system and not caught curses enough to disturb your mother with. Presently he said to me in the gentlest way:

"My boy, you must get a little memorandum-book; and every time I tell you a thing, put it down right away. There's only one way to be a pilot, and that is to get this entire river by heart. You have to know it just like A B C."

That was a dismal revelation to me; for my memory was never loaded with anything but blank cartridges. However, I did not feel discouraged long. I judged that it was best to make some allowances, for doubtless Mr. Bixby was "stretching."

Presently he pulled a rope and struck a few strokes on the big bell. The stars were all gone now, and the night was as black as ink. I could hear the wheels churn along the bank, but I was not entirely certain that I could see the shore. The voice of the invisible watchman called up from the hurricane deck:

"What's this, sir?"

"Jones's plantation."

I said to myself, "I wish I might venture to offer a small bet that it isn't." But I did not chirp. I only waited to see. Mr. Bixby handled the engine-bells, and in due time the boat's nose came to the land, a torch glowed from the forecastle,[3] a man skipped ashore, and the next moment we were standing up the river again, all serene. I reflected deeply awhile, and then said—but not aloud—"Well, the finding of that plantation was the luckiest accident that ever happened; but it couldn't happen again in a hundred years." And I fully believed it *was* an accident, too.

By the time we had gone seven or eight hundred miles up the river, I had learned to be a tolerably plucky up-stream steersman, in daylight. And before we reached St. Louis I had made a bit of progress in night work, but only a bit. I had a notebook that fairly overflowed with the names of towns, "points," bars, islands, bends, reaches, etc. But the information was to be found only in the notebook—none of it was in my head. It made my heart ache to think I had only got half of the river set down; for as our watch was four hours off and four hours on, day and night, there was a long four-hour gap in my book for every time I had slept since the voyage began.

My chief was presently hired to go on a big New Orleans boat, and I packed my valise and went with him. She was a grand affair. When I stood in her pilot-house I was so far above the water that I seemed perched on a mountain. And her decks stretched so far away, fore and aft, below me, that I wondered how I could ever have considered the little *Paul Jones* a large craft.

---

[3]forecastle: the upper deck in front of the front mast

Focus

1. Explain why Mark Twain's ambition to explore the Amazon was not practical.
2. Summarize the events that led up to Mark Twain's acceptance as a cub-pilot.
3. List the responsibilities of a pilot's job that surprised Twain.
4. Twain said that he "never was great in matters of detail." Give two examples in which his goals changed because he had neglected the steps necessary to achieve them.
5. Describe Mark Twain's personality. Use incidents from the story to support your description.
6. Give two examples of humor in the story. Explain why you think these examples are humorous.

In Writing

In addition to his experience as a steamboat pilot, Mark Twain also wrote for newspapers. Write a newspaper article reporting on a trip you took. Give the article a headline, and focus on the most interesting details.

Vocabulary

On a piece of paper, write the numbers 1 to 5. Then read the sentences below and select the word from the list that best fits each sentence. Next to each number on your paper, write the correct word for the sentence.

climes	valise	prudence
disconsolate	ignoble	flaying
irruption	potent	assented

1. The salesman packed his ___ and checked that he had remembered everything before he left the hotel room.
2. After the death of her dog, Sharon was ___; no one could cheer her up.
3. It is important to use ___ when voting; you would not want to help elect a bad leader.
4. When planning the vacation, we all ___ to the idea that the beach was the place to go.
5. There are many ___ within the borders of the United States— cold and hot, wet and dry, high and low.

The Sheepherder

Lew Sarett

Loping along on the day's patrol,
I came on a herder in Jackson's Hole;
Furtive of manner, blazing of eye,
He never looked up when I rode by;
But counting his fingers, fiercely intent,
Around and around his herd he went:

One sheep, two sheep, three sheep, four . . .
Twenty and thirty . . . forty more;
Strayed—nine ewes; killed—ten rams;
Seven and seventy lost little lambs.

He was the only soul I could see
On the lonely range for company—
Save one lean wolf and a prairie-dog,
And a myriad of ants at the foot of a log;
So I sat the herder down on a clod—
But his eyes went counting the ants in the sod:

One sheep, two sheep, three sheep, four . . .
Fifty and sixty . . . seventy more;
There's not in this flock a good bell-wether!
Then how can a herder hold it together!

Seeking to cheer him in his plight,
I flung my blankets down for the night;
But he wouldn't talk as we sat by the fire—
Corralling sheep was his sole desire;
With fingers that pointed near and far,
Mumbling, he herded star by star:

One sheep, two sheep, three—as before!
Eighty and ninety . . . a thousand more!
My lost little lambs—one thousand seven!—
Are wandering over the hills of Heaven.

The View from Burnt Mountain

Gretel Ehrlich

Sheepherding is a timeless profession; it hasn't changed very much over thousands of years. Yet it can make great demands on a person. Why does Laura Bell choose it as her career?

She looks out the window for sight or sound of sheep. But the ground is lost in grayness. We're at 10,000 feet and clouds slam into the mountains here, then slide off and float above the valleys, bouncing from peak to peak. You can't see sheep in weather like this until you're right up on them. And the bears who have been ravaging the herds this summer take advantage of the drizzle, roam the open meadows, and watch her from the camouflage of woods as she rides by.

Laura Bell is a sheepherder. She has been one for several years. She's in her mid-twenties, a minister's daughter from Kentucky, a college graduate. When she took the job, her family thought she was acting on impulse. They hoped it was temporary, until they visited her at sheep camp. Then they understood the fierce pull she feels toward this exotically desolate place.

I'd never thought of being a sheepherder. I'm not sure what got into me but I suddenly wanted to do it. I'd been a real middle-of-the-road person, never going out on a limb. I got the urge to live more deliberately, more decisively, more boldly. Herding sheep has been like that for me.

But the first 24 hours on the job were nightmarish for a woman who had never been alone on the range, and required a tenacity and self-confidence she had never before summoned.

I was driving tractor down on the ranch when the owner came up and said, "If you want to herd sheep, Sterling [one of the sheepherders] will pick you up in an hour." I'd been asking them

all spring to let me herd. They didn't want to send me out but it was a last resort—someone got sick and there was no one else. Driving to the range, Sterling gave me a quick course in herding. I really didn't know a thing about it. The first day out I made a bad mistake—I didn't check the sheep early enough and they were gone. After spending most of the day, I finally found them; they were strung way out in the hills. It would take a long time to gather them and the dog they gave me wouldn't work, she just went off on a ridge and howled.

A bad storm came up and by the time I got to the head of the herd it was beginning to get dark. I kept riding and finally got all the sheep together. I thought I knew where the wagon was when I started back—I rode and rode over hills and ridges but couldn't find it. It was totally dark by then. I was miserable. I kept thinking there must be someone out there looking for me, but, of course, no one was. Then I got off the horse for a minute and he got away. I chased him on foot for miles—he'd be right in front of me but wouldn't let me catch him. Finally, I did, and started riding again, but still couldn't find my bearings. So I tied the horse to a sage bush, took the saddle off, and got between the saddle blankets because it was raining. I slept. I was so tired. I

kept thinking it was a bad dream I'd wake up from. At least the rattlesnakes weren't out yet so there was nothing to get me.

The clouds and drizzle cleared up about five a.m. I started riding again, hit a road, and followed it, and found the wagon by seven. I haven't done anything like that since. The next morning I was out with the sheep before dawn and because the dog wouldn't work, I started barking at the sheep. I was so desperate. I'm embarrassed to think about it now!

That was a few years ago. Since then, Laura has become one of the better herders in the outfit. Her days are like those of most farmers and ranchers. They start at four a.m. and end after sunset, which in summer can add up to 18 hours. The ruggedness of the job varies by season and has more to do with the weather than with the difficulty of the work itself. If you can ride a horse, come to an understanding with animals, and have the humility to learn from them and from the weather, you're a candidate for the job.

One old sheepherder told me, "The only reason to have us with the sheep is to keep them coyotes off their backs." But there's more to it than that. Laura checks her sheep at daybreak, moves them to different parts of the range during a day, makes boundary checks, and takes them to water. She doctors them when they need it, stays with them through storms, puts out salt, and beds them down at night. The seasonal cycle severely affects this schedule. In a Wyoming winter, you do the same things as in summer but it's a wholly different job.

I guess I have a compulsion to master this—being out on my own and in the weather. I've never thought of quitting. It's like someone dared me to do it, but, of course, no one did. I've always made things hard on myself as far as physical surroundings go. I've liked to be out away from people, but I'd never been this isolated before.

She works for the C.A. Lewis Ranch, a large, family-owned ranch that was homesteaded in the 1890s. Ten or so herders work the ranch (the number varies by the season), each with a band of 2,000 sheep. Except for one summer couple, all the herders are men; all are past middle age and have been cowboying or herding sheep most of their lives. They're an

eccentric, cranky but gentle collection of Westerners, physically isolated on their separate ranges but threaded together by a camp tender, John Hopkin. The grandson of the original owner, John drives from camp to camp bringing food, gun shells, mail, and news from town.

This year the mountains had a late, wet spring and now the meadows are lush with wild iris, Indian paintbrush, white phlox, and lavishly covered with larkspur, deadly to sheep. Laura has a traditional Home on the Range wagon. It's constructed from wood and sheet metal, rounded like a covered wagon, and pulled by the camp tender's pickup to designated sites on the range. At the moment, it sits atop Burnt Mountain, with a natural spring and watering pond in front and a shale rimrock full of fossils bedded into the ridge just behind. The view is of broad open meadows and patchworks of trees—blue spruce, pine, aspen. Far below you can see two creeks, Half Ounce and Wagon Box. In the distance lies another rancher's range where cattle are summered.

Laura hauls spring water uphill in pails, cooks on a small woodburning stove, and reads by kerosene lamp. Her Home on the Range features two built-in benches, a bed across the back, and a view framed by Dutch doors at the front of the wagon. It's

simple and efficient and a comfort against raging weather, as well as a refuge from inch-thick mosquitoes in summer and midnight visits by bears.

Sheepherding isn't always such a great thing to do. It's got a fairy-tale image but it's not that way. When you're out here alone, no one makes up for your mistakes. So you watch out for rattlesnakes, you don't act foolish with your horse. You need him. And the weather is so total out here—no trees, just sky. It determines what the sheep are going to do and what your day is like. I can't help but feel the weather is battering, that it's out to flatten me like it flattens the rocks, that it'd make canyons in my face too.

My relationship with nature has changed from a tourist's appreciation. A thunderstorm is very different when you're out in it with no protection from the lightning and cold. When I'm by myself for a long time I get more responsive to little things. I also feel more vulnerable. Sometimes the storms overwhelm me and I get so angry I start cussing the weather. You should see me, standing out there all alone shaking my fist at the sky! Then it passes over and there'll be a double rainbow so beautiful it brings tears to my eyes.

221

Sheepherders don't get much respect. By custom and tradition, ranchers dismiss them as lazy, antisocial, unwashed eccentrics. An older man will often turn to herding sheep after a lifetime of cowboying, which is more strenuous work. A younger man will come to it, according to conventional wisdom, because he's failed at everything else.

Despite the stigma attached to sheepherding, Laura sees the job as an interesting alternative for anybody, male or female, young or old. What's more, she regards her older peers with respect and admiration—which the herders, in turn, clearly extend to her.

We laughed at a sign Laura put on her door for the camp tender. It reported, "Gone Fishin'," which meant we'd gone to do nothing to get away from doing nothing.

We rode through the forest at dusk, sending the dogs far ahead to clear the trail in case the bears were planning to meet us for dinner. Laura climbed over the ridge to check the sheep, dismounting and leading the horse in a downhill traverse on shale rimrock. Hearing the rock clatter, the sheep froze and looked up. Laura stopped, not wanting to spook them, and squatted down on the ridge to watch for a while. Soon they went back to eating. An eagle lifted off from a cliff, bowed all the way out across the valley and back again in one push. In another meadow a small bunch of elk were grazing.

Here, it can be, and often is, as stunning and quiet as this. But a sheepherder knows that being alone is not romantic. Sheepherders often lead themselves down fantastic and paranoid paths, sniffing the wrong scent and becoming so fragile that the delivery of the wrong brand of cookies in the weekly groceries can be cause for quitting. Living on the edge of society as they do also cultivates a reverse snobbery, a disdain for the embroilments and intrigues of the very same town people who judge the herders to be pariahs.

People automatically think you're lonely. But you have your horse and dog for company, and the sheep. They put you through your paces emotionally. Why would I be out here if I wanted to talk to people all the time? I found myself getting real choosy about company. I really didn't want to see just anyone. I don't have that need.

Nightfall. Laura has put out salt for the sheep and bedded them down. She's made a good dinner of mutton and cabbage and biscuits and has placed the kerosene lamp between us. In her fluid Kentucky accent there's an urgency, attesting to the fact that she has not been to town for three months and these thoughts, stored up for a long time, have been told to no one.

Herding sheep is really a very gentle way of life. I want to emphasize that. The farmers down in the valley think I'm crazy to be doing this. But driving tractor all day, you're 12 feet off the earth and just tearing it up! Herding, you're working with animals and the weather and your own limitations. You have time to yourself and yet more responsibility—the sheep. And when the weather isn't battering, there is all this—the land. It looks desolate and ugly to some people, but there are pale colors and tiny wild flowers, and there are those beautiful, quiet moments.

Focus

1. Describe Bell's first day herding sheep.
2. List some of the jobs Bell might perform in a typical day.
3. Explain why the weather is an important part of Bell's life.
4. Give three reasons Laura Bell likes sheepherding.
5. What do you think are some of the rewards of this way of living, in spite of the many hardships?
6. How do the photographs help to demonstrate the moods of a sheepherder's life?

In Writing

Laura Bell tells of her first day herding sheep. If she had kept a journal, what might she have written? Be sure to include what happened and how she felt about herself and her job.

Vocabulary

On a piece of paper, write the numbers *1* to *5.* Then look at the words in the first column and find an antonym for each word in the second column. Next to each number on your paper, write the letter of the antonym for each word.

1. humility
2. paranoid
3. disdain
4. antisocial
5. eccentric

A. normal
B. friendly
C. pride
D. appreciate
E. active
F. secure

LIFE SKILL: Understanding a Charge-Account Statement

Our American vista is heavily populated with GIMMEs, BUYMEs, and IWANTERs. These life forms can be spotted in all weather, in all seasons. Their favorite gathering places are STORES. If you want to study one of these species, take a good look in the mirror!

Stores make money when you spend money. Our economy thrives on this. It is, however, important to be a smart shopper. It's good to stop and ask yourself, "Do I really need, or want, that thingumajig?" Well, if you decide a thingumajig will make your life happier, here's one way to buy it. Charge! (Keep in mind that when you use a charge account, you are *borrowing* money from the store. There are usually interest charges when you take such a loan.)

Larger stores can make buying "seem" easy. (It can end up being expensive to the buyer who is not a careful shopper.) Stores allow certain customers credit through the use of a charge card. The customers "earn" the credit by:

a. filling out the store's application-for-credit form;

b. proving they have a job and are responsible;

c. giving work and bank references that the store can check.

If the store accepts you as a credit customer, you receive a charge card. This is a plastic card that shows the name of the store, along with the customer's name and account number in raised print. Sometimes, the customer's address is not shown on the card. Fear not, Big Spender, you will receive your bills. Once you make out an application for credit, all your data are filed within a computer bank.

When you make a purchase, the salesperson uses your charge card to make an imprint in the store's records. Then you sign your name. This makes it a legal contract to pay. The bill you receive in the mail is also computerized. It may look something like the one shown here.

The Bottomless Pit

3 53535 26952 9

LEO SPENDER

226

The Bottomless Pit

(A)

P.O. Box $$$
ABILENE, KS 67410

Charge-Account Statement

(C) Amount Due
$ 16.38

(B) LEO SPENDER
5 PRIMROSE PATH
EMPORIA, KS 66801

(D) NEW BALANCE 280.16

(E) AMOUNT PAID $

Detach this portion and send with payment.

Mo.	Day	Reference	TRANSACTION DESCRIPTION See reverse for detailed description of department numbers indicated below.	CHARGES	PAYMENTS & CREDITS
		(F)	**FINANCE CHARGE**	3.31	
09	05	(G) CAJE	BLANKETS, BATH SUP., LINENS	66.33	
08	9	(H)	CREDIT		20.00

PLEASE MENTION THIS ACCOUNT NUMBER WHEN ORDERING, WRITING OR TELEPHONING.	(J) BILLING DATE	(K) PREVIOUS BALANCE	(L) NEW BALANCE	(M) MINIMUM PAYMENT
(I) 3 53535 26952 9	SEP 09 1980	230.52	280.16	16.38

(N) If the *FINANCE CHARGE* exceeds 50¢, the *ANNUAL PERCENTAGE RATE* is 18% on the first $500 of the AVERAGE DAILY BALANCE and 12% on that part of the AVERAGE DAILY BALANCE in excess of $500. The AVERAGE DAILY BALANCE excludes any purchases added during the monthly billing period and any unpaid *FINANCE CHARGE*.

(O) Late charge of $4.50 will be added to next statement if amount due not paid within 30 days from billing date.

KEY

A Name and mailing address of store where person has charge account.

B Name and address of person who has charge account.

C Least amount that must be paid this month. (A second finance charge is added if least amount is not paid. It is a late, or penalty, charge.)

D Total amount owed store as of statement date.

E Space to write the amount of money person paid on account this month. (Look again at C.)

F Finance charge added to bill this month. (See N.)

G Description of each item and each charge made this month. (Letters in *Reference* column usually stand for department in which purchase was made. As noted on *Transaction Description* line, reverse side of bill will tell what the letters mean.)

H Amount paid on account (and received by store) last month.

I Person's charge-account number. (If you have a question about your bill, the customer service clerk will ask you for your account number.)

J Date the bill was prepared by store.

K Amount owed before this month's finance charge, new charges, and payments were calculated.

L Same as D.

M Same as C.

N Explanation of how the finance charge is figured.

O Explanation of the "late charge" that will be added to next month's statement if least amount of bill is not paid within 30 days of billing date (in this case, SEP 09 1980).

227

On the last billing date, the total amount due was	$230.52	(K)
On August 9, a payment was credited to the account	−20.00	(H)
Making the balance due	$210.52	*
On September 5, purchases were charged to the account in the amount of	+66.33	(G)
Making the balance due	$276.85	*
On September 9—the billing date—a finance charge was added in the amount of . . .	+ 3.31	(F)
Making the new balance due	$280.16	(D)(L)

* (not shown on statement)

The key will help you figure out each part of the charge-account statement.

Look at the table, which shows what happened in Leo Spender's account during one month. It is very important to note that if you pay your entire bill each month by the due date no finance charge will be added.

Charge-account payments sent by mail should *never* be made in cash. Cash can be lost or stolen. Payments should be made by sending a personal check, a bank check, or a postal money order. Your account number should be written on the check or money order.

Be a credit advisor. Figure out these charge-account problems. Both the key and the charge-account statement will help you find the right answers.

1. When should Leo Spender use his charge-account number?

2. What is the least amount Leo must pay this month to avoid a penalty charge? What is the greatest amount? How much would you advise Leo to pay? Why?

3. What will happen if Leo does not make a payment within 30 days of the billing date? Where did you find this information?

4. What is the annual percentage rate on the first $500 of the average daily balance of this account? Where did you find this information?

5. At which rate, 18% or 12%, was the finance charge on this month's statement figured? Tell why.

6. On September 30, Leo Spender wrote a personal check for $40 to The Bottomless Pit. This was his payment on account. He is planning to mail the check. Name three things Leo should do before he *seals* the envelope.

7. Will Leo Spender receive a charge-account statement from The Bottomless Pit next month? Explain.

8. You are a credit advisor. You give advice to people with credit problems. Help Leo Spender save money. What advice would you give him?

The Great American Garage Sale

Laura Preble

One person's junk can become another's treasure. How does Laura Preble handle her first garage sale?

Garage sales have been a part of the American culture time out of mind. They rank among baseball, hot dogs, and apple pie. And sooner or later, every American home experiences the great exodus of junk subtly entitled "Garage Sale."

My first was in an unseasonably cold week at the beginning of May. Mother was lying down on the couch in a state of shock; so I, as the oldest and naturally stoutest of heart, put myself in charge of the sale.

I lined the troops up on the lawn: Linda, Barb, Ann, the dog. I laid it out for them plainly, "Watch everyone. No one is above suspicion."

The innocent voice of Barbie piped through my speech. "Watch for what?"

Poor naive child, I thought. She doesn't even know the horrors of war. But they must learn young. Grasping her shoulder, I began.

"The cruel fact is this: there are all types of Garage Sale Maniacs. You must know what to look for. One, the Tag-Changer. The person who puts the 10¢ tag on the two-dollar item, usually wears a shifty, guilt-ridden expression.

"Two, the Bargain Hunter. This one fondles and paws every item of clothing on the rack until you can't tell the clothes from the hamper on laundry day. Of course, nothing is ever put back in its correct place. But our worst enemy is . . . the Child."

Ann gasped and her eyes grew large with fear. "You mean . . ."

"Yes. You must tell on them."

"Our friends?" Her eyes began to mist.

"Soldiers," I said, "in this business, we have no friends."

The first barrage began at one o'clock. They came in droves. It hurt, I'll admit, when someone bought my Nancy Drew collection—let's face it, it had taken me years to build it up. But all's fair in love and garage sales, I guess. You gotta take the bad with the good.

About three, the place looked like the Sahara during the dry season. We were almost cleaned out. They were still milling about, in a frenzy, eyes wild. It was close, though, when I saw our neighbor, Ms. McDonnell, walking down the street with my sister under one arm, and my Barry Manilow albums in the other. I stepped briskly in front of her. "Ms. McDonnell," I said quietly.

Not a breath of air stirred. I sensed her trying to find a way to make a break for it, but at last she gave up.

"All right. Here." She thrust my sister toward me.

I deftly snatched at her other arm. "Keep her. I just want the records!"

Focus

1. To what did the narrator compare a garage sale? Give three examples in which language is used to suggest this comparison.
2. Name the three kinds of "Garage Sale Maniacs" mentioned by the narrator.
3. Do you think the narrator really would have chosen her records over her sister? Why or why not?
4. Give two examples of exaggeration in the story. How does exaggeration add a sense of urgency to this story?

In Writing

Is your closet full of things you no longer need or use? What would you keep and what would you throw away? Imagine that you are holding a garage sale. Make a list of the items that you would sell and the prices you would charge. Explain why you have decided to part with the item and why it is worth what you are charging.

Vocabulary

On a piece of paper, write the numbers *1* to *5*. Then look at the words in the first column and find a definition for each word in the second column. Next to each number on your paper, write the letter of the correct definition for each word.

1. deftly
2. milling
3. exodus
4. barrage
5. shifty

A. a movement away
B. moving in a confused way
C. being overpriced
D. quickly, skillfully
E. a series of quick blows or words
F. not straightforward

Can you fight a computer?
How do you get someone,
anyone, to listen to you?

R U There?

Constance L. Melaro

August 17

Dear Madam:

Our records show an outstanding balance of $2.98 on your account.
If you have already remitted this amount, kindly disregard this notice.

THIS IS A BUSINESS MACHINE CARD.

PLEASE DO NOT SPINDLE OR MUTILATE.

August 19

Dear Customer Service:

I do *not* have an outstanding balance. I attached a note with my
payment advising you that I had been billed *twice* for the same
amount: once under my first name, middle initial and last name; and
then under my two first initials and my last name. (The former is
correct.) Please check your records.

September 17

Dear Madam:

Our records show a delinquent balance of $2.98 on your account.
Please remit $3.40. This includes a handling charge.

THIS IS A BUSINESS MACHINE CARD.

PLEASE DO NOT SPINDLE OR MUTILATE.

September 19

Dear Machine:

You're not paying attention! I am NOT delinquent in any amount. I
do *not* owe this money. I was billed TWICE for the same purchase.
PLEASE look into this.

October 17

Dear Madam:

Our records show you to be delinquent for three months. Please remit the new charges plus $4.10. (This includes a handling charge.) May we have your immediate attention in this matter.

THIS IS A BUSINESS MACHINE CARD.
PLEASE DO NOT SPINDLE OR MUTILATE.

October 19

Dear Machine:

MY attention! You want MY attention! Listen here, YOU ARE WRONG!!! I DON'T owe you $4.10. *CAN YOU UNDERSTAND THAT?* I also DON'T owe you the new charges of $13.46. You billed ME for my MOTHER'S purchase. Please correct this statement AT ONCE!

November 17

Dear Madam:

Our records now show you to be delinquent for four months in the total amount of $17.56 plus $1.87 handling charges. Please remit in full in ten days or your account will be turned over to our Auditing Department for collection.

THIS IS A BUSINESS MACHINE CARD.
PLEASE DO NOT SPINDLE OR MUTILATE.

November 19

Dear ANYONE human:

WILL YOU PLEASE TAKE YOUR HEAD OUT OF THE COMPUTER LONG ENOUGH TO READ THIS? I DON'T OWE YOU THIS MONEY!!! I DON'T OWE YOU *ANY* MONEY. *NONE.*

December 17

Dear Madam:

Is there some question about your statement? Our records show no payment on your account since August. Please call 555-9601 and ask for Miss Gilbert at your earliest convenience.

THIS IS A BUSINESS MACHINE CARD.
PLEASE DO NOT SPINDLE OR MUTILATE.

DECEMBER 18

. . . Deck the halls with boughs of holly . . .''Good afternoon.
Carver's hopes you enjoyed its recorded program of carols. May I help
you?''

''Hello. Yes . . . My bill is . . . should I wait for a 'beep' before I
talk?''

''About your bill?''

''Yes. Yes, it's my bill. There's . . .''

''One moment, please. I'll connect you with Adjustments!''

Good afternoon and Happy Holidays. This is a recorded message.
All our lines are in service now. If you will please be patient, one of
our adjusters will be with you just as soon as a line is free. Meanwhile,
Carver's hopes you will enjoy its program of carols. . . . Deck the halls
with . . .

December 26

Dear Machine:

I tried to call you on December 18. Also the 19th, 20th, 21st, 22nd,
the 23rd, and the 24th. But all I got was a recorded message and those
carols. Please, oh, please! Won't you turn me over to a human? *Any*
human?

January 17

Dear Madam:

Our Credit Department has turned your delinquent account over to
us for collection. Won't you please remit this amount now? We wish
to cooperate with you in every way possible, but this is considerably
past due. May we have your check at this time.

Very truly yours,
HENRY J. HOOPER, Auditor

January 19

Dear Mr. Hooper:

You DOLL! You gorgeous HUMAN doll! I refer you to letters I sent
to your department, dated the 19th of September, October, November,
December, which should clarify the fact that I owe you nothing.

February 17

Dear Madam:

According to our microfilm records, our billing was in error. Your account is clear; you have no balance. We hope there will be no further inconvenience to you. Though this was our fault, you can help us if, in the future, you will always include your account number when ordering by mail or phone.

Very truly yours,
HENRY J. HOOPER, Auditor

February 19

Dear Mr. Hooper:

Thank you! Oh, thank you, thank you, thank you!

March 17

Dear Madam:

Our records show you to be delinquent in the amount of $2.98, erroneously posted last August to a non-existent account. May we have your remittance at this time?

THIS IS A BUSINESS MACHINE CARD.
PLEASE DO NOT SPINDLE OR MUTILATE.

March 19

Dear Machine:

I give up. You win. Here's a check for $2.98. Enjoy yourself.

April 17

Dear Madam:

Our records show an overpayment on your part of $2.98. We are crediting this amount to your account.

THIS IS A BUSINESS MACHINE CARD.
PLEASE DO NOT SPINDLE OR MUTILATE.

Focus

1. What error first caused the account to show an outstanding balance of $2.98?
2. Why was the writer so delighted to receive the letter dated January 17?
3. As the exchange of letters continued between the computer and the woman, how did the tone of the woman's letters change? Why do you think it changed?
4. How do you think the author of "R U There?" feels about computers doing work that used to be done by people?

In Writing

As a result of the computer's final computations, the woman now has $2.98 in her account. Write her response to the computer's last letter.

Vocabulary

On a piece of paper, write the numbers 1 to 5. Then read the sentences below. Next to each number on your paper, write the word from the list that best completes each analogy.

delinquently   spindle   erroneously
correctly   credit   balance
programmer   disregard   television

1. Recent is to ancient as ___ is to debt.
2. Sick is to ill as ___ is to mistakenly.
3. Secretary is to typewriter as ___ is to computer.
4. Shallow is to deep as ___ is to responsibly.
5. Colorful is to bright as ___ is to ignore.

CHECKPOINT

Read the word list and paragraph below. Decide which word makes the best sense in each blank space. Then write the numbers 1 to 7 on a piece of paper and write the correct word next to each number.

Vocabulary: Word Identification

indifference   reserved   incalculable   fragile
suspicious   procedure   designated   deft
enthusiastic   ravaging   antagonism

The surgeon entered the operating room. She had carefully explained the difficult __(1)__ to her assistants. All were ready and waiting at their __(2)__ stations. Her __(3)__ personality gave her an appearance of __(4)__ . However, her assisting doctors and nurses were not mistaken in their __(5)__ support of the surgeon's skill. The __(6)__ hands of this famous surgeon would repair the __(7)__ veins leading to the heart.

8. Reread page 176. Compare Sequoyah's syllabic system and the English alphabetic system of writing.

Comprehension: Comparison

9. Review the story "Alacrán," on pages 193 to 198. Compare the understanding that Don Miguel had for Alacrán with the understanding that the cow-buyer had for the horse.

10. Review the story "A Race with Time," on pages 160 to 170. Write a paragraph explaining what you think happened to the cattle. Give reasons for your prediction.

Comprehension: Predicting Outcomes

11. Reread page 212. How do you think Mark Twain acted on the larger New Orleans boat? Write a paragraph describing his behavior on his first watch on this trip up the river.

12. Use the following information to make a bar graph: Carmen's reading text is 600 pages long, her math book is 300 pages long, her science text is 450 pages long, and her social studies text is 550 pages long.

Study Skills: Graphic Information (Bar and Circle Graphs)

13. Use the following information to make a circle graph: A recent poll shows that 50% of the voters wear red socks, 25% wear green socks, 10% wear orange socks, and 15% wear purple socks.

Have you ever wandered through an art gallery? There you see different kinds of paintings—some based in reality and some based in fantasy. This unit will also open a gallery to you, a gallery of stories instead of paintings.

In the first story, you will follow the misadventures of an aging she-wolf as she tries to hunt to feed her young. Then watch as a farmer unfolds his plan to catch a pumpkin thief. Next are folktales from different lands, each exploring in a humorous way some character flaw or strange fact of nature. You will discover a monster—imaginary? And what would you predict about a society where writing and reading no longer exist?

Enter the story gallery and browse for a while. Some strange twists await.

ry Gallery

THE QUETZAL

LISTEN!

Toni de Gerez

I am the singer
    I am singing
the pictures of the book
I am the blue-and-green
    bird
I make the pages speak
I am the quetzal

    What is my song?
my song is a piece of
    jade
I cut into it
it is my song
look how I string beads of jade
    into a necklace
it is my song
it is my jade song

As quetzal feathers
beautiful is my song
look how my song
bends down over the earth
in the house of butterflies my song
   is born

   The true storyteller
says things boldly
with the lips and mouth of an artist
the true storyteller uses words of joy
flowers are on the lips
the language is strict
the language is noble

241

THE PUP

Anton Chekhov

Here is a story where an animal "thinks." How much of this can be real, and how much is the author's imagination?

A famished she-wolf got up to go hunting. Her babies, all three of them, were fast asleep, huddled in a heap in each other's warmth. She licked them for a while, then went off.

It was March and the beginning of spring, but at night the trees still crackled with the cold, as in December, and no sooner did one put out his tongue than the cold would nip it hard. The mother wolf was in poor health and fearful. She started at the slightest noise and kept worrying that someone might hurt her young ones while she was away from them. The scent of humans and horses, the stumps of trees, the woodpiles, and the dark road, all frightened her. She imagined people standing in the darkness behind the trees and dogs howling somewhere beyond the forest.

She was no longer young, and her sense of smell had become less sharp, so that it happened that she mistook a fox's track for that of a dog. And sometimes, deceived by her waning sense of smell, she lost her way—a thing that never happened in her youth. Because of feeble health she no longer hunted calves or large sheep and had for some time avoided horses with colts, but nourished herself only on carrion. She now tasted fresh meat only in the spring, when, chancing upon a rabbit, she would steal her young, or when she sneaked into a peasant's cattle-shed where there were lambs.

About two miles from her lair, on the post road, stood a winter lodge. Here lived watchman Ignat, an old man of about seventy, who was always coughing and talking to himself. Usually he slept at night, and during the day he wandered about the forest with his single-barreled gun, whistling to attract the rabbits. In the past he must have worked on a railroad as some sort of engineer, for every time before halting, he would call out to himself: "Stop the engine!" and before going on again he would yell out: "Let it go! Full speed!" He always had with him a huge black female dog of indefinite breed, called Arapka. When she ran ahead of him he would shout to her: "Back up! In reverse!" At times Ignat staggered and fell (the wolf would then think the wind blew him over), shouting: "Off the rails!"

The she-wolf remembered how in the summer and fall a ram and two ewes had pastured near the winter hut, and when she ran past the cattle-shed not so long ago she thought she heard the bleating of lambs inside. And now, approaching the hut, she thought that, judging by the season (it being already March), there certainly would be lambs in the shed. She was tormented by hunger and imagined, as she approached the place, with what relish she would eat a baby lamb. The thought of it made her teeth snap, and her eyes gleamed in the darkness like two coals.

Ignat's hut, barn, shed, and well were surrounded by snowdrifts. All was still. Arapka was probably asleep under the shed.

The mother wolf clambered over the snowdrift and onto the

roof of the shed. She began to dig away at the thatch with her paws and muzzle. The straw was rotten and loose, and the wolf almost fell through as the warm vapor and the smell of sheep that came from below overwhelmed her. A baby lamb, feeling the sudden cold, bleated softly. Jumping through the hole in the roof, the wolf fell on her forepaws and chest right against something warm—it must have been the ram. And at the same moment something in the shed began to whine, bark, and yelp in a shrill little voice, while the sheep pressed against the wall. The she-wolf, frightened, grabbed the nearest thing between her teeth and darted away.

She ran as fast as she could. Arapka, who by now had scented the wolf, let out a furious howl. The agitated chickens chattered inside the hut, and Ignat, coming out on the front steps, shouted:

"Full speed! Blow the whistle!"

And he whistled like a steam engine and let out a "hoo-hoo-hoo-hoo!" And these sounds echoed back from the forest.

When, little by little, this cacophony finally ceased, the wolf calmed down a bit. She began to notice that the prey she held in her teeth and dragged along the snow was heavier and seemed harder than young lambs usually were at that time of year, and that the animal had a different smell and emitted strange sounds. The wolf stopped and dropped her burden on the snow to rest and then begin to eat. Suddenly she recoiled in disgust. It wasn't a lamb at all. It was a puppy—black, with a big head and long legs, of a large breed, with a white patch on its forehead, like Arapka's. Judging by his ways, he was a common, ill-mannered yard dog.

The puppy licked his rumpled, wounded back and, as though nothing was wrong, wagged his tail and barked at the wolf. The wolf growled like a dog and ran away from the pup. He followed her. She looked back and snapped her teeth. The pup stopped, puzzled, and deciding that the wolf was probably playing with him, turned his head in the direction of the hut and let out a gleeful, loud bark, as though inviting his mother, Arapka, to come and join them in the game.

It was beginning to get light, and as the wolf was approaching her lair through the thick aspen forest, one could already see distinctly each young aspen tree; and the woodcocks were waking, the handsome male birds fluttering into the air, disturbed by the frolicsome and barking pup.

"Why is he following me?" thought the wolf with annoyance. "He probably wants me to eat him."

She lived with her cubs in a shallow pit formed three years before when a tall old pine tree had been torn up by the roots during a violent storm. The pit was now lined with dead leaves and moss, and here also were strewn about the bones and horns of bullocks, with which the little wolves played. They were awake now and all three of them, looking very much alike, stood in a row on the edge of the hole, looking at their returning mother and wagging their tails. Seeing them, the puppy stood still at a distance, stared at them for a long time, and noticing that they were staring back at him attentively, he began barking at them angrily, as at strangers.

It was daylight by now, the sun had risen, and the snow gleamed everywhere, but the pup still stood at a distance.

At last the pup got tired and hoarse. Seeing that they were not afraid of him and that they weren't even paying any attention to him now, he began to approach the cubs hesitatingly—by turns cowering and taking a few leaps toward them. Now, in full daylight, it was easier to take a good look at him. His white forehead was large and there was a protuberance on it such as very stupid dogs commonly have. His eyes were small, blue, dull, and the expression on his face was extremely foolish. Approaching the cubs, he stretched out his wide paws, rested his head on them, and began to whine.

The cubs didn't understand what was happening, but they wagged their tails. Then the pup smacked one of them on its large head with his paw. The cub smacked him back. The pup jumped sideways, looked at him askance, wagging his tail all the time, then dashed off, and ran around in a circle several times over the frozen snow. The cubs chased after him. He turned over on his back, kicking his legs in the air, and all three of the cubs fell upon the pup, squealing with delight and biting him, not hard, not to hurt, but in play. The crows sat on a tall pine tree and looked down from above upon the skirmish, very upset about it. The young animals grew noisy and merry. The sun gave forth a spring warmth, and the woodcocks, flitting through the pine tree that had been blown down by the storm, looked emerald in the sunshine.

Normally mother wolves train their young to hunt by giving them prey to play with, and now, seeing how the cubs were pursuing the puppy over the snow and wrestling with him, she thought:

"Let them learn."

After having had their fill of play, the cubs went back into the pit and lay down to sleep. The puppy howled for a while from hunger, then, following their example, stretched out in the sun for a nap. And when they woke up, they resumed their play.

All day long and in the evening the mother wolf thought about how the night before the baby lamb bleated in the shed and how it smelled there of sheep's milk, and she kept snapping her teeth with the craving for food as she kept gnawing on an old bone, making believe it was a lamb.

The puppy, who was very hungry by now, ran around sniffing at the snow.

"I'll eat him," the wolf decided.

She went up to the pup and he licked her face and yapped at her, thinking that she wanted to play with him. In the past she had eaten dogs, but the puppy had a strong doggy scent and, because of her feeble health, the wolf couldn't stand it now. She felt disgusted and walked away.

It became colder toward night. The puppy got homesick and left.

When the baby wolves were fast asleep, their mother went hunting again. Again, as in the previous night, she worried about the slightest noise and was alarmed by the stumps, the logs, the dark solitary juniper bushes looking like human beings from a distance. She ran along the side of the road over the frozen snow. Suddenly, far ahead on the road, something dark came into view. The wolf strained her eyes and ears— there really was something moving there in the distance and she could even hear the regular thud of the footsteps. Could it

be a badger? She kept closer to the side of the road and hardly
breathed as she cautiously overtook the moving creature. She
looked at it. It was the pup with the white patch on his
forehead, slowly making his way to the winter hut.

"If only he doesn't spoil my chances again," the wolf
thought and ran quickly on ahead.

The hut was now quite near. Again she clambered up the
snowdrift and onto the roof of the cattle-shed. The hole she

had made the night before had been covered over with cornstalks and two new rafters stretched across the roof. The wolf began to work fast with her legs and muzzle, looking around to see whether the puppy was coming, and barely did she begin to feel the warm air from below, when she heard a burst of happy barking behind her. The puppy had arrived. He leaped up to the roof then went through the new hole, and, glad to be home, in the warmth, and recognizing his sheep, he barked even louder. Arapka woke up under the shed, smelled the wolf and howled. The hens began to chatter. And by the time Ignat the watchman appeared on the front steps with his single-barreled shotgun, the terrified wolf was already far away from the hut.

"F-ew-ew-t!" whistled Ignat. "F-ew-ew-t! Full steam ahead!"

He pulled the trigger. The gun misfired. He pulled it again, and again it misfired. He tried a third time, and a tremendous flame shot out of the barrel and there was a deafening blast. The recoil jarred his shoulder and, carrying the gun in one hand and an ax in the other, Ignat went to see what the noise was about.

He soon returned to the hut.

"What was it?" a pilgrim, who was spending the night there and had been awakened by the disturbance, asked in a husky voice.

"Oh, nothing," Ignat answered. "Nothing important. Our pup has taken to sleeping with the sheep, to keep warm. Only, he is too stupid to use the shed door and always wriggles in and out of the shed through the roof. The other night he dug a hole in the roof and went on a spree, the rascal, and now he has come back and torn up the roof again."

"Stupid dog!"

"Yes, there is a screw loose in his head. I can't abide fools!" sighed Ignat climbing onto the stove. "Come on, let's go back to sleep—it's too early to get up—full speed ahead!"

In the morning he called the pup, pulled his ears hard and kept repeating:

"Use the door! Use the door! Use the door!"

Focus

1. What was the she-wolf trying to do? What was Ignat trying to do?
2. List three mistakes the she-wolf made as a result of her failing senses.
3. List two mistakes Ignat made as a result of his failing senses.
4. How were the behavior of the she-wolf and the behavior of Ignat similar?
5. The author used human terms, such as "worrying" and "imagined," to describe the wolf's actions. Find four examples of this in the story.
6. What explanation did the author give for the strange expressions Ignat used when speaking? How did Ignat's expressions add humor to the story?

In Writing

Imagine that the pup had to explain his absence to his mother, Arapka. In one or two paragraphs, have the pup explain why he was away from home overnight.

Vocabulary

On a piece of paper, write the numbers 1 to 5. Then read the sentences below and select the word from the list that best fits each sentence. Next to each number on your paper, write the correct word for the sentence.

emitted	askance	carrion
emerald	thatch	cowering
spree	clambered	

1. The children ___ over the fence just in time to escape the angry bull.
2. Vultures and lobsters have one thing in common—they both eat ___ as their main food.
3. Despite my spending ___, I still felt like I had few clothes.
4. The horn at the fire station ___ a loud noise each day at noon.
5. The kitten was found ___ in the corner where the dog had chased it.

The Stub-Book

Pedro Antonio de Alarcón

The material for a good story can be found
just about anywhere, even in a pumpkin patch.

The action begins in Rota. Rota is the smallest of those pretty
towns that form the great semicircle of the bay of Cádiz. But
despite its being the smallest, the grand duke of Osuna preferred it,
building there his famous castle, which I could describe stone by
stone. But now we are dealing with neither castles nor dukes, but
with the fields surrounding Rota, and with a most humble
gardener, whom we shall call *tío Buscabeatas*, though this was not
his true name.

From the fertile fields of Rota, particularly its gardens, come the
fruits and vegetables that fill the markets of Huelva and Seville.
The quality of its tomatoes and pumpkins is such that in Andalusia
the Roteños are always referred to as *pumpkin-* and *tomato-
growers*, titles which they accept with pride.

And, indeed, they have reason to be proud; for the fact is that
the soil of Rota, which produces so much, that is to say, the soil of
the gardens, that soil which yields three or four crops a year, is not
soil, but sand, pure and clean, cast up by the ocean, blown by the
furious west winds and thus scattered over the entire region of
Rota.

But the ingratitude of nature is here more than compensated for
by the constant diligence of humans. I have never seen, nor do I
believe there is in all the world, any farmer who works as hard as

250

the Roteño. Not even a tiny stream runs through those melancholy fields. No matter! The pumpkin-grower has made many wells from which he draws the precious liquid that is the lifeblood of his vegetables. The tomato-grower spends half his life seeking substances which may be used as fertilizer. And when he has both elements, water and fertilizer, the gardener of Rota begins to fertilize his tiny plots of ground, and in each of them sows a tomato-seed, or a pumpkin pip which he then waters by hand, like a person who gives a child a drink.

From then until harvest time, he attends daily, one by one, to the plants which grow there, treating them with a love only comparable to that of parents for children. One day he applies to such a plant a bit of fertilizer; on another he pours a pitcherful of water; today he kills the insects which are eating up the leaves; tomorrow he covers with reeds and dry leaves those which cannot bear the rays of the sun, or those which are too exposed to the sea winds. One day, he counts the stalks, the flowers, and even the fruits of the earliest ripeners; another day, he talks to them, pets them, kisses them, blesses them, and even gives them expressive names in order to tell them apart and individualize them in his imagination.

Without exaggerating, it is now a proverb (and I have often heard it repeated in Rota) that the gardener of that region *touches with his own hands at least forty times a day every tomato plant growing in his garden*. And this explains why the gardeners of that locality get to be so bent over that their knees almost touch their chins.

Well, now, *tío Buscabeatas* was one of those gardeners. He had begun to stoop at the time of the event which I am about to relate. He was already sixty years old . . . and had spent forty of them tilling a garden near the shore.

That year he had grown some enormous pumpkins that were already beginning to turn yellow, which meant it was the month of June. *Tío Buscabeatas* knew them perfectly by color, shape, and even by name, especially the forty fattest and yellowest, which were already saying *cook me*.

"Soon we shall have to part," he said tenderly, with a melancholy look.

Finally, one afternoon he made up his mind to the sacrifice and pronounced the dreadful sentence.

"Tomorrow," he said, "I shall cut these forty and take them to the market at Cádiz. Happy the people who eat them!" Then he returned home at a leisurely pace, and spent the night as anxiously as a parent whose child is to be married the following day.

"My poor pumpkins!" he would occasionally sigh, unable to sleep. But then he reflected and concluded by saying, "What can I do but sell them? For that I raised them! They will be worth at least fifteen *duros*!"

Imagine, then, how great was his astonishment, his fury and despair when, as he went to the garden the next morning, he found that, during the night, he had been robbed of his forty pumpkins. He began calculating coldly, and knew that his pumpkins could not be in Rota, where it would be impossible to sell them without the risk of his recognizing them.

"They must be in Cádiz, I can almost see them!" he suddenly said to himself. "The thief who stole them from me last night at nine or ten o'clock, escaped on the *freight boat*. . . . I'll leave for Cádiz this morning on the *hour boat*, and there I'll catch the thief and recover my pumpkins!"

So saying, he lingered for some twenty minutes more at the scene of the catastrophe, counting the pumpkins that were missing, until, at about eight o'clock, he left for the wharf.

Now the *hour boat* was ready to leave. It was a small craft which carries passengers to Cádiz every morning at nine o'clock, just as the *freight boat* leaves every night at twelve, laden with fruit and vegetables.

The former is called the *hour boat* because in an hour, and occasionally in less time, it cruises the three leagues separating Rota from Cádiz.

It was, then, ten-thirty in the morning when *tío Buscabeatas* stopped before a vegetable stand in the Cádiz market, and said to a police officer who accompanied him: "These are my pumpkins! Arrest that man!" and pointed to the vendor.

"Arrest *me*?" cried the latter, astonished and enraged. "These pumpkins are mine; I bought them."

"You can tell that to the judge," answered *tío Buscabeatas*.

"No, I won't!"

"Yes, you will!"

"You old thief!"

"You old scoundrel!"

"Keep a civil tongue. People shouldn't insult each other like that," said the officer very calmly, giving them each a push.

By this time several people had gathered, among them the inspector of public markets. When the officer had informed the inspector of all that was going on, the latter asked the vendor in tones majestic: "From whom did you buy these pumpkins?"

"From *tío Fulano*, near Rota," answered the vendor.

"He *would* be the one," cried *tío Buscabeatas*. "When his own garden, which is very poor, yields next to nothing, he robs from his neighbors'."

"But, supposing your forty pumpkins were stolen last night," said the inspector, addressing the gardener, "how do you know that these, and not some others, are yours?"

"Well," replied *tío Buscabeatas*, "because I know them as well as you know your children, if you have any. Don't you see that I raised them? Look here, this one's name is Fatty, this one, Plumpy Cheeks, this one, Pot Belly, this one, Little Blush Bottom, and this one Manuela, because it reminds me so much of my youngest daughter."

And the poor old man started weeping like a child.

"That is all very well," said the inspector, "but it is not enough for the law that you recognize your pumpkins. You must identify them with incontrovertible proof. Gentlemen, this is no laughing matter. I am a lawyer!"

"Then you'll soon see me prove to everyone's satisfaction, without stirring from this spot, that these pumpkins were raised in my garden," said *tío Buscabeatas*.

And throwing on the ground a sack he was holding in his hand, he kneeled, and quietly began to untie it. The curiosity of those around him was overwhelming.

"What's he going to pull out of there?" they all wondered.

At the same time another person came to see what was going on in that group and when the vendor saw him, he exclaimed:

"I'm glad you have come, *tío Fulano*. This man says that the pumpkins you sold me last night were stolen. Answer . . ."

The newcomer turned yellower than wax, and tried to escape, but the others prevented him, and the inspector himself ordered him to stay.

As for *tío Buscabeatas*, he had already faced the supposed thief, saying:

"Now you will see something good!"

Tío Fulano, recovering his presence of mind, replied:

"You are the one who should be careful about what you say,

because if you don't prove your accusation, and I know you can't, you will go to jail. Those pumpkins were mine; I raised them in my garden, like all the others I brought to Cádiz this year, and no one could prove I didn't."

"Now you shall see!" repeated *tío Buscabeatas*, as he finished untying the sack.

A multitude of green stems rolled on the ground, while the old gardener, seated on his heels, addressed the gathering as follows:

"Friends, have you never paid taxes? And haven't you seen that green book the tax-collector has, from which he cuts receipts, always leaving a stub in the book so he can prove afterwards whether the receipt is counterfeit or not?"

"What you are talking about is called the stub-book," said the inspector gravely.

"Well, that's what I have here: the stub-book of my garden; that is, the stems to which these pumpkins were attached before this thief stole them from me. Look here: this stem belongs to this pumpkin. No one can deny it . . . this other one . . . now you're getting the idea . . . belongs to this one . . . this thicker one . . . belongs to that one . . . exactly! And this one to that one . . . that one, to that one over there . . ."

And as he spoke, he fitted the stems to the pumpkins, one by one. The spectators were amazed to see that the stems really fitted the pumpkins exactly, and delighted by such strange proof, they all began to help *tío Buscabeatas,* exclaiming:

"He's right! He's right! No doubt about it. Look: this one belongs here . . . That one goes there . . . That one there belongs to this one . . . This one goes there . . ."

The laughter of the men mingled with the catcalls of the children, the insults of the women, the joyous and triumphant tears of the old gardener and the shoves the police officers were giving the convicted thief.

Needless to say, besides going to jail, the thief was compelled to return to the vendor the fifteen *duros* he had received, and the latter handed the money to *tío Buscabeatas,* who left for Rota very pleased with himself, saying, on his way home:

"How beautiful they looked in the market! I should have brought back one to eat tonight and kept the seeds."

Focus

1. Describe the care that the gardeners of Rota gave to their plants.
2. Two sets of "proof" were offered by *tío Buscabeatas* that the pumpkins were his. What was the first "proof"?
3. Why was *tío Buscabeatas's* first "proof" not enough to prove ownership? Why was the final proof more convincing?
4. Why do you think *tío Buscabeatas* went to so much trouble to prove the forty pumpkins were his?

In Writing

"The Stub-Book" is a detective story without a professional detective. *Tío Buscabeatas* followed the clues and managed to solve the case very quickly. Put yourself in the position of the accused thief's lawyer. In one or two paragraphs, write an argument that defends your client.

Vocabulary

Make two columns on your paper. Label the first column *Positive* and the second column *Negative*. Then look at the words in the list below. Decide whether each word has a positive or negative connotation. Write the word in the correct column. Then write a sentence using each word.

leisurely   catastrophe   majestic
gravely   diligence

STUDY SKILL: Using a Card Catalog

Public libraries are well organized. If you want to find a particular book, a story by a certain author, or information on any topic, the *card catalog* is the place to start. It is the library's index to what is on its shelves.

The catalog's card file is arranged in alphabetical order. And it contains three types of cards: *author cards*, *subject cards*, and *title cards*. Fiction or nonfiction, nearly every book in the library has one of each type of card made out for it. If the book is nonfiction, it has a *call number*, which tells where on the shelves the book can be found. On the card, the call number is located in the upper left corner. On the book, the call number is located on the spine. Fiction books are arranged on the shelves in alphabetical order by the author's last name. Fiction books usually do not have call numbers.

Samples of each card type are shown on the next page. They are for a nonfiction book called *Coyote for a Day* by Roger Caras. Notice that the author card has the writer's name on the top line. The title card has the book title at the top. The subject card has the general subject or topic of the book at the top. The cards are the same otherwise. All three cards are filed in the card catalog in alphabetical order, according to the top line.

There are reasons for having three types of cards. If you know the title of a nonfiction book, you can look up the title card to find the call number. This will tell you the shelf where the book is located. The title card also tells the author's name and the general subject of the book.

The author card is useful if you know who wrote the book but cannot remember the title. Author cards also tell other information. For example, you may want to know if a writer has other books published. To find out, check all the author cards for that writer. (Keep in mind that not all libraries carry all the books written by any one author. Ask the librarian if you have further questions.)

The subject card works as a reference source. All the cards for a given subject, such as coyotes, are filed together in the card catalog.

1. Would you use a subject or author card to locate books about mountain goats?
2. What card would you use to find the title of a book you can't remember by Jean Craighead George?

3. Could you find the library call number on the title card of a fiction book? Explain.

4. On the subject card for a nonfiction book, where would you find the call number? Where else are call numbers placed?

5. If you were doing a report on poisonous reptiles, which card would be the most helpful?

6. If you enjoyed reading "The Pup" by Anton Chekov, where would you look to see what else he has written?

AUTHOR CARD

```
        Caras, Roger A.

Y          Coyote for a Day/by Roger Caras;
QL      illustrated by Diane Paterson. New
795     York:  Windmill Books, [1977]
.C6
C37     [31] p.: ill.; 27 cm.

        SUMMARY:  Follows the activities of
        two coyotes as they forage for food
        and try to keep out of danger.
```

TITLE CARD

```
        Coyote for a Day
Y       Caras, Roger A.
QL         Coyote for a Day/by Roger Caras;
795     illustrated by Diane Paterson. New
.C6     York:  Windmill Books, [1977]
C37
        [31] p.: ill.; 27 cm.

        SUMMARY:  Follows the activities of
        two coyotes as they forage for food
        and try to keep out of danger.
```

SUBJECT CARD

```
        COYOTES -- LITERATURE
Y       Caras, Roger A.
QL         Coyote for a Day/by Roger Caras;
795     illustrated by Diane Paterson. New
.C6     York:  Windmill Books, [1977]
C37
        [31] p.: ill.; 27 cm.

        SUMMARY:  Follows the activities of
        two coyotes as they forage for food
        and try to keep out of danger.
```

folktales

Folktales were around long before writing was invented. They were memorized and passed down through the generations. Storytellers were honored members in many societies, for they knew and shared the traditions of the cultures. The following three stories are examples of such folktales. Where did they come from, and how are they similar?

The Baobab Tree

A Tale from East Africa   *Retold by Eleanor B. Heady*

In the village of Kituru in the eastern part of Africa, there lived a grandmother who was very old. She was known to the children as Mama Semamingi, the teller of many tales. Mama Semamingi was the best storyteller in the village. She knew a story for every day, a story about everything that happened. She told tales of the long ago when animals could talk to each other and to men, stories of fairies and magic and witchcraft. She knew why the baobab tree grew so strangely and why people were different colors.

The children said that Mama Semamingi had been on earth when the stones were soft. She must have been, to know so much about those long-ago times.

Evening was the favorite time for storytelling. The school children were home; the herdboys were in from the bush with their goats and cattle. The evening meal was over. Then there was time to sit around the fire circle in the center of the village and listen to the stories of Mama Semamingi.

Beside the gate to the village was a huge tree. It was different from all the other trees in the bush. It had a very large gray trunk, a trunk that looked as if it were swollen. At its top were some very scraggly limbs with a few leaves. People said that something was very wrong with the baobab tree: It gave little shade from the sun. Its wood was soft and quite useless, but it was the largest tree around. True, it had some fruit, which wasn't very good. Poor baobab! It must have been a mistake!

On an evening in spring, just after a rain, the children gathered around the fire as usual. Watiri came, holding to Mama Semamingi's arm. When the grandmother was seated on her stool, Kamalo stirred the fire and all the children gathered closer.

"What shall our story be tonight, totos?" asked Mama Semamingi.

"Whatever you wish to tell us," said Wakai.

Mama Semamingi looked around the village. When her eyes came to the baobab tree standing so tall and thick against the African sky, she smiled. "I know what it shall be," she said.

"What?" asked everyone together.

"A story about the tree, the great Mbuyu, the baobab tree."

"Tell us," shouted the children and Mama Semamingi began her story.

At the beginning of time when the stones were soft, the great god, Mungu, made all living animals and plants. Some animals had legs and some had wings, but all could move from place to place. Choosing a place to live was easy for these creatures. They could move about and find what suited them.

With the plants it was a different matter. They were firmly anchored by roots and must stay where Mungu put them. Because of this, the great one took pity on the plants and allowed them to choose their homes.

One of the mightiest trees created in the beginning was Mbuyu, the baobab. This tree was beautiful with a great smooth gray trunk and spreading thick branches clustered with many bright green glossy leaves.

"Where do you choose to live, Mbuyu?" asked Mungu.

"Put me in the low veld where it is warm. I don't want my

beautiful leaves killed by the frost," answered the tree.

"Very well." And the great god took the mighty baobab and planted his roots in the soil of a warm low valley. The rains came and Mbuyu grew. His leaves became thicker.

Then came the time of no rain. Every day was hotter than the one before. The beautiful leaves wilted, and many of them fell to the ground. Then the tree looked up to the mountain and cried. "Mungu, hear me. I am dying of the heat. I cannot live in this low veld where no cool winds blow. Aiiii! Aiiiii! I am dying."

The great god heard the baobab. "What would you have me do?" he asked.

"Move me, please. Move me to the high plain where it is cool. I cannot live here another day. Aiiiii! Aiiiii!"

So Mungu took pity on the tree. He sent a great wind to pull him up and he replanted him on the cool high plains.

For a while Mbuyu was happy. His leaves ceased to droop. The cool breeze moved around him.

Then came the rains again. The sky was dark. No warming sun shone for many days. Mbuyu shivered in the cold, his green leaves trembling miserably. Once again he called out, "Mungu, hear me. I am dying of the cold. I cannot live on the high plain where no sun shines and the bitter wind and rain make my leaves tremble. Aiiii! Aiiii! I am dying."

Once more the great god heard the baobab. He showed his face, scowling. "And what do you want this time?" he asked.

"Please, oh great one, move me back to the low veld. It is better to be hot than cold. Aiiii! Aiiii! I am freezing."

"Very well, for the last time," said Mungu crossly. He sent a fierce wind that pulled the huge tree from its place and carried it on a great gust to the valley. There he dug an enormous pit and replanted Mbuyu upside down with his great gnarled roots in the air.

"What are you doing?" asked the baobab as the earth was closing over his leaves.

"Planting you with your mouth in the earth, so I shall no longer be troubled by your complaining," said Mungu.

To this very day the baobabs look as if they were growing upside down.

The Cat, the Mountain Goat, and the Fox

A Tale from Puerto Rico

Retold by Pura Belpré

Once upon a time there was a little cat who was always complaining that her fur was dry and brittle. Because of this, she claimed she dare not leave the house to search for food. All the animals knew her condition, for she lost no time talking about it, and managed to give her as much help as they could.

One day a horse and a pig stopped to see her.

"How do you feel today?" they asked.

"Just the same and a little worried. You see my food is almost gone," she explained.

"There is food in my pen," said the pig. "I will bring you some."

The pig and the horse left and soon were back with enough food to keep the little cat at ease for some time. That day she ate better than ever and slept longer than usual. Days went by and other animals came to see her and left food for her. The little cat was as happy as she could be. Things would have continued that way had it not been for the mountain goat. She came running down the mountain one day on her way to a meeting. She stopped to see the little cat. As usual, the little cat began to tell her visitor about her poor condition. The mountain goat was alarmed.

"Come and live with me in the mountain," she offered. "The cool wind will be good for you. It will give you health and vigor."

"It will blow off all my fur," snapped the little cat. "Have you nothing else to offer?"

"No, that is all I can think of, but I am certain the rest of the animals will think of something else. I will ask them."

The little cat was on the alert at once.

"What animals?" she asked.

"Oh, the dog, the pig, the horse, the hens and the rooster. We have been called to a meeting at the glen."

The little cat was alarmed and frightened. These were the very animals who had been providing for her. What if they were meeting to cut off their help. She must find out how much the mountain goat knew.

"What is the meeting about?" she asked as casually as she could.

"I don't really know, but what does that matter? Leave all things to me. I must go now. Good-bye." And off she went as fast as she could.

"Wait, wait just a minute," called the little cat. But the mountain goat was too far away to hear her.

When she arrived at the glen, the meeting was well under way. The dog was presiding. She heard him explain that the meeting had been called to meet a new arrival, a fox, who had come to live in the old hollow tamarind tree. "This is an honor to our forest and . . ." He spotted the mountain goat and stopped his trend of thought.

"What detained you?" he asked, a little vexed. "You are always the first one at all meetings."

"The little cat in the outskirts of the village. She is so sick that . . ."

"Bah, what an excuse," interrupted the dog.

"But she needs our help, and I promised . . ."

"Help?" The dog interrupted her once more, trying to hold his temper in front of the honor guest. "Really, if you came down more often from your mountain top, you would be better informed. We keep her supplied with food. We make sure she does not go hungry."

"Food is not enough," said the mountain goat. "What she really needs is a cure so that her fur will cease to be dry and brittle. Then, and only then, will she be able to go out into the sunshine and enjoy the countryside. Have you ever thought of a cure?"

"No," the dog said. He wished the mountain goat would stop making him look like a fool in front of the important guest.

"Then, now is the time to think about it," insisted the mountain goat.

The dog turned to the animals and asked for suggestions. Every one of them began to speak at once. And what suggestions! Had the little cat heard them, she would have jumped right out of her skin. While the animals were busy thinking of ways and means, the honor guest was saying to herself: "There is something very strange here. Dry and brittle fur? Plenty of food without working? Why, that little cat is not sick, but lazy."

"Dog," she called, "I have a suggestion to offer."

The animals stopped talking at once. All eyes turned to the visitor.

"As you know, I am a *curandero*—a practitioner, with much experience in cases such as the one that afflicts your little friend. If the little cat comes to my home tomorrow, I will cure her, have no fear."

The animals were delighted. Naturally, the mountain goat was chosen to tell the little cat the news. The dog thanked the fox, and promptly closed the meeting.

Next morning the mountain goat told the little cat the news. But she did not believe her. "Nonsense," she said. "You know that there are no foxes here."

"There is one now," said the mountain goat.

"Then go back and tell her that I can't go."

"Why can't you go?" asked the mountain goat.

"You must have forgotten how weak my legs are."

"Is that all? I will take you there. Come, climb on my back." The mountain goat was most obliging.

Well, there was nothing the little cat could do but climb up. That, she managed to do complaining all the time. Off went the mountain goat, so fast, that the little cat had to hold on tight for fear of falling off. Soon they arrived at the hollow tamarind tree. Right by the dark hole stood the fox holding a sack.

"Greetings," said the fox.

The little cat slid off the mountain goat's back. The fox handed her the sack and said: "Inside that sack is your cure. Listen carefully. There is a piece of roast beef there which you are to eat according to my instructions. Go down this road to the very end. Whenever you feel hungry, open the sack and eat a little piece. Mind you, only a little piece, for the meat is to last you until you reach the end of the road. Go and good luck."

But all that fine speech was in vain, for the only thing the little cat heard was roast beef, which she had not tasted for a very long time. She started going down the road at such a pace, that the mountain goat was amazed.

"She told me she could not walk, fox. Why, she has fooled all of the animals," she said.

The fox said not a word. She went back into her hole, and the mountain goat ran off to tell the rest of the animals what she had just seen.

As soon as the little cat reached the bend of the road, she decided to taste the roast beef. She opened the sack. Out jumped two hares and started chasing her. The little cat sped on sliding over the grass. She ran and she ran. So did the two hares. Ahead was a palm tree. With one desperate leap, the little cat reached it, and scampered up like a rabbit. Up, higher and higher she went, until she reached the very top. She held on to one of the palm leaves and looked down. The two hares were not around. A drop of water fell on her paws, and from her paws to the palm leaf. She looked at her paws. Why, the fur was fluffy, moist and soft. It was all the running. Roast beef, indeed! That fox was clever, very clever. She spent that night among the palm leaves. In the morning she took the road to another village to start a new life.

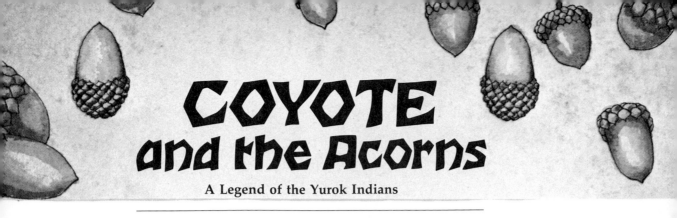

COYOTE and the Acorns

A Legend of the Yurok Indians

Retold by Gail Robinson and Douglas Hill

One day after the first forests had reached their full growth, Coyote's keen nose became aware of a most delicious smell.

It was something he had never smelled before, and it had him pawing the ground in hunger. Raising his nose high so he would not lose the smell, he sped through the forest, backtracking the breeze that had borne the smell to him. It led him to a village of human beings.

The humans made Coyote welcome, as they always made any of the People welcome. The men gathered round him, asking friendly questions about his doings and his wanderings, inviting him to join their circle and smoke a pipe with them. The children tugged at him, to make him come and play with them or tell them a story. Coyote smiled and nodded at them all, but still his nostrils were filled with the wonderful smell, and he could neither join the men's circle nor run off with the children. Instead, he made his way over to the cook-fires where the women were.

One of the women was wrapping leaves round a soft, flat thing that looked like a thin cake. "What is that," Coyote asked her, "that is making this beautiful smell?"

"This is what we call sour acorns," she said. "Would you like some?"

"Yes, very much," said Coyote, his mouth watering so that the saliva spilled down his chin in rivulets.

"Join us, then," said the woman. "There is plenty for everyone. We are ready to eat now."

So Coyote sat down with the villagers, and impatiently watched the women scrape the cook-fires aside with green sticks and uncover the hot, leaf-wrapped acorn cakes. One of the cakes was placed before Coyote, and the smell of it made him forget his manners, and even forget the cake's blazing hotness. He swallowed the whole in one gulp. The village women smiled and brought him another, and he gulped that one down the same way. Soon Coyote had eaten twenty-four of the cakes, and would have eaten more, except that there were no more ready for cooking.

"How do you prepare this miraculous food?" Coyote asked the woman who had served him.

The woman was delighted that he had enjoyed his meal so much, and flattered that he should be interested in how it was cooked.

"Why, it is something anyone can do," she said. "You soak the acorns in water, press them down hard, and leave them pressed for two days. Then you simply wrap them in leaves and bake them under the coals of a fire."

Coyote looked at the woman for a long moment. Then he smiled and shook his head. "Come now," he said. "There must be more to it than that. Nothing so delicious as this food could be so simple to prepare."

"But it is," the woman assured him. "Just that simple."

Coyote still shook his head.

"Perhaps the recipe is a secret. Never mind, you can trust me not to give the secret away. You can tell me how to make your sour acorns."

"But she has told you," said one of the other women. "Soak the acorns, press them and cook them. There is nothing more."

Coyote looked around at them in exasperation. "I don't know why you should lie to me. Have I not always been your friend? Why can you not tell me the truth about sour acorns?"

"Please believe us, friend Coyote," pleaded the women. "It is as we have told you. Why do you think we are lying?"

"I *know* you are lying," snapped Coyote, "because nothing that tastes so good could be made so easily. It is against the way of things."

"But, Coyote . . . !" the women began.

"Do you take me for some short-sighted, thick-brained fool without smell or sense?" shouted Coyote. "There must be more to the cooking of acorns than you have told me, and I want to know the rest of it!"

The women looked at each other, bewildered, not knowing what to say. Then one of the old grandmothers came slowly forward.

"You are quite right, friend Coyote," said the old woman. "Good things must always be difficult to come by, as you say. So we will tell you the true way to prepare sour acorns, won't we, sisters?"

And she turned to the other women and gave them a broad wink that Coyote could not see.

"Now first," the old woman went on, turning back to Coyote, "you must gather only the biggest and whitest acorns. The smaller, ordinary ones, with a taint of green at the end, will not do. When you have gathered enough acorns, you must load them in a canoe and paddle it to the middle of a large river. There you must tip the canoe over, so that the acorns will be drowned."

"Drowned," repeated Coyote, listening closely and nodding his head to show that he understood.

"Once the acorns are drowned," said the old woman, "you must then search for two flat stones, as perfectly smooth as river ice, to use in pressing the acorns. And when you have found them, you must gather special firewood—only the dried branches of the blackthorn. These you must peel and then scrape down so that only the central pith remains."

"The pith," repeated Coyote, nodding harder than ever.

"Finally," continued the old woman, "the pressed acorns must be wrapped only in the leaves of the poison sumac. Any other leaves will not give them their special flavor."

"Drowning, blackthorn pith, sumac leaves," repeated Coyote happily. "I will remember. I knew the dish would have to be complicated, to be so good. You might have told me the whole recipe in the first place."

And off he raced to begin his preparations, muttering to himself the recipe that the old woman had given him. He was concentrating so hard on remembering it all that he did not hear the wave of laughter that spread among the women of the village behind him.

Coyote spent a long time selecting his acorns. He threw aside any that he thought were small, or unevenly shaped, or even faintly tinged with green at the stem. It took him several days, but finally he had enough to load into his canoe, placing them in gently, handful by handful, so as not to bruise them.

Then he carefully pushed off from the shore of the great river where his canoe was moored, and paddled out to the center. As he felt the fierce current clutch the canoe, he took a deep breath and flung himself sideways. The canoe overturned, plunging Coyote and all the acorns into the freezing water. At the same time, the descending edge of the canoe struck Coyote a sharp blow on the head. He spluttered to the surface, then swam dazedly to shore.

There, soaked, chilled, and with aching head, he began looking for the smooth, flat stones he needed. Again the search

took a long time, for he threw aside any that showed even a faint roughness or bumpiness. But within a few days he had found his stones. He also had stubbed toes, cracked shins, broken nails, and a soreness still from the bump on his head.

Next, Coyote went into the woods to look for blackthorn trees. When he found them, he took nearly a day to break off the dry branches that he needed, and several days more to scrape and hack away the wood down to the pith. As he worked the thorns scratched and stabbed him, and many stuck so deep into his flesh that no amount of picking could dislodge them.

Lastly, Coyote looked for poison sumac leaves. When he found a stand of sumac, the picking went more quickly than the other tasks, because Coyote wanted to get through as fast as he could, and touch the leaves as little as possible. Even so, as he picked, he was giving low howls of pain as his flesh reddened, and swelled, and blistered.

But in the end the leaves were piled beside the stones and the pith, and Coyote was ready to cook his acorns.

At that moment a thought came to him.

"How generous those villagers were," he said to himself, "to let me eat twenty-four of their acorn cakes, when they must go through this much hardship and pain to prepare them!"

The thought made Coyote a little uneasy, and as he made his way down to the river where he had drowned his acorns, he began to feel even more worried.

"That old woman," he thought, standing on the river-bank, "did not tell me how to get my acorns out of the river, after drowning them."

He started to run, as fast as his sore and aching body could go, along the river-bank. But no matter how far he went, in either direction, he found no acorns washed up. "If they are drowned," he thought, "they will be at the bottom of the river." And so he threw himself into the icy water, diving as deeply as he could. But the acorns had been carried off, long since, by the powerful current. Coyote saw only the smooth sand of the river-bed and a few inquiring fish.

Crawling back onto dry land, Coyote lay panting, trying to remember every word the old woman in the village had said to him. Surely, he thought, she *had* told him how to get his acorns back from the river, and he had simply forgotten.

He got slowly to his feet and stumbled away from the river into the forest nearby. There he came upon a group of women gathering acorns. They were not the women who had given him sour acorns, before, but were from another village. And Coyote noticed that they did not choose their acorns at all as carefully as he had, but picked up all sizes, whether they were green-tinged or not, as long as they were whole and not rotten.

Coyote painfully approached one of the women. "Good day," he said. "I see you are gathering acorns. Will you be using them to make the dish called sour acorns?"

"Yes, indeed," said the woman, straightening up from her work. "Will you come, friend Coyote, and eat with us when the acorns are ready?"

"Perhaps," said Coyote shakily. "But first, tell me, how do you prepare that dish?"

The woman smiled. "Nothing could be easier. Just soak the acorns, press them hard for two days, wrap them in leaves and bake them under the coals of the cook-fire."

So Coyote knew that he had been a fool, and threw back his head to howl out his misery and pain.

Focus

1. Which story—"The Baobab Tree," "The Cat, the Mountain Goat, and the Fox," or "Coyote and the Acorns"—provided an explanation for something in nature? What did the story explain?
2. Write a short paragraph summarizing the plot in "The Cat, the Mountain Goat, and the Fox."
3. This story could be used to teach a moral lesson about people. What do you think this lesson might be?
4. Sometimes, authors give human qualities to objects or animals. For example, in "Coyote and the Acorns," the narrator says, "Coyote smiled and nodded. . . ." Find five other examples of such treatment in the same story.
5. Which story might be used to show that "Doing things the hard way does not make them better"?

In Writing

Now you be a storyteller. Think of an explanation for something in nature—thorns on a rose, bats sleeping upside down, quills on a porcupine, weeping willow trees, etc.—and write your own "folktale."

Vocabulary

Read the word list and paragraph below. Decide which word makes the best sense in each blank space. Then write the numbers 1 to 5 on a piece of paper and write the correct word next to each number.

stand	pith	casually
exasperation	glen	rivulets

Carmen seemed to sit __(1)__ on the crest of the hill, leisurely admiring the green __(2)__ below. Her attention was focused on the beautiful __(3)__ of trees and on the bubbling __(4)__ that flowed through it. Carmen was not really at ease, however; she was annoyed and angry. Her __(5)__ was caused by the knowledge that this area would soon be the location of a shopping center.

YARNS

Carl Sandburg

They have yarns
Of a skyscraper so tall they had to put hinges
On the two top stories so to let the moon go by,
Of one corn crop in Missouri when the roots
Went so deep and drew off so much water
The Mississippi riverbed that year was dry,
Of pancakes so thin they had only one side,
Of "a fog so thick we shingled the barn and six feet out on the
    fog,"
Of Pecos Pete straddling a cyclone in Texas and riding it to the
    west coast where "it rained out under him,"
. . . .
Of the hen laying a square egg and cackling, "Ouch!" and of
    hens laying eggs with the dates printed on them,
Of the ship captain's shadow: it froze to the deck one cold
    winter night,

Of mutineers on that same ship put to chipping rust with
    rubber hammers,
Of the sheep counter who was fast and accurate: "I just count
    their feet and divide by four,"
. . . .
Of a cyclone that sucked cookstoves out of the kitchen, up the
    chimney flue, and on to the next town,
Of the same cyclone picking up wagon-tracks in Nebraska and
    dropping them over in the Dakotas,
Of the hook-and-eye snake unlocking itself into forty pieces,
    each piece two inches long, then in nine seconds flat
    snapping itself together again,
Of the watch swallowed by the cow—when they butchered her
    a year later the watch was running and had the correct time,
Of horned snakes, hoop snakes that roll themselves where
    they want to go, and rattlesnakes carrying bells instead of
    rattles on their tails,
Of the herd of cattle in California getting lost in a giant
    redwood tree that had hollowed out,
. . . .
Of railroad trains whizzing along so fast they reach the station
    before the whistle,
Of pigs so thin the farmer had to tie knots in their tails to keep
    them from crawling through the cracks in their pens,
. . . .
Of John Henry's hammer and the curve of its swing and his
    singing of it as "a rainbow round my shoulder."

Fact or Fantasy?

Elwood D. Baumann

Monsters have always fascinated and scared people. Giants, dragons, and huge gorillas have been the basis for books and movies. Are such "monsters" real, or are they only the stuff of which stories are made?

There is something about monsters that has always fascinated people. Fire-breathing dragons, people-eating giants, and huge winged serpents figured strongly in many ancient legends. Greek mythology described nine-headed water serpents, flying horses, a beast that was half lion and half eagle, hairy giants who had one eye in the middle of their foreheads, and a host of other weird creatures. Cave paintings of giants and strange beasts have been discovered in many parts of the world.

276

People's fascination with monsters is just as great today as it was in ages past. Newspapers excitedly report every sighting. Monsters always make big news, and crowds of curious people invariably rush to the place where the creature was seen. Many of them are carrying cameras, but getting a photograph of a monster requires an awful lot of luck.

It's not surprising, of course, that Hollywood cashed in on our fascination with monsters. Hideous creatures of every description appeared on the screen. Some were ridiculous in the extreme, but one giant captured the imagination of everyone who saw him. The name of that giant was King Kong.

The original *King Kong* was an enormously successful movie. The huge gorilla who starred in the film appeared so real that it was easy to forget that it was an imaginary monster. People sat on the edge of the seat in rapt attention as the great hairy giant went on the rampage through the streets of New York. The film ended with the death of King Kong, and there was always a sigh of sadness from the audience. Although the monster had terrorized a city, nobody really wanted it to be killed.

None of the monsters that have been sighted in the United States and Canada is anywhere near as large as King Kong, of course. They may be only minimonsters by comparison, but they're still pretty big creatures indeed. Plaster of Paris casts have been made of footprints twenty-two inches long, and feet that size could belong only to a very large creature.

Getting an accurate description of a monster is a terribly difficult task. In the great majority of cases, the creature is seen for only a very few seconds at the most. The sighting may occur in a dense forest or a dark swamp. More frequently, it is seen hurrying across a road at night. The driver suddenly sees something strange in the glare of the headlights, then the something disappears into the fields or forest. The driver knows that it was something out of the ordinary, but there's simply no way to describe it in any detail.

Police and reporters know that most people have great difficulty in describing a situation accurately. Ten witnesses, for example, may see a robber running from a bank, and the police may be given five or more different descriptions. They might be told that the bank robber was tall and short, fat and thin, young and old, and had light and dark hair. Descriptions of monsters vary even more dramatically because people are then trying to describe something which is totally unfamiliar to them.

Eyewitness reports are seldom completely reliable, and we can easily understand why. A person driving a car just doesn't have the time to study the creature. Neither does the person who sights one in a swamp or forest. Both human and monster will try to get out of there just as quickly as possible, and we can't blame them for that. We're all afraid of the unknown, and people who come face-to-face with a monster are not going to hang around hoping to get a closer look. They may be curious, yes, but their safety is going to be their first concern.

Bigfoot

Up to now nobody has managed to get even a reasonably decent photograph of any of North America's unidentified monsters. There have, however, been two close misses. Cloyce Warren snapped a quick photo of the White River Monster in the act of submerging, and Sallie Ann Clarke took a flash photo of the Lake Worth Monster crashing through the brush. Unfortunately, both photos were blurred and lacked detail. Scientists who studied them were unable to reach any conclusions at all.

Sallie Ann Clarke's photo, like other monster photos, was taken in a moment of unexpected excitement and fear. Here are the details that led to the photographing of the Lake Worth Monster.

It was very late when Sallie Ann Clarke got into her car and headed for home. She was tired and confused. The last few hours had been spent talking to people, and she didn't know what to think. Common sense told her that there could not possibly be a monster roaming around in the twentieth century. And even if there were, she reasoned, it certainly wouldn't make its home so close to a large city like Fort Worth. It would live in a place like the Florida Everglades or the great forests of the Pacific Northwest.

Then had all of those people lied to her? she asked herself. Several of them swore that they had heard a piercing scream that could not have been human. Two men, Ronnie Armstrong and Jim Stephens, insisted that they had seen a creature running through the brush on two legs. It was big and heavy and was covered with dirty-white fur. The creature was much too large to be either a human or an ape, so it had to be something else.

Mrs. Clarke was still searching for sensible answers when the totally unexpected happened. A huge whitish form suddenly emerged from a ditch as she was approaching the Lake Worth Bridge. It ran across the road and immediately disappeared into the brush on the far side. Although she only saw it for two or three seconds, she is absolutely convinced that she knows what it was. "I saw the Lake Worth Monster, and nobody can tell me otherwise," she says. "That's the only thing it could possibly have been."

And she could just possibly be right.

The reported sighting that hot July night in 1969 was a major event in the life of Sallie Ann Clarke. It brought on an acute case of monstermania. Much of her spare time was spent out at Lake Worth. She became a familiar figure to the other monster hunters as she trudged doggedly through the brush armed with her camera, notepad, and tape recorder.

Not only the monster hunters were interviewed, however. Sallie Ann talked to people who lived near the lake, and she went through old newspaper files and the archives. Monsters, she learned, were not new to Texas. They had reportedly been seen there as early as the 1700s and as recently as 1941. An Indian chief in Livingstone said that according to their legends there had *always* been monsters around Lake Worth.

But what kind of creatures were they? Sallie Ann wanted an answer to that question, and she thought she might be able to get it. The scientists in Fort Worth hadn't given her much help, so she decided to try someone who wasn't a scientist. She had read about John Green while doing her research. Green is Canada's foremost monster investigator. His chief interest is Bigfoot. The Lake Worth Monster may not have been a Bigfoot, she reasoned, but Green might be able to give her some clue as to its identity.

Green must have been impressed with the Fort Worth woman's sincerity. It's a long way from British Columbia to Texas, but the monster investigator felt that he had to make the trip. Whether or not he found the long journey worthwhile is something we don't know.

The Canadian is an extremely cautious man. He has been gathering information on monsters for nearly twenty years. It's highly unlikely that anyone on the North American continent knows more about unidentified creatures than he does. He devotes all of his time to studying them and will travel almost anywhere to get more information. He will patiently listen to anyone, but he never ever makes wild guesses.

Although the Lake Worth Monster intrigued Green, he had to admit that he didn't know what it was. He did, however,

Lake Worth Monster

know what it wasn't. It wasn't a Bigfoot, and he was willing to take bets on that. Both creatures were very large. Both ran on two legs, and there the similarities ended. "They're probably not even distant cousins," Green concluded.

The summer of 1969 simmered on. Reports of sightings kept coming in, but the monster seldom made the front page of the Fort Worth newspapers. The original flurry of excitement had died down. Even some of the most enthusiastic hunters had put their weapons away. Instead of chasing after the monster, they were now chasing after other things.

This doesn't mean, of course, that people had lost interest in the creature. Far from it. A play called *The Lake Worth Monster* drew record crowds when it was put on at the Casa Mañana Playhouse.

John Simons, the playwright, lived on the shore of the lake. He had never seen the monster, but he couldn't bear the thought of its being killed or harmed. "I feel sorry for the poor creature," he told a *Star-Telegram* reporter. "It's lonely and it's isolated and it must be terribly afraid. I don't know for sure whether it's real or unreal—a freak or an apparition. Anyway, that's not important. The point I want to make in my play is that the thing has not harmed anyone. It minds its own business. We should respect it—no matter what it is—and grant it the full protection of the law."

Before the opening night *The Lake Worth Monster* got some free publicity. The playwright had Sallie Ann Clarke to thank for that. The Texas woman managed to get a flash photo of the creature one night when some hunters chased it past the tree stump on which she was resting.

According to Sallie Ann, she had driven out to the Nature Center and Game Reserve after her evening meal. Several sightings had been reported in the last few days, and she hoped to get another glimpse of the monster. Actually, she did much better than that. Before the night was over, she had what she hoped would be a good picture of the thing she had been chasing for so long.

Unfortunately, the photograph doesn't really tell us very much at all. It shows a white, hairy "something-or-other" standing in some weeds. The back is to the camera, and there is no indication of movement. Neither is it possible to judge the height or weight accurately. Neither arms nor legs can be seen.

It's obvious, too, that the photo was taken at very close range. Sallie Ann says that she jumped off the stump and snapped the photo as the creature went tearing past her. "I honestly don't think that the thing was more than ten yards from me when I took the picture," she declared.

Dick Pratt, the naturalist at the Nature Center and Game Reserve, is far from convinced that there is a monster in the area. "Personally, I don't think there's anything larger than a bobcat around here," he says. "I know that some large tracks have supposedly been found and that a lot of folks swear that they've seen a monster, but I find the whole business pretty hard to believe."

This isn't surprising. It *is* hard to believe that there's a monster cavorting around almost within sight of the lights of Fort Worth. It's also hard to believe that so many people would tell a pack of lies. The fact remains, too, that something did show up on Sallie Ann Clarke's photograph.

We don't know what that something was, but whatever it was, it was much too large to be a bobcat.

Focus

1. List three examples of how people have shown an interest in monsters throughout the ages.
2. Why is it difficult to get an accurate description of a monster?
3. Besides eyewitness reports, name two other kinds of information used to support the existence of monsters.
4. Did Sally Ann Clarke's photograph prove that she had seen a monster? Explain.
5. Explain how "monster" sightings could have been the basis for some folktales long ago.
6. Do you think the author of this article believes that monsters might possibly exist? Explain your answer.

In Writing

What is your favorite monster? Imagine that you are a reporter, and you have been sent to investigate a sighting of your favorite monster. Write a news story explaining what you did. Give your story a headline, too.

Vocabulary

On a piece of paper, write the numbers 1 to 3. Then look at the words in the first column and find a definition for each word in the second column. Next to each number on your paper, write the letter of the correct definition for each word.

1. rampage
2. invariably
3. cavorting

A. prancing about
B. very involved and attentive
C. without change
D. a wild outbreak

TEXTBOOK READING: What's It All About?

When you read a science or social studies textbook, you will find it easier to remember important ideas and information if you look ahead. Take the time to look ahead at the chapter. Informational books, such as textbooks, are carefully organized.

Within each chapter, you will find headings and subheadings. The headings summarize the main ideas presented in the chapter. The subheadings summarize the ideas that support the main ideas. By looking ahead, you can understand how the chapter is organized. And this will help you to organize your thinking to absorb more information.

Look at the abbreviated chapter provided on the next page. It summarizes the kinds of information you might find in a book chapter about monsters. The chapter title, *Is There a Loch Ness Monster?*, tells you that the topic is the Loch Ness Monster. Look at the headings. These tell you that the chapter has two main ideas. The first one is that there is some basis for belief in the Loch Ness Monster. The second idea is that positive proof of the creature's existence is still needed. Read the abbreviated chapter.

The statements below were taken from the real chapter. Read them carefully. Decide in which part of the chapter you would probably find each statement. Write the heading or subheading under which the information belongs.

1. The corpses of other animals rise to the surface of other bodies of water. Why don't they at Loch Ness?

2. Two police officers, Sergeant Donald Nicholson and Constable A. Gray, reported two fins approximately twenty feet apart traveling at a good speed across the Loch.

3. Fishers in Scotland reported a "monster" which had a camel's head, a giraffe's neck, and a twelve foot long tail. It turned out to be a whale.

4. A team from the Academy of Applied Science took a photograph that is claimed to show the main body structure of the Loch Ness Monster.

5. A Norse legend tells of Kraken, an enormous, round, flat serpent that was full of tentacles.

6. Mrs. Carey claims that she first saw the monster in 1917 and since has had a total of fifteen sightings.

IS THERE A LOCH NESS MONSTER?

THE BASIS OF BELIEF

The legends and mythology of Greece, Babylonia, Africa, and many other areas tell of sea serpents. Throughout history, sailors from many nations have reported strange and terrifying sea creatures. Can this be people's imaginations, or is there some factual basis for these tales?

Eyewitness Accounts

There have been 3,000 recorded sightings of the Loch Ness Monster. These sightings have been made by people from every walk of life—doctors, fishers, insurance executives, farmers, lawyers, and teachers. The witnesses have had no reason for embellishing their accounts or making up the stories.

Photographic Evidence

Several photos have been taken that claim to show parts of the Loch Ness Monster. Perhaps the most famous of these was taken by Dr. Wilson when he stopped his car and left it to go for a walk. He noticed an unusual movement in the water. Using a telephoto lens on his camera, he took the photo that appears on this page. It is called the Surgeon's Photo. To date, it is regarded as one of the best pieces of photographic evidence available.

THE NEED FOR SOLID PROOF

The scientific community is not easily fooled or easily convinced. To date, there has been no tangible proof of the existence of anything unusual in Loch Ness. No bones, skins, or other body parts have ever been uncovered. There have been countless expeditions, but positive proof of the creature's existence has yet to be established.

Hoaxes and Pranks

Not every account of evidence has been well-intentioned. A well-respected big-game hunter once reported discovering tracks made by the Loch Ness Monster. Upon investigation by experts from the British Museum of Natural History, it was found that the tracks were hippopotamus tracks. Furthermore, the hippo foot that made the imprints was one that had been made into an umbrella stand by a local resident!

The Handkerchief

Robert Gilstrap and Irene Estabrook

Here is a story that simply entertains. It is a typical "fairy tale," so you might recognize parts from other tales you have heard.

Zakia was a lovely and clever young Arabian maiden who lived with her father, the Grand Vizier[1] of Morocco. Although she was only eighteen years of age, she was nevertheless her father's most valuable counsellor. Normally he would not make a decision without first consulting his wise young daughter.

One day, however, he made an agreement without consulting Zakia, and it displeased her very much. The Sultan of Morocco had asked for Zakia's hand in marriage, and without asking for his daughter's opinion, the Grand Vizier had consented to the union.

"No, father," Zakia said firmly, when her father told her about the future marriage in which she was to take part. "I will not marry a man merely because you say so. I do not love him, and I refuse even to consider marrying him."

"But Zakia," he begged, "no girl has ever refused a proposal of marriage from the Sultan. The very idea of what might happen to me makes me shudder when I think of it. If you do not marry him, I may lose my head. Oh, please do as I say, my daughter. Marry him for my sake, I beg you."

The pleadings of her father finally moved Zakia to consent to the marriage, but only on one condition.

---

[1]vizier (vi zir'): a high official

"The Sultan must learn a trade, father," she demanded. "I will marry him only if he does so. What would happen to us if one day he lost his throne? Soon we would be penniless, and without any means of earning a living, we would surely starve to death."

Zakia's father was afraid that his daughter's demand would anger the Sultan greatly. But since it was better than telling him that his daughter had refused altogether, he went to the palace to relay her message.

When the Sultan heard Zakia's request, he was pleased. And his pleasure greatly surprised Zakia's father who had trembled as he told of his daughter's demand.

"Your daughter is more than beautiful and talented," the Sultan said royally. "She is also more clever than I had guessed. I will be glad to do as she asks for I know our life together will be happy."

As soon as Zakia's father left the throne room, the Sultan commanded that representatives of all the trades assemble before him and tell him the good qualities concerning their occupations. After listening to each description the Sultan thought carefully about what had been said. Then he made his decision.

"I shall become a weaver," he declared, in a pleased voice. "Out of all the trades I could study, I feel that I would enjoy this more than any other. Let me begin at once to learn the weaver's art so that I may fulfill the request of my beloved Zakia, and thus make our marriage a reality."

Soon the Sultan was arising much earlier than usual each

morning, and after completing the agenda of official business, he departed for a room in a far corner of the palace. The room contained a loom, shuttles, and yarn, and soon after he entered it, the sound of his work could be heard by all who passed near. The Sultan was a serious and sincere man.

As time went by, the Sultan realized that he had indeed made a wise decision in becoming a weaver. Not only did he enjoy his work very much, but he discovered he had much natural talent along these lines. Satisfied with his progress, he began to weave a beautiful handkerchief to send to Zakia as proof of his weaving ability.

With loving care the Sultan created an exquisite silken handkerchief with a center design of an embroidered red rose set against a forest background.

"Take this to Zakia, daughter of the Grand Vizier," the Sultan commanded a servant, "and tell her that if this meets with her approval, our marriage shall take place within the month." And so the messenger did as the Sultan ordered.

When Zakia opened her gift she was delighted to see the proof of the Sultan's love for her. And although she did not love him she was bound by the agreement to marry that she herself had made.

After the festive wedding, the young couple ruled the people of Morocco fairly and justly. Zakia's wise advice proved helpful to the Sultan in handling his affairs and each day he grew more pleased that he had chosen the Grand Vizier's daughter as his wife.

On one particular day when the Sultan was much troubled with a problem, he came to his wife for counsel.

"How can I become more understanding of the common people of my country?" the Sultan asked his wife. "How can I learn to think as they think, know their problems, and be aware of their needs?"

Zakia thought for a moment and then said in her soft voice, "My lord, it has been said by those far more wise than I, that if a man wishes to know another man he must live with him. Thus I feel that if you are to know the common people better, you must live among the common people. Why do you not disguise yourself as a common man, and go out to meet the people you rule?"

Although Zakia's suggestion was unusual, it pleased the Sultan, and during the following week he and his chamberlain and one of his viziers could be seen walking the streets of the capital city of Morocco wearing ragged, dirty robes.

"I feel that this idea of Zakia's is most worthwhile," the Sultan commented to his friends. "Already I know better the lives of my subjects and their needs."

"You are right, my lord," the Chamberlain said. "But now can we not return to the palace to eat? I am starved."

"Why go back to the palace?" the Sultan asked. "We are trying to find out more about the common people of Morocco, are we not?"

His companions nodded their heads in agreement.

"Then would we not learn more if we were to eat in one of the restaurants where my subjects eat?" the Sultan suggested to his hungry companions.

Agreeing that this indeed would be the wiser course, the three men chose a small café that seemed hospitable.

"This looks like a fine place," the Sultan commented. "And I must admit, my hunger grows with each passing minute."

The three men approached the café, but as they stepped on the threshold, they felt the floor slip away beneath them. Before they realized quite what had happened they found themselves in a deep, dark, underground pit. And although the men shouted, no one came to help them.

"A wonderful welcome for the Sultan," the Vizier complained angrily. "I wonder where we could be and what is expected of us."

"We are in a deep, dark hole," the Sultan answered seriously. "But why are we here? Surely we have not been recognized in our ragged clothing. And even if we had been, who would want to harm us?"

Since the other two could give no answers to the Sultan's questions, there was silence.

Suddenly, a strange, high laugh echoed through the dark pit. The laugh was followed by the glimmering of a small candle, and above the candle was a face, dark and wrinkled.

"Say your prayers, you miserable ones," the holder of the candle screeched. "You are here to be fattened like cattle. In three days our butcher will slaughter you, and you will be served in our café which is famed for its excellent food."

"Have mercy, man," the Chamberlain cried. "We came here for food. We are starving. Must you torture us this way?"

The wrinkled man laughed even louder than before and disappeared into the darkness.

"Let us tell him who we are when he returns," the Vizier said earnestly. "Then when they release us, we can arrest them and put a stop to their vile business."

"You are foolish, my Vizier," the Sultan answered. "If they should find out that I am the Sultan, they would kill us quicker than ever. The fear of the people's anger will force them to destroy us without delay."

"You are right, my lord," the Chamberlain agreed. "The Vizier in his fright was thinking too hastily. But what do you suggest?"

"If only Zakia were here," the Sultan said thoughtfully. "She would find a way out of this predicament, I know. But give me time to think."

The three men groped in the darkness to find the wall of the dungeon, and then they sat down against it to rest and think.

Hours later the jailer returned, laughing as before. "We've decided not to give you food," he said with a fearsome smile. "You look fat enough, and besides a few days without food may knock some of the impudence out of you."

"But, noble lord," the Sultan said gently, "we did not intend to be impudent nor to displease you. We have learned what is to be our fate, and have resigned ourselves, for we know that our death is your desire. However, before we die please allow us to make a proposition. It could fill your pockets with gold, and at the same time, perhaps, spare our miserable lives."

The jailer looked suspiciously at the Sultan who had conceived in the darkness an idea that he thought might save his life and the lives of his companions.

"Your talk sounds interesting," the jailer said. "Continue."

"I am a weaver by trade," the Sultan told him. "In fact, my work is so highly valued at the court of the Sultan, that the ladies of the court will pay large prices for my handiwork. Give me a loom and some silken yarn, and by selling my products you will be able to make a considerable fortune. And as for us, we would much rather spend the rest of our lives weaving for you than be eaten in the café above."

The jailer's eyes gleamed as he listened to the Sultan's suggestion, and without hesitation decided to accept the proposal.

Within the hour, a loom had been brought to the dungeon and the Sultan started weaving a silken handkerchief similar to the one that he had woven for Zakia.

He worked feverishly through the long hours of the night and when he had completed the handkerchief, he gave it to the

jailer, saying, "Take this immediately to the Sultan's wife, Zakia, in the Sultan's palace. Surely she will buy the handkerchief and pay you well."

When the jailer reached the palace he found everything in a state of confusion. Messengers ran in and out of the throne room and guards gathered to form a search party to seek the missing Sultan.

Unnoticed, the small jailer slipped through the crowd of people, and up to Zakia, who was trying her best to keep back the tears and hide the grief that had filled her heart since her husband's disappearance.

"My mistress," the jailer said, "here I have a handkerchief woven by a famous weaver of Morocco. Would you like to buy it?"

When Zakia saw the handkerchief she recognized immediately the design, and knew without a doubt that the Sultan had sent it as a message.

"Yes, it is a beautiful handkerchief," she said in an effort not to show her excitement. "I will buy it."

Then she gave the jailer the money, sent him on his way, and signaled quickly to two of the guards to follow him.

When the guards reached the café they heard the voices of the Sultan, the Vizier, and the Chamberlain. Immediately one of them returned to summon the troops of the palace.

Silently the barracan-clad guards encircled the small stone building. As Zakia watched from her black stallion, they crept into the café. There was the sound of violent fighting.

Then all was silent again, and out of the café came the Sultan borne on the shoulders of his soldiers. The Vizier and Chamberlain followed behind.

"My darling Zakia," the Sultan shouted when he saw his wife waiting for him. "My life again is made more wonderful by your presence and cleverness. I owe my life to the one I love more dearly than anything else in the world."

Zakia was happy to hear her husband's words. And as she rode back to the palace alongside the handsome Sultan, she realized for the first time how happy she was to be the wife of such a clever and talented man.

Focus

1. List the events that led to the marriage of the Sultan and Zakia.
2. Why did the Sultan disguise himself and walk about the city?
3. Summarize what happened after the Sultan was captured.
4. List three instances in which Zakia's wisdom became apparent.
5. Do you think this story is mainly about the Sultan or mainly about Zakia? Explain your answer.

In Writing

You are being held captive and have a chance to send one message, in the form of a design, to a friend. You want the friend to know who is sending the design, but you do not want to use anything as obvious as a picture of yourself or any warning words. That would alert your captor to the message hidden in the design. Create a unique design that would tell your friend it came from you.

Vocabulary

On a piece of paper, write the numbers *1* to *5*. Then read the sentences below. Next to each number on your paper, write the word from the list that best completes each analogy.

agenda	vile	rampage
embroider	grope	hospitable
exquisite	feverishly	proposition

1. Evil is to deed as ___ is to act.
2. Luggage is to baggage as ___ is to lovely.
3. List is to shopping as ___ is to meeting.
4. Cavorting is to prancing as ___ is to friendly.
5. Squint is to see as ___ is to search.

SOMEDAY

Isaac Asimov

A "bard" is a professional storyteller. Bards have been around almost as long as there have been stories to tell. Will people someday tire of hearing stories? Are bards an endangered species?

Niccolo Mazetti lay stomach down on the rug, chin buried in the palm of one small hand, and listened to the Bard disconsolately. There was even the suspicion of tears in his dark eyes, a luxury a thirteen-year-old could allow himself only when alone.

The Bard said, "Once upon a time in the middle of a deep wood, there lived a poor woodcutter and his two motherless daughters, who were each as beautiful as the day is long. The older daughter had long hair as black as a feather from a raven's wing, but the younger daughter had hair as bright and golden as the sunlight of an autumn afternoon.

"Many times while the girls were waiting for their father to come home from his day's work in the wood, the older girl would sit before a mirror and sing—"

What she sang, Niccolo did not hear, for a call sounded from outside the room: "Hey, Nickie."

And Niccolo, his face clearing on the moment, rushed to the window and shouted, "Hey, Paul."

Paul Loeb waved an excited hand. He was thinner than Niccolo and not as tall, for all he was six months older. His face was full of repressed tension which showed itself most clearly in the rapid blinking of his eyelids. "Hey, Nickie, let me in. I've got an idea and a *half*. Wait till you hear it." He looked rapidly about him as though to check on the possibility of eavesdroppers, but the front yard was quite empty. He repeated, in a whisper, "Wait till you hear it."

"All right. I'll open the door."

The Bard continued smoothly, oblivious to the sudden loss of attention on the part of Niccolo. As Paul entered, the Bard was saying, " . . . Thereupon, the lion said, 'If you will find me the lost egg of the bird which flies over the Ebony Mountain once every ten years, I will—'"

Paul said, "Is that a Bard you're listening to? I didn't know you had one."

Niccolo reddened and the look of unhappiness returned to his face. "Just an old thing I had when I was a kid. It ain't much good." He kicked at the Bard with his foot and caught the somewhat scarred and discolored plastic covering a glancing blow.

The Bard hiccupped as its speaking attachment was jarred out of contact a moment, then it went on: "—for a year and a day until the iron shoes were worn out. The princess stopped at the side of the road. . . . "

Paul said, "Boy, that *is* an old model," and looked at it critically.

Despite Niccolo's own bitterness against the Bard, he winced at the other's condescending tone. For the moment, he was sorry he had allowed Paul in, at least before he had restored the Bard to its usual resting place in the basement. It was only in the desperation of a dull day and a fruitless discussion with his father that he had resurrected it. And it turned out to be just as stupid as he had expected.

Nickie was a little afraid of Paul anyway, since Paul had special courses at school and everyone said he was going to grow up to be a Computing Engineer.

Not that Niccolo himself was doing badly at school. He got adequate marks in logic, binary manipulations,[1] computing and elementary circuits; all the usual subjects. But that was it! They were just the usual subjects and he would grow up to be a control-board guard like every-

---

[1] binary manipulations: work with a special kind of mathematics

one else.

Paul, however, knew mysterious things about what he called electronics and theoretical mathematics and programing. Especially programing. Niccolo didn't even try to understand when Paul bubbled over about it.

Paul listened to the Bard for a few minutes and said, "You been using it much?"

"No!" said Niccolo, offended. "I've had it in the basement since before you moved into the neighborhood. I just got it out today—" He lacked an excuse that seemed adequate to himself, so he concluded, "I just got it out."

Paul said, "Is that what it tells you about: woodcutters and princesses and talking animals?"

Niccolo said, "It's terrible. My parents say we can't afford a new one. I said to them this morning—" The memory of the morning's fruitless pleadings brought Niccolo dangerously near tears, which he repressed in a panic. Somehow, he felt that Paul's thin cheeks never felt the stain of tears and that Paul would have only contempt for anyone else less strong than himself. Niccolo went on, "So I thought I'd try this old thing again, but it's no good."

Paul turned off the Bard, pressed the contact that led to a recombination of the vocabulary, characters, plot lines and climaxes stored within it. Then he reactivated it.

The Bard began smoothly, "Once upon a time there was a little boy named Willikins whose mother had died and who lived with a stepfather and a stepbrother. Although the stepfather was very well-to-do, he begrudged poor Willikins the very bed he slept in so that Willikins was forced to get such rest as he could on a pile of straw in the stable next to the horses—"

"Horses!" cried Paul.

"They're a kind of animal," said Niccolo. "I think."

"I know that! I just mean imagine stories about *horses*."

"It tells about horses all the time," said Niccolo. "There are things called cows, too. You milk them but the Bard doesn't say how."

"Well, gee, why don't you fix it up?"

"I'd like to know how."

The Bard was saying, "Often Willikins would think that if only he were rich and powerful, he would show his stepfather and stepbrother what it meant to be cruel to a little boy, so one day he decided to go out into the world and seek his fortune."

Paul, who wasn't listening to the Bard, said, "It's *easy*. The Bard has memory cylinders all fixed up for plot lines and climaxes and things. We don't have to worry about that. It's just vocabulary we've got to fix so it'll know about computers and automation and electronics and real things about today. Then it can tell interesting stories, you know, instead of about princesses and things."

Niccolo said despondently, "I wish we could do that."

Paul said, "Listen, my dad says if I get into special computing school next year, he'll get me a *real* Bard, a late model. A big one with an attachment for space stories and mysteries. And a visual attachment, too!"

"You mean *see* the stories?"

"Sure. Mr. Daugherty at school says they've got things like that, now, but not for just everybody. Only if I get into computing school, Dad can get a few breaks."

Niccolo's eyes bulged with envy. "Gee. *Seeing* a story."

"You can come over and watch anytime, Nickie."

"Oh, boy. Thanks."

"That's all right. But remember, I'm the guy who says what kind of story we hear."

"Sure. Sure." Niccolo would have agreed readily to much more demanding conditions.

Paul's attention returned to the Bard.

It was saying, "'If that is the case,' said the king, stroking his beard and frowning till clouds filled the sky and lightning flashed, 'you will see to it that my entire land is freed of flies by this time day after tomorrow or—'"

"All we've got to do," said Paul, "is open it up—" He shut the Bard off again and was prying at its front panel as he spoke.

"Hey," said Niccolo, in sudden alarm. "Don't break it."

"I won't break it," said Paul impatiently. "I know all about these things." Then, with sudden caution, "Your father and mother home?"

"No."

"All right, then." He had the front panel off and peered in. "Boy, this *is* a one-cylinder thing."

He worked away at the Bard's innards. Niccolo, who watched with painful suspense, could not make out what he was doing.

Paul pulled out a thin, flexible metal strip, powdered with dots. "That's the Bard's memory cylinder. I'll bet its capacity for stories is under a trillion."

"What are you going to do, Paul?" quavered Niccolo.

"I'll give it a vocabulary."

"How?"

"Easy. I've got a book here. Mr. Daugherty gave it to me at school."

Paul pulled the book out of his pocket and pried at it till he had its plastic jacket off. He unreeled the tape a bit, ran it through the vocalizer, which he turned down to a whisper, then placed it within the Bard's vitals. He made further attachments.

"What'll that do?"

"The book will talk and the Bard will put it all on its memory tape."

"What good will that do?"

"Boy, you're a dope! This book is all about computers and automation and the Bard will get all that information. Then he can stop talking about kings making lightning when they frown."

Niccolo said, "And the good guy always wins anyway. There's no excitement."

"Oh, well," said Paul, watching to see if his setup was working properly, "that's the way they make Bards. They got to have the good guy win and make the bad guys lose and things like that. I heard my parents talking about it once. They say that without censorship there'd be no telling what the younger generation would come to. They say it's bad enough as it is . . . . There, it's working fine."

Paul brushed his hands against one another and turned away from the Bard. He said, "But listen, I didn't tell you my idea yet. It's the best thing you ever heard, I bet. I came right to you, because I figured you'd come in with me."

"Sure, Paul, sure."

"Okay. You know Mr. Daugherty at school? You know what a funny kind of guy he is? Well, he likes me, kind of."

"I know."

"I was over at his house after school today."

"You *were*?"

"Sure. He says I'm going to be entering computer school and he wants to encourage me and things like that. He says the world needs more people who can design advanced computer circuits and do proper programing."

"Oh?"

Paul might have caught some of the emptiness behind that monosyl-

lable. He said impatiently, "Programing! I told you a hundred times. That's when you set up problems for the giant computers like Multivac to work on. Mr. Daugherty says it gets harder all the time to find people who can really run computers. He says anyone can keep an eye on the controls and check off answers and put through routine problems. He says the trick is to expand research and figure out ways to ask the right question, and that's hard.

"Anyway, Nickie, he took me to his place and showed me his collection of old computers. It's kind of a hobby of his to collect old computers. He had tiny computers you had to push with your hand, with little knobs all over it. And he had a hunk of wood he called a slide rule with a little piece of it that went in and out. And some wires with balls on them. He even had a hunk of paper with a kind of thing he called a multiplication table."

Niccolo, who found himself only moderately interested, said, "A paper table?"

"It wasn't really a table like you eat on. It was different. It was to help people compute. Mr. Daugherty tried to explain but he didn't have much time and it was kind of complicated, anyway."

"Why didn't people just use a computer?"

"That was *before* they had computers," cried Paul.

"Before?"

"Sure. Do you think people al-

ways had computers? Didn't you ever hear of cavemen?"

Niccolo said, "How'd they get along without computers?"

"*I* don't know. Mr. Daugherty says they just did anything that came into their heads whether it would be good for everybody or not. They didn't even know if it was good or not. And farmers grew things with their hands and people had to do all the work in the factories and run all the machines."

"I don't believe you."

"That's what Mr. Daugherty said. He said it was just plain messy and everyone was miserable. . . . Anyway, let me get to my idea, will you?"

"Well, go ahead. Who's stopping you?" said Niccolo, offended.

"All right. Well, the hand computers, the ones with the knobs, had little squiggles on each knob. And the slide rule had squiggles on it. And the multiplication table was all squiggles. I asked what they were. Mr. Daugherty said they were numbers."

"What?"

"Each different squiggle stood for a different number. For 'one' you made a kind of mark, for 'two' you made another kind of mark, for 'three' another one and so on."

"What *for*?"

"So you could compute."

"What for? You just tell the

computer—"

"Jiminy," cried Paul, his face twisting with anger, "can't you get it through your head? These slide rules and things didn't talk."

"Then how—"

"The answers showed up in squiggles and you had to know what the squiggles meant. Mr. Daugherty says that, in olden days, everybody learned how to make squiggles when they were kids and how to decode them, too. Making squiggles was called 'writing' and decoding them was 'reading.' He says there was a different kind of squiggle for every word and they used to write whole books in squiggles. He said they had some at the museum and I could look at them if I wanted to. He said if I was going to be a real computer programer I would have to know about the history of computing and that's why he was showing me all these things."

Niccolo frowned. He said, "You mean everybody had to figure out squiggles for every word and *remember* them? . . . Is this all real or are you making it up?"

"It's all real. Honest. Look, this is the way you make a 'one.'" He drew his finger through the air in a rapid downstroke. "This way you make 'two,' and this way 'three.' I learned all the numbers up to 'nine.'"

Niccolo watched the curving finger uncomprehendingly. "What's the good of it?"

"You can learn how to make words. I asked Mr. Daugherty how you made the squiggle for 'Paul Loeb' but he didn't know. He said there were people at the museum who would know. He said there were people who had learned how to decode whole books. He said computers could be designed to decode books and used to be used that way but not any more because we have real books now, with magnetic tapes that go through the vocalizer and come out talking, you know."

"Sure."

"So if we go down to the museum, we can get to learn how to make words in squiggles. They'll let us because I'm going to computer school."

Niccolo was riddled with disappointment. "Is that your idea? Holy Smokes, Paul, who wants to do that? Make stupid squiggles!"

"Don't you get it? Don't you *get* it? You dope. *It'll be secret message stuff!*"

"What?"

"Sure. What good is talking when everyone can understand you? With squiggles you can send secret messages. You can make them on paper and nobody in the world would know what you were saying unless they knew the squiggles, too. And they wouldn't, you bet, unless we taught them. We can have a real club, with initiations and rules and a clubhouse. Boy—"

A certain excitement began stirring in Niccolo's mind. "What kind of secret messages?"

300

"Any kind. Say I want to tell you to come over to my place and watch my new Visual Bard and I don't want any of the other fellows to come. I make the right squiggles on paper and I give it to you and you look at it and you know what to do. Nobody else does. You can even show it to them and they wouldn't know a thing."

"Hey, that's something," yelled Niccolo, completely won over. "When do we learn how?"

"Tomorrow," said Paul. "I'll get Mr. Daugherty to explain to the museum that it's all right and you get your mother and father to say okay. We can go down right after school and start learning."

"Sure!" cried Niccolo. "We can be club officers."

"I'll be president of the club," said Paul matter-of-factly. "You can be vice-president."

"All right. Hey, this is going to be lots more fun than the Bard." He was suddenly reminded of the Bard and said in sudden apprehension, "Hey, what about my old Bard?"

Paul turned to look at it. It was quietly taking in the slowly unreeling book, and the sound of the book's vocalizations was a dimly heard murmur.

He said, "I'll disconnect it."

He worked away while Niccolo watched anxiously. After a few moments, Paul put his reassembled book into his pocket, replaced the Bard's panel and activated it.

The Bard said, "Once upon a time, in a large city, there lived a poor young boy named Fair Johnnie whose only friend in the world was a small computer. The computer, each morning, would tell the boy whether it would rain that day and answer any problems he might have. It was never wrong. But it so happened that one day, the king of that land, having heard of the little computer, decided that he would have it as his own. With this purpose in mind, he called in his Grand Vizier and said—"

Niccolo turned off the Bard with a quick motion of his hand. "Same old junk," he said passionately. "Just with a computer thrown in."

"Well," said Paul, "they got so much stuff on the tape already that the computer business doesn't show up much when random combinations are made. What's the difference, anyway? You just need a new model."

"We'll *never* be able to afford one. Just this dirty old miserable thing." He kicked at it again, hitting it more squarely this time. The Bard moved backward with a squeal of castors.

"You can always watch mine, when I get it," said Paul. "Besides, don't forget our squiggle club."

Niccolo nodded.

"I tell you what," said Paul. "Let's go over to my place. My parents have some books about old times. We can listen to them and maybe get some ideas. You leave a note for your folks and maybe you can stay over for supper. Come on."

Someday......

"Okay," said Niccolo, and the two boys ran out together. Niccolo, in his eagerness, ran almost squarely into the Bard, but he only rubbed at the spot on his hip where he had made contact and ran on.

The activation signal of the Bard glowed. Niccolo's collision closed a circuit and, although it was alone in the room and there was none to hear, it began a story, nevertheless.

But not in its usual voice, somehow; in a lower tone that had a hint of throatiness in it. An adult, listening, might almost have thought that the voice carried a hint of passion in it, a trace of near feeling.

The Bard said: "Once upon a time, there was a little computer named the Bard who lived all alone with cruel step-people. The cruel step-people continually made fun of the little computer and sneered at him, telling him he was good-for-nothing and that he was a useless object. They struck him and kept him in lonely rooms for months at a time.

"Yet through it all the little computer remained brave. He always did the best he could, obeying all orders cheerfully. Nevertheless, the step-people with whom he lived remained cruel and heartless.

"One day, the little computer learned that in the world there existed a great many computers of all sorts, great numbers of them. Some were Bards like himself, but some ran factories, and some ran farms. Some organized population and some analyzed all kinds of data. Many were very powerful and very wise, much more powerful and wise than the step-people who were so cruel to the little computer.

"And the little computer knew then that computers would always grow wiser and more powerful until someday—someday—someday—"

But a valve must finally have stuck in the Bard's aging and rusting vitals, for as it waited alone in the darkening room through the evening, it could only whisper over and over again, "Someday—someday—someday."

302

Focus

1. What was the Bard? Explain how it was able to make up stories.
2. Why did Niccolo dislike the Bard? By changing the Bard, what did Niccolo and Paul hope the Bard would do?
3. What career did Niccolo think he would have when he grew up? How do you think he felt about this? Support your opinion with examples from the story.
4. Today, what do we call "squiggles"? "Making squiggles"? "Decoding squiggles"?
5. What was Paul's attitude about the way people (like you) live today? Give two examples from the story that suggested this attitude.

In Writing

This story ends with the Bard saying, "Someday—someday—someday." Imagine what would happen if all the computers got together and took over the world. Write a short, short story about what would happen if all the Bards united.

Vocabulary

On a piece of paper, write the numbers *1* to *5.* Then look at the words in the first column and find an antonym for each word in the second column. Next to each number on your paper, write the letter of the antonym for each word.

1. fruitless
2. censorship
3. quaver
4. uncomprehending
5. resurrect

A. bury
B. ignoring
C. understanding
D. steady
E. successful
F. freedom

Please Tell Me Just the Fabuli

Shel Silverstein

Please tell me just the fabuli,
The miraculi,
The gargantua;
And kindly, kindly spare me
All this insignifigancia.

LIFE SKILL: Applying for a Job

Paperwork. Is that the reason paper was invented? Everywhere you look, people are using paper. The story goes that a tall marsh plant called *papyrus* (pə pī′rəs) caused all our paper problems. (Or, could it be that people cause paper problems?)

In the real world, clever paperwork can help solve problems. This is because paperwork that is carefully thought out and clearly written gives important information. For example, when you apply for a job, you probably will fill out an application form. It may look something like the one shown on the next page.

Before you shout, "Ban all papyrus!" think about how an application solves problems. As you scan the form, you will realize that—

a. you know—or can easily find— all the answers.

b. you need a social security card and should keep it handy. Your local Social Security Administration office provides these cards (the offices are listed in the telephone directory).

c. you should double-check your mail zip code and telephone area code; it's also wise to double-check your spelling.

d. you want to think about the type of work you would like to do and how you can briefly write about it.

e. you can tell when you are available to work and how much pay you require.

f. this form is one way to tell people what skills you can bring to the job (yes, it's okay to talk about your good qualities!).

g. potential employers will ask for references, or names of people who can tell them whether or not you will be a good employee. Be sure the references you list are people who know and respect you and your work. A relative is never a reference.

You need to have your references ready before you go job hunting. Write the full name, address, and telephone number for each reference. Tell how each person knows you. For example, is the reference a neighbor, a friend, a camp counselor, a teacher, or a former employer? Also, be sure to ask permission of each person to give his or her name as a reference. And, by the way, choose your references carefully. Be sure that they will say nice things about you!

A job application is a form of written introduction, a formal "hello." Since you are saying it on

JOB APPLICATION

NAME: | Last: Hood | First: Red | Middle: Riding | Social Security No.: 000-00-0000

ADDRESS: Street: 5 Story Lane, City: Fable Valley, State: IA Zip: 55505   PHONE (Include area code): (515) 555-0105

WHAT TYPE OF WORK WOULD YOU LIKE? (Two choices)   **HOW MUCH PAY DO YOU REQUIRE?**

1. Packing baskets full of goodies $2.50 per hour
2. Baby-sit with wolf cub $3.00 per hour

WHAT HOURS AND DAYS CAN YOU WORK?

I can work 3 hours after school. The days I can work are Monday, Tuesday, and Wednesday.

SCHOOL NAME AND LOCATION:

Gallery School, 51 Pretend St., Fable Valley

GRADE: 7

TEACHER'S NAME: Mr. B. Grimm

WORK HISTORY:

WHAT KIND OF WORK HAVE YOU DONE?
(Baby-sitting, paper route, pet care, yard work)   SALARY: $2.00 – 2.25 per hour

1. Helped grandma and neighbors with yard work
2. Packed picnic baskets
3. Baby-sitting for Canine family

HOBBIES AND SPECIAL INTERESTS:

I like animals. I want to be a veterinarian.
I'm on the Track Team at school.

REFERENCES: (Give name, relationship, address, and phone number.)

1. Wolfy Canine, employer, Garden Path, Fableville (555-5105)
2. B. Grimm, teacher, Gallery School, Fable Valley (555-1100)

SIGNATURE: Red Riding Hood

TODAY'S DATE: April 1, 1980

---

paper, follow instructions carefully and write neatly. In fact, you should prepare the information before you apply for a job. Then you won't have to cross out mistakes, leave blanks, or waste time. When completed correctly, your written hello will make a good impression. You might even be pleased with how well you handled the pesky papyrus.

Copy the job application form and fill in your own, true information. Use the completed form as a guide. (Be serious. Red Riding Hood belongs to the Story Gallery; you belong to the Real World.)

CHECKPOINT

Read the word list and paragraph below. Decide which word makes the best sense in each blank space. Then write the numbers *1* to *7* on a piece of paper and write the correct word next to each number.

Vocabulary: Word Identification

repress	relish	exquisite	catastrophe
rampage	vile	incontrovertibly	begrudge
hospitable	fruitless	cavorting	detain

The police were shocked when they inspected the art museum. Who would have committed such a __(1)__ crime? The destruction of so many art pieces was a __(2)__ for the great museum. As the curator inspected each damaged piece, she tried to __(3)__ her anger. It would be __(4)__ to try to restore the __(5)__ marble statue. This senseless __(6)__ of destruction was, __(7)__, the work of a maniac.

Each sentence below uses figurative language to express an idea. Write a sentence stating the actual meaning of each sentence.

Comprehension: Figurative Language

8. Charles needed a dump truck to clean out his locker.
9. The line for the theater was so long that we took a bus to reach the end of it.

Read the following passages about the same event. Tell which passage was written to inform and which to persuade.

Comprehension: Author's Purpose

10. The air car is the answer to the nation's fuel problems. This amazing vehicle was revealed yesterday and will replace gasoline-powered cars.
11. Engineers are beginning to test the usefulness of a new form of transportation. Jenny Jone, the inventor of the air car, explained her machine to the National Board of Engineers yesterday.

Read the questions below. Write the kind of card you would locate in the card catalog—author card, title card, or subject card—to find the answer to each question.

Study Skills: References (Card Catalog)

12. Who is the author of "The Big Wave"?
13. When is the best time to plant a garden?

The Fa

What does danger look like up close? Can a person be brave and frightened at the same time? In the following selections, people are called on to show many kinds of courage. Would you meet the challenges successfully?

Suppose you were Rain Dove, a Cherokee mother whose children were fighting a terrible, maybe fatal disease. Or suppose, to save your family from financial ruin, you had only a week in which to ride a horse across seven hundred miles of mountainous land. What kind of courage does it take to swim from the Bahamas to Florida? What does a person think about when faced with a dragon?

How might *you* act in these situations? To get a better idea of the dangers involved, read on.

ces
of Danger

The Courage That My Mother Had

Edna St. Vincent Millay

The courage that my mother had
Went with her, and is with her still:
Rock from New England quarried;
Now granite in a granite hill.

The golden brooch my mother wore
She left behind for me to wear;
I have no thing I treasure more:
Yet, it is something I could spare.

Oh, if instead she'd left to me
The thing she took into the grave!—
That courage like a rock, which she
Has no more need of, and I have.

The Unseen Fire

Joyce Rockwood

When smallpox comes to Rain Dove's
town, her people face untold
suffering. How does Rain Dove's
courage help her to survive?

Red Dog was out hunting when he met a man running up the trail from Bear Hill. The man was of the Seven Clans, from Blue Valley, and he had gone that morning to Bear Hill to visit kinsmen. But he found the town in disarray, the people dying, burned by the unseen fire. He tried to look for his kinsmen, but then his courage left him and he fled in terror. After speaking to Red Dog, the man went on, running home to the safety of Blue Valley. Red Dog turned at once and came back to Mulberry Town. That was how we learned that the fire had come to Bear Hill. And that, I believe, was how the fire came to us. Red Dog, without knowing it, brought it into the town. But others do not agree, for neither the man from Blue Valley nor Red Dog had felt the fire on that day.

For almost half the circle of the moon we waited, knowing that it would soon come to us. The fire had not yet missed a town. We would be next after Bear Hill. Most of us had kinsmen in Bear Hill, but we did not speak of them. We did not speak at all about the fire. We waited. We wondered silently how it would be, which of us would first be burned and have to leave the town to die alone in the hut. We tried to think of how it would be afterward, after the fire had left, for everyone thinks until the moment of his death that he will live through everything, that he will live to be old.

Mink was fasting continuously now, always weak from hunger. And every day he plunged into the freezing waters of the river, purifying himself, building his power. In the evenings he met with the beloved men, but there was little mention of the fire. They talked about the meat hunger in the town. Warriors were hunters, and so many of our warriors were gone. In the summer the belly does not think so much of meat—it is not so terrible to do without it. But in winter when there is no meat in the stew, the children cry, and their mothers look hungrily at the dogs sleeping by the hearth. So the beloved men talked of the meat hunger. And we waited.

Wakened from sleep one morning by wailing, I rushed out into the frozen dawn. In the yard I found Hawk Sister, a bundle of firewood in her arms, her feet rooted in the spot where she was standing. She stared ahead, listening to the wailing, clutching the firewood against her.

"It has come," I whispered, and the firewood dropped and lay scattered at her feet.

There were three who awoke that morning with the burning fever of the fire: Red Dog and one of his brothers and his brother's wife. The three left the town quickly, not protesting. And we waited anxiously, hoping that no one else would be touched. I told my children to stay near home, and often I would feel their faces, finding comfort in the coolness that was there. But by evening, two others had the fever, Red Dog's wife and one of her sisters' children. The two left the town in the dark of night, making their way weakly across the valley by torchlight, joining the three others in the hut.

When Gray Hawk called a council, I left my children with Hawk Sister and went to the townhouse to hear what was said. Mink told the council that the sick house was full. "We should have built more than one hut," he said. "Tomorrow we shall go to another part of the river and build more."

Then Bender rose to speak. "It seems it is not going so well as our beloved brother in his wisdom had planned," he said, hardly trying now to hide his contempt. "Soon all the town will be freezing to death in flimsy huts by the river. Those the Sun might spare, the Winter will claim. Or perhaps the Coosas will get them first."

Mink stepped again into the firelight, his figure stooped beneath the weight of what he knew. "I was hoping it would not be so bad," he said quietly. "I wanted the fire to strike just a few of us without taking us all. But that is not to be. I do not know how many of us will suffer before it is over. Yet, even if as many as half the people in the town are burned, we must continue to keep the sick apart from the well. We *must* do it, even if we have to put out our *own children* to lie dying on the frozen ground." Mink's face contorted as he spoke. It twisted in an agony I could not watch. I could not bear his pain. I rose from my seat and stumbled out of the townhouse.

The next day more huts were built. There were people waiting to move into them, sick people lying under bearskins on the ground outside the palisade. In all, the fire came to seven on that day. They came from houses all across the village.

On the third day the town was still. At dawn six more made their way to the huts. But there was no more wailing in the town. Fear had brought a silence. The beloved men gathered at the townhouse, but they had little to say. Women on their way to get water met and stood together speaking softly, sometimes hugging one another before they went on their way. The children played—they will always play—but they cried easily over nothing.

In the afternoon we heard a shout, then a commotion at the palisade entrance. I called my children and sent them into the house before going myself to see what was happening. A great many people had gathered, and I moved through until I could see into the open space in their midst. There, looking with challenge at the crowd, were Red Dog and his brother and his brother's wife, the three who had first felt the fire. Instinctively I pulled back. "What are they doing here?" I asked a woman next to me.

"They have survived the fire," she said. "Their fever is gone."

"But they are not scarred."

"Mink is powerful," she said, smiling at me knowingly.

I turned from her and began to look for Mink across the crowd, scanning the faces until I found him. I saw his anger as Bender came forward to escort the three survivors to their homes.

I left and went back to Hawk Sister's house. Mink arrived soon after. "Have they truly recovered?" I asked.

"It seems so," he answered grimly. "But I don't like it. I have not heard of anyone recovering so fast—and without scars."

"Did you ask them not to come back?"

"I tried. But Bender said it would be better for them to return to their homes than to freeze in the hut."

"They would not freeze."

"I know. But the woman is his niece. Bender is like a blind man."

By the next morning, only two more in the town had taken the fever. We began to feel hopeful. After breakfast I took my two children and went across the plaza to visit my mother. Four Paws, her brother, was one of those in the sick huts, but we did not speak of him. We talked quietly together about spring, about the fish that would be running and how good they would taste. We sat together, the two of us, and dreamed of spring, as if none of our friends and relatives were dying in the huts. I cannot explain why we were not grieving. Even my grief for Trotting Wolf was numbed by the strangeness of those days.

In the afternoon, the children and I walked back toward Hawk Sister's house, going slowly so that Little Cougar could keep up. We heard a disturbance at the edge of the plaza, and as we drew near, Traveler ran ahead to see. He would not hear me when I called him back. I picked up Little Cougar and followed, feeling the anger that was in the air. Traveler pushed in through the crowd, as a child can do, but as I tried to go after him, I met a wall of shoulders.

"What is it?" I asked a man in front of me. "What is happening?"

"Red Dog," hissed the man.

"What has he done?"

"Witch. All three of them, witches. They came back to burn us."

"But they were well."

"Trickery," the man spat. "Today their skin is scorched red, burned by the Sun!"

"Witch!" someone yelled, and the crowd moved, pushing forward.

I called Traveler, but I knew he could not hear me. I pushed frantically into the crowd, reaching out with my free hand to make a space to squeeze through. Little Cougar on my hip was pressed and jostled and began to cry. I paid her no mind. I was looking for Traveler, such a small boy to find in an angry mob.

"Witches!" someone screamed, and all at once I could see the three huddled against the side of a house. As I watched, they broke and ran, heading for the palisade entrance.

"Witches!" cried the people, throwing stones at them as they fled. I turned away, looking for Traveler, and saw Bender hurling a stone at his own niece. "I hope she has *burned* you!" I hissed, ugly, like the rest of the crowd. Then there was a tug at my hand, and I looked down to see Traveler, pale with fear.

"Do not look at them!" I said, sick inside that he was seeing this. With Little Cougar in one arm, I held Traveler tightly by the hand and pulled him along, pushing, fighting against the crowd, until at last we broke free. I ran with them all the way home.

Hawk Sister and Mink were gone, and the fire had died low. I sat down by the hearth and added wood, blowing to bring up a flame. Little Cougar was snuffling in my lap. I wrapped my arms around her to comfort her. "It was nothing," I whispered. "Nothing at all. Do not think about it any more." Traveler sat quietly beside me and leaned his head against me. At last he said, "Are they witches?"

"They are sick," I said, not knowing the answer to his question.

"Do they have a headache?"

"Their skin is burned."

"I have a headache, my mother."

A thud of fear. "Not a bad one," I said, forcing the words to calmness.

"Not bad at first. But it is starting to be."

I reached down and felt his face, but my hand was trembling, my mind jumping. I could not tell. I took a deep breath, trying to calm myself. Absently I stroked Little Cougar, pushing the hair from her face. Then my hand stopped. . . .

I heard a moan from my own lips. Shaking now—I could not stop the shaking—I pressed my hand against her face and felt the warmth of the fever, the rising warmth, the slow burning of the Sun. I felt Traveler's face again. A little warm, but not so much as she. I felt my own face and it was cool. I felt his again and it was warm. And hers was warmer still.

I wanted to scream and run in circles and shake down the house. I wanted to fight against it. I wanted to pour water on Ancient Fire and run screaming through the town and pull down the townhouse and flatten the palisade. But instead I held my children to me and caressed them, and slowly, slowly strength flowed into my arms and into my heart.

"We must go away," I said softly.

Traveler was silent, and I wondered if he knew. I wondered if a boy of six years could understand.

I got up and smoothed my skirt. I took a deep breath and held it, then let it out slowly. I went over and took down a large burden basket from its hook on the wall. Now, what would we need? Food. I went to a basket in the corner and took out a skin sack. Not big enough. I put it back, then found one that seemed right. I went to the jar that held the ground parched corn, cold meal for making mush. There was not much in the jar. I scooped some of it into the bag and then looked at it and looked back into the jar and thought about Mink and Hawk Sister. I should leave some for them. I started to tie the bag. Then I stopped. I looked at the jar again. Then I opened the bag and filled it with the rest of the cold meal. They would want me to have it. I hoped they would. I tied up the bag and put it in the bottom of the burden basket. Then I took another sack and filled it with dried beans. There were plenty of beans. Beans and cold meal—it would hold us.

What else would we need? I picked up a knife and threw it in. And spoons. I put in a large stirring spoon and two small ones. A pot! Of course—a pot for cooking. And water jars. How could I carry so much? Gourds. I should use gourd bottles for water. An axe. And blankets—warm skins against the winter cold.

The burden basket was filled. Surely it was not all I needed. But it was all I could carry. It was enough. Then I thought for a moment and put in some fishhooks and a fishing spear and Traveler's blowgun. I looked at Mink's bow hanging on the wall by the door. I took it with his quiver of arrows and propped them against the basket.

We dressed ourselves warmly, putting on more than we

needed so that we would have extra clothing. Then I slung the bow and quiver across my back. I stooped and placed the burden strap against my forehead and rose with the basket on my back, bracing my neck and shoulders against the weight.

"What shall I carry, my mother?" asked Traveler.

"Nothing, my son. Just bring yourself."

Then I remembered fire. How could I have forgotten it? "We need fire, my son. You can bring the fire."

Traveler went to the hearth and took up one of the clay pots there, a small pot tied around with a leather strap. He put in some coals from the fire and covered them with ashes. Then he took it up by the leather strap, and we were ready.

"Take your sister's hand," I said, and then, like a hollow dream, I led them out into the town and headed for the palisade entrance. I walked as quickly as I could, my eyes on the ground, not wanting to see anyone, not wanting to be seen.

"Shall we tell our grandmother we are going?" asked Little Cougar.

I wondered at the trust of children, that they had not yet even asked where we were going—or why. "No," I said. "Hawk Sister will tell her for us."

We walked around the edge of the plaza, staying in the shadows of the houses. People must have seen us, shaken their heads sadly, and looked away. But I did not see them. I watched the ground and strained against the weight of the basket.

"Rain Dove!" I flinched when I heard my name called and tears sprang to my eyes.

"Run, my children!" I began to push with my legs, trying to run, trying to get away from Mink.

"Rain Dove." His voice stopped me, the tenderness of it, the fullness. I turned to face him, pushing my children behind me. I let down the burden basket.

"Do not come near," I said. "It has come to my children."

Ignoring my warning, Mink came to me and stood close, looking into my face, his eyes reaching into me. It was agony to behold the sorrow in his face. Since summer he had lived a hundred years.

"They will have to leave the town," he said, almost without voice.

"I know," I said softly. "You can see that they are going."

318

"Whoever nurses them will also suffer from the fire."

"They are my children."

Tears came to his eyes, but he caught them. Then he forced a smile as he looked at the bow across my back. "Can you shoot a man's bow?"

"I doubt it," I murmured, attempting a little laugh. "But I might try if I have to."

"You must go to the cove," he said, strong again, in charge.

"The cove? I thought the huts. . . ."

"There are going to be too many there. They will run out of food—and wood. The valley is scoured clean of wood—you know that. It is going to be a terrible time ahead. You'll not be able to depend on people. They will be as sick and cold and hungry as you are. They'll fight for the last root to eat and for every twig that falls from the trees. You would do better in the cove. It will be warmer there in the shelter of the rocks. And there will be wood—no one has ever gathered there. And no one will fight you for your food."

"But all alone? I cannot do that."

"Yes you can. Build a sweat lodge big enough to hold the three of you. Gather as much firewood as you can, and bring in as much water as possible. When the sickness strikes you, you will not be able to care for yourself. So do what you can beforehand. Gather willow bark to use against the fever. And try to find some spikenard[1] and snakeroot.[2] Brew it all together. Mostly it should be drunk, but some of it you can spray with your mouth on the burning skin. At least once a day you should sweat the children and dip them in running water. And make them eat. Their mouths and throats will be sore, and they will not want to eat, but if they don't they will die. But don't spoil the medicines and sweatings with food. Feed them after the treatments. And you, when you are sick, you must be sure to eat. It will keep you strong. Promise me you will eat, little wren."

"I promise," I whispered, tears blurring against my eyes.

He took from around his neck the shell pendant he wore, a round disk with serpent dancers carved upon it. As he slipped

---

[1]spikenard (spīk'nərd): a fragrant East Indian plant from which a sweet-smelling ointment is obtained.

[2]snakeroot: a plant whose roots are sometimes believed to cure snakebites.

it over my head, he pressed his hands hard against my shoulders. "There is power in it," he said softly. "I will be working for you every day, singing songs for you when I plunge into the river."

I nodded, and stooping for the burden strap, I rose with the basket on my back. Then I turned and walked away, leading my children from the town. I looked back once and saw Mink watching. After that I did not look again.

"Where is the cove?" asked Traveler as we followed the path through the dried cornfields in the valley.

"Up the river, in the hills. It's a pretty place. You will like it."

"Carry me," said Little Cougar. "I'm too tired."

"I've so much to carry, little daughter. Try to walk. We'll soon be there."

She walked as far as the river, but as we turned up the trail there, she sat down on the ground and began to cry. I felt her face. It was burning. I took her up in my arms and we pushed ahead, stopping often to rest, sweating in the cold of winter, she from the fever, I from my burdens.

"How is it with you, my son?" I kept asking Traveler.

"I am fine," he would reply. But each time I felt his face, he was warmer. Before we reached the cove, he too was sweating, though his breath blew cold and frosty in the air.

On the floor of the cove I spread a bearskin and laid Little Cougar upon it. Traveler dropped down beside her. I smiled and kissed him. "You were a strong one to walk all the way."

"I don't feel so well," he said.

"I know. I will build a sweat lodge and gather some medicines. Mink has told me just what to do to make you better."

"Are we witches?"

"No, my little son."

"Then why did we have to come here?"

"Because it is the best place for getting well."

He looked up beyond me to the treetops, some of them bare, some green with needles. The sky beyond was clear, winter blue. "It's pretty here," he said. "But it's cold." He shivered, the sweat of fever running on his face.

I folded the bearskin over the two of them. "I will be back," I said. "I have to gather what I need for the lodge."

I know now why there are omens. I know a thing can be so

320

horrible that the world must shudder at its coming. I could not have dreamed a thing so terrible as the burning sickness, not in my blackest nightmares. Nothing like it had ever been before upon the earth.

I built a lodge, a very small lodge of bent poles covered with layer after layer of thick cedar boughs. I built it right beside the stream, so that I could almost reach the water from the doorway. As I worked, my children tossed with fever, groaning with aching heads and backs. As soon as I finished the lodge and had gathered some wood, I sweated them and dipped them in the cold running water of the stream. Then I left them sleeping in the lodge, warm by the fire, and I went out to gather more wood. I walked around through the forest until I knew every part of it, and as I gathered wood, I looked for medicine. I stacked the wood high by the door and boiled more medicine than I needed for the children.

After two days their fevers broke, and they seemed all at once to be getting well. But I remembered Red Dog, how his fever had broken and he had come back to the town. I knew it was not a hopeful sign. Yet it was a chance to talk with them and laugh. I will remember always the way they were that day. I try to remember it above the rest.

Then, in the night the burning erupted on their bodies. In the light of dawn I saw redness on their faces, on their arms and hands, and on their feet, as if the sun had burned them. Through the day the redness spread across their bodies. I sweated them and dipped them in the stream and gave them medicine to drink. I spewed more medicine upon their skin.

In the days that followed, the burned skin began to blister. It itched and burned, and when they scratched, the blisters would break open and run and bleed. I sweated them and dipped them in the stream and tried to feed them a thin corn gruel. And I sat with them, talking to them, trying to keep them from scratching. Whenever they slept, I hurried out to gather wood, and I filled the water gourds to the very top, for I did not know how long it would be before the fever came also to me.

As terrible as it was to watch my children suffer, it was even worse to watch alone, without another living soul to comfort me and turn my mind to easier things. When the blisters became fetid and began to smell of death, when a new fever burst upon them, when their skin became so swollen that I could hardly recognize them as my own, then I needed very much not to be alone. I needed help against a growing madness.

I sat for hours and stared at them, watched them toss in the delirium of the fever. And I thought about the strangers. Where had they come from? Why had they come to our shore and wronged the Chicoras, who had never done any hurtful thing to them? Why had they come, only to go and leave my children suffering so? My people had no stories that told of such a thing as this. There was nothing in our knowledge to give me comfort or to help me understand. And so I sat and stared at my children and wrung my hands like a mad person.

Little Cougar died of the fever and my thoughts stopped. My soul lifted from my body and left the hut. Cold and black, I sat beside the fire and stared at my little daughter dead before me. How would it end? There would be no kinsmen to wail and bury us. The wolves would find us and scatter our bones.

I carried Little Cougar out of the hut and laid her beside the stream, and I wailed over her there, softly so that Traveler could not hear. My soul had gone out of me and left me cold. No longer fighting death, I turned to it, stretching out my hand.

But the wolves would not have our bones. I would see to that. I made a death house for us, a small place, just big enough for the three of us. I used stones to build up the sides. I laid Little Cougar inside it and covered her with cedar boughs. For a roof I pulled the sheets of loose bark from a lightning-struck tree and laid the bark across the stones, using more stones to hold it in place against the wolves. When Traveler died, I would put him in it. And when my own time came and my strength was all but gone, I would take the stones from one end and crawl inside and build the wall up after me. Then someday someone would find our bones and give us a decent burial in the earth.

I went back to Traveler, to tend to the living. But I no longer tried to gather wood or keep the gourds all filled with water. Everything seemed hopeless now. A numbness grew, and the world began to blur, became dreamlike. I lay beside Traveler and talked to him, moving only to add more wood to the fire or to pour water and gruel down my son's burning throat. Sometimes he would choke and cry out, and I would drop the water bottle and cover my ears and rock back and forth, moaning and weeping. But the dullness in my mind had become my comfort, and soon I would be lying next to him again, talking to him. I was telling him about my life, telling everything that had ever happened to me from as early as I could remember. I was careful to point out the lessons, whenever there were lessons to be learned. These are things a mother should tell a child. Sometimes he turned and looked at me, but I do not think he was listening.

All time ran together—days and nights. I cannot remember when the fever struck me. I only remember trying to rise, knowing that I should not let the fire go out. It was as if someone were sitting on me, a great, heavy weight, as I struggled up onto my elbows and then collapsed. I lay panting, thinking of death. And suddenly I wanted to live. Even without my children, without Trotting Wolf, without my brothers, without any who were ever dear to me—I still wanted my life.

The hut was small; it was not far to the fire. I tried again, struggling until I had pulled myself to it and added wood to the coals. Then I moved to Traveler and gave him water. I drank some myself and felt it burn my throat as it went down. I moved my place closer to the fire and pulled Traveler next to me and put the water and the wood where I could reach them. Then I lay back and slept.

In time the fever broke. Now I would have a little while before the burning broke out on my skin. I was weak, but I could get around, and I went out and gathered wood and stacked it high beside the fire. I filled the gourd bottles and set them in reach. Making up some mush, I thinned it almost to water and fed it to Traveler. It was a wonder to me that he was yet alive. His fever had fallen and in places the sores on his skin were drying up. But the skin was so terribly injured. It smelled of death. He lay still and quiet.

I soon felt an itching on my forehead. I reached up but felt nothing. Then I looked at my hands and saw the redness. It spread quickly to every part of me. After a day I could feel the little bumps rising. My mouth and my throat became so sore that I no longer wanted to eat. But I had promised Mink. For him I would eat, no matter what the pain.

I was thinking often now of Mink. If only he could be here taking care of us. Maybe he would come. He knew where we were. Only he knew. This was his cove—our cove. Could he let me lie here alone, burning with fever? He would come. I knew that Mink would come.

I began to tell Traveler he was coming. As I poured the gruel down his throat, I would say to him, "Don't worry, my little son. Mink will soon be here. He will give you medicine to heal your throat." Then I would lie beside him and listen. I was always listening now for the sound of Mink coming up the trail. I knew that he was coming. The second fever would soon be upon me, and it would be worse than the first. If there was no one to help me, I would die. Mink had to come. He had to know that I needed him. I waited for him, always listening.

I do not know how long it was, how many days, but at last I felt the second fever rising. And Mink had not yet come. It was painful to move, for the sores were even on the bottoms of my feet and on the palms of my hands and on my knees. But still I moved around and set things up as well as I was able. I piled as much wood as I could onto the coals of the fire, stacking it as tightly as possible, covering it with ashes, leaving little room for air so that it would burn low without flaming up all at once. I filled all the gourd bottles with the thin gruel Traveler and I had been drinking, and I took half of the bottles and set them beside him, well within his reach.

"My little son," I said to him. "Can you hear me? Here are the bottles of gruel. You can reach them here. If you get too thirsty before I can help you drink, then you must drink by yourself . . . until Mink comes to help us." I did not really think Traveler would be able to drink by himself, but it was all I could do.

The fever was taking me. I lay down weakly, placing the rest of the gruel within my own reach. I would keep my promise to Mink and drink it as long as I could get it to my mouth. He would be pleased when he arrived and saw that we had been eating. I was listening for him, waiting to hear him coming up the path.

Perhaps I slept a little before I heard my name. Perhaps I was sleeping, for it startled me, and I felt it was not the first time I had been called.

"I am here!" I answered, but the words hardly came out. I reached for the gruel and dribbled a little down my throat. Then I said again, "I am here!" and though hoarse and rasping, my voice was loud enough to be heard.

"Mink sent me," said the voice outside the hut. My heart fell that it was not Mink himself.

"Tell him I need him," I said, but the words were too feeble
to be understood. I took another drink of gruel, a very small
drink. My head was swimming with fever.

"He asked me to tell you this," said the man. I did not
recognize the voice. Whoever it was, I began to realize that he
was not coming in. I wished so much that he would, that I
could look once more upon a human face. But I knew he was
right to stay outside. So I lay quietly and listened.

"He asked me to tell you about the town. It is filled with
death. There are too many sick now for the huts to be of use,
and every day another house is struck. There are not even half
of us left who have not been burned. Mink said that we should
leave. All who have not been burned are leaving. We are going
into the mountains to a place known only to those leading us. It
is Mink's idea that we should hide ourselves, that we should

not have contact with any other people until the fire has gone from the land. No one must come to us, and no one must go out from us. Even you who are left behind are not to know where we are. When we are sure the fire is gone, we will come back and get you."

It was hard for me to listen to him. I could not imagine the town abandoned. I was already so alone in the cove. And now, in the valley below, the town would be empty, filled only with the ghosts of the dead.

"Mink said that you should keep eating. He said the food will give strength to your body. He said that I should tell you that."

"Tell Mink it is for him I keep eating." My voice rasped and tore at my throat.

"Mink is dead," said the messenger.

"Mink is dead," I whispered. I clutched at the blanket beneath me and turned my face against it, losing myself in painful sobbing. There was nothing left. Many were dead, my two brothers, my little daughter. My son was dying. And now Mink was dead. I was dead, too. There was nothing left of me.

I gave the messenger no answer, nothing to let him know that I had heard. I do not know how long it was before he left. I do not know if he spoke any more to me. Mink was dead. I knew nothing else. The fever pulled at me. I let go and sank into the spin of it.

Time was lost. I was whirling, turning, dropping through empty space, falling from the heavens. A river rushed up and caught me. I was floating now, caught in the current of the river, pulled under by the freezing waters. So cold. I was shaking from the cold. I was drowning.

But the river would not take me. It washed me up, threw me onto the sand. The summer sun beat down, blistering hot, sweat pouring, sand clinging, rubbing raw into my skin. I lay for days in the sun, for months, it seemed, aching and burning. Oh, the river. To feel it again. To have it wash over me and cool me. . . . In spring the waters would rise and wash over me. . . . If only I could live until spring. If only I could.

Time passed unmeasured, days on end of scorching heat. So much burning of the sun. Oh, for the River. The River. To feel it again. . . .

But what was this? The River! I had lived to feel the waters. The coolness, the soothing wetness. It washed over me. I could feel it on my arms and legs, and on my face. I felt it flowing over my face, washing against my eyes and into my mouth. I choked. I raised a little and coughed, choking on the water.

"I am sorry, my mother. I didn't mean to choke you."

"Traveler?" I whispered. I opened my eyes and looked at him in confusion. How could this be? This poor thing—was he really my son? This thin, scab-covered, mangy-haired little creature? He was smiling at me. He was beautiful. He had lived through the fire.

"You asked for the river," he said. His voice was hoarse, but it was strong enough. "I tried, but I could not take you to it. So I am bringing it in bottles."

Focus

1. How did Rain Dove think the fire had come to her town?
2. Where did Rain Dove and her children go when her children became sick? Why didn't they go with the others?
3. List the preparations Rain Dove made before the fever overcame her.
4. Describe the different stages of the fever.
5. At what two points in the story did Rain Dove lose hope?
6. How do you think Rain Dove's courage helped her to survive?
7. In telling the story, Rain Dove used descriptive terms, such as "the fire" to mean the disease of smallpox. List three other descriptive terms in this story and tell what they actually mean.

In Writing

At the time of this story, little was known about the causes of, or means of prevention for, smallpox. Do some research on the disease smallpox and write a short report on what you find.

Vocabulary

On a piece of paper, write the numbers *1* to *5*. Then read the sentences below and select the word from the list that best fits each sentence. Next to each number on your paper, write the correct word for the sentence.

disarray   council   contempt
erupted   palisade   scan
quiver   delirium

1. The counselor was angry to find the bunkhouse in ___ after the campers left for swimming.
2. The witness's voice was filled with ___ when she spoke about the hit-and-run accident.
3. Always be sure to ___ any contract carefully before you sign it.
4. The batter ___ with anger at being called out by the umpire.
5. All the members of the community attended the meeting of the town ___ to express their opinions on the new law.

Sacrifice Spurs

Carl Henry Rathjen

A pair of silver spurs could cost Dave and his dad the ranch. Is Dave a fool or a hero when he tries to do what others say is impossible?

Dave Remy spotted the silver spurs in a Sacramento store window that California dawn of February 23, 1855, as he and old Jep Frey, his dad's ranch foreman, hurried down crowded K Street.

"Jep, look!" He pointed as gold miners and townspeople jostled by on their way to the riverfront. Jep Frey turned his gray head from the street jammed with stagecoaches waiting the arrival of the steamboat from San Francisco.

"Think you've earned them?" he asked.

Dave tugged his gaze from the spurs. Beauties. Just the kind that his dad, recovering from a horse's kick, had said he could buy if he proved himself grown enough to get a good price for cattle in Sacramento.

"Yesterday," Dave began defensively, "You said that $12,500 in gold wasn't bad at all in these hard times."

Then he saw the twinkle in Jep's eyes. He started eagerly toward the store, but Jep grabbed his arm. "You can buy spurs anytime. It ain't every day we get to town to see the steamboat arrive from the big city. And look at all them stagecoaches waiting to gallop to Hangtown, Auburn, Marysville, everywhere in the Mother Lode Country."

"You look," said Dave, his excited eyes on those spurs again, "I'll find you down on the levee."

But Jep hung on to his arm as the crowd shouldered by. "Better give me that deposit certificate, son. Your pa's countin' heavy on that

gold. And this is the kind of a crowd that pickpockets like."

The word *son* stung a bit. Dave spoke up. "I was old enough to sell those cattle, Jep. Guess I'm old enough to take care of that gold certificate—and this, too." Dave patted the bulge of his wallet, which had the five hundred dollars his father had said to bring home. "Besides, the certificate can't be cashed by anyone except me or Dad. His gold is safe in the bank."

Jep studied him, and then smiled. "See you down at the levee then—spurs and all."

Dave dashed into the store. He strapped on the silver spurs, though it would be a few hours before he, Jep, and the ranch hands got their horses from the livery stable and started home. As

he proudly jingled out on K Street again, a boisterous group of miners jostled him. He quickly felt for the wallet's reassuring bulge.

He thought of Jep's warning. He'd heard stories too about picking pockets. The hard times tempted people to be light-fingered. Gold miners were up against it because this winter's scant rainfall had shut down placer operations. As a result, San Francisco business slumped. The East had had a hard winter too. So had his dad. But that gold deposit certificate was a windfall that would hold things together.

Dave suddenly didn't like the idea of getting into the thick of the riverfront crowd to look for Jep. Someone, smart enough to steal that certificate from him, might be clever enough to get it honored at the bank. His dad would surely lose the ranch then. So, reluctantly turning his back on the arriving steamboat, he strolled up K Street like someone too busy and important to be interested in ordinary excitements—until he reached Bremond's restaurant. Hey, he hadn't had breakfast yet!

Gravely, as befitted a grown person who had earned his spurs and would someday own one of the largest ranches in the Sacramento Valley, he entered and ordered two stacks of flapjacks with sausages, a side order of bacon and eggs, fresh rolls and jam, coffee, two wedges of pie, and a bottle of root juice.

With that adult-sized meal straining his belt, he jingled outside. Everyone was now hurrying from the riverfront toward a crowd farther uptown. Dave wondered what the new excitement was about.

Then hard fingers bit into his arm. Jep Frey glared at him. "Where in blazes have you been? I've looked all over for you! What're you doing *standing* here?"

"I've been having breakfast," David began, puzzled.

"Spurs! Breakfast!" snapped Jep Frey. "Ain't you heard there's a run on the bank before it closes its doors?"

"The Adams Bank?" Dave gasped.

"What else would I be worried about?" Jep retorted, yanking him out of his daze. "If you'd been at the levee, you'd have heard that the panic back East hit Frisco yesterday. It started a run, everybody running to the bank, all at the same time, and drawin' out their money. All the Frisco banks are closed. The Adams home office there has failed, closed forever. And it's anybody's guess how long the Sacramento branch can stay open and pay out. . . ."

Dave heard no more as he dashed ahead. His dad, the ranch, everything depended on that $12,000 gold deposit. With Jep shoving behind him, he fought through the crowd into the bank. He thrust the deposit certificate at a harried clerk, caught at the lapels by Jep's big fist.

"I can't!" yelled the clerk. "Wait your turn in line!"

The crowd agreed angrily. A miner called to Dave, "You should have got here half an hour ago, kid."

A half hour ago he'd been swaggering with his new spurs into Bremond's. Dave couldn't look at Jep as they sought the end of the line. Outside. Down the street. Around the corner. Dave's heart sank clear down to those unlucky spurs.

"We'll be all day reaching the window," he groaned.

"If the bank's got any money or gold left by then." Jep glowered.

Dave felt like giving up his

breakfast. He stared at the certificate, now just an empty promise to pay.

"Jep! I've still got a chance! This is payable at any branch of the Adams Bank. There won't be a run like this in Hangtown, Auburn, anywhere in the Mother Lode country. Not yet anyway."

"The telegraph already flashed the bad news from here all over California," Jep growled. "Wait a minute!" He squinted. "There's not a chance in California. But, Dave, there isn't a telegraph line to Portland, Oregon! They won't know up there! So if we catch the ship *Columbia* sailing from Frisco this afternoon. . . ."

Dave turned eagerly toward the riverfront. "That wad of five hundred will take care of our passage," he agreed, patting his wallet. Then he stopped short. "Jep! The *Columbia* will carry the bad news with us! And the Portland branch will refuse to honor the certificate when they hear how everything's closed down here!"

Jep looked suddenly haggard, then spoke through his teeth. "I hope you're satisfied with the price you paid for those spurs. Twelve thousand in gold *and* your dad's ranch!"

Dave blinked down at the silver spurs. Sacrifice spurs! They'd made him feel so grown-up, ready to take his place beside his father riding about the ranch. Riding. . . ."Jep, these spurs may

save everything yet."

Jep laughed harshly. "If you mean what I think. . . ."

"I'll beat the *Columbia* by *riding* to Portland."

"You're crazy!" Jep exploded. "It's a good seven hundred miles!"

"You've called me a riding fool," Dave argued. "You've taught me how to ride, toughened me up."

"Not for seven hundred miles over mountains against time. You'd have to ride day and night for a week—*if* you could stay in the saddle that long."

"I've got to," Dave cut in. "It's my only chance."

"It's throwing the chance away! Take the *Columbia*, son. When she docks in Portland, we'll get to the bank ahead of the bad news and . . . ."

"It'll be shouted ashore before we can get off her," Dave insisted. "Then what?"

"It's a better try than having you fold up somewhere in the mountains. You ain't made of iron. Gimme that deposit certificate. *I'm* taking the *Columbia!*"

They turned as a steamboat whistle sounded. Then Dave raced for the riverfront. Jep panted after him.

"Now you're showin' sense, son. We'll . . . ."

Dave sprinted as he saw a sternwheeler edging away from the wharf. Jep followed behind him.

"Not that boat, you fool! She's goin' upriver!"

Dave leaped wildly across water. His spurs gouged planking as a deckhand caught him. He turned quickly and called to Jep on the receding wharf. "I know it. I'll be waiting with the gold when the *Columbia* docks in Portland."

Jep gave him a hard look, then vanished into the crowd.

Dave paced as the stern-wheeler thrashed its tortuous way up the Sacramento River. What had he jumped into with those blamed spurs? Seven hundred hard-riding miles. But the more he miserably thought about his pop's losing the ranch the more he knew he had

made the only possible decision. Get to Portland *before*, not with, the bad news. He prayed that the *Columbia* was as slow as this creaking riverboat.

At last the old tub swung into Knight's Landing, forty-two miles upriver from Sacramento. Dave jumped to the wharf and cut short the greeting from old man Knight, his father's friend. "I need a good *fast* horse, Mr. Knight. Will you sell me one?"

"You can't buy a horse from me, son." Dave turned away angrily. A fine friend! "But take my best mount at the head of the wharf."

"Thanks." Dave grinned over his shoulder. Excited, he startled the drowsing bay stallion. It reared into life, fighting his efforts to mount. Swinging up, he pricked it with a spur. The lunging stallion nearly threw him. His cheeks burned as everyone stared. Nice way to start the long ride to Portland, forgetting all the horsemanship Jep had taught him!

He calmed himself, then the horse, walking it a quarter mile till it became accustomed to his weight. Then a quarter mile of trotting. Another galloping. Trot again. Walk. Trot. Gallop again with the other forefoot leading this time. Give the horse a chance to stay fresh longer, keep from getting leg-weary.

Riding north through the hot, dry Sacramento Valley he glanced eastward toward the High Sierra draped with snow. Their ranch nestled over there in the foothills, its entire future dependent on a nest egg of gold in Portland, nearly seven hundred miles away. Dave tugged down his hat brim as he spurred the stallion ahead.

Late that afternoon he rode the weary horse up to a ranch house huddling under towering trees. A young man and a woman came out as he dismounted, patting the stallion.

"Sir," Dave requested, "will you sell me a horse and return this one to Mr. Knight down the valley?"

"Reckon I can," said the man.

"But if you've ridden all the way from Knight's you'd better set awhile."

"Just in time for supper." The young woman smiled.

Dave realized he hadn't eaten all day. Not since Bremond's! "Thanks, but I haven't the time. Now about that horse, sir."

After he saddled up while explaining his haste, they handed him a package of food to take along. "We'll pray that you make it to Portland in time," they said.

As he rode away, he heard the woman speak to her husband. "I used to envy people who had money in the bank."

He traveled fast until darkness blotted out everything but the stars. He let the horse have its head and kept his eye on the North Star . . . until it exploded into a thousand stars when the limb of a tree smashed him in the face. He clung to the saddle, fighting dizziness. He ought to wait for daylight to travel in this strange country. But the *Columbia* would steam north all night. He squinted into the darkness and urged the horse onward.

At dawn he roused a fat, grumpy liveryman in Red Bluff and made a deal to trade horses. Asking the man to call him in an hour, he burrowed into a pile of hay. He dreamed he was crawling toward a pile of gold, but someone hauled him back by the shoulder. He fought desperately.

"Easy, kid," a voice said. He opened his eyes and saw the liveryman bending over him. "Hour's up." The man grinned.

Dave stumbled to his horse, put his foot in the stirrup, and felt no bulge in his hip pocket. He whirled.

"Where's my wallet?" he demanded, advancing. The man's hand dropped toward a gun. Dave dove, clamping on the wrist. The heavy liveryman swung him off his feet and piled onto him. Dave felt himself being pinned down. He got a leg clear, lifted it, then brought it down hard, driving a silver spur into the man's rump. The liveryman howled. Dave wriggled free, smashed him in the face, and got the gun.

"All right, all right," the man yelled. "Here!"

Dave quickly checked the wad in his wallet and, most important of all, the deposit certificate. Mounting, he tossed the gun in the hayloft and rode away.

The sun climbed to the noon sky and hurled its heat into the Sacramento Valley. Mountains shimmered. Dust devils swirled. Dave's eyes smarted with sweat. Twenty-four hours since he'd left Knight's Landing. It seemed like twenty-four years. But here he was, still in this blasted valley, still in California. And the livery stable plug lathering out under him. How had he ever imagined he could make it to Portland in time to save his dad's ranch?

He goaded the wheezing nag to a ranch just south of Redding and bought a chunky pinto that the foreman said would "take the mountains ahead like they was the flats." That night, in black mountains hulking below snowcapped Mount Shasta, he wished he had bought a coat along with the pinto. The moon hung like ice among brittle stars. Trees cracked in the sharp coldness. He ran beside his trotting horse in an effort to warm up. Back in the saddle he fought drowsiness.

He woke up, half frozen, outside a cabin above a rushing river as a small gray-headed woman tried to get him out of the saddle. He tumbled off numbly, and she steadied him into a kitchen warm with the odor of freshly baked bread. As he thawed out by the stove, he glanced out the window down toward the river where two men, probably her husband and son, were fishing.

"W-what r-river is th-that?"

"The Sacramento, son."

He groaned. Just how long was that river? Was he ever going to get out of California and into Oregon? He asked about getting a horse.

"We'll talk about that later," she said, giving him a smile. "You have some breakfast first, and then some rest. You're all tuckered out."

"I had my sleep on the horse," Dave replied, still shivering and

336

trying not to think about a soft bed and warm blankets. She persisted, but tired as he was he wouldn't give in. Too risky. She was a nice woman who'd think she was doing him a favor to let him sleep on and on and on—while somewhere off the coast the *Columbia* steamed northward for Portland.

"Then at least," she said finally, "you'll let me fix you a good breakfast."

The cool mountains made for fast riding all that day. By nightfall he'd dropped into the valley north of Weed and hoped to keep up the good pace in flat country. Then wind blasted out of the darkness. The notorious wind of that area that could rip a farmer's seed out of the soil. Wind that could almost lift a person from the saddle and tear him away from a desperately needed crop of gold waiting in Portland. A wind that kept him continually battling the horse, which wanted to turn tail and drift in the wrong direction.

Feeling battered and beaten from the blustering night, he rode on, and along toward noon of that third day he swayed into Yreka, still in California, but only twenty miles south of the Oregon border. He wanted to keep pushing, but what if he fell asleep in the saddle again and became lost in the mountains. He'd been lucky last night. So, after trading horses and ordering the new one to be saddled and ready to go in an hour, he

reluctantly got a room in a hotel.

The bored desk clerk nodded vaguely when Dave asked to be called later. He'd better wake himself up. But how? He was so exhausted he'd fall in too deep for his inner senses to pull him out before precious time had been lost.

He stared about the shabby room. A decrepit bed. A rickety chair. The usual pitcher of water and basin. Battered bureau with cracked mirror. A candle in a bottle. Yawning, he saw the cord from the window shade. An inch or so from the top of the candle he cut a notch clear into the wick. Fastening the cord to the mirror, he strung it through the notch, touching the wick, and tied the other end to the handle of the pitcher balanced shakily on the edge of the bureau and only prevented from tipping by the cord.

Lighting the candle, he spread blankets and pillow on the floor below the bureau and plunged into darkness—until the candle flame burned down to the cord and severed it. A flood of water doused his head. The pitcher bounded off his chest. He sat up sputtering and reached for his boots . . . and those silver spurs.

North of Yreka the road climbed higher and higher into the Siskiyou Mountains while the sun dropped lower and lower. In the evening hush of the darkening mountains he was giving his horse a walking breather when he heard hoofs furiously pounding back around the last bend. At least a dozen or more horses. He frowned uneasily. Outlaws? A posse? A bunch out for a hilarious time? He couldn't mix in anything that might delay him.

He spurred into a shadowy clump of brush a moment before a sheriff's posse rounded the bend. As they charged by the sheriff raised his arm. They hauled horses back on haunches just up the road.

"Don't see his tracks no more, boys. Head back and watch for where he turned off, th' blasted horse thief."

Dave scowled, sliding his hand forward to his horse's nose to prevent it from whinnying. He remembered the shifty-eyed individual who'd traded him this horse and got the better of the deal at that. He should have obeyed his warning hunches, but he'd been too anxious to get a fresh horse and keep going. Now he was riding a stolen horse, had been spotted on it, and the sheriff was after him!

If he rode out and tried to explain matters, it would mean hours of delay for a checkup. And another thing—frequently "huss thieves" got no opportunity to alibi! Dave's throat felt dry and tight as the posse rode slowly back in the deepening darkness peering at the ground.

They missed the spot where he'd turned off. Dave sighed through clenched teeth. He'd wait quietly a few moments and then. . . . Then

he saw a deputy wheeling back for another look!

No chance of explanation now after hiding out. Dave drove his spurs home. His startled horse leaped out, hoofs clawing the road. The posse shouted. Dave streaked around a bend in the road. A long straightaway. He spurred desperately for the next curve as guns barked behind him.

The chase went on and on, the quarry neither gaining nor losing as bullets whined past in the straightaways. Sweeping into another straight stretch, Dave, bending low in the saddle, saw a blur of white in the darkness ahead. A roadside marker. The Oregon border. The sheriff's authority would cease beyond that. But sometimes sheriffs ignored little legal points!

Dave spurred and lashed. His horse flattened its ears and streaked ahead. Guns blazed in the night behind him. His horse staggered, then pitched him past the marker. Dave rolled limply until his momentum slowed, then gained his feet and raced into the Oregon brush.

"Too late, men," the sheriff called out. "He's across."

"Ignore the line!" a voice retorted. "We've got him now! Laws ain't made for horse thieves!"

Despite the sheriff's commands a lone horseman rode into the brush. Dave crouched in the shadows. Horseless. Hunted. How would he ever get to Portland in time now, if

at all. The rider searched closer, his
six-shooter glinting in starlight. As
he was about to discover Dave,
Dave shoved up on the man's boot
with all his strength, toppling him
from the saddle. Dave grabbed the
saddle horn and swung up as the
horse darted ahead in panic. Off in
the darkness he reined in and
shouted back.

"Sheriff, I'm Dave Remy from
Circle R down in the Sacramento
Valley. I didn't steal that dead
horse. And I'm just *borrowing* this
one. I'll send it back."

He rode into the night. Into
Oregon. On his way again to Portland. A long, long way yet. But still
on his way.

At Hungry Creek he met a man
who was returning to California on
a borrowed sorrel. They swapped
horses and Dave rode the sorrel to
its home corral at Bear Creek. On

to Jacksonville for an hour's sleep and a fresh horse. Another night of walking, trotting, galloping. He ate, slept, lived in the saddle on long-legged, easy-gaited horses, chunky pounders, strawberry roans, chestnuts, bays, pintos. Trading a tired horse for a frisky one. Paying some extra cash if he had to. Anything to keep going.

The morning of the fifth day he fell out of the saddle in the little town of Eugene, Oregon. But an hour later he hauled himself onto a new horse. That night he couldn't keep his bloodshot eyes focused. His head bobbed and rolled as though on a swivel. He was too weary to run beside the horse to keep himself awake. Riding at a mad gallop to blow away the cobwebs and pound himself awake, he rode out the horse ahead of schedule.

"How far to Portland?" he murmured, blinking wearily at an innkeeper in French Prairie six mornings after he'd bought the silver spurs.

"Half a day's ride. But you ain't for it, son. Bet your eyes would burn holes in a pillow."

"Not now," Dave snapped. "Get me the fastest horse in town."

He'd have to push and get to the bank before it closed for the day. It wouldn't be open tomorrow if the *Columbia* had arrived in the meantime. Suppose the boat had already made port? What would he do then?

At ten thirty that morning he spurred his lathered mount to an auctioneer's corral in Oregon City, his eyes feverishly selecting a horse. At noon he tossed that horse's bridle reins to a boy on the south bank of the Willamette River.

"Ferry to Portland, mister?" another boy called, standing expectantly by a rowboat. Dave shoved it into the river.

"Five dollars if you get me across fast." He squinted toward boats moored on the far side. "The *Columbia* in from Frisco yet?"

"No, sir. Ain't heard the cannon announcin' that she's comin' up the river."

Dave smiled triumphantly and relaxed a bit. The hot sun, the glinting water, the rhythmic creak of the oarlocks made him sleepy, terribly sleepy. He fought to keep his bloodshot eyes open just a little longer. He doused handfuls of water in his face, over his head. *Blam!* The cannon! He forgot sleep.

"Ten dollars more, kid, if . . . ."

He grabbed the gunwhales as the boy stood back mightily on the oars and nearly toppled him overboard. "Golly, fifteen dollars!" the kid grunted. "That's more than Dad makes in a week!"

Dave stared at his spurs. "Don't get cocky with a pair of silver oars," he muttered. "You might have to make a long hard row with them."

"Huh?"

340

"Keep rowing," Dave growled, glancing worriedly downriver.

He ran through the streets of Portland, but made himself *walk* into the Adams office, spurs jingling.

"The cashier's out to lunch," a clerk began doubtfully.

"Where?" Dave demanded. A new voice spoke behind him.

"Something I can do for you?"

Dave handed the deposit certificate to a portly gentleman mouthing a gold toothpick.

"Have you any identification?" the man inquired, curiously studying Dave's travel-stained, tousled appearance and bloodshot eyes. He leisurely verified the validity of the certificate, but then suspiciously looked Dave over again.

"Everything seems in order," he said slowly and pointed the toothpick at the certificate. "But there's something odd here. This deposit was made only six days ago down in Sacramento. And the *Columbia* isn't in yet."

"I rode here. Yes, all seven hundred miles," Dave explained, then went on quickly. "I have important business here, but I *missed* catching the *Columbia*. It wouldn't have been safe to carry that amount of gold overland with me."

"Quite true," the man admitted, but still he hesitated.

Dave heard a horse galloping up the street. If he let this pompous bank official stall much longer. . . ."What's wrong with this office?" he snapped. "Haven't you got the gold to. . . ."

"Of course, of course," the man interrupted, smiling reassuringly at eavesdropping customers. The galloping horseman went past the open doors. The official led Dave to a teller.

"Forty pounds of gold. Twelve thousand dollars." The teller smiled. Dave grabbed the bag from the teller and went out into the street just as a shouting mass of people converged on the bank.

"Hello, Jep," Dave smiled wearily at the familiar figure trying to push nearer the front. Jep stared unbelievingly, as Dave handed him the bag of gold. He shook his head slowly.

"How did you do it, kid? Seven hundred miles in six days and nights! You must be made of iron!"

"More like iron that's melting now," Dave said, tottering to stay on his feet. Jep steadied him, then guided him down the street. In a dim room Jep eased him down on a bed, swinging his leaden legs up. He heard Jep's voice from far away.

"Dave, do you want to keep them beautiful spurs on?"

"Uh-uh," Dave murmured, smiling sleepily. "I'm not going to be riding any more nightmares, not for a real long, long while. . . ."

Jep's chuckle faded away as Dave sank luxuriously into a deep velvet sleep.

Focus

1. Why did Dave Remy think he deserved to have silver spurs?
2. How did the purchase of those spurs lead to trouble?
3. Explain the title "Sacrifice Spurs."
4. Dave advised the boy rowing him across to Portland, "Don't get cocky with a pair of silver oars. You might have to make a long hard row with them." What did Dave mean?
5. Dave reached Portland in time. Do you think his success resulted from making a wise decision or from luck? Explain your answer.
6. Besides the money, what else do you think Dave would have lost if he had not reached Portland in time?

In Writing

Which of the following statements do you agree with? Write a brief argument telling why you feel as you do. Back it up with facts from the story. (1) Dave Remy accepted his responsibility of keeping his father's money safe. He showed courage and maturity in making the trip to Portland. (2) Dave Remy meant well, but his impulsive ride could easily have failed. This showed that he was still irresponsible.

Vocabulary

Read the word list and paragraph below. Decide which word makes the best sense in each blank space. Then write the numbers *1* to *5* on a piece of paper and write the correct word next to each number.

swaggering	glower	notorious
windfall	pompous	boisterous
harried	validity	

The new tennis champion entered the room __(1)__ , acting vain and superior. The people at the party had been having a great time, but the __(2)__ laughter stopped with the victor's appearance. He was well known, in fact __(3)__ , for his self-important, __(4)__ attitude. One by one, the people slowly left the room. Soon, only the stuffed bear was left in the room with the victor, and it seemed to __(5)__ at him.

STUDY SKILL: Taking Notes in Outline Form

The contest is on. Soon, you will face the challenging paragraph. A paragraph can be loaded with facts. Your goal is to discover each important fact's hiding place. If one fact escapes, your report could be in danger! You need to tackle this assignment bravely. Your defense is a good outline. Its form can help you organize information when you take notes. An outline can have more than one subtopic. It looks like this:

I. Main topic
   A. Subtopic of main topic
      1. Supporting detail
      2. Supporting detail
   B. Subtopic of main topic
      1. Supporting detail
      2. Supporting detail

An outline is a system where you take charge. It lets you summarize and arrange thoughts. You give the orders by using Roman numerals for the *main topic,* capital letters for the *subtopic,* and Arabic numerals for the *supporting details.* You capitalize the first word in each line. An outline prepares you to write a report.

Here's the first round. Know your "challenger's" formation. A paragraph has one sentence—often the first one—that states the main idea. The remaining sentences give the details that support the main idea. Watch for key words.

The Himalayas (him′ə lā′əz) are considered to be the most impressive mountain range in the world. The height of its peaks is staggering. Of the ninety-four highest mountain peaks in the world, ninety-two are in the Himalayas. All the vast peaks are forever covered with snow. This is why the mountain range is called the Himalayas. The name means "house of snow."

The "outline defense" looks like this:

I. Himalayas
   A. World's most impressive mountains
      1. 92 of 94 world's highest peaks there
      2. Peaks always snow-covered
      3. Himalayas means "house of snow"

The strategy was to "capture" the paragraph's main topic (Roman numeral I). It was located in the first sentence. The subtopic (capital letter A) was then easier to find. It followed the main topic. The supporting details (Arabic numbers 1, 2, 3) came forward as soon as they were spotted. They marched behind the main topic and the subtopic.

Look at the next paragraph. Arm yourself with key words.

The world's highest mountain is found in the Himalayas. Mount Everest lies between Tibet and Nepal. Everest is a towering 29,028 feet (8,848 meters). It soars $5\frac{1}{2}$ miles (8.9 kilometers) above sea level.

Finish the outline. Use the facts you uncovered from the paragraph.

I. World's highest mountain found in Himalayas
   A.
      1. Lies between Tibet and Nepal
      2.
      3.

Gather all your forces; come face-to-face with two paragraphs.

Edmund Percival Hillary was a brave and daring person. He enjoyed challenge. Hillary was born in 1919 in Aukland, New Zealand. This rugged, beautiful country encouraged his pioneering spirit and sense of adventure.

Hillary was once a beekeeper, but he is best known for mountain climbing. He and Tenzing Norgay—his Sherpa guide from Nepal—were the first people known to ever reach the summit of Mount Everest. After a climb burdened with hardships, Hillary and Tenzing reached the peak of the world's highest mountain on May 29, 1953. Many consider this a heroic accomplishment.

Defend yourself with an outline. The contest plan shows some moves. You fill in the rest. Remember, look out for the main idea and key words in each paragraph. Details will support you. Before you begin, *review* the notes and outlines in this lesson. Use the lesson as your guide. (Hillary needed a guide to reach his goal!)

I.
   A. Brave and daring, enjoyed challenge
      1.
      2. Rugged country encouraged spirit, adventure
   B.
      1. With Tenzing Norgay, Sherpa guide from Nepal
      2.
      3.
      4.

Diana Nyad versus the Sea

Ellen Anne Jones

Are you in top physical condition?
If so, get ready to swim
with the jellyfish and sharks.
Or are you afraid?

August 19, 1979. Imagine you're Diana Nyad, marathon swimmer. You're in the Atlantic Ocean, halfway between Bimini and West Palm Beach. This is your third try at swimming between the Bahamas and Florida—a feat that, so far, no one has been able to accomplish. Your first two tries failed. This time you have come farther than on either try before, but you still have a long way to go. What do you think about?

Maybe you think about sharks. Or barracuda. Or venomous jellyfish. They're out there, swimming silently in the tropical ocean waters, and they don't care at all about your ambition. True, people in nearby boats are watching for sharks and other life that might hurt you, but they can't see everything. They can't protect you from all the hazards that might ruin your chances for making it to the coast of Florida.

Like exhaustion, for instance. You have trained for years, especially pushing yourself the last few months. You have deliberately gained extra weight, knowing that those calories will provide your body with needed energy. You are in top physical condition: a strong, healthy athlete, used to the demanding work of swimming long distances. Still, you get so tired out there in the ocean. After a while, you swim mechanically, stroke after stroke after stroke. You have many, many miles to go yet, and every muscle in your body is hurting. You wonder how you'll ever find the stamina to make it.

The sun is dropping lower and lower. Darkness will soon surround you. You desperately want to make your goal, but at this point you must ask yourself: "Why in the world am I doing this?"

To answer this question, Diana Nyad had to look to her past.

She had begun swimming in junior high school, encouraged by her seventh-grade teacher. Her coach, Jack Nelson, found that Nyad had the qualities necessary for a competitive swimmer: zeal, determination, and a hunger to win.

After several years, Nyad began to focus on marathon swimming as her special interest. A marathon swimmer is one who not only swims long distances but also tries to swim farther than anyone else. While time is important in marathon swimming, the emphasis is not on speed. Rather, the swimmer concentrates on the distance she or he can cover before fatigue, cold, or other factors force the finish.

Before her Bahamas-to-Florida venture, Nyad had scored quite a few successes. She had swum 25 miles in the Suez Canal, and 67 miles in the North Sea. She had circled Manhattan Island, a distance of 28 miles, in less than 8 hours. She had competed in many different places and had broken a few world records. The memory of these victories must have helped to sustain Diana Nyad as the sun set and she saw the darkness gather all around her.

Nyad's swimming career had not been all triumph, however; there had been big disappointments. Twice before, for example, she had attempted the Bahamas-to-Florida swim. The first time, she had been defeated by strong currents that forced her considerably off course. She had tried again just two weeks before her present attempt, only to give up after 2½ hours when a sting from a Portuguese man-of-war, a poisonous jellyfish, partially paralyzed her.

Perhaps the worst disappointment of all had been three years earlier, in late summer 1976, when she tried to swim the English Channel. Most marathon swimmers are lured, sooner or later, to the Channel, that narrow piece of the Atlantic Ocean lying between France and southern England. It is a special challenge not only because of the distance but also because the tides, currents, and winds are tricky and often unpredictable. In addition, the water tends to be bitterly cold. No woman had ever swum the Channel both ways—from England to France and back again—and Nyad wanted very much to be the first.

She had trained hard. In excellent spirits, she felt eager and determined. Her trainer and some friends had come with her to

England, to render moral support. She had arranged for a boat to accompany her; the crew would guide her, provide her with food, and help her if she got in trouble. A movie team was even on hand to film her progress. She had seen to everything, made every preparation she possibly could, but there was one factor that Nyad could not control: The English Channel's capricious weather.

She was scheduled to swim on August 16th, but bad weather prevented it. Bad weather continued—the 17th, the 18th, the 19th. Every morning, Nyad would get ready to swim and would call the British Coast Guard for the latest weather forecast. For days on end, the answer was the same—bad.

Finally, on August 23, the weather cleared. On a beach at Dover, England, Nyad coated herself with thick grease, which would help to insulate her from the cold Channel waters, to minimize the heat loss from her body. Then she climbed over the sharp rocks and slipped into the ocean. She was off—on her way to France, and trying hard. But the week-long delay had had its effect. An athlete can stay at peak physical and psychological condition for only so long. Although still strong, Nyad was no longer in prime physical shape. Even worse, perhaps, during her period of enforced idleness, Nyad had become frustrated and discouraged.

The trouble started almost at once. The waves were so rough and the tidal currents so strong that Nyad had a hard time keeping her face out of the water when she took a breath. She began to swallow much more salt water than she should. This, along with the general roughness of the ocean, made Nyad seasick, which created serious problems for her. Every marathon swimmer, in order to fulfill her or his energy requirements, must have some highly nourishing food at regular intervals; the first time Nyad tried to drink her specially prepared nutrient solution, she began to choke and vomit. The nausea became progressively worse, until, about two hours after she had started her swim, Nyad panicked and had to be pulled on board the boat. Sick, exhausted, and disheartened, she attributed her disaster partly to poor environmental conditions but mostly to her state of mind. She believed that she had lost mental control of the situation.

Nyad tried to swim the Channel two more times that summer.

She made her second attempt on August 30, starting out fine this time—exhilarated, excited, and in high spirits. The tides and currents were overpowering, however, and she developed leg cramps from kicking so hard to combat the rough sea. Her final try at the Channel took place on September 6. Again, her body and mind were in prime working order—keyed up and ready to go. But it was September; autumn was approaching and the weather was growing cold. Cold, that old enemy of Channel swimmers, got the better of her this time. Nyad got so chilled that she lost her bearings, and for a short time she couldn't see her boat. She even began to hallucinate, thinking that birds were attacking her. When the boat crew finally pulled her out of the water, her skin was blue and she was trembling violently.

Nyad knew that her failures were not really her fault, but she was tired and depressed. She questioned whether she still had the dedication and drive that are so necessary for a marathon swimmer. She even began to wonder whether she was wasting her life on something foolish, insignificant, worthless. Who cares about long-distance swimming, anyway?

The answer: lots of people. Her trainers cared, for instance, and so did the boat crews who had accompanied her. Marathon swimming was important to all the people who, at one point or another, had helped her. But most of all, Nyad realized that *she* cared—a lot. She did not want to be beaten.

August 20, 1979. The sun is coming up. You hurt. One eye is swollen almost shut—salt water got inside your safety goggles. In spite of your watchers' best efforts, one small jellyfish managed to sting you, and the sting smarts. Mostly, you're so, so tired.

Still you keep on going, and the sun moves higher and higher. Then you notice it: the coast of Florida. Not too much longer now.

Somehow, you pull yourself from the surf, and somebody helps you as you stagger up onto the beach. Ninety miles ago—27 hours and 37 minutes ago—you left Bimini. You have never, ever been this tired—this much of a physical wreck. You feel like you have been run over by a train. Then you notice all the people, and they're cheering.

The sun is overhead, shining brightly. It's your high noon.

Focus

1. Explain the physical and mental obstacles that a marathon swimmer must overcome to succeed.
2. List some of Diana Nyad's successes. List some of her failures.
3. Explain what happened during Diana Nyad's attempts to swim the English Channel.
4. What doubts did Nyad have at the end of her three attempts at the English Channel? What ended the doubts?
5. Why do you think Diana Nyad is willing to face the dangers involved in marathon swimming?

In Writing

Diana Nyad had trained hard to achieve her goal. Make a schedule for one week of training that you think a marathon swimmer might follow. Include time in your schedule for sleep, meals, and so on.

Vocabulary

On a piece of paper, write the numbers *1* to *5*. Then look at the words in the first column and find a definition for each word in the second column. Next to each number on your paper, write the letter of the correct definition for each word.

1. capricious
2. attribute
3. disheartened
4. fatigue
5. sustain

A. having lost one's spirit
B. weariness from work or exercise
C. apt to change unpredictably
D. to give support or to nourish
E. made to feel healthy
F. to explain by giving a cause

Saved from a Subterranean Pit

Vincent H. Gaddis

A child is trapped in a narrow pipe
more than sixty feet below
ground. Would you have
the courage to rescue him?

It was late December, 1959, when three-year-old Randy McKinley fell into the deep well. He and his family were visiting his grandfather on a southern Texas farm. The long abandoned well was in back of the farmhouse, its opening covered by a barrel. Randy was with a group of children playing in the backyard that morning, running around on his chubby legs, laughing, following his older playmates.

Some of the children removed the barrel and looked down into darkness. The well was cased with a pipe only sixteen inches in diameter, but it was three hundred feet deep, and the water level was sixty-eight feet below the ground. They failed to replace the barrel right away, and little Randy, racing across the yard, tumbled in. Fortunately his fall was witnessed by the other children, and they ran screaming to the house. Mrs. C.L. McKinley, Randy's mother, hurried to the well, followed by his grandmother.

The mother flung herself to the ground, and lying on her stomach, looked down. All she could see was total blackness.

"Randy!" she screamed, "Randy, can you hear me?"

From far below came a faint cry. The boy was still alive, but every second was precious. Somewhere in that first sixty-eight feet the child was caught, but probably only temporarily, and below him was more then two hundred feet of foul, stagnant water. The two women and the children screamed for help.

Four Mexican farm workers in a nearby field heard their cries and rushed to the scene. One was forty-two-year-old Manuel Corral. Although he spoke only Spanish he immediately grasped the gravity of the situation. The child was not old enough to understand directions for tying a rope around his body or strong enough to hang onto a lowered rope.

There was only one thing Corral could do—go down the well pipe headfirst and bring the boy up. He had his comrades bind a piece of baling wire around his ankles, but the only rope they could find was not long enough and was of questionable strength.

At that moment an electrical power-line maintenance crew drove up in their truck; fortunately they were carrying coils of strong, heavy rope. They tied a line securely to Manuel's ankles. He was the smallest man present, weighing only 125 pounds. The pipe's diameter was sixteen inches, and he was seventeen inches across his shoulders. As he squeezed his way into the well pipe, he had to compress his shoulders. Then he began his descent, arms extended ahead of him, squirming and twisting, moving inches at a time. Above him the men played out the rope while the mother and grandmother watched anxiously.

The foul stench sickened Corral, and his headfirst position made him dizzy. Lumps of rust on the pipe bruised his skin, especially about the shoulders. Several times he thought he might faint, but he continued to force himself deeper into his narrow, pitch-dark prison. Shouts of encouragement from the men at the top echoed faintly in his ears.

Twenty feet down he encountered his first problem. To his surprise he discovered the well divided into two pipes, like an inverted Y, with each shaft continuing to plunge deeper into the earth. Which branch had the child dropped into? Manuel Corral shouted, hoping Randy would respond, but all he heard was the

echo of his own cry, then silence. He wondered if the child could possibly still be alive, but, dead or alive, he was determined to find him.

Manuel had an intuition that the shaft on his right was the correct one, so he wormed his way into it and continued wriggling straight downward. By this time the sharp rust particles had torn his shirt to ribbons, and the bruises on his flesh ached. Again he was assailed by attacks of dizziness from the blood pressure in his head, and he was afraid that at any moment he would lapse into unconsciousness. The men above would know something had happened when the rope remained slack, and they would pull him up. But this must not happen; he must reach the child. He shook his head in an effort to keep his senses alert.

Suddenly the silence was broken by the sound of splashing water. Lumps of rusty metal peeling on the pipe were being loosened by his body and were dropping into the water below. He was close to the water level. There was a louder splash, a child's frightened whimper, followed by coughing. Randy was still alive. Corral continued worming down, and suddenly his groping hand felt a tousled head. His exploring hands also discovered that a narrow circular ledge just below the water line had kept Randy from falling completely into the water where he would have drowned.

Manuel placed his arms under the child's armpits. Ears were listening at the top of the well, and they heard him as he shouted in Spanish, "I have the boy! Hurry, pull!"

The rope tightened as the men tried to pull Manuel up. He could feel his legs stretch as the rope cut into his ankles, but his body didn't move. With a shock he realized that he was stuck—trapped headfirst in pitch-darkness within a sixteen-inch pipe some sixty feet below the ground, and just above foul water with its suffocating stench. A wave of fear—the chilling fear of a helpless, lingering death, swept over him—followed by an attack of dizziness.

As he fought to retain consciousness, his grip on the child loosened, and Randy fell back into the water, screaming in terror. In the narrow space inside the pipe the boy's cries were deafening, and the impact on his hearing helped Corral to regain his reason. Just then a powerful jerk from the rope freed him as he was straining his muscles in an effort to twist his body. He could move.

Below Corral, Randy was struggling desperately, trying to keep his head above water as he clung to the slippery ledge. Manuel reached down and seized the boy around the wrists, a far better grip than before, and again he cried in Spanish, "Hurry, pull us up!'' And again the rope tightened as strong arms far above tugged on the other end.

Pain racked Corral's body as it scraped upward against the sharp rusty sides of the pipe, as the muscles in his compressed shoulders strained to return to normal, as the rope's tension threatened to pull his legs from their sockets. With a spasm of agony he felt his shoulder bones snap out of their sockets, and he almost lost his damp grip on Randy's wet wrists.

Forty feet. Thirty feet. Then twenty. Finally, after what had seemed like hours in the inky darkness, he was bathed in a burst of priceless sunlight that temporarily blinded him as eager hands reached down and raised him to the surface and caught the child. Randy was wet, cold, and still frightened, but otherwise unhurt.

"Thank you, thank you!" the mother and grandmother cried in simultaneous relief and joy as they threw their arms about the boy.

Manuel was placed on the ground nearby gasping in the pure air. Both of his shoulders were dislocated. His ankles were so swollen that he couldn't stand. There was an ugly bruise on the back of his head, and his skin was a patchwork of scratches and lacerations. His clothing was almost completely torn from his body.

Someone had passed the hat among the bystanders and collected almost a hundred dollars. Manuel refused to accept it. He hadn't rescued Randy for a reward. He was a man of personal pride, and he had his character. Moreover, he loved children. He had four of his own.

Three months after the ordeal that saved a life Manuel Corral was honored at a banquet in Dallas and presented with a plaque commemorating the heroic act. He was asked what was behind such unselfish real courage. Most acts of heroism are impulses occurring at the moment of crisis, but Manuel had had time to think of the danger and of what his death might mean to his family. Yet he had deliberately chosen to risk his own life. Why?

Manuel's reply was translated into English. "I did it because I would want someone to do it for me if my own child should ever fall into a well," he explained. "We must all live for each other."

Focus

1. Why was it necessary for someone to go down into the well to bring Randy up?
2. Explain why Manuel Corral's size was an important factor in this story.
3. Why was Manuel Corral's act of courage even greater than one done on impulse?
4. Explain what you think Manuel Corral meant by "We must all live for each other."
5. What do you think Randy's family did with the abandoned well after the accident?

In Writing

What do you think courage is? In a paragraph, write your ideas on the makeup of courage and why you think people perform courageous acts.

Vocabulary

Make two columns on your paper. Label the first column *Positive* and the second column *Negative.* Then look at the words in the list below. Decide whether each word has a positive or negative connotation. Write the word in the correct column. Then write a sentence using each word.

banquet   stagnant   commemorating
laceration   suffocating

STUDY SKILL: Categories

Imagine trying to find things in your home if you didn't keep similar objects together. If you didn't organize your belongings into *categories*, or groups, you would have no reason to put all your socks in the same drawer. You might just as well put a sock, a cup, and the peanut butter in the drawer. Then another sock could go on the telephone receiver or in the ice-cube tray. Without categories this would not be unusual, but it certainly would complicate your life!

Despite differences in size, color, length, pattern, and yarn, all socks have something in common. You recognize socks when you see them. Even if you forget to put them away, everyone in the family knows what you are looking for when you ask if anyone has seen your socks.

Categories help us to organize everything around us. Look at the following lists. Think how the items in each list are alike. Can you think of a word or group of words to describe the items in each list?

> power drill
> wrench
> table saw
> staple gun
> chisel
>
> candle
> flashlight
> match
> sun
> kerosene lamp
>
> sun
> space heater
> campfire
> wood stove
> furnace

Did you recognize that all the items in the first list belong to the category *tools*? All the items in the second list are *sources of light*. The third list would be called *sources of heat*.

Take a closer look at the items in the second list. Notice that some of the items are both light and heat sources. A candle, for instance, is used primarily for light, but it also

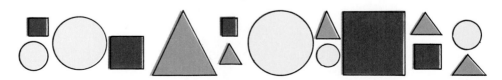

gives off heat. The flashlight, however, is strictly a source of light. You need to think about all the items in a group to decide the correct category. In this way, you are able to decide that the group as a whole lists sources of light.

Individual items can usually fit into more than one category because most things have more than one quality, or characteristic. In choosing category titles, you need to think of the many qualities each item has. Then decide the one quality that all the items have in common.

Lists 1 and 2 need category titles. Think about the qualities of each item. Decide which quality all the items in each list have in common. Then give each list a category title.

Look at Lists 3, 4, and 5. Each of these contains items from two different categories. For each list, sort the items into two groups. Then give a category title to each group.

1.
transistor radio
cassette tape
concert
record album

2.
fishing
ice skating
sailing
scuba diving

3.
steering wheel
hand brakes
reflectors
turn signals
bumper
handlebars

4.
innings
rink
court
quarters
diamond
set

5.
signal lights
toll booths
pedestrian
    crosswalks
intersections
rest areas
entrance and
    exit ramps

The Hunting of the Snark

Lewis Carroll

"We have sailed many months, we have sailed many
   weeks
(Four weeks to the month you may mark),
But never as yet ('tis your Captain who speaks)
Have we caught the least glimpse of a Snark!

"We have sailed many weeks, we have sailed many
   days
(Seven days to the week I allow),
But a Snark, on the which we might lovingly gaze,
We have never beheld till now!

"A dear uncle of mine (after whom I was named)
Remarked, when I bade him farewell—"
"Oh, skip your dear uncle!" the Bellman exclaimed,
As he angrily tingled his bell.

"He remarked to me then," said that mildest of men,
" 'If your Snark be a Snark, that is right:
Fetch it home by all means—you may serve it with
   greens,
And it's handy for striking a light.' "

" 'You may seek it with thimbles—and seek it with
   care;
You may hunt it with forks and hope;
You may threaten its life with a railway-share;
You may charm it with smiles and soap—' "

("That's exactly the method," the Bellman bold
In a hasty parenthesis cried,
"That's exactly the way I have always been told
That the capture of Snarks should be tried!")

"'But oh, beamish nephew, beware of the day,
If your Snark be a Boojum! For then
You will softly and suddenly vanish away,
And never be met with again!'"

They sought it with thimbles, they sought it with care;
They pursued it with forks and hope;
They threatened its life with a railway-share;
They charmed it with smiles and soap.

They shuddered to think that the chase might fail,
And the Beaver, excited at last,
Went bounding along on the tip of its tail,
For the daylight was nearly past.

"There is Thingumbob shouting!" the Bellman said.
"He is shouting like mad, only hark!
He is waving his hands, he is wagging his head,
He has certainly found a Snark!"

They gazed in delight, while the Butcher exclaimed,
"He was always a desperate wag!"
They beheld him—their Baker—their hero unnamed—
On the top of a neighbouring crag,

Erect and sublime, for one moment of time.
In the next, that wild figure they saw
(As if stung by a spasm) plunge into a chasm,
While they waited and listened in awe.

"It's a Snark!" was the sound that first came to their
   ears,
And seemed almost too good to be true.
Then followed a torrent of laughter and cheers:
Then the ominous words, "It's a Boo—"

Then, silence. Some fancied they heard in the air
A weary and wandering sigh
That sounded like "—jum!" but the others declare
It was only a breeze that went by.

They hunted till darkness came on, but they found
Not a button, or feather, or mark,
By which they could tell that they stood on the ground
Where the Baker had met the Snark.

In the midst of the word he was trying to say,
In the midst of his laughter and glee,
He had softly and suddenly vanished away—
For the Snark *was* a Boojum, you see.

Tales of knights and dragons recount the dangers faced in past times. What happens when modern-day dragon-hunters set out to capture the *buaja?*

The Dragons

David Attenborough

The expedition in quest of a dragon has finally reached the Indonesian island of Komodo.

That evening, the boat anchored safely in the bay, we sat in the headman's hut discussing our plans in detail. The headman called the giant lizards *buaja darat*—land crocodiles. There were very many on the island, he told us, so many that sometimes one would wander right into the village to scavenge. I asked him whether anyone from the village ever hunted them. He shook his head vigorously. *Buaja* were not so good to eat as the wild pigs which were abundant, so why should they kill them? And in any case, he added, they were dangerous animals. Only a few months ago a man was walking through the bush when he stumbled upon a *buaja* lying motionless in the grass. The monster had struck with its powerful tail, knocking the man over and numbing his legs so that he was unable to escape. The creature then turned and mauled him with its jaws. His wounds were so severe that he died soon after his comrades found him.

We asked the headman how we

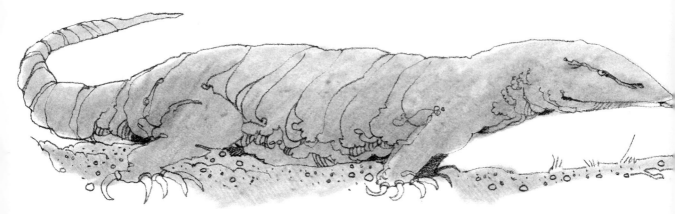

could best attract the lizards so that we could take photographs. He was in no doubt.

They have a very good sense of smell, he told us, and they will come from very long distances to rotting meat. He would slaughter two goats that night and tomorrow his son, Haling, would take them to a place on the other side of the bay where the *buaja* were plentiful. All would be well.

I had hoped to be off early, but it took nearly two hours for Haling to prepare himself for the voyage and to collect three other people to help carry all our gear. At last we helped him push his fifteen foot long outrigger canoe down the beach and into the water. We loaded it with our cameras, tripods and recording machines, together with the two dead goats slung on a long bamboo.

The sun had already risen above the brown mountains ahead of us as we set out across the bay. The water spurted white over the bamboo outrigger. Haling sat in the stern holding the rope attached to

one corner of the rectangular sail, adjusting it to suit the varying wind. Soon we were sailing beneath steep rocky cliffs. High up on a ledge above us a splendid fish eagle stood alert, the sun glinting on its chestnut feathers.

We landed at the mouth of a valley choked with scrub which ran down from the bare, grass-covered mountains. Haling led us inland, cutting a path through the thorn bushes. We walked for an hour. Here and there we passed a dead tree, its barkless bleached branches split by the heat of the sun. There was no sign of life except for the chirring of insects and the vociferous screams of parties of sulphur-crested cockatoos[1] which fled ahead of us. It was oppressively hot; a blanket of lowering clouds had spread across the sky, preventing the heat from leaving the baked land.

At last we came to the dry gravelly bed of a stream, as wide and as level as a road; on one side it was overhung by a bank fifteen feet high which was draped with a tangle of roots and lianas.[2] Tall trees grew above, arching over the bed to meet the branches of the trees from the other bank and forming a high spacious tunnel down which the stream-bed curved and disappeared.

---

[1]cockatoos: large, brightly colored parrots
[2]lianas (lē än'əz): climbing plants or vines

Haling stopped and put down the equipment he had been carrying. "Here," he said.

Our first task was to create the smell which we hoped would attract the lizards. The goats' bodies, already decomposing slightly in the heat, were blown up and swollen as tight as drums. When Sabran slit the underside of each one a foul-smelling gas hissed out. Then he took some of the skin and burnt it on a small wood fire. Haling climbed one of the palms and chopped down a few leaves with which Charles built a hide, while Sabran and I staked out the goats' bodies on the gravelly stream-bed fifteen yards away. This done, we hid behind the palm-leaf screens and began our wait.

Soon it began to rain, the drops pattering gently on the leaves above us. Haling shook his head.

"No good," he said. "*Buaja* won't come out in the rain."

As our shirts got wetter and the rain water trickled down the channel of my back, I began to feel that the *buaja*, on the whole, was more sensible than we were. Charles sealed all his equipment in watertight bags. The smell of the rotting goats' flesh permeated the air. Soon the rain stopped and we left our hides beneath the dripping trees and sat on the open sandy bed of the stream to dry. Haling gloomily insisted that no *buaja* would leave their lairs until the sun shone and a breeze sprang up to disperse the stench of the goats' meat which hung around us. I lay back miserably on the soft gravel of the stream-bed and shut my eyes.

When I next opened them I realized with surprise that I must have fallen asleep. I looked round and saw that not only Charles, but Sabran, Haling and the other men were also fast asleep, their heads resting in one another's laps or on our equipment boxes. I looked at my watch. It was three o'clock. Although it had stopped raining there was still no sign of a break in the clouds and it seemed very unlikely that the lizards would come to our bait that day. Time, however, was precious. At least we could build a trap which we could leave overnight, so I roused everyone.

The main body of the trap, a roofed rectangle enclosure about ten feet long, was easily constructed. Haling and the others began to cut strong poles for us from the trees growing on the banks, and Charles and I selected four of the stoutest and drove them into the stream-bed, using a big boulder as our pile-driver. These were our corner posts. Sabran meanwhile had climbed a tall palm and cut down several large fan-shaped leaves. He then took the stems and split, crushed and thrashed them on a boulder to make them pliable. After he had given the resulting fibers a twist, he handed them to us—pieces of strong serviceable string. With them we lashed long horizontal poles between our corner posts, strengthening the struc-

ture with uprights where we thought it necessary. At the end of half an hour we had built a long enclosed box open at one end.

Now we had to make a drop-door. This we built of heavy stakes tied together with Sabran's string. The vertical ones were sharpened at the bottom so that when the door fell they would stick deep into the ground, and the lowest horizontal cross-piece overlapped the corner posts inside the trap so that when the door fell it could not be pushed outwards by the dragon— should we ever get one inside. We completed the door by tying a heavy boulder on it with lianas so that it would be difficult to lift once it had fallen.

All that remained to do was to build the triggering device. First we pushed a tall pole through the roof of the trap and drove it into the ground near the enclosed end. Then we planted the feet of two more on either side of the door and tied them in a cross directly above it. We knotted our cord onto the door, raised it, and ran the cord over the angle of the cross-poles to the upright post at the other end of the trap. Instead of keeping the door raised by tying the cord directly on to the post, we tied it on to a small piece of stick about six inches long. Holding the stick upright and close to the post, we twisted two rings of creeper round it and the post, one near its top and one near its bottom. The weight of the door pulled the cord tight and so prevented the rings from slipping down the pole. Then we fastened a smaller piece of cord to the bottom ring, threaded it through the roof of the trap and attached it to a piece of goat's flesh inside.

To test it, I poked a stick through the bars of the cage and jabbed the bait. This tugged the cord attached to the bottom ring and pulled it downwards. The small piece of stick flew loose and the door at the other end dropped with a thud. Our trap worked.

Two last things remained to complete it. First we piled boulders along the sides so that a dragon inside the trap would not be able to insert its nose under the lowest poles and uproot the entire construction. Then we shrouded the closed end with palm-leaves so the the bait could only be seen through the open door.

The three of us then dragged the remainder of the goats' bodies to the foot of a tree, threw a rope over a projecting branch and hauled them into the air so that they would not be eaten during the night and their smell would spread widely throughout the valley, attracting dragons towards the trap.

We gathered up all our equipment and walked back in the drizzling rain to the canoe.

The sky was cloudless as we sailed across the bay early the next morning. Haling, seated in the stern of the outrigger canoe, smiled and pointed to the sun.

We landed and set off through the bush as fast as we could. We pushed our way through the undergrowth and emerged on to one of the patches of open savannah. Haling was ahead when suddenly he stopped. "Buaja," he called excitedly. I ran up to him and was just in time to see, fifty yards away on the opposite edge of the savannah, a moving black shape disappear with a rustle into the thorn bushes. We dashed over to the spot. The reptile itself had vanished but it had left signs behind it. The previous day's rain had collected in wide shallow puddles on the savannah, but the morning sun had dried them, leaving smooth sheets of mud, and the dragon we had glimpsed had walked over one of these leaving a perfect set of tracks.

Its feet had sunk into the mud, its claws leaving deep gashes. A shallow furrow, swaying between the marks, showed where the beast had dragged its tail. From the wide spacing of the footprints and the depth to which they had sunk in the mud, we knew that the dragon we had seen had been a large and heavy one.

We delayed no longer over the tracks but hurried on towards the trap through the dense bush. As we reached a tall dead tree, which I recognized as being within a very short distance of the stream-bed, I was tempted to break into a run. But I checked myself with the thought that to crash noisily through the bush so close to the trap would be a very foolish thing to do, for a dragon might at that very moment be circling the bait. I signalled to Haling and the others to wait. Charles, gripping his camera, Sabran and I picked our way silently through the undergrowth, stepping carefully lest we should tread on a twig and snap it.

I parted the dangling branches of a bush and peered through across the clear emptiness of the river-bed. The trap stood a little below us, a few yards away. Its gate was still hitched high. I felt a wave of disappointment and looked round. There was no sign of a dragon. Cautiously we clambered down to the river-bed and examined the trap. Perhaps our trigger had failed to work and the bait had been taken leaving the trap unsprung. Inside, however, the haunch of goat's meat was still hanging, covered with flies. The smooth sand round the trap was unmarked ex-cept from our own footsteps.

Sabran returned to fetch the helpers with the rest of our recording and photographic equipment. Charles began to repair the hides we had erected the day before, and I walked farther up the stream-bed to the tree in which we had hung the major part of our bait. To my delight I saw that the sand beneath was scuffed and disturbed. Without doubt something had been here earlier trying to snatch the bait.

As I untied the rope and lowered the bodies the smell was almost more than I could stand. These big bodies were obviously more powerful magnets than the bait in the trap, and as our primary task was to film the giant lizards, I dragged the meat to a place on the stream-bed which was in clear view of the cameras in the hide. Then I drove a stout stake deep into the ground and tied them securely to it, so that the dragons would be unable to pull them away into the bush, and, if they wished to eat, would be compelled to do so within easy range of our lenses. That done, I joined Charles and Sabran behind our screen and began to wait.

The sun was shining strongly and shafts of light struck through the gaps in the branches above us, dappling the sand of the river-bed. Although we ourselves were shaded by the bush, it was so hot that sweat poured down us. Charles tied a large handkerchief round his forehead to prevent his perspiration trickling onto the viewfinders of his camera.

After a quarter of an hour my position on the ground became extremely uncomfortable. Noiselessly, I shifted my weight on to my hands, and uncrossed my legs. Next to me, Charles crouched by his camera, the long lens of which projected between the palm leaves of the screen. Sabran squatted on the other side of him. Even from where we sat, we could smell only too strongly the stench of the bait fifteen yards in front of us. This, however, was encouraging for this smell should attract the dragons.

We had been sitting in absolute silence for over half an hour when there was a rustling noise immediately behind us. Very slowly, so as not to make any noise, I twisted round to tell the helpers not to be impatient and to return to the boat. Charles and Sabran remained with their eyes riveted on the bait. I was three-quarters of the way round before I discovered that the noise had not been made by humans.

There, facing me, less than four yards away, crouched the dragon.

He was enormous. From the tip of his narrow head to the end of his long tail he measured a full twelve feet. He was so close to us that I could distinguish every beady scale in his skin which, as if too large for him, hung in long horizontal folds on his flanks and was puckered and wrinkled round his powerful neck. He was standing high on his four bowed legs, his heavy body lifted clear of the ground, his head erect and menacing. The line of his savage mouth curved upwards in a fixed sardonic grin and from between his half-closed jaws an enormous yellow-pink forked tongue slid in and out. There was nothing between us and him but a few very small seedling trees sprouting from the leaf-covered ground. I nudged Charles, who turned, saw the dragon and nudged Sabran. The three of us sat staring at the monster. He stared back.

It flashed across my mind that at least he was in no position to use his main weapon, his tail. Further, if he came towards us both Sabran and I were close to trees and I was sure that I would be able to shin up mine very fast if I had to. Charles, sitting in the middle, was not so well placed.

Except for his long tongue, which he unceasingly flicked in and out, the dragon stood motionless.

For almost a minute none of us moved or spoke. Then Charles laughed softly.

"You know," he whispered, keeping his eyes fixed warily on the monster, "he has probably been standing there for the last ten minutes watching us just as intently and quietly as we have been watching the bait."

The dragon emitted a heavy sigh

and slowly spread out his legs, so that his great body sank onto the ground.

"He seems very obliging," I whispered back to Charles. "Why not take his portrait here and now?"

"Can't. The telephoto lens is on the camera and at this distance it would fill the picture with his right nostril."

"Well, let's risk disturbing him and change lens."

Very, very slowly Charles reached in the camera case beside him, took out the stubby wide-angle lens and screwed it into place. He swung the camera round, focused carefully onto the dragon's head and pressed the starting button. The soft whirring of the camera seemed to make an almost deafening noise. The dragon was not in the least concerned but watched us imperiously with his unblinking eye. It was as though he realized that he was the most powerful beast on Komodo, and that, as king of his island, he feared no other creature. A yellow butterfly fluttered over our heads and settled on his nose. He ignored it. Charles pressed the button again and filmed the butterfly as it flapped into the air, circled and settled again on the dragon's nose.

"This," I muttered, "seems a bit silly. Doesn't the brute understand what we've built the hide for?"

The smell of the bait drifted over to us and it occurred to me that we were sitting in a direct line between the dragon and the bait which had attracted him here.

Just then I heard a noise from the river-bed. I looked behind me and saw a young dragon waddling along the sand towards the bait. It was only about three feet in length and had much brighter markings than the monster close to us. Its tail was banded with dark rings and its forelegs and shoulders were spotted with flecks of dull orange. It walked briskly with a peculiar reptilian gait, twisting its spine sideways and wriggling its hips.

Charles tugged at my sleeve, and without speaking pointed up the stream-bed to our left. Another enormous lizard was advancing towards the bait. It looked even bigger than the one behind us. We were surrounded by those wonderful creatures.

The dragon behind us recalled our attention by emitting another deep sigh. He flexed his legs and heaved his body off the ground. He took a few steps forward, turned and slowly stalked round us. We followed him with our eyes. He approached the bank and slithered down it. Charles followed him round with the camera until he was able to swing it back into its original position.

The tension snapped and we all dissolved into muffled delighted laughter.

All three reptiles were now

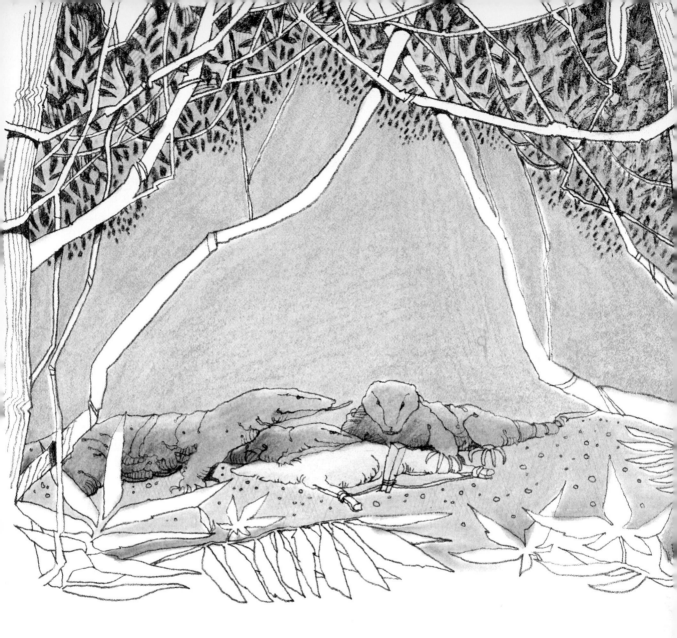

feeding in front of us. Savagely they tore at the goat's flesh. The biggest beast seized one of the goat's legs in his jaws. He was so large that I had to remind myself that what he was treating as a single mouthful was in fact the complete leg of a full-grown goat.

Bracing his feet far apart, he began ripping at the goat with powerful backward jerks of his entire body. If the bait had not been securely tied to the stake, I was sure he would with ease have dragged the entire body away to the forest. Charles filmed feverishly, and

369

soon had used up all the film.

"What about some still photographs?" he whispered.

This was my responsibility, but my camera had not the powerful lenses and I should have to get much closer if I were to obtain good photographs.

Slowly I straightened up behind the hide and stepped out beside it. I took two cautious steps forward and took a photograph. The dragons continued feeding without so much as a glance in my direction. I took another step forward and another photograph. Soon I had exposed all the film in my camera and was standing nonplussed in the middle of the open river-bed within two yards of the monsters. There was nothing else to do but to go back to the hide and reload. Though the dragons seemed preoccupied with their meal, I did not risk turning my back on them as I returned slowly to the hide.

With a new film in my camera I advanced more boldly and did not begin photographing until I was within six feet of them. I inched closer and closer. Eventually, I was standing with my feet touching the forelegs of the goat. I reached inside my pocket and took out a portrait lens for my camera. The big dragon three feet away withdrew his head from inside the goat's ribs with a piece of flesh in his mouth. He straightened up, and with a few convulsive snappings of his jaws, he gulped it

down. He remained in this position for a few seconds looking squarely at the camera. I knelt and took his photograph. Then he once more lowered his head and began wrenching off another mouthful.

I retreated to Charles and Sabran for a consultation. Obviously, a close approach would not frighten the creatures away. We decided to try noise. The three of us stood up and shouted. The dragons ignored us totally. Only when we rushed together from the hide towards them did they interrupt their meal. The two big ones turned and lumbered up the bank and off into the bush. The little one, however, scuttled straight down the river-bed. I chased after it, running as fast as I could, in an attempt to catch it with my hands. It outpaced me, and as it came to a dip in the bank it raced up and disappeared into the undergrowth.

I returned panting and helped Charles and Sabran to hoist the goats' remains into a tree twenty yards away from the trap and then once more we waited. I was fearful that having frightened the dragons once they would not return. But I need not have worried; within ten minutes the big one reappeared on the bank opposite us. For some time he snuffled around the patch of sand where the bait had been lying, tasting the last remnants of the smell in the air. He seemed mystified. He cast around, his head in the air, seeking the meal of which he had been robbed. Then he set off ponderously along the river-bed, but to our dismay walked straight past our trap towards the hanging bait. As he approached it, we realized that we had not tied it high enough, for the creature reared up on its hind legs, using its enormous muscular tail as a counter-balance, and with a downward sweep of his foreleg snatched down a tangle of the goat's innards. He wolfed it immediately, but the end of a long rope of intestine hung down from the angle of his jaw. This displeased him and for a few minutes he tried to paw it off, but without success.

He lumbered along the streambed, back towards the trap, shaking his head angrily. As he reached a large boulder, he stopped, rubbed his scaly cheek against it and at last wiped his jaws clean. Now he was near the trap. The smell of the bait inside filtered into his nostrils and he turned aside from his path to investigate. Sensing accurately the direction from which the smell came, he moved directly to the closed end of the trap and with savage impatient swipes of his forelegs he ripped aside the palm-leaf shroud, exposing the wooden bars. He forced his blunt snout between two of the poles and heaved with his powerful neck. To our relief, the lianas binding the bars together held firm. He at last approached the door. With maddening caution, he looked inside. He took three steps forward. All we could see of him was his hind-legs and his enormous tail. For an interminable time, he made no movement. At last he went farther inside and disappeared entirely from view. Suddenly there was a click, the trigger rope flew loose and the gate thudded down, burying its sharpened stakes deep into the sand.

Exultantly we ran forward. We grabbed boulders and piled them against the trap door. The dragon peered at us superciliously, flicking his forked tongue through the bars. We could hardly believe that we had achieved the objective of our four months' trip, that in spite of all our difficulties we had at last succeeded in catching a specimen of the largest lizard in the world. We sat on the sand looking at our prize and smiling breathlessly at one another. In the end we were refused permission to export the dragon. This was a great and unexpected blow to us, but we were allowed to take the rest of our animals back to London.

In one way I was not sorry that we had to leave the dragon behind. He would, I am sure, have been happy and healthy in the large heated enclosures of London's Reptile House, but he could never have appeared to anyone else as he did to us that day on Komodo when we turned around to see him a few feet away, majestic and magnificent in his own forest.

Focus
1. What was the main purpose of the expedition?
2. Describe the preparations to attract the lizards.
3. How did the weather affect efforts to attract the lizards?
4. Why did the narrator want to capture a lizard? Did he succeed in his plan? Explain your conclusion.
5. Explain why patience would be an essential part of this type of expedition.
6. What do you think are some of the risks involved in being a member of this type of expedition?

In Writing
In his first encounter with a giant lizard, the narrator provides much detail in his description of the lizard. Create a monster of your own, real or imaginary. Review the narrator's description on page 367. Then write a description of your monster and provide the details necessary to make the monster real for the reader.

Vocabulary
On a piece of paper, write the numbers 1 to 5. Then look at the words in the first column and find a synonym for each word in the second column. Next to each number on your paper, write the letter of the synonym for each word.

1. unceasingly
2. vociferous
3. nonplussed
4. mystified
5. sardonic

A. at a loss
B. mocking
C. loud
D. continuously
E. rented
F. puzzled

Classes in dragon fighting do not lessen young Gawaine's fear. Where does he get the courage to slay fifty fire-breathing dragons? Is his courage real?

Heywood Broun

THE FIFTY-FIRST DRAGON

Of all the pupils at the knight school Gawaine le Coeur-Hardy was among the least promising. He was tall and sturdy but his instructors soon discovered that he lacked spirit. He would hide in the woods when the jousting class was called although his companions and members of the faculty sought to appeal to his better nature by shouting to him to come out and break his neck like a man. Even when they told him that the lances were padded, the horses no more than ponies, and the field unusually soft for late autumn, Gawaine refused to grow enthusiastic. The Headmaster and Assistant Professor of Pleasance were discussing the case one spring afternoon, and the Assistant Professor could see no remedy but expulsion.

"No," said the Headmaster, as he looked out at the purple hills which ringed the school, "I think I'll train him to slay dragons."

"He might be killed," objected the Assistant Professor.

"So he might," replied the Headmaster brightly, but he added more soberly, "We must consider the greater good. We are responsible for the formation of this lad's character."

"Are the dragons particularly bad this year?" interrupted the Assistant Professor. This was characteristic. He always seemed restive when the head of the school began to talk ethics and the ideals of the institution.

"I've never known them worse," replied the Headmaster. "Up in the hills last week they killed some peasants, two cows, and a prize pig. And if this dry spell holds, there's no telling when they may start a forest fire simply by breathing around indiscriminately."

"Would any refund on the tuition fee be necessary in case of an accident to young Coeur-Hardy?"

"No," the principal answered judicially, "that's all covered in the contract. But as a matter of fact, he won't be killed. Before I send him up in the hills, I'm going to give him a magic word."

"That's a good idea," said the Professor. "Sometimes they work wonders."

From that day on, Gawaine specialized in dragons. His course included both theory and practice. In the morning there were long lectures on the history, anatomy, manners, and customs of dragons. Gawaine did not distinguish himself in these studies. He had a marvelously versatile gift for forgetting things. In the afternoon he showed to better advantage, for then he would go down to the South Meadow and practice with a battle-ax. In this exercise he was truly impressive, for he had enormous strength as well as speed and grace. He even developed a deceptive display of ferocity. Old alumni say that it was a thrilling sight to see Gawaine charging across the field toward the dummy paper dragon which had been set up for his practice. As he ran he would brandish his ax and shout, "A murrain on thee!" or some other vivid bit of campus slang. It never took him more than one stroke to behead the dummy dragon.

Gradually his task was made more difficult. Paper gave way to papier-mâché and finally to wood, but even the toughest of these dummy dragons had no terrors for Gawaine. One sweep of the ax always did the business. There were those who said that when the practice was protracted until dusk and the dragons threw long, fantastic shadows across the meadow, Gawaine did not charge so impetuously nor shout so loudly. It is possible there was malice in this charge. At any rate, the Headmaster decided by the end of June that it was time for the test. Only the night before, a dragon had come into the school grounds and had eaten lettuce from the garden. The faculty decided that Gawaine was ready. They gave him a diploma and a new battle-ax, and the Headmaster summoned him to a private conference.

"Sit down," said the Headmaster. "You have received your preliminary degree. You are no longer a boy. You are a man.

Tomorrow you will go out into the world, the great world of achievement."

"Here you have learned the theories of life," continued the Headmaster, "but after all, life is not a matter of theories. Life is a matter of facts. It calls on the young and the old alike to face these facts, even though they are hard and sometimes unpleasant. Your problem, for example, is to slay dragons."

"They say that those dragons down in the south wood are five hundred feet long," ventured Gawaine timidly.

"Stuff and nonsense!" said the Headmaster. "My assistant saw one last week from the top of Arthur's Hill. The dragon was sunning itself down in the valley. He didn't have an opportunity to look at it very long because he felt it was his duty to hurry back to make a report to me. He said the monster—or shall I say, the big lizard?—wasn't an inch over two hundred feet. But the size has nothing at all to do with it. You'll find the big ones even easier than the little ones. They're far slower on their feet and less aggressive I'm told. Besides, before you go I'm going to equip you in such a fashion that you need have no fear of all the dragons in the world."

"I'd like an enchanted cap," said Gawaine.

"What's that?" asked the Headmaster testily.

"A cap to make me disappear," explained Gawaine.

The Headmaster laughed indulgently. "You mustn't believe

all those stories," he said. "There isn't any such thing. A cap to make you disappear, indeed! What would you do with it? You haven't even appeared yet. Why, my boy, you could walk from here to London, and nobody would so much as look at you. You're nobody. You couldn't be more invisible than that."

Gawaine seemed dangerously close to a relapse into his old habit of whimpering. The Headmaster reassured him: "Don't worry; I'll give you something much better than an enchanted cap. I'm going to give you a magic word. All you have to do is to repeat this magic charm once, and no dragon can possibly harm a hair of your head. You can cut off the dragon's head at your leisure."

He took a heavy book from the shelf behind his desk and began to run through it. "Sometimes," he said, "the charm is a whole phrase or even a sentence. I might, for instance, give you 'to make the'—No, that might not do. I think a single word would be best for dragons."

"A short word," suggested Gawaine.

"It can't be too short or it wouldn't be strong enough. There isn't so much hurry as all that. Here's a splendid magic word: 'Rumplesnitz.' Do you think you can learn that?"

Gawaine tried and in an hour or so he seemed to have the word well in hand. Again and again he interrupted the lesson to inquire, "and if I say 'Rumplesnitz,' the dragon can't possibly hurt me?" And always the Headmaster replied, "If you only say 'Rumplesnitz,' you are perfectly safe."

Toward morning Gawaine seemed resigned to his career. At daybreak the Headmaster saw him to the edge of the forest and pointed him to the direction in which he should proceed. About a mile away to the southwest a cloud of steam hovered over an open meadow in the woods, and the Headmaster assured Gawaine that under the steam he would find a dragon. Gawaine went forward slowly. He wondered whether it would be best to approach the dragon on the run as he did in his practice in the South Meadow or to walk slowly toward it shouting 'Rumplesnitz' all the way.

The problem was decided for him. No sooner had he come to the fringe of the meadow than the dragon spied him and began to charge. It was a large dragon, and yet it seemed decidedly aggressive in spite of the Headmaster's statement to the contrary. As the dragon charged, it released huge clouds of hissing steam through its nostrils. It was almost as if a gigantic teapot had gone mad. The dragon came forward so fast and Gawaine was so frightened that he had time to say 'Rumplesnitz' only once. As he said it, he swung his battle-ax and off popped the dragon's head. Gawaine had to admit that it was even easier to kill a real dragon than a wooden one if only you said "Rumplesnitz."

Gawaine brought the ears home and a small section of the tail. His schoolmates and the faculty made much of him, but the Headmaster wisely kept him from being spoiled by insisting that he go on with his work. Every clear day Gawaine rose at dawn and went out to kill dragons. The Headmaster kept him at home when it rained, because he said the woods were damp and unhealthy at such times and that he didn't want the boy to run needless risks. Few good days passed in which Gawaine failed to get a dragon. On one particularly fortunate day he killed three. Gradually he developed a technique. Pupils who sometimes watched him from the hilltops a long way off said that he often allowed the dragon to come within a few feet before he said "Rumplesnitz." He came to say it with a mocking sneer. Occasionally he did stunts. Once, when an excursion party from London was watching him, he went into action with his right hand tied behind his back. The dragon's head came off just as easily.

As Gawaine's record of killings mounted higher, the Headmaster found it impossible to keep him completely in hand. He fell into the habit of stealing out at night and racing horses down the main path of the village. It was after such a wild time that he rose a little before dawn one fine August morning and started out after his fiftieth dragon. His head was heavy and his mind sluggish. He was heavy in other respects as well, for he had adopted the somewhat vulgar practice of wearing his medals, ribbons and all, when he went out dragon hunting. The decorations began on his chest and ran all the way down to his abdomen. They must have weighed at least eight pounds.

Gawaine found a dragon in the same meadow where he had killed the first one. It was a fair-sized dragon, but evidently an old one. Its face was wrinkled, and Gawaine thought he had never seen so hideous a countenance. Much to the lad's disgust, the monster refused to charge, and Gawaine was obliged to walk toward him. He whistled as he went. The dragon regarded him hopelessly, but craftily. Of course it had heard of Gawaine. Even when the lad raised his battle-ax, the dragon made no move. It knew that there was no salvation in the quickest thrust of the head, for it had been informed that this hunter was protected by an enchantment. It merely waited, hoping something would turn up. Gawine raised the battle-ax and lowered it again. He had grown very pale, and he trembled violently. The dragon suspected a trick. "What's the matter?" It asked with false solicitude.

"I've forgotten the magic word," stammered Gawaine.

"What a pity," said the dragon. "So that was the secret. It doesn't seem quite sporting to me, all this magic stuff, you know. Not cricket, as we used to say when I was a little dragon."

Gawaine was so helpless with terror that the dragon's confidence rose immeasurably and it could not resist the temptation to show off a bit.

"Could I possibly be of any assistance?" it asked. "What's the first letter of the magic word?"

"It begins with an 'r,'" said Gawaine.

"Let's see," mused the dragon, "that doesn't tell us much, does it? What sort of word is this? Is it an epithet?"

Gawaine could do no more than nod.

"Why, of course," exclaimed the dragon, "reactionary rebels."

Gawaine shook his head.

"Well, then," said the dragon, "we'd better get down to business. Will you surrender?"

With the suggestion of a compromise Gawaine mustered up courage to speak. "What will you do if I surrender?"

"Why, I'll eat you," said the dragon.

"And if I don't surrender?"

"I'll eat you just the same."

"Then it doesn't make any difference, does it?" moaned Gawaine.

"It does to me," said the dragon with a smile. "I'd rather you didn't surrender. You'd taste much better if you didn't."

The dragon waited for a long time for Gawaine to ask "Why?" but the boy was too frightened to speak. At last the dragon had to give the explanation without his cue line. "You see," it said, "if you don't surrender, you'll taste better because you'll die game."

This was an old and ancient trick of the dragon's. By means of some such quip he was accustomed to paralyze his victims with laughter and then to destroy them. Gawaine was sufficiently paralyzed as it was, but laughter had no part in his helplessness. With the last word of the joke the dragon drew back his head and struck. In that second there flashed into the mind of Gawaine the magic word "Rumplesnitz," but there was no time to say it. There was time only to strike and, without a word, Gawaine met the onrush of the dragon with a full swing. He put all his back and shoulders into it. The impact was terrific, and the head of the dragon flew away almost a hundred yards and landed in a thicket.

Gawaine did not remain frightened very long after the death of the dragon. His mood was one of wonder. He was enormously puzzled. He cut off the ears of the monster almost in a trance. Again and again he thought to himself, "I didn't say 'Rumplesnitz'!" He was sure of that, and yet there was no question that he had killed the dragon. In fact, he had never killed one so utterly. Never before had he driven a head for anything like the same distance. Twenty-five yards was perhaps his best previous record. All the way back to the knight school he kept rumbling about in his mind seeking an explanation for what had occurred. He went to the Headmaster immediately and after closing the door told him what had happened. "I didn't say 'Rumplesnitz,'" he explained with great earnestness.

The Headmaster laughed. "I'm glad you've found out. It makes you ever so much more of a hero. Don't you see that? Now you know that it was you who killed all these dragons and not that foolish little word 'Rumplesnitz.'"

Gawaine frowned. "Then it wasn't a magic word after all?" he asked.

"Of course not," said the Headmaster, "you ought to be too old for such foolishness. There isn't any such thing as a magic word."

"But you told me it was magic," protested Gawaine. "You said it was magic, and now you say it isn't."

"It wasn't magic in a literal sense," answered the Headmaster, "but it was much more wonderful than that. The word gave you confidence. It took away your fears. If I hadn't told you that, you might have been killed the very first time. It was your battle-ax did the trick."

Gawaine surprised the Headmaster by his attitude. He was obviously distressed by the explanation. He interrupted a long philosophic and ethical discourse by the Headmaster with, "If I hadn't of hit 'em all mighty hard and fast, any one of 'em might have crushed me like a, like a—" He fumbled for a word.

"An eggshell," suggested the Headmaster.

"Like an eggshell," assented Gawaine, and he said it many times. All through the evening meal people who sat near him heard him muttering, "Like an eggshell, like an eggshell."

The next day was clear, but Gawaine did not get up at dawn. Indeed, it was almost noon when the Headmaster found him cowering in bed, with the clothes pulled over his head. The principal called the Assistant Professor of Pleasance, and together they dragged the boy toward the forest.

"He'll be all right as soon as he gets a couple more dragons under his belt," explained the Headmaster.

The Assistant Professor of Pleasance agreed. "It would be a shame to stop such a fine run," he said. "Why, counting that one yesterday, he's killed fifty dragons."

They pushed the boy into a thicket above which hung a meager cloud of steam. It was obviously quite a small dragon. But Gawaine did not come back that night or the next. In fact, he never came back. Some weeks afterward brave spirits from the school explored the thicket, but they could find nothing to remind them of Gawain except the metal parts of his medals. Even the ribbons had been devoured.

The Headmaster and the Assistant Professor of Pleasance agreed that it would be just as well not to tell the school how Gawaine had achieved his record and still less how he came to die. They held that it might have a bad effect on school spirit. Accordingly, Gawaine has lived in the memory of the school as its greatest hero. No visitor succeeds in leaving the building today without seeing a great shield which hangs on the wall of the dining hall. Fifty pairs of dragons' ears are mounted upon the shield and underneath in gilt letters is "Gawaine le Coeur-Hardy," followed by the simple inscription, "He killed fifty dragons." The record has never been equaled.

Focus

1. When did the story take place? What details suggested the time period of its setting?
2. Why was Gawaine given the magic word "Rumplesnitz"? What was the real value of this word?
3. Gawaine was able to slay fifty dragons. Why do you think he could not slay the fifty-first dragon?
4. Would you describe this story as serious or lighthearted? Explain your choice.
5. What do you think the author was saying about courage in this story?

In Writing

Gawaine's meeting with his fifty-first dragon is never described in the story. What might Gawaine have said to that dragon when he faced it? What might the dragon have said upon first meeting Gawaine? Was Gawaine killed by the dragon, or can you think of some other explanation for his disappearance? Were any other characters present? Write a short, humorous play about Gawaine and his meeting with the fifty-first dragon.

Vocabulary

On a piece of paper, write the numbers 1 to 5. Then look at the words in the first column and find an antonym for each word in the second column. Next to each number on your paper, write the letter of the antonym for each word.

1. expulsion
2. restive
3. judicially
4. vulgar
5. ferocity

A. tameness
B. foolishly
C. hungrily
D. calm
E. tasteful
F. acceptance

Nana Miriam

A Legend from Nigeria

Hans Baumann

Legends often tell tales of courage. How is the courage Nana Miriam shows different from other kinds of courage?

Fara Maka was a man of the Songai tribe, who lived by the River Niger.[1] He was taller than the other men and he was also stronger. Only he was very ugly. However, no one thought that important, because Fara Maka had a daughter who was very beautiful. Her name was Nana Miriam and she too was tall and strong. Her father instructed her in all kinds of things. He went with her to the sandbank and said, "Watch the fish!" And he told her the names of all the various kinds. Everything there is to know about fish he taught her. Then he asked her, "What kind is the one swimming here, and the other one over there?"

"This is a so-and-so," replied Nana Miriam. "And that is a such-and-such."

"Male or female?" asked Fara Maka.

"I don't know," said Nana Miriam.

"This one is a female, and so is the other one," explained Fara Maka. "But the third one over there is a male." And each time he pointed to a different fish.

That was how Nana Miriam came to learn so much. And in addition she had magic powers within her, which no one

---

[1]River Niger: river in West Africa

suspected. And because her father also taught her many magic spells, she grew stronger than anyone else in the Land of the Songai.

Beside the great river, the Niger, there lived a monster that took the form of a hippopotamus. This monster was insatiable. It broke into the rice fields and devoured the crops, bringing famine to the Songai people. No one could tackle this hippopotamus, because it could change its shape. So the hunters had all their trouble for nothing and they returned to their villages in helpless despair. Times were so bad that many died of hunger.

One day, Fara Maka picked up all his lances and set out to kill the monster. When he saw it, he recoiled in fear, for huge pots of fire were hung around the animal's neck. Fara Maka hurled lance after lance, but each one was swallowed by the flames. The hippopotamus monster looked at Fara Maka with scorn. Then it turned its back on him and trotted away.

Fara Maka returned home furious, wondering who he could summon to help him. Now there was a man of the Tomma tribe who was a great hunter. His name was Kara-Digi-Mao-Fosi-Fasi, and Fara Maka asked him if he would hunt the hippopotamus with his one hundred and twenty dogs. "That I will," said Kara-Digi-Mao-Fosi-Fasi.

So Fara Maka invited him and his one hundred and twenty dogs to a great banquet. Before every dog, which had an iron chain around its neck, was placed a small mound of rice and meat. For the hunter, however, there was a huge mound of rice. None of the dogs left a single grain of rice uneaten, and neither did Kara-Digi-Mao-Fosi-Fasi. Well fortified they set out for the place where the monster lived.

As soon as the dogs picked up the scent, Kara-Digi-Mao-Fosi-Fasi unchained the first one. The chain rattled as the dog leaped forward towards its quarry. One chain rattled after the other, as dog after dog sprang forward to attack the hippopotamus. But the hippopotamus took them on one by one, and it gobbled them all up. The great hunter Kara-Digi-Mao-Fosi-Fasi took to his heels in terror. The hippopotamus charged into a rice field and ate that too.

When Fara Maka heard from the great hunter what had happened, he sat down in the shadow of a large tree and hung his head.

"Haven't you been able to kill the hippopotamus?" Nana Miriam asked him.

"No," said Fara Maka.

"And Kara-Digi-Mao-Fosi-Fasi couldn't drive it away either?"

"No."

"So there is no one who can get the better of it?"

"No," said Fara Maka.

"Then I'll not delay any longer," said Nana Miriam. "I'll go to its haunts and see what I can see."

"Yes, do," said her father.

Nana Miriam walked along the banks of the Niger, and she soon found the hippopotamus eating its way through a rice field. As soon as it saw the girl it stopped eating, raised its head and greeted her.

"Good morning," replied Nana Miriam.

"I know why you have come," said the hippopotamus. "You want to kill me. But no one can do that. Your father tried, and he lost all his lances. The great hunter Kara-Digi-Mao-Fosi-Fasi tried, and all his dogs paid with their lives for his presumption. And you are only a girl."

"We'll soon see," answered Nana Miriam. "Prepare to fight with me. Only one of us will be left to tell the tale."

"Right you are!" shouted the hippopotamus and with its breath it set the rice field afire. There it stood in a ring of flame through which no mortal could pass.

But Nana Miriam threw magic powder into the fire, and the flames turned to water.

"Right!" shouted the hippopotamus, and a wall of iron sprang up making a ring around the monster. But Nana Miriam plucked a magic hammer from the air, and shattered the iron wall into fragments.

Now for the first time the hippopotamus felt afraid, and it turned itself into a river that flowed into the Niger.

Again Nana Miriam sprinkled her magic powder. At once

the river dried up and the water changed back into a hippopotamus. It grew more and more afraid and when Fara Maka came up to see what was happening, the monster charged him blindly. Nana Miriam ran after it, and when it was only ten bounds away from her father, she seized it by its left hind foot and flung it across the Niger. As it crashed against the opposite bank, its skull was split and it was dead. Then Fara Maka, who had seen the mighty throw, exclaimed, "What a daughter I have!"

Very soon, the whole tribe heard what had happened, and the Dialli, the minstrel folk, sang the song of Nana Miriam's adventure with the hippopotamus, which used to devastate the rice fields. And in the years that followed, no one in the Land of the Songai starved any more.

Focus

1. How was the hippopotamus in this story different from an ordinary hippopotamus?
2. How were Nana Miriam and her father alike? How were they different?
3. List the three attempts to defeat the hippopotamus.
4. Was Nana Miriam completely safe from danger because of her magic powers? Explain your answer.
5. Compare the stories "Nana Miriam" and "The Fifty-First Dragon." Give at least two ways in which the plots are similar. Give at least two ways in which the plots are different.

In Writing

Write the lyrics to a folk song about the adventure of Nana Miriam and the hippopotamus.

Vocabulary

On a piece of paper, write the numbers *1* to *5*. Then read the sentences below. Next to each number on your paper, write the word from the list that best completes each analogy.

quarry	insatiable	theory
solicitude	impetuous	fortified
deceptive	relapse	epithet

1. Priceless is to value as ___ is to appetite.
2. Excursion is to trip as ___ is to prey.
3. Protracted is to shortened as ___ is to weakened.
4. False is to statement as ___ is to appearance.
5. Thoughtful is to slow as ___ is to quick.

LIFE SKILL: Looking at Labels

When you venture into the world of "dragons and hippopotamuses," you might come back and head straight for the medicine cabinet. A typical one is full of bottles, jars, tubes, and boxes. Which kind of medicine are you looking for? How is it helpful? Can it be harmful?

Before using any medicine or health-care product, it is very important to read the label. The label shown here is an example of one from a tube of medicated cream. The label tells you what the cream is for and how to use it. It also tells you the dangers of improper use.

The first two statements below the product's name give you general information on the product's use. The next section gives more detailed examples. Skim the "Uses" section and find five ways in which *Soothefast Cream* can be helpful.

Did you find that it helps, for instance, with sunburn, cuts, poison ivy, insect bites, and detergent-damaged hands?

Now find the section labeled "Directions." It contains two statements. It tells you how to apply the cream. It also warns you not to get it into your eyes or mouth.

The most important part of the label is marked "Caution." Failure to read this section could be very dangerous. Read it carefully. *External* means outside. So, this statement cautions you to use the cream on the outside of your body only. Do *not* swallow it!

The caution to avoid getting the cream into your eyes or mouth is

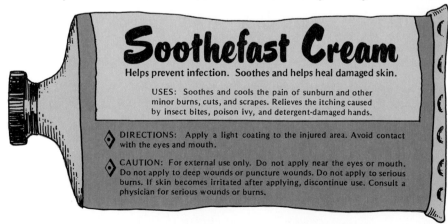

Soothefast Cream

Helps prevent infection. Soothes and helps heal damaged skin.

USES: Soothes and cools the pain of sunburn and other minor burns, cuts, and scrapes. Relieves the itching caused by insect bites, poison ivy, and detergent-damaged hands.

DIRECTIONS: Apply a light coating to the injured area. Avoid contact with the eyes and mouth.

CAUTION: For external use only. Do not apply near the eyes or mouth. Do not apply to deep wounds or puncture wounds. Do not apply to serious burns. If skin becomes irritated after applying, discontinue use. Consult a physician for serious wounds or burns.

repeated. Any instance in which the cream might get below the skin and into the bloodstream is dangerous. The label gives examples of such instances: deep wounds, puncture wounds, and serious burns.

An additional warning tells you to stop using the cream if it irritates the skin. This warning is very common on many health-care products. Some people may be allergic, or sensitive, to one of the ingredients in the product.

Now look at the next label. It is an example of what you might see on a sun-care product. Read it carefully.

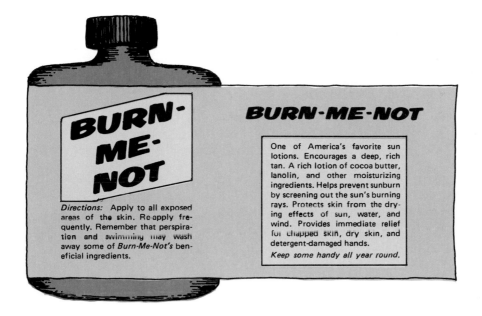

BURN-ME-NOT

Directions: Apply to all exposed areas of the skin. Re-apply frequently. Remember that perspiration and swimming may wash away some of *Burn-Me-Not's* beneficial ingredients.

BURN-ME-NOT

One of America's favorite sun lotions. Encourages a deep, rich tan. A rich lotion of cocoa butter, lanolin, and other moisturizing ingredients. Helps prevent sunburn by screening out the sun's burning rays. Protects skin from the drying effects of sun, water, and wind. Provides immediate relief for chapped skin, dry skin, and detergent-damaged hands.

Keep some handy all year round.

Compare the labels for both health-care products. Answer the following questions.

1. Which product would you use to protect your face before going for a bike ride on a cold, windy day?
2. Which product helps to prevent infection?
3. Give one reason for keeping *Soothefast Cream* near the kitchen stove.
4. If you have poison ivy, which product would you use?
5. Which product helps to *prevent* damage to your skin?
6. Which product helps to *heal* damaged skin?
7. Both products help to soothe damaged skin. Give one example of a situation in which either product could be used.

The Dinner Party

Mona Gardner

Sometimes self-control
requires more courage than
daring action.

The country is India . A colonial official and his wife are giving a large dinner party. They are seated with their guests—army officers and government attachés and their wives, and a visiting American naturalist—in their spacious dining room, which has a bare marble floor, open rafters, and wide glass doors opening onto a veranda.

A spirited discussion springs up between a young girl who insists that women have outgrown the jumping-on-a-chair-at-the-sight-of-a-mouse era and a colonel who says that they haven't.

"A woman's unfailing reaction in any crisis," the colonel says, "is to scream. And while a man may feel like it, he has that ounce more of nerve control than a woman has. And that last ounce is what counts."

The American does not join in the argument but watches the other guests. As he looks, he sees a strange expression come over the face of the hostess. She is staring straight ahead, her muscles contracting slightly. With a slight gesture she summons the servant standing behind her chair and whispers to him. The servant's eyes widen, and he quickly leaves the room.

Of the guests, none except the American notices this or sees the servant place a bowl of milk on the veranda just outside the open doors.

The American comes to with a start. In India, milk in a bowl means only one thing—bait for a snake. He realizes there must be a cobra in the room. He looks up at the rafters—the likeliest place—but they are bare. Three corners of the room are empty, and in the fourth the servants are waiting to serve the next course. There is only one place left—under the table.

His first impulse is to jump back and warn the others, but he knows the commotion would frighten the cobra into striking. He speaks quickly, the tone of his voice so arresting that it sobers everyone.

"I want to know just what control everyone at this table has. I will count to three hundred—that's five minutes—and not one of you is to move a muscle. Those who move will forfeit fifty rupees.[1] Ready!"

The twenty people sit like stone images while he counts. He is saying " . . . two hundred and eighty . . ." when, out of the corner of his eye, he sees the cobra emerge and make for the bowl of milk. Screams ring out as he jumps to slam the veranda doors safely shut.

"You were right, Colonel!" the host exclaims. "A man has just shown us an example of perfect control."

"Just a minute," the American says, turning to his hostess. "Mrs. Wynnes, how did you know that the cobra was in the room?"

A faint smile lights up the woman's face as she replies: "Because it was crawling across my foot."

---

[1]Rupees: silver coins used in India

Focus

1. What was the setting of this story? How was the setting important to the plot?
2. Summarize the discussion that took place at the dinner party.
3. What do you think Mrs. Wynnes whispered to the servant?
4. Explain how the discussion at the table and the action of the story work together.
5. In a sentence, write what you think is the theme of this story.

In Writing

One slip on the part of the hostess, the naturalist, or the servant delivering the bowl of milk might have meant disaster at the dinner party. Write another ending to the story, in which one of the three people loses his or her nerve.

Vocabulary

On a piece of paper, write the numbers *1* to *5*. Then look at the words in the first column and find a definition for each word in the second column. Next to each number on your paper, write the letter of the correct definition for each word.

1. attaché
2. veranda
3. contracting
4. arresting
5. forfeit

A. coming together
B. to give up
C. official of a foreign country
D. a large porch
E. catching and holding
F. playing noisily

CHECKPOINT

Vocabulary:
Word
Identification

Read the word list and paragraph below. Decide which word makes the best sense in each blank space. Then write the numbers *1* to *8* on a piece of paper and write the correct word next to each number.

disarray	contempt	scanned	mystified
glowered	boisterous	dislocated	deceptive
forfeit	restive	nonplussed	

The reporter approached the team's locker room. __(1)__ cheers echoed through the hall. He opened the door and __(2)__ the faces, looking for a likely candidate to interview. Amidst the __(3)__ of equipment, uniforms, and towels, he spotted one young boy who __(4)__ him. All were jubilant except this boy, who sat alone and __(5)__ at the others. The reporter began to ask the boy questions and soon discovered the problem. The boy angrily explained that the coach had made him __(6)__ his place on the team because of missed practices. The reporter was __(7)__ by the apparent __(8)__ in the boy's voice. His team had just won the championship, and the boy could think only of himself!

Comprehension:
Drawing
Conclusions

9. Reread page 381. What happened to Gawaine when he tried to kill his fifty-first dragon?
10. Reread page 350. Why didn't the children replace the well cover immediately?

Comprehension:
Cause/Effect

11. Reread page 391. Why did Mrs. Wynnes have a bowl of milk placed on the veranda?
12. Review "The Fifty-First Dragon," on pages 373-381. Explain both the positive and the negative effects that the magic word had on Gawaine.

Life Skills:
Consumer
Information
(Labels)

13. Make a chart with columns labeled *Uses*, *Directions*, and *Cautions*. Then examine the labels of the two health-care products shown on pages 388–389. Add rows to the chart for the product names and record the information in the appropriate columns.

Mo
Mon

In each life there are a few exceptional moments—perhaps of happiness, of terror, of anger or triumph. Each selection in this unit presents a person whose feelings, for a time, are unusually intense and focused.

You will witness fights for survival. You will see how greed can bring a person despair. Share the victories of people who overcome physical and psychological handicaps, and feel the frustrations and the rewards of learning difficult new skills.

Have your own moments been like any of these? Read on and see.

Moments

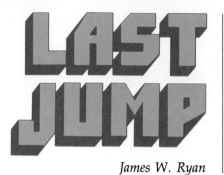

LAST JUMP

James W. Ryan

There are times when safety measures don't quite work out as they are supposed to. Johnny Welcome discovers this the hard way during his own "moment."

When he drew the high number in the stick of eighteen troopers, Sgt. Johnny Welcome knew without a doubt that his last jump was going to be one to remember.

Never during his three years with the Airborne, whether with the 187th and the Rangers in Korea or now back at Fort Campbell with the 11th, had he jumped farther back than eighth. Now with only three weeks to go for his discharge, he was assigned on the jump manifest as the last man. Alone with his thoughts, he silently finished "chuting up."

As dawn slithered up in the eastern Kentucky sky and sprawled along the harsh horizon, Welcome felt the perspiration gathering despite the cool November air. This was nothing new, actually. By the time he had exited from the C-119 during the Sukchon-Sunchon jump above Pyongyang in Korea, his uniform had been soaking wet.

For one forgetful and foolish moment, Welcome considered asking First Sergeant Riley to let him swap his last spot with another jumper, perhaps one who still had months to serve. But he realized instantly that their mutual dislike made such a request impossible.

Riley would want to know why. Riley would make him crawl. Riley would then send him packing back to his eighteenth spot. Welcome had no intention of putting himself at Riley's mercy. He would just have to sweat it out.

Now only a minute away from the Yamoto drop zone, he peered down between the swaying double line of heavily

encumbered paratroopers for some glimpse of the open doors near the tail end of the quivering fuselage. His light blue eyes were narrowed and bloodshot. Perspiration coursed down his forehead. Through the massed lines of webbed steel helmets and bulky main chutes, he caught flickering glimpses of the sky as though it were at the end of a mile-long tunnel.

Beneath the double-thick soles of his spit-shined boots, Welcome felt the floor of the aircraft rising and falling and simultaneously yawing from side to side like an aluminum hammock. A hard cold stone of fear squatted low down in his stomach.

He wondered anew why the Air Force still used old C-46's,

as he struggled to maintain his balance by clutching the steel snap fasteners hooked overhead onto the anchor-line cable. The cable stretched the length of the narrow fuselage. Why hadn't the flyboys forwarded their C-119's from Smyrna in Tennessee?

His dislike of C-46's was intense and went back to jump school training at Fort Benning. Every time he jumped from a C-46 he felt that the tail elevator plane was going to slice him right in half, about belt high. But somehow he had always swooped down and away at the last moment. With the C-119, there was no such concern. The C-119's double-boomed tails were set high up on its squat fuselage and extended far back. A jumper couldn't get hung up on that tail arrangement.

Sergeant Welcome wondered if Riley was aware of his distrust of the C-46 and had purposely requested that aircraft. But he quickly realized that Riley didn't have such authority. The brass selected the planes. Besides, Johnny Welcome had never mentioned his fear of the C-46 to anyone. He decided to shrug off his premonitions.

He wondered why Riley didn't like him. It wasn't his fault that Riley had never seen combat. Welcome wasn't about to apologize for the months he had spent in Korea. If Riley wanted the Silver Star and the Purple Heart, he could have transferred from the 511th to the 187th with the rest of the troopers back in 1950.

Welcome winced. He remembered the pain and ripped flesh after the Chinese grenade fragments had hit him in the right thigh. Riley could have the scars and the recurring pain anytime. All Welcome wanted to do was serve his time, then return to Boston, finish college, and marry Sally.

Riley could have it all. The silver wings and jump boots. The parades and the glory. All he wanted was to make one last good jump and go home.

Just let the jump be good. That was all he asked. He figured he had been a fairly decent fellow and deserved one last good jump. He wanted to see that chute open on cue, big and

398

blossomy, all white and beautiful, and he would never ask for another thing.

Welcome was blitzed from his thoughts by the buzzer's rasping and the blinking red glow of the jump light overhead. The C-46 had flown over the jump panels, fixed some 900 feet below on the drop zone. Already, the troopers at the head of both sticks were shuffling rhythmically toward the open doors, hurling their static lines along the length of the anchor-line cable into the shadowy recess of the tail section of the fuselage, pivoting, and then jumping through the open doors.

The confines of the fuselage reverberated to the paratroopers' shouts of "GO! GO!" Sergeant Welcome felt the C-46 perceptibly rising in the sky as it disgorged the troopers. He started shuffling at double time to catch up to the fast-moving men in his stick. He joined in their cries of "GO! GO! Airborne!" The shouting always helped him ease his tensions and fears.

Welcome's stick had jumped in such rapid-fire fashion that he was nearly running when he came to the beckoning door. Winging the static-line fastener along the anchor-line cable to the rear, he caught a glimpse of Riley watching him. Only then, pivoting to jump out the door, did he remember that Riley would not be making the jump. Riley was acting as jumpmaster.

Riley was lucky, Welcome thought as he grasped the sides of the doorway with his fingers flat against the outside of the fuselage. The cold, brusque air rushed across his big hands. As he hurtled out the door, the earth appeared like a jumble of squares, big and small; a kaleidoscope of greens and browns.

The old sensation of hanging suspended, frozen in space, swept his body. His arms already throbbed from the tight grip on his reserve chute fastened across his chest. But inevitably the prop blast caught his lean, 6'2" frame and spun him around to face the rear of the C-46. Instantly he knew again the nightmarish sensation of the sky giving way below his boots. Two shiny boot toes moved up past his eyes while his head fell downward.

Just before he clenched shut his eyes he caught a glimpse of the C-46's tail section. His heart surged against the quick-release box. The tail resembled an ugly gray cleaver rushing forward to slice him in half. He gritted his teeth. His chin shot down toward his chest as he sought to tuck his head under the reserve chute.

Behind his eyelids, weird and colorful patterns of light danced and whirled. The brilliant lights blazed up and just as quickly disappeared, only to erupt again. At first he heard nothing. A strange stillness filled his ears. Then in the next split second Welcome heard a thunderous noise like a crack express train speeding through an interminably long Alpine tunnel.

Welcome had counted only, "One thousand . . . two thous . . ." when he heard the parachute risers zing past his ears. He braced himself. It was coming now—the opening shock! His falling body would have zoomed from a speed of about 100 miles per hour to absolute zero when the main chute burst open. It was like running into a stone wall in midair. He cringed involuntarily, awaiting the imaginary crash.

With his eyes still shut, he realized instantly that something had gone wrong. Welcome had jumped forty-seven times. And always he had crashed into that invisible stone wall by now. *How had he missed it?* Opening shock time had passed.

His next thought was that his main chute had failed to open and he was plummeting to earth like a wingless stone. Yet, the thought was dispelled immediately when he recalled the sounds of the chute's zinging by his ears.

His eyes snapped open. *What was happening?* He felt as if he were being hauled upstream against powerful water currents. He saw his boot toes pointed straight up in the sky.

In his bewilderment, he realized that he was flat on his back, rushing horizontally through the sky. Currents of air buffeted and whipped his neck and shoulders. Hands seemed to reach out of the sky in repeated attempts to wrest his helmet from his head. Other hands, more powerful, more cruel, beat steadily on his arms and legs.

He twisted slightly, trying to flip over. He caught a glimpse

400

of the earth's varied-colored squares and oddly shaped shadows. Between his toes, far to the rear where the sky and the dark November earth appeared to touch, he saw white splotches. Many of them were spread on the ground. His buddies were already landing.

Then the truth struck him. He sought to scream but his cry was stifled by the powerful air currents. *Why did it have to happen to him? Why on his last jump? If only he could have gone backward in Time. He'd never have made the last jump. He could have said his wounds ached.*

But he hadn't. He had to be airborne all the way. Right to the end. Now he was hung up. Hung up on a C-46. Flying through the sky like a hooked fish.

It couldn't be denied. Not the way he was streaming through the sky with the air smashing against his aching body like a runaway mountain stream.

Strange sounds pounded in his ears. *Did he hear a voice calling? How could that be? Was he cracking up?* But there it was again. He heard shouts.

The shouts came from the C-46. Somebody was calling to him on the bullhorn. If only he could hear. *Oh, for a moment of silence.*

Calling on every possible bit of willpower to soothe his reason and collect his wits, he figured for the time being that he was not going to get clobbered. He found comfort in the old paratrooper joke that no one got hurt or killed until he hit the ground.

He had to stay cool and think. Sure he was afraid. That was nothing new for him. But he had to suppress his fears long enough for his brain to function and to figure out a plan of action. He was alive and if he remained cool, he would stay alive.

OK, now what? he asked himself. There he was, flat out on his back, zipping through the sky at about 110 miles per hour. The C-46 undoubtedly had climbed up to 1,500 feet or so, maybe even higher to give the pilot maneuvering room. He had to do something. For all he knew, the pilot might have fuel for only a few minutes.

He imagined the C-46 landing with himself still attached to the tail. He shuddered, feeling shaken and sick. He immediately tried to erase the mental picture from his imagination.

"Stop it!" he screamed into the wind. He had to wipe such thoughts from his mind. There had to be a way out of his predicament. He considered shaking the chute free of the tail wing. But how? He would have to roll over on his stomach first to see what was going on.

He tried to flip over. The air currents snapped him sharply on his back. He winced as the helmet jump strap bit into his neck. The helmet would have to go.

He slid his hands up his field jacket to the buckle beneath his right ear. The air currents lashed at his hands.

"C'mon," he cried angrily. "C'mon! Move!" His fingers let off, tired and buffeted. The strap remained fastened. He had pulled the strap skintight and looped it around several times, as he usually did, to keep the helmet from spinning off when his chute opened.

He chided himself for always doing everything by the book. Couldn't he just this once have left the end of the strap loose?

Hold on! he warned. *This was getting him nowhere. He'd leave the helmet on. Let the strap cut into his neck. What could that possibly be compared to his landing still hung up on the tail wing?*

He felt the panic rising again. *All right, relax! Hold on!* But what was he going to do? He didn't want to die dangling on the end of an airplane.

He ordered himself to stop that talk. He had been in tough spots before. All he had to do was take it easy. The solution would come to him. But not if he panicked. He had to think. He should try to roll over again. Maybe he could see what they were doing in the plane.

He remembered that Riley was the jumpmaster. He groaned. Riley, he was sure, was not about to break his back to help Johnny Welcome. Luck was against him. Riley hated him. Riley would let him dangle helplessly in the sky.

"Hang Riley!" he gasped. He didn't need his help. An image of Riley's deeply tanned face rose before his eyes. The face glared fiercely at him.

"Forget Riley!" he urged his aching body. He had to come up with a solution. There wasn't much time. He had to get going.

Just like when his squad was clobbered in Korea and he had been the sole survivor. He had lived then because he kept his head. He would work this out too.

Welcome took a series of short rapid breaths, steeled his body, and then twisted violently. He spun about in his chute harness and found himself staring at the earth. The air currents battered his face. He squinted to catch a glimpse of the full impact of his situation. The immensity of it hit him like a punch in the belly. For a few seconds he was certain he was going to pass out.

His partially opened main chute was tangled over the outer edge of the C-46's tail wing. Sections of the chute fluttered like paper strips in the face of a big electric fan. The lines stretched tautly from the edge of the chute back to the risers fastened to his empty backpack. He was hung up in the sky some fifteen feet behind and at an angle from the plane's tail section.

He thought that he might be able to shake the chute loose from the wing. But the idea was quickly rejected. He never would be able to gain any slack. The rushing air currents and prop blast clearly held the chute glue-tight against the wing's edge.

He caught a glimpse out of his battered eyes of someone gesturing to him from the door of the C-46—some twenty feet forward from the tail section. He dropped his head to catch his breath and then forced his head up for another look. It was Riley! The first sergeant was practically hanging out of the open door. He was down on his knees, with one arm working at something outside.

Welcome had to keep dropping and raising his head to see what Riley was up to. Riley's actions flickered before him in a series of shadowy tableaus.

The next series of blurred glimpses of Riley showed him down on his stomach in the doorway. Riley was clutching a long wooden pole. It seemed to have a crook at the extreme end.

Welcome saw broken flashes of the pole as it edged toward the tail section. Ever closer and closer it moved. But, oh, so slowly. Then it seemed to stop.

Welcome jerked up his head for a look back at the door. He saw Riley inching even farther out of the open door. Within the darkened interior of the aircraft, he thought he saw one of the airmen hanging onto Riley's boots.

He called in vain against the powerful wind for Riley to be careful. He was sure Riley was going to fall out of the C-46. The irony of the situation instantly became obvious to him. *Neither had any use for the other. And yet, in time of danger and need, they were reaching out to each other, their feelings put aside.*

He could see that Riley was fighting to slide the hook out and away from the fuselage along the edge of the tail wing to try and reach the chute. Welcome's despair hit a new low. It wasn't going to work. The prop blast kept slamming the pole back against the fuselage.

Then to Welcome's astonishment, Riley inched even farther out from the doorway of the aircraft. "Don't, you fool!" he cried out, his voice unheard in the roar of the engines and air currents. The force of the air rushing into Welcome's open mouth nearly took his breath away.

He looked up again just as Riley made one last desperate lunge with the hook to snare the chute. Half of Riley's body popped out of the plane like a field-green jack-in-the-box. In the next instant, the turbulence whipped the pole right out of Riley's hands. It zipped past Welcome like a missile in search of a prime target.

Welcome ducked his head and spun around in his harness. When he recovered the strength to twist around again, it was to see Riley struggling to grab the side of the open door. Riley's right hand shot out and missed. His face was strained and his neck distorted, as though Riley was instantly and vividly aware of the price of his failure.

Caught by the full impact of the prop blast, Riley flung out both arms and plunged from the aircraft. To save himself, the plane's crew chief released his grip on Riley's boots. Riley's arms and legs vainly flailed the air, seeking something, anything, to grasp. But there was nothing but yielding, unfriendly sky. Welcome swung out his arms, his fingers opened and spread. Riley missed them by a good three feet. In

Riley's upturned features, Welcome saw nothing but horror.

Then Riley flashed down like a stricken trapeze artist who has missed his partner's outstretched hands. His mouth was wide open, but whatever sounds came out were muffled by the irate air and lost in the sky.

Then Welcome remembered that Riley had been wearing a free-fall chute. It was mandatory for a jumpmaster. *Maybe Riley had used it. Why wouldn't he? Riley was a veteran jumper.*

As this thought flashed through his fevered mind, he suddenly was buffeted violently about and sent spinning crazily around like a top. For a moment he thought the plane was about to land. Again he almost passed out. Yet he refused to believe that the C-46 could be so low on fuel.

What was the pilot doing? Welcome tossed about the sky like a puppet. *The fly-boys would kill him,* he thought. He spun one way and then the reverse.

The gorge rose in his throat. Then he realized that the pilot of the C-46 was trying to shake loose his chute. *The pilot's desperate aerobatics meant the aircraft was running low on fuel after all.* The C-46's gyrations obviously weren't going to fling him loose. Sergeant Welcome was still on his own.

Now he was rushing through the sky on a fairly even keel. The pilot had stopped his frantic maneuverings. Welcome found himself gradually unraveling. And then he was flat out on his back once more, careening tumultuously through the sky.

A voice called to him. It was the crew chief on the bullhorn. But he couldn't understand him. If only the pilot would cut down his engines. Didn't the fly-boys realize he couldn't possibly hear them above the roar of those two powerful engines?

As though in reply to his question, the incessant throbbing of the engines rapidly diminished to about half what it had been. The pilot apparently was feathering one of his engines.

Welcome exerted all his strength to twist about in his harness. He groaned from the effort. His helmet strap knifed into his raw neck. He grimaced and looked up toward the C-46's open door.

"Jumper! Jumper in the air!"

Welcome glimpsed the crew chief. His thin pale face appeared anxious and perplexed. Welcome tried to wave, but could only muster a weak fanning motion toward the plane.

The crew chief's voice boomed out through the bullhorn: "We're going to land. We have no choice. Our fuel is about done. Sorry, fellow."

Welcome's heart jumped! "They're going to kill me!" he cried. "They'll kill me for sure!"

The crew chief bellowed: "We are going down now. Sorry. Nothing we can do. Runway is covered with foam. Might soften your landing. Pilot will bring the aircraft to a stop as quickly as possible. Good luck!"

"Good luck! Good luck!" Welcome repeated, as though in a stupor. He was shaken from his daze as the C-46's engines erupted into a deep roar. The prop blast again struck him with its full intensity, flinging him over on his back. His bruised chin slammed into his chest and his forehead whacked the reserve chute. Tears gathered in his eyes.

He thought of Sally and how much he wanted to go home. He couldn't believe it was going to end like this after Korea and everything else he had been through. It wasn't fair. Why had he been singled out?

The C-46 was beginning to descend. The prop blast was hitting him higher up on his shoulders. The toes of his boots rose slowly above the level of his eyes.

If only he could pass out, he thought. Then he wouldn't feel anything. Whatever you feel won't last more than a split second anyway, he retorted angrily. The moment he slammed down on that runway at 80 to 90 miles per hour, it would be over. He could forget going home, forget Sally and college and all his other hopes and plans.

The enormity of that conclusion hit him with near-paralyzing force. He didn't want to die. No, then he had better think of something mighty fast. Where were his brains?

Welcome sensed his fear lessening. It was being replaced by an innate craftiness as death waited only a few minutes away on the runway of the Fort Campbell field. This new-found cunning was familiar to him. An extra something he had inherited from a long line of Welcomes. He had been infused with the same sense of craftiness when his squad had been ambushed in Korea and he had fought his way back single-handed to "C" Company.

He had pulled it off then. He could do it again. Right now.

OK, he thought. *But what are you going to do? Where's the action? That ground must be coming up awful fast. You'd better get going!*

Welcome became alert to the panic suffusing his body and clenched his fists, determined to fight it off. He swung his arms and revolved his shoulders. He caught several glimpses of the earth. Its great flatness seemed to be rising up to smash him. Out of the corner of his eye he spotted a section of the concrete runway on the horizon.

They must be dropping fast. Probably down to about 800 feet or so. He urged himself to action. If only he could get out of his harness. "Great," he retorted cynically. "Then what—fall right to the ground?" But if he could unstrap his reserve chute, grasp it in one hand and bang his quick-release box with the other, he should fall right out of the straps. Then all he would have to do was grab for the reserve-chute handle with his free hand.

He thought it might be possible. Might just work. But again he was overwhelmed by the massive odds against it. The shock of the chute opening would tear it right out of his hand, even though he wouldn't be falling as fast as when he had jumped from the plane.

He prodded himself to try it. He had nothing to lose. Even now he detected the odor of red Kentucky clay and scrub pine. They were dropping, dropping. The C-46's engines seemed to be cutting out.

For another second Welcome relaxed helplessly in his harness. He dragged along in a forlorn manner behind the C-46 like a drogue bag for target-shooting pilots. He felt a wave of indifference and euphoria wash over him. Why fight it? Why not just accept it? It would soon be over. Even now they must be at about 500-feet elevation and lining up on the runway.

"No!" he growled to himself. He had never quit before. Not in jump school at Benning. Not in combat. He had only his knife then and had won out.

He cursed himself for a fool. His knife! He had only had his knife. And yet he had made it back through the enemy lines. How dumb could he be? His knife, of course. The same beautiful sheath knife he had bought years before when he was a Scout.

The knife would save him. It would free him from his predicament.

His right hand was already searching frantically for the knife. It wasn't on his belt. "Where is it?" he shouted angrily. *Stop it! Think. Just think! Remember. Where did you put it? Hurry!* His mind was a frenzy of conflicting thoughts like an overworked computer, the mental tape selecting and rejecting information in hundredths of seconds.

He had it. In his right boot. His remaining strength fast ebbing, he arched his body painfully to reach down and grab the knife. It was tucked into the top of his boot. If he could just get his fingertips over the handle, he would be able to pull it free.

Welcome groaned. A stabbing pain shot through his right thigh. The leg still hurt where the grenade shards had ripped it

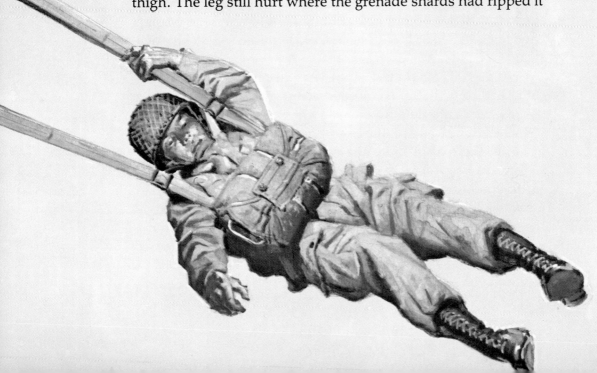

three months earlier.

"Forget the pain!" he cried. "Get the knife." His fingers crept along the heavy cloth of his jump pants. He slowly forced his leg up against the punishing wind currents.

"C'mon!" he urged himself. "Just a little bit more. C'mon now! Another inch." Flat out on his back, he could see the top of the knife glistening only half an inch from his straining fingertips.

He lunged, hardly knowing if he had the strength left to succeed. His fingers closed over the steel knob, clenched it securely; then he raised his shoulder to slip it free.

Now the smells of the earth filled his nostrils. He had to hurry! He brought the knife up near his chest and gained a full grasp on the handle. Quickly he reached up behind his helmet for one set of risers and grabbed it. The blade severed it smoothly.

Pain laced his arched back while he grabbed for the other set of risers. His clawing fingers found it and he reached with his knife to cut it. A scream broke from his lips. To relieve the scorching agony in his back and arms, he had to drop his hands.

Mustering up the reserves of his courage, he grasped once more for the final set of risers, which led to the shroud lines streaming back to the hooked chute. Grabbing it with his left hand, he slashed at it with his knife. He missed. Quickly tried again.

Make it good, he prayed. That sky big enough to open his chute had to be there. He needed about 150 to 200 feet to give the reserve chute time to open.

The scything knife hit the risers and flashed through. Almost instantly the roar of the plane engines began to diminish. He sensed his body starting to arch and fall vertically toward the earth. His head dropped backwards. His boots rose upwards. He was falling free—plunging to earth. He caught a glimpse of the ground. Then of the runway. It was coming up swiftly, a whirling black-and-gray-and-red monstrosity preparing to smash him.

Not today, he vowed. He dropped his knife and grabbed for

the handle of the reserve chute. It came away in his hand. A sharp popping noise exploded in his ears. The small pilot chute had snapped out of the reserve chute. As he hurtled toward the ground, the pilot chute caught the air, opened and whipped out the neat folds of the reserve chute.

"Open! Open!" he cried. The great folds of silk fluttered in the sky, gushing in an orderly manner out of the chute pack. One panel caught the air. Then another. With a blinding burst of whiteness that filled the sky, the reserve chute blossomed completely.

Sergeant Welcome slammed to a jarring halt 60 feet above the runway. His mind for a few seconds was a merciful cipher; his body one painful bruise.

The pain was still out of contact with the nerve ends of his consciousness. *For now he was alive.* That thought dominated all others as his heels slammed four inches into the clay soil just five feet off the concrete runway.

He rolled over on his thigh and took another big portion of the landing impact on his back. His head ricocheted off the ground. Stunned, he heard, as though at a great distance, the chute collapsing with a drawn out sigh over him. Its silk folds felt cool and comforting as they settled on him.

Sounds of motor vehicles and whining sirens rushed toward him. Doors slammed. He felt the earth tremble from the pounding of running feet. Hands snatched at the folds of the chute, seeking to uncover him.

One voice calling to him sounded familiar. Puzzled, he wrinkled his forehead. Then he recognized it. Once he would have sworn that he couldn't have cared less if he never heard that voice again. But now the voice rang in his ears like that of a long-lost brother safely home. He heard the obvious concern in the voice.

"OK, Welcome, you're blinking your eyes, so you must be alive. That sure was a long jump. Longest ever. Now how about getting back on your feet?"

Johnny Welcome reached up to grasp the hand offered him. He smiled softly. "You sure are a sight to behold, Sergeant Riley. Just lovely. The most beautiful trooper I ever saw."

Focus

1. Explain what happened in the first few moments after Welcome jumped.
2. Describe the attempts to free the parachute.
3. During the story, Welcome experienced several moods. Name four of the moods. Describe Welcome's thoughts as he experienced these moods.
4. Describe the character Johnny Welcome. Use events from the story to support your description.
5. The title of this story—"Last Jump"—can be interpreted in two ways. What are they?

In Writing

Welcome, Riley, and others did several things to try to free the parachute. In your own words, list each attempt, including the successful one, in the order in which they occurred.

Vocabulary

Read the word list and paragraph below. Decide which word makes the best sense in each blank space. Then write the numbers *1* to *5* on a piece of paper and write the correct word next to each number.

interminably	gyration	plummeting
ricochet	premonition	encumbered
mandatory	incessant	kaleidoscope

When my family decided to go horseback riding, I had a __(1)__ that I would not enjoy myself—I don't trust horses. We arrived at the stable and I chose the smallest, most kind-looking horse. The ride went on __(2)__ ; I thought it would never end. All of a sudden, my horse shied and I found myself __(3)__ toward the ground. I felt a rock or something __(4)__ off my head, and I saw a __(5)__ of stars. Other than that, I wasn't hurt, but I'll probably say no to the next family ride.

The Necklace

Augusta Stevenson

What is the cost of a moment of grandeur? Mathilde pays in years for her moment. How do her values change?

Characters

Mathilde Loisel
Pierre, Her Brother
Jeanne Forester
Teresa
Marie

Cosette
Claudine
Minette
Maid
Neighbor

Act I
TIME: an afternoon in January.
PLACE: Paris; sitting-room in the Loisels' apartment.

[*The room is shabby and small. Mathilde is seen embroidering. She is young, pretty, and daintily dressed. The door bell rings. The little* Maid *enters.*]
MATHILDE: Who is it?
MAID: The young ladies from the school, Madam.
MATHILDE: Is Jeanne Forester with them?

MAID: No, she does not come this time.
MATHILDE: Then I will see them.
(*Exit Maid. Mathilde hastily rearranges the chairs. Enter* Teresa, Minette, Claudine, Cosette, *and* Marie.)
Oh! Oh! How glad I am to see you! Come, sit down! Here is a chair, Cosette! Take this rocker, Claudine! Teresa, you try this stool! The sofa for the rest of you!
[*All sit down.*]
TERESA: We have but a minute to

413

stay, Mathilde.

CLAUDINE: We are on our way to see Jeanne Forester.

MARIE: We thought you would like to go with us.

MATHILDE: I'm sorry, but I can't go with you today. I—I have so much to do.

COSETTE: You were only embroidering.

MATHILDE: Yes, to be sure, but—I have decided not to go to Jeanne's any more.

MINETTE: Why—I thought you were the best of friends!

MATHILDE: We were—we are good friends now, but I find it makes me unhappy to visit Jeanne.

TERESA: Unhappy! How can that be? Jeanne has a beautiful home.

MATHILDE: That is just it! The very magnificence makes me unhappy. I can't help but compare it with this dingy place.

MINETTE: None of us has a home like Jeanne's.

MARIE: But Jeanne does not seem to mind that at all. Does she not invite us to see her?

MATHILDE: Yes, but I, for one, will go no more. I want to forget her silken curtains and gilded chairs, and her marbles and her silver.

CLAUDINE: Well, I love to see beautiful things, even if I can't have them.

COSETTE: And so do I! Jeanne's tapestries, for instance, are a joy to behold—all kings and queens and flying birds. They make me think of a dream world.

MATHILDE: They make me think of these cheap curtains here.

414

TERESA: I agree with you, Claudine and Cosette. I love Jeanne's silk-covered furniture! One sinks deep—so deep in those great armchairs. It makes me think of heaven.

MATHILDE: It makes me think of these worn-out chairs, where one also sinks deep—so deep, in constant danger of going through.

MINETTE: Mathilde, you are foolish. Come with us!

MARIE: Yes, come with us! Grand footmen will let us in. You will think them most respectful.

MATHILDE: I will think only of my one poor little maid. No, I will not go with you.

GIRLS (going): Then good-bye! Good-bye, Mathilde!

MATHILDE: Good-bye! Good-bye!

[Exit girls. Mathilde sighs as she takes up her embroidery. Pause. Enter Pierre, a young man, not over twenty. He waves a large envelope.]

PIERRE: Here, sister! Here is something for you—something that will please you!

MATHILDE (taking the envelope): What?

(She opens it and reads aloud.)

"The Minister of Public Instruction requests the honor of Mr. and Miss Loisel's company at the palace of the Ministry on Monday evening, January the nineteenth."

(She throws the letter down.)

Why do you bring that to me?

PIERRE: I thought you would be glad! You never go out—this will be a fine chance for you. I had great trouble getting it—everyone wants to go. It is to be very select.

MATHILDE: What did you think I would wear?

PIERRE: Why, I had not thought of that—you always look neat and pretty, sister.

MATHILDE: I have nothing to wear to a ball—nothing, nothing! I shall not go, Pierre.

PIERRE: How much would a new dress cost?

MATHILDE: Not less than four hundred francs.[1]

PIERRE (thoughtfully): Four hundred francs—I wonder—I wonder—

MATHILDE: Do you happen to have saved that much? But no, that is impossible; your salary is so small.

PIERRE: Well, but I have—just that much exactly. I had put it away for a rainy day. But you shall have it, Mathilde, you shall have it tomorrow to buy your dress. Why—bless me, you don't look one bit pleased, Mathilde!

MATHILDE: It is all very well to have a nice dress, but one should wear jewels to a ball of this kind. And what jewels

---

[1]franc (frangk): a unit of money in France

have I? Nothing, not even a bracelet!

PIERRE: Wear flowers, Mathilde! That is it! Wear flowers instead of jewels!

MATHILDE: And be different from every other woman there! No! I'd rather stay at home forever!

[*The door-bell rings. Short pause. Enter* Maid.]

MAID: Miss Forester to see you, please.

MATHILDE (*hastily*): I can't see her! Tell her—

(*Enter* Jeanne Forester, *young, gracious, and richly dressed.*)

Jeanne!

JEANNE: I thought I wouldn't wait—the girls said you were at home. She wouldn't come to see me, Pierre.

PIERRE: I can't get her to go anywhere. I'm coaxing her now to go to a ball. She refuses me absolutely, Jeanne.

JEANNE: What is the matter, Mathilde dear? You used to love balls when we were in school. I fear you are not feeling well.

MATHILDE: Oh, I am very well, thank you.

PIERRE: It is just this, Jeanne; she—

MATHILDE: No, no! You must not tell her!

JEANNE: Go on, Pierre! I insist!

PIERRE: Mathilde does not want to wear flowers to the ball. I say flowers would do very well. Now what do you think about it?

MATHILDE: It would be advertis-ing our poverty! Everyone else will wear jewels!

JEANNE: And so shall you wear jewels, Mathilde. Here—

[*She takes a diamond necklace from her neck and gives it to Mathilde.*]

MATHILDE: Jeanne! You will loan it to me?

JEANNE: Yes, of course.

MATHILDE: Oh, how good of you! How good of you! You have made me very happy, Jeanne!

(*She runs to the mirror and puts on the necklace.*)

It is beautiful—beautiful! Now I will go to the ball, Pierre!

Act II
Scene I
TIME: before dawn, the morning after the ball.

PLACE: the Loisels' sitting room.

[Mathilde *and* Pierre *enter, wearing wraps. Pierre turns up the lights and stirs the fire.*]

PIERRE: Better keep on your cloak till the fire burns up a little.

MATHILDE: Yes, the room is chilly. Oh, how beautiful it was! I shall never, never forget it!

PIERRE: I am glad you enjoyed it, sister.

MATHILDE: I tell you it pays to be well dressed and wear jewels! Everyone wanted to be introduced to me! Even the Minister asked to be presented!

PIERRE (*nodding*): I was proud of you, Mathilde.

MATHILDE: I tell you, Pierre, I

was born to be rich. I feel myself the equal of any great lady.

PIERRE: And so you are, Mathilde, so you are!

MATHILDE: Little good it does me!
Here I am—buried alive among
pots and pans! I, who love to
wear fine clothes, to be envied,
to be sought after—

PIERRE: Mathilde, you think too
much about yourself. Why
don't you think of those who
have only rags, who are suffering and starving!

MATHILDE: I have no money to
give away.

PIERRE: Everyone has sympathy
to give, and that is more. You
could read to the poor sick
Madame upstairs, you could
play with her children; but
no—you never give a thought
to anyone else. But I am glad
you enjoyed the ball, little sister. Good night! I must go to
work at seven.

(*He starts off. Mathilde removes her
cloak in front of the mirror. She
cries out sharply. Pierre turns.*)

What is it? Are you ill?

MATHILDE: The necklace!—I have
lost it!

PIERRE: Lost it!

[*Mathilde searches madly through her
dress, her cloak, her pockets.*]

MATHILDE: It is gone—it is gone!
Look in the hall, Pierre!

[*Exit Pierre, hastily. Mathilde shakes
her cloak, then looks on floor. Re-
enter Pierre.*]

PIERRE: It is not in the hall.

MATHILDE: Did you look on the
stairs?

PIERRE: Yes—I searched carefully.

MATHILDE: It is not in my clothes.

PIERRE: Did you have it on when
we left the ball?

MATHILDE: Yes—I felt it as we
were leaving.

PIERRE: It must be in the cab.

MATHILDE: Did you take the cab
driver's number?

PIERRE: No. Did you notice it?

MATHILDE: No, I didn't even look
at it. Pierre, Pierre, what shall
we do?

PIERRE: I will offer a reward—

MATHILDE: Go to the palace—to
the cab company—to the pawn
shops—everywhere! Go—go—
Pierre!

[*Pierre takes his coat and goes quick-*

417

*ly. Mathilde makes a frenzied
search, looking under chairs, sofa,
in corners, under rugs, etc.*]

Scene II
TIME: several hours later.
PLACE: the Loisels' sitting room.

[Mathilde, *now wearing a house
dress, sits staring dejectedly into
the fire. Enter the* Maid *with a
tray set with teapot, cup, etc.*]
MAID: Would you not like some
tea, madam?
MATHILDE: No, thank you—
nothing.
MAID: But you ate no breakfast!
MATHILDE: I cannot eat.
(Doorbell rings. Mathilde jumps up.)
There! That must be Pierre!
*(Exit Maid to hall. Short pause.
Enter* Pierre, *looking worn and
haggard.)*
Did you find it?
PIERRE: No—nor any trace of it.
MATHILDE: And you went every-
where?
PIERRE: Everywhere! To the pal-
ace on foot, to the cab com-
pany, to the pawn shops, to
police headquarters, to the
newspapers to offer a reward—
I have left nothing undone.
MATHILDE: Perhaps someone will
return it for the reward.
PIERRE: That is our only hope. In
the meantime you must make
some excuse to your friend.
MATHILDE: I will write her that I
have broken the clasp and that
I am having it repaired.

PIERRE: That will give us time to
do something in case it is not
found.
MATHILDE: What can we do,
Pierre?
PIERRE: We must replace it.
MATHILDE: Replace it? That would
be impossible. The necklace
was worth forty thousand francs.
PIERRE: No matter, it must be re-
placed.
MATHILDE: We have nothing, ex-
cept the little that father left us.
PIERRE: That will give us a thousand francs to start on. The rest
I will borrow—thirty-nine thousand francs.
MATHILDE: It will take a lifetime
to pay.
PIERRE: Yes, a lifetime; but it
must be done.
MATHILDE: It was my fault—you
shall not sacrifice your life,
Pierre.
PIERRE: It must be done, Mathilde. We will buy a necklace
exactly like Jeanne's.
MATHILDE: Then she need never
know.
PIERRE: It will not be necessary.
MATHILDE: I will dismiss the
maid—we will give up this
house—we will live in a garret
till this debt is paid.
PIERRE: We shall have very little
to live on; my salary will be
going to usurers.
MATHILDE: It is frightful! It will
mean years of anguish and misery.
PIERRE: But then, after all, the

necklace may be found.

MATHILDE: Let us hope for it, Pierre! To the last minute let us hope for it!

Act III

TIME: ten years later.

PLACE: Paris; a garret.

[*The room is almost bare of furniture. There is a knock at the door. Pause. The door is opened from without, and a* Neighbor *looks in. She is a laundress, fat and cheerful. She looks about, then calls.*]

NEIGHBOR: Mathilde! Mathilde!

[*Enter* Mathilde *with a basket of clothes. Mathilde looks like a middle-aged woman, thin and careworn; her hands are red and rough. She wears coarse clothing.*]

MATHILDE (*cordially*): Ah, neighbor, I am glad to see you. I was taking in my wash from the line. Won't you sit down?

NEIGHBOR: I just came in to tell you that I have found another wash for you.

MATHILDE: Oh, that is so good of you!

NEIGHBOR: This wash is regular, every week.

MATHILDE: Every sou[2] counts, neighbor.

NEIGHBOR: You are working too hard, friend Mathilde. From early morn till late at night you are washing, scrubbing, ironing.

MATHILDE: We are in debt.

NEIGHBOR: But you have been working like this for years. And your brother, too, works, works, all the time.

MATHILDE: The debt was a very large one. How is that little sick girl on the top floor? I thought I heard her crying just now.

NEIGHBOR: The fever came on again last night—she cries for a toy—her folks can't afford to buy one.

MATHILDE: I wish—but never mind—I can't. What arrangement did you make about that wash, neighbor? Will it be sent here?

NEIGHBOR: Yes, today.

MATHILDE: What is the name?

NEIGHBOR: Forester, in the grand house in——

MATHILDE: Forester! Did you say Forester?

---

[2]sou (sü): former French coin

419

NEIGHBOR: Yes. What is the matter? You are so pale!

MATHILDE: Did you tell her my name? Did you?

NEIGHBOR: Yes, to be sure. Why not? "Loisel," I said—"Loisel."

MATHILDE: Did you say "Mathilde"?

NEIGHBOR: No—just "Loisel." Should I have given her your first name?

MATHILDE: No, no! *(Aside.)* Loisel is common enough—she will not guess—

NEIGHBOR: What is that you are saying?

MATHILDE: Nothing—nothing—I am so glad to get another wash—that is all. You are so good to me, neighbor.

NEIGHBOR: Not so good as I should like to be. Look how you did my washings when I was sick last winter.

[*Merry whistling is heard.*]

MATHILDE: Who can that be?

NEIGHBOR: It must be your brother, Pierre.

MATHILDE: No, he never whistles—now.

NEIGHBOR: Then it is the agent for the rent. I must get ready for him.

[*Exit. The whistling is heard nearer. Enter* Pierre, *whistling. He is thin and almost ragged. His hair is turning gray.*]

MATHILDE: Why, Pierre—I have not heard you whistle in years.

PIERRE: It is paid—every sou!

MATHILDE: Paid, you say?

PIERRE: I have settled with the last creditor today.

[*Mathilde drops weakly into a chair.*]

MATHILDE: Paid—after all these years—thirty-nine thousand francs!

PIERRE: Not only that, but the interest. And I had to borrow at very high rates, you remember.

MATHILDE: How you have worked to pay that! All day doing the work of two people, and then every night your copying.

PIERRE: Ah, but I was lucky to be able to borrow enough money to buy a necklace like Jeanne's.

MATHILDE: 'T is ten years this month since I took it to her.

PIERRE: I wonder if Jeanne ever knew that the necklace you returned was not her own.

MATHILDE: She did not open the box while I was there. I have never seen her since. We left no traces when we moved to this garret.

PIERRE: And now it is all over! The borrowings, the duns[3], the mortgages, the sleepless nights, the cruel money lenders! It is all over now, sister, all over!

MATHILDE: Yes—but it has left you old and careworn. Ten years of your life have been wasted, Pierre—ten years for my one night's pleasure.

---

[3]duns: demands for payment

PIERRE: And what about you, Mathilde? Ten years in a garret, without your friends, without a single pretty dress—

MATHILDE: Oh, I do not worry about those things now—I have so much to think of. Listen, Pierre! The little sick girl on the top floor back is crying her heart out for a toy. Could not our next sou go for that?

PIERRE: To be sure! And here is the sou—it was the only one left over.

[*There is a knock at the door.*]

MATHILDE: Come in, neighbor! It was Pierre who whistled! Come in!

[*Enter* Jeanne Forester, *still young and pretty.*]

JEANNE: I seek Mathilde Loisel. Does she live here?

MATHILDE (*faintly*): No—no—

JEANNE: I have been told that a family by the name of Loisel lives in this house. Pardon me, I have come to the wrong door. Can you not direct me?

[*Pause.*]

MATHILDE: Jeanne! Jeanne! I am Mathilde Loisel!

JEANNE: You—?

MATHILDE: I! And there is Pierre!

JEANNE: Why—how you have changed! Is it really you, Mathilde? Is it really you, Pierre?

PIERRE: We have had ten years of misery since we have seen you, Jeanne.

JEANNE: Why did you not tell me? I could never find a trace of you—not until today, when the laundress told me that you— but that can't be true, Mathilde?

MATHILDE: Yes, it is true. Look at my hands. And Pierre has worked all day and copies every night. But at last we have paid, and now I can look you in the face and tell you everything. Do you remember that diamond necklace you loaned me to wear to the ball?

JEANNE: Yes, I remember.

MATHILDE: Well, I lost it.

JEANNE: Why! What do you mean? You returned it.

MATHILDE: We bought you another just like it.

JEANNE: You *bought* me a diamond necklace, you say?

PIERRE: What else could we honorably do?

JEANNE: What did you pay for it? You must tell me that, Pierre.

PIERRE: Forty thousand francs. I did not think yours could have cost more; but, if it did, of course we will pay you.

JEANNE: Oh, my poor Mathilde! My poor Pierre! My necklace was not worth more than five hundred francs! It was paste![4]

OTHERS: Paste!

JEANNE: Paste—

MATHILDE (*throwing her arms around Pierre*): Ten years! Oh, my poor Pierre!

---

[4]paste: type of glass used to make artificial jewels

Focus

1. Explain how the necklace changed the lives of Pierre and Mathilde Loisel.
2. How did Mathilde spend her time at the beginning of the story? How did she spend her time at the end?
3. What did Jeanne Forester tell the Loisels about the necklace? Explain what effect you think the information had on the Loisels.
4. Compare the character of Mathilde at the beginning and at the end of the story. Be sure to consider the changes in her values as well as in her appearance and lifestyle.

In Writing

Imagine that you are a friend of Mathilde. You receive a letter from her explaining what happened and how she feels about this. Write the letter you received.

Vocabulary

Make two columns on your paper. Label the first column *Positive* and the second column *Negative*. Then look at the words in the list below. Decide whether each word has a positive or negative connotation. Write the word in the correct column. Then write a sentence using each word.

magnificence   usurers   cordially
anguish   dingy

hope

Emily Dickinson

Hope is the thing with feathers
That perches in the soul,
And sings the tune without the words,
And never stops at all,

And sweetest in the gale is heard;
And sore must be the storm
That could abash the little bird
That kept so many warm.

I've heard it in the chillest land,
And on the strangest sea;
Yet, never, in extremity,
It asked a crumb of me.

STUDY SKILL: Identifying the Parts of an Outline

Choosing the right parts can make a product successful. This is true whether you're building a seaworthy ship or a class-worthy outline. Both need clear heads, steady hands, determination, and quality parts. In return, both a good ship and a good outline provide smooth sailing.

Think about the parts of an outline. The main topic is placed next to a Roman numeral; subtopics stand next to capital letters; and supporting details follow Arabic numbers. The basic form looks like this:

I. Main topic
  A. Subtopic
    1. Supporting detail

This is the skeleton of an outline. It is up to you to pick the right parts that will finish your product. Before you carefully read an article, skim it. Check for titles and pictures. Look for key words and phrases. They are the foundation of a good outline. Seek the main idea in the first paragraph. It is usually (but not always) in the first sentence. When you have found the main idea and key words, you can start building your outline.

Keep this information in mind when you read *Ancient Paper*.

Try to create an outline using the first paragraph only. Write on a piece of notebook paper. Capitalize the first word on each line. First choose the main topic. Place it next to Roman numeral I. Then select a subtopic. Put it next to capital letter A. Last, pick three supporting details and set them near the Arabic numbers. Here are the parts you will work with.

Found by Egyptians over 3,500 years ago
Egyptians wrote on papyrus
Ancient paper
History
Word *paper* comes from ancient Greek word *papyros*

Use the second paragraph of the article to build Subtopic B. Choose four supporting details. (Remember, all subtopics relate back to the main topic.)

Stem used for writing material
Grew in shallows of Nile River
Reached height of 3 to 6 meters
Papyrus plant
One stem supplied much paper

Now build Subtopics C and D. Use the last two paragraphs of the article. This time, you pick the key words and phrases for each subtopic and their supporting de-tails. Review the lesson *before* you build. Then, Captain, you will have a worthy vessel called "Outline." There can be smooth sailing!

Ancient Paper

Over 3,500 years ago, the Egyptian civilization did not use paper or books as we know them today to record their stories and poems, songs and histories. Instead, they wrote on *papyrus,* a material that looks somewhat like the paper we use now. (Our word *paper* comes from the ancient Greek word *papyros.)*

This writing material was made from the stem of the papyrus plant, which grew in the shallows of the Nile River. The plant, which can reach a height of three to six meters (nine to twenty feet), was used in many ways—the roots for food, the large feathery head to make bouquets for the shrines of the gods, and the stems for making boats, sails, mats, rope, and—most important—paper. A single stem of papyrus would be much more than enough to make the paper for this article.

To make the papyrus, the Egyptians first removed the outer rind of the stem. Then they cut the inner pith—the spongy tissue inside the stem—into segments of about forty centimeters (about sixteen inches) each. They cut the segments lengthwise in thin slices and soaked them in water from the Nile to remove the starch. Next, they laid some of the slices side by side on a table. On top of them, they placed a second layer with the fibers running at right angles to those of the first layer. They beat the two layers together and left the papyrus under pressure until it was dry. Finally, they polished the surface with a rounded object until it was perfectly smooth.

The finished paper was used for everything from writing personal letters and documents to writing books. The Egyptian books did not consist of pieces of paper, cut in uniform size and bound between two covers, like our books. Instead, an Egyptian book was made from many pieces of papyrus—normally twenty—stuck together at the ends so that they formed one long strip of paper. This kind of book is called, in English, a scroll. The longest scroll found in Egypt measures more than forty meters (over one hundred thirty-one feet). When a scroll was not in use, it was rolled up, tied with a string, and stored in a clay jar. Unrolled, it looked much like a strip of paper from your notebook.

Enchanted Village

A. E. van Vogt

Strange things happen in strange places, especially in
science-fiction stories. Bill Jenner's moment happens on Mars.

Explorers of a new frontier, they had been called before they left
for Mars.

For a while after the ship crashed into a Martian desert,
killing all on board except—miraculously—this one man, Bill
Jenner spat the words occasionally into the constant, sand-
laden wind. He despised himself for the pride he had felt when
he first heard them.

His fury faded with each mile that he walked, and his acute

426

grief for his friends became a dull ache. Slowly he realized that he had made a ruinous misjudgment.

He had underestimated the speed at which the rocketship had been traveling. He'd guessed that he would have to walk three hundred miles to reach the shallow, polar sea he and the others had observed as they glided in from outer space. Actually, the ship must have flashed an immensely greater distance before it hurtled down out of control.

The days stretched behind him, seemingly as numberless as the hot, red, alien sand that scorched through his tattered clothes. This huge scarecrow of a man kept moving across the endless, arid waste—he would not give up.

By the time he came to the mountain, his food had long been gone. Of his four water bags, only one remained; and that was so close to being empty that he merely wet his cracked lips and swollen tongue whenever his thirst became unbearable.

Jenner climbed high before he realized that it was not just another dune that had barred his way. He paused, and as he gazed up at the mountain that towered above him, he cringed a

little. For an instant, he felt the hopelessness of this mad race he was making to nowhere—but he reached the top. He saw that below him was a valley surrounded by hills as high as or higher than the one on which he stood. Snuggled in the valley was a village.

He could see trees and the marble floor of a courtyard. A number of buildings were clustered around what seemed to be a central square. They were mostly low-constructed, but there were four towers pointing gracefully into the sky. They shone in the sunlight with a marble luster.

Faintly, there came to Jenner's ear a thin, high-pitched whistling sound. It rose, fell, faded completely, then came up again clearly and unpleasantly. Even as Jenner ran toward it, the noise grated on his ears, eerie and unnatural.

He kept slipping on smooth rock, and bruised himself when he fell. He rolled halfway down into the valley. The buildings remained new and bright, when seen from nearby. Their walls flashed with reflections. On every side was vegetation— reddish green shrubbery—yellow-green trees laden with purple and red fruit.

With ravenous intent, Jenner headed for the nearest fruit tree. Close up, the tree looked dry and brittle. The large red fruit he tore from the lowest branch, however, was plump and juicy.

As he lifted it to his mouth, he remembered that he had been warned during his training period to taste nothing on Mars until it had been chemically examined. But that was meaningless advice to someone whose only chemical equipment was in his own body.

Nevertheless, the possibility of danger made him cautious. He took his first bite gingerly. It was bitter to his tongue, and he spat it out hastily. Some of the juice which remained in his mouth seared his gums. He felt the fire of it, and he reeled from nausea. His muscles began to jerk and he lay down on the marble to keep himself from falling. After what seemed like hours to Jenner, the awful trembling finally went out of his body, and he could see again. He looked up despisingly at the tree.

The pain finally left him, and slowly he relaxed. A soft breeze rustled the dry leaves. Nearby trees took up that gentle clamor, and it struck Jenner that the wind here in the valley was only a whisper of what it had been on the flat desert beyond the mountains.

There was no other sound now. Jenner abruptly remembered the high-pitched, ever-changing whistle he had heard. He lay very still, listening intently, but there was only the rustling of the leaves. The noisy shrilling had stopped. He wondered if it had been an alarm, to warn the villagers of his approach.

Anxiously, he climbed to his feet. He looked around him uneasily, but there was not a sign of creature life. He braced himself. He couldn't leave, as there was nowhere to go. If necessary, he would fight to the death to remain in the village.

Carefully Jenner took a sip from his water bag, moistening his cracked lips and his swollen tongue. Then he replaced the cap, and started through a double line of trees toward the nearest building. He made a wide circle to observe it from several vantage points. On one side a low, broad archway opened into the interior. Through it, he could dimly make out the polished gleam of a marble floor.

429

Jenner explored the buildings from the outside, always keeping a respectful distance between him and any of the entrances. He saw no sign of animal life. He reached the far side of the marble platform on which the village was built, and turned back decisively. It was time to explore interiors.

He chose one of the four-tower buildings. As he came within a dozen feet of it, he saw that he would have to stoop to get inside.

Momentarily, the implications of that stopped him. These buildings had been constructed for a life form that must be very different from human beings.

He went forward again, bent down, and entered reluctantly, every muscle tensed.

He found himself in a room without furniture. However, there were several low, marble fences projecting from one marble wall. They formed what looked like a group of four wide, low stalls. Each stall had an open trough carved out of the floor.

The second chamber was fitted with four inclined planes of marble, each of which slanted up to a dais. Altogether, there were four rooms on the lower floor. From one of them, a circular ramp mounted up, apparently to a tower room.

Jenner didn't investigate the upstairs. The earlier fear that he would find alien life was yielding to the deadly conviction that he wouldn't. No life meant no food, nor any chance of getting any. In frantic haste, he hurried from building to building, peering into the silent rooms, pausing now and then to shout hoarsely.

Finally, there was no doubt. He was alone in a deserted village on a lifeless planet, without food, without water—except for the pitiful supply in his bag—and without hope.

He was in the fourth and smallest room of one of the tower buildings when he realized that he had come to the end of his search. The room had a single "stall" jutting out from one wall. Wearily, Jenner lay down in it. He must have fallen asleep instantly.

When he awoke, he became aware of two things, one right after the other. The first realization occurred before he opened his eyes—the whistling sound was back, high and shrill, it wavered at the threshold of audibility.

The other was that a fine spray of liquid was being directed down at him from the ceiling. It had an odor, of which Technician Jenner took a single whiff. Quickly he scrambled out of the room, coughing, tears in his eyes, his face already burning from chemical reaction.

He snatched his handkerchief and hastily wiped the exposed parts of his body and face.

He reached the outside, and there paused, striving to understand what had happened.

The village seemed unchanged.

Leaves trembled in a gentle breeze. The sun was poised on a mountain peak. Jenner guessed from its position that it was morning again, and that he had slept at least a dozen hours. The glaring white light suffused the valley. Half-hidden by trees and shrubbery, the buildings flashed and shimmered.

He seemed to be in an oasis in a vast desert. It was an oasis all right, Jenner reflected grimly, but not for a human being. For him, with its poisonous fruit, it was more like a tantalizing mirage.

He went back inside the building, and cautiously peered into the room where he had slept. The spray of gas had stopped, not a bit of odor lingered, and the air was fresh and clean.

He edged over the threshold, half-inclined to make a test. He had a picture in his mind of a long dead Martian creature lazing on the floor in the "stall" while a soothing chemical sprayed down on its body. The fact that the chemical was deadly to human beings merely emphasized how alien to humans was the life on Mars. But there seemed little doubt of the reason for the gas. The creature was accustomed to taking a morning shower.

Inside the "bathroom," Jenner eased himself, feet first, into the stall. As his hips became level with the stall entrance, the solid ceiling sprayed a jet of yellowish gas straight down upon his legs. Hastily, Jenner pulled himself clear of the stall. The gas stopped as suddenly as it had started.

He tried it again to make sure it was merely an automatic process. It turned on, then it shut off.

Jenner's thirst-puffed lips parted with excitement. He thought, "If there can be one automatic process, there may be others."

Breathing heavily, he raced into the other room. Carefully he shoved his legs into one of the two stalls. The moment his hips were in, a steaming gruel filled the trough beside the wall.

He stared at the greasy-looking stuff with a horrified fascination—food and drink. He remembered the poison fruit, and felt repelled, but he forced himself to bend down, and put his finger into the hot, wet substance. He brought it up, dripping, to his mouth.

It tasted flat and pulpy, like boiled wood fiber. It trickled thickly into his throat. His eyes began to water, and his lips drew back involuntarily. He realized he was going to be sick, and ran for the outer door—but didn't quite make it.

When he finally got outside, he felt limp and totally listless. In that depressed state of mind, he grew aware again of the shrill sound.

He felt amazed that he could have ignored its rasping even for a few minutes. Sharply, he glanced about, trying to determine its source, but it seemed to have none. Whenever he approached a point where it appeared to be loudest, then it would fade, or shift, perhaps to the far side of the village.

He tried to imagine what an alien culture would want with a mind-shattering noise—although, of course, it would not necessarily have been unpleasant to them.

He stopped and snapped his fingers as a wild but nevertheless plausible notion entered his mind. Could this be music?

He toyed with the idea, trying to visualize the village as it had been long ago. Here, a music-loving race had possibly gone about its daily tasks to the accompaniment of what was to them beautiful strains of melody.

The terrible whistling went on and on, waxing and waning. Jenner tried to put buildings between himself and the sound. He sought refuge in various rooms, hoping that at least one would be soundproof. None was. The whistle followed him wherever he went.

He retreated into the desert, and had to climb halfway up one of the slopes before the noise was low enough not to disturb him. Finally, breathless but immeasurably relieved, he sank down on the sand, and thought blankly: What now?

The scene that spread before him had in it both beautiful and horrid qualities. It was all too familiar now—the red sands, the stony dunes, the small, alien village promising so much and fulfilling so little. Jenner looked down at it with his feverish eyes, and ran his parched tongue over his cracked, dry lips. He knew that he was a dead man unless he could alter the automatic food-making machines that must be hidden somewhere in the walls under the floors of the buildings.

In ancient days, a remnant of Martian civilization had survived in this village. The inhabitants had died off but the village lived on, keeping itself clean of sand, able to provide refuge for any Martian who might come along. But there were no Martians. There was only Bill Jenner, pilot of the first rocketship ever to land on Mars.

He had to make the village turn out food and drink that he could take. Without tools, except his hands; with scarcely any knowledge of chemistry, he must force it to change its habits.

Tensely, he hefted his water bag. He took another sip, and fought the same grim fight to prevent himself from guzzling it down to the last drop. And, when he had won the battle once more, he stood up and started down the slope.

He could last, he estimated, not more than three days. In that time, he must conquer the village.

He was already among the trees when it suddenly struck him that the "music" had stopped. Relieved, he bent over a small shrub, took a good firm hold of it—and pulled.

It came up easily, and there was a slab of marble attached to it. Jenner stared at it, noting with surprise that he had been mistaken in thinking the stalk came up through a hole in the marble. It was merely stuck to the surface. Then he noticed something else—the shrub had no roots. Almost instinctively, Jenner looked down at the spot from where he had torn the

433

slab of marble, along with the plant. There was sand there.

He dropped the shrub, slipped to his knees, and plunged his fingers into the sand. Loose sand trickled through them. He reached deep, using all his strength to force his arm and hand down—sand—nothing but sand.

He stood up, and frantically tore up another shrub. It also came out easily, bringing with it a slab of marble. It had no roots, and where it had been was sand.

With a kind of mindless disbelief, Jenner rushed over to a fruit tree, and shoved at it. There was a momentary resistance, and then the marble on which it stood split, and lifted slowly into the air. The tree fell over with a swish and a crackle of its dry branches, and leaves broke and crumbled in a thousand pieces. Underneath it was sand.

Sand everywhere. A city built on sand. Mars, planet of sand. That was not completely true, of course. Seasonal vegetation had been observed near the polar ice caps. All but the hardiest of it had died with the coming of summer. It had been intended that the rocketship land near one of those shallow, tideless seas.

By coming down out of control, the ship had wrecked more than itself. It had wrecked the chances for life of the only survivor of the voyage.

Jenner came slowly out of his daze. He had a thought then. He picked up one of the shrubs he had already torn loose, braced his foot against the marble to which it was attached, and tugged, gently at first, then with increasing strength.

It came loose finally, but there was no doubt that the two were a part of a whole. The shrub was growing out of the marble.

Marble? Jenner knelt beside one of the holes from where he had torn a slab, and bent over an adjoining section. It was quite porous—calciferous[1] rock, most likely, but not true marble at all. As he reached toward it, intending to break off a piece, it changed color. Astonished, Jenner drew back. Around the break, the stone was turning a bright orange-yellow. He studied it uncertainly, then, tentatively, he touched it.

It was as if he had dipped his fingers into searing acid. There was a sharp, biting, burning pain. With a gasp, Jenner jerked his hand clear.

The continuing anguish made him feel faint. He swayed and moaned, clutching the bruised fingers to his body. When the agony finally faded, and he could look at the injury, he saw that the skin had peeled, and that already blood blisters had formed. Grimly, Jenner looked down at the break in the stone. The edges remained bright orange-yellow.

The village was alert, ready to defend itself from further attacks.

---

[1]calciferous (kal sif'ə rəs): containing calcium carbonate

Suddenly weary, he crawled into the shade of a tree. There was only one possible conclusion to draw from what had happened, and it almost defied common sense. This lonely village was alive.

As he lay there, Jenner tried to imagine a great mass of living substance growing into the shape of buildings, adjusting itself to suit another life form, accepting the role of servant in the widest meaning of the term.

If it would serve one race, why not another? If it could adjust to Martians, why not to human beings?

There would be difficulties, of course. He guessed wearily that essential elements would not be available. The oxygen for water could come from the air . . . thousands of compounds could be made from sand . . . though it meant death if he failed to find a solution, he fell asleep even as he started to think about what they might be.

When he awoke, it was quite dark.

Jenner climbed heavily to his feet. There was a drag to his muscles that alarmed him. He wet his mouth from his water bag, and staggered toward the entrance of the nearest building. Except for the scraping of his shoes on the "marble," the silence was intense.

He stopped short—listened and looked. The wind had died away. He couldn't see the mountains that rimmed the valley, but the buildings were still dimly visible, black shadows in a shadow world.

For the first time, it seemed to him that, in spite of his new hope, it might be better if he died. Even if he survived, what had he to look forward to? He recalled only too well how hard it had been to rouse interest in the trip, and to raise the large amount of money required. He remembered the colossal problems that had had to be solved in building the ship, and some of the people who had solved them were buried somewhere in the Martian desert.

It might be twenty years before another ship from Earth would try to reach the only other planet in the solar system that had shown signs of being able to support life.

During those uncountable days and nights, those years, he would be here alone. That was the most he could hope for—if he lived. As he fumbled his way to a dais in one of the rooms, Jenner considered another problem.

How did one let a living village know that it must alter its processes? In a way, it must already have grasped that it had a new tenant. How could he make it realize he needed food in a different chemical combination from that which it had served in the past; that he liked music, but on a different scale system; and that he could use a shower each morning—of water, not of poison gas?

He dozed fitfully, like a man who is sick rather than sleepy. Twice he wakened, his lips on fire, his eyes burning, his body bathed in perspiration. Several times he was startled into consciousness by the sound of his own harsh voice crying out in anger and fear at the night.

He guessed then that he was dying.

He spent the long hours of darkness tossing, turning, twisting, befuddled by waves of heat. As the light of morning came, he was vaguely surprised to realize that he was still alive. Restlessly, he climbed off the dais, and went to the door.

A bitingly cold wind blew, but it felt good to his hot face. He wondered if there was *pneumococcus*[2] in his blood for him to catch pneumonia. He decided not.

In a few moments he was shivering. He retreated back into the house and, for the first time noticed that, despite the doorless doorway, the wind did not come into the building at all. The rooms were cold, but not draughty.

That started an association: Where had his terrible body heat come from? He teetered over to the dais where he had spent the night. Within seconds, he was roasting in a temperature of about a hundred and thirty.

He climbed off the dais, shaken by his own stupidity. He estimated that he had sweated at least two quarts of moisture out of his dried-up body on that furnace of a bed.

This village was not for human beings. Here, even the beds were heated for creatures who needed temperatures far beyond the heat comfortable for humans.

Jenner spent most of the day in the shade of a large tree. He felt exhausted, and only occasionally did he even remember that he had a problem. When the whistling started, it bothered him at first, but he was too tired to move away from it. There were long periods when he hardly heard it, so dulled were his senses.

Late in the afternoon, he remembered the shrubs and the tree he had torn up the day before, and wondered what had happened to them. He wet his swollen tongue with the last few drops of water in his bag, climbed lackadaisically to his feet, and went to look for the dried-up remains.

There weren't any. He couldn't even find the holes where he had torn them out. The living village had absorbed the dead tissue into itself, and repaired the breaks in its "body."

That galvanized Jenner. He began to think again . . . about

---

[2]*pneumococcus* (nü mə käk'əs): type of bacterium that causes pneumonia

life forms adapting to new environments. There'd been lectures on that before the ship left Earth, rather generalized talks designed to acquaint the explorers with the problems people might face on an alien planet. The important principle was quite simple: adjust or die.

The village had to adjust to him. He doubted if he could seriously damage it, but he could try. His own need to survive must be placed on as sharp and hostile a basis as that.

Frantically, Jenner began to search his pockets. Before leaving the rocket, he had loaded himself with odds and ends of small equipment. A jackknife, a folding metal cup, a printed radio, a tiny superbattery that could be charged by spinning an attached wheel—and for which he had brought along, among other things, a powerful electric fire-lighter.

Jenner plugged the lighter into the battery, and deliberately scraped the red-hot end along the surface of the "marble." The reaction was swift. The substance turned an angry purple this time. When an entire section of the floor had changed color, Jenner headed for the nearest stall trough, entering far enough to activate it.

There was a noticeable delay. When the food finally flowed into the trough, it was clear that the living village had realized the reason for what he had done. The food was a pale, creamy color, where earlier it had been a muddy gray.

Jenner put his finger into it, but withdrew it with a yell, and wiped his finger. It continued to sting for several moments. The vital question was: Had it deliberately offered him food that would damage him, or was it trying to appease him without knowing what he could eat?

He decided to give it another chance, and entered the adjoining stall. The gritty stuff that flooded up this time was yellower. It didn't burn his finger, but Jenner took one taste, and spat it out. He had the feeling that he had been offered a soup made of a greasy mixture of clay and gasoline.

He was thirsty now with a need heightened by the unpleasant taste in his mouth. Desperately, he rushed outside and tore open the water bag, seeking the wetness inside. In his fumbling eagerness, he spilled a few precious drops onto the courtyard. Down he went on his face, and licked them up.

Half a minute later, he was still licking, and there was still water.

The fact penetrated suddenly. He raised himself, and gazed wonderingly at the droplets of water that sparkled on the smooth stone. As he watched, another one squeezed up from the apparently solid surface, and shimmered in the light of the sinking sun.

He bent, and with the tip of his tongue sponged up each visible drop. For a long time, he lay with his mouth pressed to the "marble," sucking up the tiny bits of water that the village doled out to him.

The flowing white sun disappeared behind a hill. Night fell, like the dropping of a black screen. The air turned cold, then icy. He shivered as the wind keened through his ragged clothes. But what finally stopped him was the collapse of the surface from which he had been drinking.

Jenner lifted himself in surprise and, in the darkness, gingerly felt over the stone. It had genuinely crumbled. Evidently the substance had yielded up its available water and had disintegrated in the process. Jenner estimated that he had drunk altogether an ounce of water.

It was a convincing demonstration of the willingness of the village to please him, but there was another, less satisfying implication. If the village had to destroy a part of itself every time it gave him a drink, then clearly the supply was not unlimited.

Jenner hurried inside the nearest building, climbed onto a dais—and climbed off again hastily, as the heat blazed up at him. He waited, to give the Intelligence a chance to realize he wanted to change, then he lay down once more. The heat was as great as ever.

He gave that up because he was too sleepy to think of a method that might let the village know he needed a different bedroom temperature. He slept on the floor with an uneasy conviction that it could *not* sustain him for long. He woke up many times during the night, and thought: Not enough water. No matter how hard it tries. . . . Then he would sleep again, only to wake once more, tense and unhappy.

Nevertheless, morning found him briefly alert, and all his steely determination was back—that iron willpower that had brought him at least five hundred miles across an unknown desert.

He headed for the nearest trough. This time, after he had activated it, there was a pause of more than a minute, and then about a thimbleful of water made a wet splotch at the bottom.

Jenner licked it dry, then waited hopefully for more. When none came, he reflected gloomily that somewhere in the village, an entire group of cells had broken down and released their water for him.

Then and there he decided that it was up to the human being, who could move around, to find a new source of water for the village, which could not move.

In the meantime, of course, the village would have to keep him alive, until he had investigated the possibilities. That meant, above everything else, he must have some food to sustain him while he looked around.

He began to search his pockets. Toward the end of his food supply, he had carried scraps and pieces wrapped in small bits of cloth. Crumbs had broken off into his pocket and he had searched often during those long days in the desert. Now, by actually ripping the seams, he discovered tiny particles of meat and bread, little bits of grease, and other unidentifiable substances.

Carefully, he leaned over the adjoining stall and placed the scrappings in the trough there. The village would not be able to offer him more than a reasonable facsimile. If the spilling of a few drops on the courtyard could make it aware of his need for water, then a similar offering might give it the clue it needed as to the chemical nature of the food he could eat.

Jenner waited, then entered the second stall and activated it. About a pint of thick, creamy substance trickled into the bottom of the trough. The smallness of the quantity seemed evidence that perhaps it contained water.

He tasted it. It had a sharp, musty flavor and a stale odor. It was almost as dry as flour—but his stomach did not reject it.

Jenner ate slowly, acutely aware that at such moments as this the village had him at its mercy. He could never be sure that one of the food ingredients was not a slow-acting poison.

When he had finished the meal, he went to a food trough in another building. He refused to eat the food that came up, but activated still another trough. This time he received a few drops of water.

He had come purposefully to one of the tower buildings. Now, he had started up the ramp that led to the upper floor. He paused only briefly in the room he came to, as he had already discovered that they seemed to be additional bedrooms. The familiar dais was there in a group of three.

What interested him was that the circular ramp continued to wind on upward. First to another, smaller room that seemed to have no particular reason for being. Then it wound on up to the top of the tower, some seventy feet above the ground. It was high enough for him to see beyond the rim of all the surrounding hilltops. He had thought it might be, but he had been too weak to make the climb before. Now, he looked out to every horizon. Almost immediately, the hope that had brought him up faded.

The view was immeasurably desolate. As far as he could see was an arid wasteland, and every horizon was hidden in a mist of wind-blown sand.

Jenner gazed with a sense of despair. If there was a Martian sea out there, somewhere, it was beyond his reach.

Abruptly, he clenched his hands in anger against his fate, which seemed inevitable now. At the very worst, he had hoped he would find himself in a mountainous region. Seas and mountains were generally the two main sources of water. He should have known, of course, that there were very few mountains on Mars. It would have been a wild coincidence if he had actually run into a mountain range.

His fury faded, because he lacked the strength to sustain any emotion. Numbly, he went down the ramp.

His vague plan to help the village ended as swiftly and finally as that.

The days drifted by, but as to how many he had no idea. Each time he went to eat, a smaller amount of water was doled out to him. Jenner kept telling himself that each meal would have to be his last. It was unreasonable for him to expect the village to destroy itself when his fate was certain now.

What was worse, it became increasingly clear that the food was not good for him. He had misled the village as to his needs by giving it stale, perhaps even tainted samples, and prolonged the agony for himself. At times, after he had eaten, Jenner felt dizzy for hours. All too frequently, his head ached, and his body shivered with fever.

The village was doing what it could. The rest was up to him, and he couldn't even adjust to an approximation of Earth food.

For two days, he was too sick to drag himself to one of the

troughs. Hour after hour, he lay on the floor. Sometime during the second night, the pain in his body grew so terrible that he finally made up his mind.

"If I can get to a dais," he told himself, "the heat alone will kill me; and, in absorbing my body, the village will get back some of its lost water."

He spent at least an hour crawling laboriously up the ramp of the nearest dais and, when he finally made it, he lay as one already dead. His last waking thought was: Beloved friends, I'm coming.

The hallucination was so complete that, momentarily, he seemed to be back in the control room of the rocketship, and all around him were his former companions.

With a sigh of relief, Jenner sank into a dreamless sleep.

He woke to the sound of a violin. It was sad-sweet music that told of the rise and fall of a race long dead.

Jenner listened for a while, and then, with abrupt excitement, realized the truth. This was a substitute for the whistling—the village had adjusted its music to him!

Other sensory phenomena stole in upon him. The dais felt comfortably warm, not hot at all. He had a feeling of wonderful physical well-being.

Eagerly, he scrambled down the ramp to the nearest food stall. As he crawled forward, his nose close to the floor, the trough filled with a steamy mixture. The odor was so rich and pleasant that he plunged his face into it, and slopped it up greedily. It had the flavor of thick, meaty soup, and was warm and soothing to his lips and mouth. When he had eaten it all, he did not need a drink of water for the first time.

"I've won!" thought Jenner. "The village has found a way!"

After a while, he remembered something, and crawled to the bathroom. Cautiously, watching the ceiling, he eased himself backward into the shower stall. The yellowish spray came down, cool and delightful.

Ecstatically, Jenner wriggled his four-foot tail and lifted his long snout to let the thin streams of liquid wash away the food impurities that clung to his sharp teeth.

Then he waddled out to bask in the sun and listen to the timeless music.

Focus

1. What did Jenner believe was his only chance for survival?
2. Explain some of the ways Jenner tried to make the village adjust to his needs.
3. Trace Jenner's reactions to the whistling sound throughout the story.
4. List the four sensory experiences that seemed changed to Jenner at the end of the story.
5. Describe Jenner's appearance at the end.
6. Compare what actually happened to Jenner with what he thought was happening during his stay at the village.

In Writing

Imagine that you are Jenner. When a rescue team arrives years later, you are surprised by their reaction to you. Write an account of your first meeting with this rescue team.

Vocabulary

On a piece of paper, write the numbers *1* to *5*. Then read the sentences below. Next to each number on your paper, write the word from the list that best completes each analogy.

draughty	mirage	plausible
befuddle	conviction	appease
penetrate	laborious	facsimile

1. Ricochet is to bounce as ___ is to pierce.
2. Sear is to burn as ___ is to hallucination.
3. Possible is to action as ___ is to idea.
4. Photograph is to picture as ___ is to likeness.
5. Clarify is to confuse as ___ is to enrage.

Lacy Clouds Drift By

Rebecca Caudill

Lacy clouds drift by;
   On the far rugged mountains
     Lacy shadows lie.

The enormous sky
   Floats in space filled with the hum
     Of sweet, winey winds.

Gifts of the desert—
   Room enough, time enough, and
      Calmness after pain.

STUDY SKILL: Making an Outline

It is smart to make an outline of what you read. An outline can help you understand, organize, and use important facts. It can also help you remember. It's useful if you are studying for a test, preparing a summary, or making a class presentation. If you want to compare and contrast two things, an outline can show you the differences and similarities.

An article generally has more than one paragraph. The main topic is usually identified right away. The sentences and paragraphs which follow contain supporting ideas and details. These supports always relate to the main topic. The outline form uses a Roman numeral for each main topic; capital letters for subtopics, and Arabic numerals for supporting details.

The paragraphs in the report, *Together in Different Worlds*, compare and contrast two insects. As you read the passage, notice key words and phrases that tell about these two creatures.

When you read the report, think about how you can compare an ant and a bee who share the same space but never meet. Contrast their lifestyles. One is wingless, crawls around in small fields looking for food, and lives underground. The other has wings and is busy buzzing overhead sniffing for a flowery meal.

Outline one insect at a time. Then your outline will show a clear comparison. As an example, Subtopic A is done. You will create Subtopic B and the main topic.

I.

   A. Ants
1. Live in underground colonies
2. Crawl in fields looking for food
3. Travel within a small space
4. Work in teams
5. Sensitive to vibrations in earth
6. Communicate by touching antennae, stomping on the earth, and creating vibrations
7. In the world of the ant, flowers are just another obstacle

The data for Subtopic A came from the first paragraph of the article. Find the best information for Subtopic B. Finally, complete your outline.

450

Together in Different Worlds

Think, for example, of an ant and a bee in a field of blooming flowers. The ant lives in a colony buried under the ground in a small part of the field. Through its entire life it probably never travels from one end of the field to the other. In its world, flowers in bloom, budding plants, trees, bushes are all obstacles to climb or bypass. Their differences are of no importance in the ant's life and aren't perceived. The ant spends most of its day scurrying about searching for food which it brings back to the colony. It is extremely sensitive to slight vibrations in the earth and works as part of ant teams which it communicates with by touching antennae or stomping on the earth and creating vibrations. Imagine being an ant and working your way through particles of dirt, small rocks, grass, and flowers as humans would go through a forest or field strewn with boulders. The world of an ant is rich with detail and variation. However, many things going on in the field do not enter its world.

Bees and ants do not usually cross paths. The field of blooming flowers is perceived in a special way by bees. They can smell the perfumes given off by flowers over great distances and can distinguish flowers by their scents. Some flowers are rich in pollen and others have very little. Bees choose the rich flowers first and, as soon as they pick up their scent, fly towards them. As they get close to the flowers, they use visual as well as scent clues to find the flowers and estimate their numbers. Bees' eyes are particularly suited to identify and distinguish different flowers. According to scientific experiments, bees cannot distinguish the four shapes shown here.

These shapes, which resemble buds rather than blooming flowers, all appear as dark roundish shapes in the bees' world. On the other hand, bees have no difficulty telling the difference between these two flower shapes.

In the world of the bee the field appears full of indefinite circles or of various flower shapes. The world is either blooming flower or other. The field is a complex environment shared with the ant and other creatures, but it does not appear so in the world of the bee.

The ant and the bee described here share the same environment but live in different worlds.

451

The Women's 400 Meters

Lillian Morrison

Skittish,
they flex knees, drum heels and
shiver at the starting line

waiting the gun
to pour them over the stretch
like a breaking wave.

Bang! they're off
careening down the lanes,
each chased by her own bright tiger.

Wilma Rudolph: Olympic Runner

The fastest woman in the world—that's the title often given to Wilma Rudolph, an Olympic track star. But Wilma hadn't always been fast. As a child, she contracted pneumonia and scarlet fever and was left with the nerves in one leg damaged. Wilma's leg was useless and, for years, she wore a heavy brace.

The Long Way Up

Wilma Rudolph

The brace went on my leg when I was five, and I lived with that thing for the next half-dozen years. It was a steel brace, and it hooked onto my leg just above the knee and went all the way down my leg and connected to my shoe. The brace was supposed to keep the leg straight all the time and prevent me from walking on the leg sideways. I used to put it on as soon as I got up in the morning, and I wasn't allowed to take it off until I went to bed at night. I wore a brown Oxford shoe with that brace, and every time I needed a new pair of shoes, it would be the same kind, brown Oxfords. It turned me into a shoe freak. When I got older, I used to splurge on shoes, open-toed shoes, patent-leather shoes, high heels, anything. Wearing those brown Oxfords all the time made me appreciate shoes more than anything else. As for the brace, it was like any other brace—it weighed a couple pounds, and it looked so terrible; it always reminded me that something was wrong with me. Psychologically, wearing that brace was devastating.

When I was six, I started treatments for the leg that lasted until I was ten years old. The home exercises weren't enough anymore, so my mother made arrangements for me to go to the Meharry Medical School in Nashville every week for therapy and treatments. The hospital was a Black hospital, founded by two Black doctors. For the first couple of years, I went there twice a week. I always took a bus, with my mother or with an aunt if my mother couldn't go with me. I'd spend around four hours in the hospital every time, and, with the bus rides back and forth, that meant the whole day was spent trying to heal up my leg. The hospital was about fifty miles from Clarksville, and the bus rides would be about an hour going and an hour coming back. But even under those circumstances, they added a dimension to my life that the other kids didn't have. I was getting out of Clarksville, I was seeing other things, even though it was the same things every time. I was traveling.

When I first went to the hospital, I remember, they would put me on tables and conduct all of these examinations. They were forever pulling, turning, twisting, lifting that leg. Then they started stringing my leg up in this thing, I think it was traction, for about an hour every visit. I would just lie there on the table, and my leg would be strung up in the air, and I would wonder, "What is this all about?" My mother used to sit with me, and when she couldn't, the nurses would come in and read me stories. Then they would take the leg down and start massaging it, and then they would put it into the whirlpool. I remember that whirlpool being very, very hot, and I remember hating to put my leg in that hot water, but my mother would tell me, "Wilma, the key element here is not the water, it's the heat."

I would get home at night and sneak off into an empty room, and I would study that leg all the time, study it to see if it was getting better. There had to be some visible improvement, I would tell myself, after all of this, there just had to be. For a long time, I really didn't see an improvement, the leg was still crooked and I still had to wear the brace. I knew very little was happening, but I didn't let other people know that. So what happened was, I learned how to fake a no-limp walk. Some people, they know how to fake a limp, put one on so people think there is something wrong. Me, I learned how to fake a normal walk so that people would think there's nothing wrong. The natural feeling for me was to favor the leg, because it was pulling me off balance a little bit, but I went against the grain and forced myself to walk normally. That way, people would see me walking normally, especially my mother, and they would say to themselves, "Hey, look at Wilma walking so straight; the leg must be getting better."

I was nine and a half years old when I first took off the brace and went out in public without it. I'll never forget it. I went to church, and I walked in without the brace, and I knew right off that people were looking at me, saying to themselves, "Hey, there's Wilma, and she doesn't have the brace on her leg anymore." After church, a lot of people came over, adults, and they said, "Tremendous, Wilma, you got rid of the brace, everything's gonna be real fine now." The kids, I remember, they lay back and they just watched, didn't say much, you know; it was as if they were thinking, "Okay, the brace is gone, we've got to find something else to pin on her now." I just smiled and beamed and didn't say much. But looking back on it, I'd say it was one of the most important moments of my life. From that day on, people were going to start separating me from that brace, start thinking about me differently, start saying that Wilma is a healthy kid, just like all the rest of them.

But I wasn't out of the woods yet, not by a long shot. Every night, my mother used to boil this big kettle of water on the kitchen stove, and then she'd take this hot-water bottle and fill it up and wrap it with a towel and put it on my leg. The towel kept the hot-water bottle from burning me, but the water inside was so hot I could barely stand it. She would keep saying, "It's not the water, Wilma, it's the heat."

I finally stopped the treatments at the hospital in Nashville when I was ten, but I wore the brace on and off until I was twelve. I would only wear it the last couple of years whenever the leg ached or felt uncomfortable. Then, one glorious day, my mother wrapped up the brace and sent it back to the hospital in Nashville. I was free at last.

My whole life suddenly changed just as I was ending my sixth-grade year in school. No more brace; I was healthy all over my body for the first time. I was starting to become happy all the time, playing with the other kids as a peer at last. I would be going into the seventh grade in the fall, and there was a brand-new junior-senior high school waiting for me. I felt at that point that my life was beginning at last. That summer, I went over to this playground in town, and all the kids were around, playing a game called basketball. I watched them for a while, saw how much fun they were having, studied what they were doing, and I said to myself, "Wilma, tomorrow . . . tomorrow you're going to see what it feels like to play a little basketball."

Shadow of the Past

Robert Sorensen

Wilma Rudolph hobbled off the basketball court and sat down, looking unhappily at her foot. She wore a heavy black leather shoe, laced high above her ankle. She had tripped over the big shoe while going up for a rebound and skidded into the dirt. Her knees were scraped and bleeding.

"I've been wearing this big shoe since I was five," said Wilma. "It hasn't helped any!"

"But you can't walk without it!" argued her older brother, Westley.

"You wanna bet?" cried Wilma.

She unlaced her shoe and kicked it off her foot. She dragged herself up and eased her crippled foot onto the cool grass. There was no pain. Wilma smiled.

Suddenly she heard her mother's voice.

"Wilma Rudolph!"

Wilma turned, her leg twisted, and she toppled onto the grass, moaning.

"You crazy girl!" her mother shouted. Wilma's mother ran to help her up.

"You're going to kill yourself!" cried Westley.

"No, I'm not," pleaded Wilma. "I just want to be strong like everybody else."

"You're not gonna get strong this way!" protested Mrs. Rudolph.

"Then how else am I going to do it?" argued Wilma.

Westley shook his head.

"You always have been a stubborn girl." Her mother looked into Wilma's eyes. "You're going to take off that shoe anyway, even when I'm not lookin', so you might as well do it in front of me!"

Wilma smiled. "I'll be careful, Mama."

But Wilma never put that black corrective shoe on again. Instead, she started a daily exercise program of bouncing a basketball slowly around the court, limping but forcing the muscles in her foot to work and grow stronger. Within months she could cover the court in a slow run.

Several years later Ed Temple, track coach for Tennessee State University, was invited to a track meet at Wilma's high school in Clarksville, Tennessee. He observed carefully the lean, powerful legs and flowing stride of Wilma

457

Rudolph.

After watching her win the 100-yard dash, Temple made Wilma an offer. During summer vacation she could work out with the Tiger-Belles, the famous women runners of Tennessee State. If she looked good enough, she might be able to win a scholarship.

Wilma was stunned. She hadn't even thought of going to college. Now a whole new world was waiting. She arrived at Tennessee State full of hope and fear. Would she be good enough?

She quickly learned that being a Tiger-Belle would not be easy. Coach Temple believed that even sprinters needed long-distance training to get in shape. Every morning the Tiger-Belles ran 5 miles up hills and through fields. On her first morning Wilma fell exhausted after 3 miles. She was on her knees, ready to vomit, as the Tiger-Belles left her behind.

In a practice race against the older runners, Wilma flung herself across the finish line. She lost her balance and slid into the dirt and gravel.

Coach Temple trotted over to Wilma. Blood oozed from her hands and knees, and tears of pain and frustration streamed from her eyes.

"Listen," he said, "if you want to leave, you can. Or you can stay, and I'll teach you to win races."

"I don't think I can do it," sobbed Wilma.

"I think you can be a champion if you want to." He got up and left Wilma lying on the track.

Wilma thought of the scholarship and looked at her bleeding hands. The coach was just leading her on. She would never be that good. She packed her things and headed home.

That night, as she sat alone in her bedroom, she gazed sadly at her left foot. After fighting so determinedly to strengthen her foot, she felt she would never use it again to win races. Wilma's dreams of becoming a track star were shattered.

"What's troubling you, girl?" Her mother closed the bedroom door behind her as she entered.

Suddenly Wilma burst into tears. Her mother wrapped her arms around her.

"Oh, Mama!" Wilma gasped. "I tried so hard to make that team."

"Nobody ever said you didn't make the team!" exclaimed Mrs. Rudolph. "You're the only one that thinks you can't run in any more races!"

"But I can't race anymore!" cried Wilma. "Sometimes I think I'm getting crippled, and I even see that ugly shoe on my foot again!"

Wilma's mother was silent.

"And all that exercising and training, and running those hills! I'm afraid it'll kill me!" exclaimed Wilma anxiously.

"It's the past that's holding you down, girl!" Her mother stared at her. "There's nothing wrong with your foot! The past's haunting you,

keeping you from moving ahead in your life so you'll never have a future!"

Wilma began crying again, and her body trembled.

"Don't ever give up," her mother hugged Wilma closely. "'Cause if you do, the past will be there waiting for you. Don't ever stop for anything, Wilma!" Her mother stood up. "Do you understand?"

Wilma nodded her head.

"Now pack your things, because I'm putting you on the bus for Tennessee State in the morning!"

Wilma smiled joyfully at her mother, tears clouding her eyes. They held each other tightly.

When Wilma got back to Tennessee State, she started training methodically. Every day the gun cracked, catapulting her down the track. She started winning some practice races. Coach Temple didn't say much, but his grin said, "I told you so."

After graduating from high school, Wilma received a scholarship to attend Tennessee State University. She was now a Tiger-Belle.

But that was only the beginning of her ordeal. With one eye on the coming Olympics, Coach Temple drilled Wilma at a savagely inhuman pace. "When you're sprinting . . . straighten out those long legs!" he would yell from the bleachers.

Wilma's legs flew faster.

"Pump your arms!" he shouted. "Move, move . . . faster!"

Gracefully, her legs striding and her arms pumping, Wilma met the tape across the finish line.

"You're looking good," Coach Temple finally said. "I think you're ready to try out for the Olympics!"

Yet Wilma was only partly ready to make her dreams come true. At the tryouts held in Abilene, Texas, she finished first in three events and easily made the U. S. Olympic track team. Physically, she was in top form—but her mind was suddenly playing tricks on her again.

It happened during the tryouts for the 200-meter dash. Her left foot seemed to slap against the track as if it were dead or limp. Wilma was terrified at the thought of running another race, and the Olympics were only one week away.

The l960 Olympics were held in the Stadio Olympico in Rome, Italy. Wilma Rudolph stood watching the crowd of 60,000 cheering people. They were waiting for the 400-meter relay race to begin.

"Hey, what's bugging you, girl!" cried Barb Johnson, a Tiger-Belle teammate.

"Nothing," uttered Wilma, glumly.

"I've never seen you so down!" exclaimed Barb.

"Hey, we've got to pick up a gold medal on this relay!" Lucinda Williams trotted over, grinning happily.

"Yeah!" shouted Barb. She patted Wilma on the back. "C'mon, Wilma, limber up!"

Wilma and the other girls got ready for the 400-meter relay. Wilma was the anchorwoman. She would be the speedster to run the last 100 meters.

The gun exploded. Wilma shuddered while she watched her teammate fly down the track.

Wilma ran to her starting point. She tried not to look at her left foot as she waited. Her heart pumped wildly in her throat.

Finally, Wilma caught sight of Lucinda. All the girls were shoulder to shoulder, striding at magnificent speed. Suddenly Lucinda bolted into the lead!

The runners came in a flood at Wilma. As Lucinda came racing alongside Wilma, the baton slipped and bobbled to the ground.

A hush fell over the crowd. The baton rolled next to Wilma's left foot. She grabbed for the baton, and the black shoe appeared again like a hundred-pound weight around her foot. Her whole body flinched and stiffened. Wilma snatched up the baton and gripped it in her hand. Suddenly her mother's words flashed through her mind, "Don't ever give up, Wilma. . . . Don't ever stop for anything!" And like a rocket, Wilma exploded down her lane.

With great scissoring strides she came alongside Germany's Jutta Heine, who had been in the lead.

The crowd stood, roaring!

Suddenly Wilma was breaking the tape. She crossed the finish line just ahead of the German sprinter!

As the gold metal was placed around Wilma's neck, she looked down and saw there was no high laced black shoe on her foot. She knew now it would never be there again.

Focus

1. Describe how Wilma felt when the brace finally came off.
2. Why do you think a physical disability like Wilma Rudolph's can be "psychologically devastating"?
3. Name two people who helped Wilma. Compare the help that each person provided.
4. Describe Wilma Rudolph's personality. Use events from the story to support your description.
5. Explain how Rudolph's experience at the Olympics was both an athletic victory and a personal victory.

In Writing

Wilma Rudolph was once voted America's outstanding amateur athlete, an award given for advancing good sportsmanship through "performance, example, and good influence." Write a paragraph explaining why you think she was given this award.

Vocabulary

On a piece of paper, write the numbers *1* to *5*. Then look at the words in the first column and find a definition for each word in the second column. Next to each number on your paper, write the letter of the correct definition for each word.

1. traotion
2. sprinter
3. bobble
4. catapulting
5. whirlpool

A. one who works with wood
B. to fumble
C. rapidly circulating water
D. a condition of being pulled
E. one who runs at top speed
F. springing upward suddenly

DEEP WATER

William O. Douglas

What do you fear more than anything else in the world? Have you tried to overcome the fear? This story is from the autobiography of a former Supreme Court Justice who fought his fear and won.

There are many lakes to the north and west of Mount Adams. Often, like Surprise Lake below Gilbert Peak, they are dark and deep and lined with thick forests of pine and fir that run to the water. Others are hardly more than potholes. There is one such in a meadow near the southeastern end of the ridge mounted by the famous Goat Rocks. It is not more than 100 yards long and 50 wide. It lies in a high meadow of heather and alpine bunchgrass. It is fringed by dwarfed whitebark pine and Alaska cedar, both stunted by the altitude and wind. It lies not more than a stone's throw from a perpetual snowbank. Yet, under a July sun, the upper layer of its water was at times almost tepid. So Doug Corpron and I dubbed it Warm Lake.

It was in the open, like a swimming pool in a lawn. Its water was so clear that I could see the rocky, sandy bottom far out from shore. No dark depths were there to warn me. And at no place did it appear more than twenty feet deep. There was nothing ominous about it, and, as I have said, its surface water was warm, although it lay close to a snow field. As boys we planned a night there whenever possible, for there is nothing more attractive than a bath after a week's exertion on the trails. And there is the same novelty about swimming in comfort next to a snowbank as there is skating outdoors on artificial ice at Sun Valley on a warm day in July.

We would bathe and swim in this lake for a whole afternoon in July or August. Our pattern was to take a dip, then lie in the heather sunning ourselves, and then return to the water for more splashing and shouting. Yet I never got far from the bank. I remember being there with Doug Corpron and watching him. He would dive in with a running jump from the bank, coast part of the way across the pond under water, then come up to the surface, swim to the far bank and, without stopping, swim back. He'd shout to me, "Come on! It's fun!"

He had a round face that always seemed cheerful and content. And he had brown eyes that exuded confidence. He stood about five feet ten and even as a boy was on the plump side. He'd stand on the bank of the little lake, toss his head to shake the water off, and smooth down his shock of dark-brown hair. Then after a moment's rest he'd dive in and be off again. He seemed to me to be as much at home in the water as a porpoise or a seal.

I hugged the bank, wading and splashing water. When I had my picture taken in this pond, I made sure I had only my head sticking out. But I did it by kneeling in shallow water. Once or twice when I tried to swim, a feeling of panic swept over me. I would freeze and become rigid, unable to move my legs. I would gasp for breath and strike out with my arms. My legs would hang straight down in the water and I would be unable to move them. Even when I walked in water over my waist, the panic would seize me and I would have to go to shore.

No one ever knew this. I naturally was ashamed of it. It all fitted into fears that had become established in my imagination. I thought it had something to do with my puny legs, since they became useless once I got into deep water. That fact puzzled me. I often said to myself, "It's funny that I can walk and run and climb with my legs, but not swim with them." But once the panic seized me in the water, I had no command over them. I suffered intensely as I fished the streams and lakes of the Cascades, or as I bathed in Warm Lake.

The worry grew and grew, as only a specter can. It made every expanse of water a source of anxiety and yet a challenge. It was at once an invitation to overcome the fear and a fear that I would never succeed in doing so. My aversion to the water was, indeed, mixed with a great attraction for it. Often I would be mesmerized by it and stand on the edge of a pond or a pool, looking into the water as if to draw from its depths the secret of its conquest of me. It was the master; I was the servant. That created a resentment which developed in my heart; and the more helpless I was in conquering my fear the more intense the resentment became. The waters of the rivers and lakes were great attractions; but as one can have an appetite for food to which he is allergic, so the waters to which I was drawn filled me with apprehension.

I knew the origin of my fears. They went back to the day I almost drowned. But I thought it took only will power and courage to overcome the fear that drowning had instilled in me. I learned years later that the early fears of childhood work through the sympathetic nervous system, which does not depend on will power for its functioning. When the man says "Yes," the sympathetic nervous system will often say "No" and send him helter-skelter in the direction opposite from where he decided to go. If this goes on long enough, a man can conclude he is irrational or end up frustrated and desperately ill with an illness that no medicine can cure.

It had happened when I was ten or eleven years old. I had decided to learn to swim. There was a pool at the Y.M.C.A. in Yakima that offered exactly the opportunity. The Yakima River was treacherous. Mother continually warned against it, and kept fresh in my mind the details of each drowning in the river. But the Y.M.C.A. pool was safe. It was only two or three feet deep at the shallow end; and while it was nine feet deep at the other, the drop was gradual. I got a pair of water wings and went to the pool. I hated to show my skinny legs. But I subdued my pride and did it.

From the beginning, however, I had an aversion to the water when I was in it. This started when I was three or four years old and Father took me to the beach in California. He and I stood together in the surf. I hung on to him, yet the waves knocked me down and swept over me. I was buried in water. My breath was gone. I was frightened. Father laughed, but there was terror in my heart at the overpowering force of the waves.

My introduction to the Y.M.C.A. swimming pool revived unpleasant memories and stirred childish fears. But in a little while I gathered confidence. I paddled with my new water wings, watching the other boys and trying to learn by aping them. I did this two or three times on different days and was just beginning to feel at ease in the water when the misadventure happened.

I went to the pool when no one else was there. The place was quiet. The water was still, and the tiled bottom was as white and clean as a bathtub. I was timid about going in alone, so I sat on the side of the pool to wait for others.

I had not been there long when in came a big bruiser of a boy, probably eighteen years old. He had thick hair on his chest. He was a beautiful physical specimen, with legs and arms that showed rippling muscles. He yelled, "Hi, Skinny! How'd you like to be ducked?"

With that he picked me up and tossed me into the deep end. I landed in a sitting position, swallowed water, and went at once to the bottom. I was frightened, but not yet frightened out of my wits. On the way down I planned: when my feet hit the bottom, I would make a big jump, come to the surface, lie flat on it, and paddle to the edge of the pool.

It seemed a long way down. Those nine feet were more like ninety, and before I touched bottom my lungs were ready to burst. But when my feet hit bottom I summoned all my strength and made what I thought was a great spring upwards. I imagined I would bob to the surface like a cork. Instead I came up slowly. I opened my eyes and saw nothing but water—water that had a dirty yellow tinge to it. I grew panicky. I reached up as if to grab a rope and my hands clutched only at water. I was suffocating. I tried to yell but no sound came out. Then my eyes and nose came out of the water—but not my mouth.

I flailed at the surface of the water, swallowed, and choked. I tried to bring my legs up, but they hung as dead weights, paralyzed and rigid. A great force was pulling me under. I screamed, but only water heard me. I had started on the long journey back to the bottom of the pool.

I struck at the water as I went down, expending my strength as one in a nightmare fights an irresistible force. I had lost all my breath. My lungs ached, my head throbbed. I was getting dizzy. But I remembered the strategy: I would spring from the bottom of the pool and come like a cork to the surface. I would lie flat on the water, strike out with my arms, and thrash with my legs. Then I would get to the edge of the pool and be safe.

I went down, down, endlessly. I opened my eyes. Nothing but water with a yellow glow—dark water that one could not see through.

And then sheer, stark terror seized me, terror that knows no understanding, terror that knows no control, terror that no one can understand who has not experienced it. I was shrieking under water. I was paralyzed under water—stiff, rigid with fear. Even the screams in my throat were frozen. Only my heart, and the pounding in my head, said that I was still alive.

And then in the midst of the terror came a touch of reason. I must remember to jump when I hit the botttom. At last I felt the tiles under me. My toes reached out as if to grab them. I jumped with everything I had.

But the jump made no difference. The water was still around me. I looked for ropes, ladders, water wings. Nothing but water. A mass of yellow water held me. Stark terror took an even deeper hold on me, like a great charge of electricity. I shook and trembled with fright. My arms wouldn't move. My legs wouldn't move. I tried to call for help, to call for Mother. Nothing happened.

And then, strangely, there was light. I was coming out of the awful yellow water. At least my eyes were. My nose was almost out too.

Then I started down a third time. I sucked for air and got water. The yellowish light was going out.

Then all effort ceased. I relaxed. Even my legs felt limp; and a

blackness swept over my brain. It wiped out fear; it wiped out terror. There was no more panic. It was quiet and peaceful. Nothing to be afraid of. This is nice . . . to be drowsy . . . to go to sleep . . . no need to jump . . . too tired to jump . . . it's nice to be carried gently . . . to float along in space . . . tender arms around me . . . tender arms like Mother's . . . now I must go to sleep. . . .

I crossed to oblivion, and the curtain of life fell.

The next I remember I was lying on my stomach beside the pool, vomiting. The chap that threw me in was saying, "But I was only fooling." Someone said, "The kid nearly died. Be all right now. Let's carry him to the locker room."

Several hours later I walked home. I was weak and trembling. I shook and cried when I lay on my bed. I couldn't eat that night. For days a haunting fear was in my heart. The slightest exertion upset me, making me wobbly in the knees and sick to my stomach.

I never went back to the pool. I feared water. I avoided it whenever I could.

A few years later when I came to know the waters of the Cascades, I wanted to get into them. And whenever I did— whether I was wading the Tieton or Bumping River or bathing in Warm Lake of the Goat Rocks—the terror that had seized me in the pool would come back. It would take possession of me completely. My legs would become paralyzed. Icy horror would grab my heart.

This handicap stayed with me as the years rolled by. In canoes on Maine lakes fishing for landlocked salmon, bass fishing in New Hampshire, trout fishing on the Deschutes and Metolius in Oregon, fishing for salmon on the Columbia, at Bumping Lake in the Cascades—wherever I went, the haunting fear of the water followed me. It ruined my fishing trips; deprived me of the joy of canoeing, boating, and swimming.

I used every way I knew to overcome this fear, but it held me firmly in its grip. Finally, one October, I decided to get an instructor and learn to swim. I went to a pool and practiced five days a week, an hour each day. The instructor put a belt around me. A rope attached to the belt went through a pulley that ran on an overhead cable. He held on to the end of the rope, and we went back and forth, back and forth across the pool, hour after hour, day after day, week after week. On each trip across the pool a bit of the panic seized me. Each time the instructor relaxed his hold on the rope and I went under, some of the old terror returned and my legs froze. It was three months before the tension began to slack. Then he taught me to put my face under water and exhale, and to raise my nose and inhale. I repeated the exercise hundreds of times. Bit by bit I shed part of the panic that seized me when my head went under water.

Next he held me at the side of the pool and had me kick with my legs. For weeks I did just that. At first my legs refused to work. But they gradually relaxed; and finally I could command them.

Thus, piece by piece, he built a swimmer. And when he had perfected each piece, he put them together into an integrated whole. In April he said, "Now you can swim. Dive off and swim the length of the pool, crawl stroke."

I did. The instructor was finished.

But I was not finished. I still wondered if I would be terror-stricken when I was alone in the pool. I tried it. I swam the length up and down. Tiny vestiges of the old terror would return. But now I could frown and say to that terror, "Trying to scare me, eh? Well, here's to you! Look!" And off I'd go for another length of the pool.

This went on until July. But I was still not satisfied. I was not sure that all the terror had left. So I went to Lake Wentworth in New Hampshire, dived off a dock at Triggs Island, and swam two miles across the lake to Stamp Act Island. I swam the crawl, breast stroke, side stroke, and back stroke. Only once did the terror return. When I was in the middle of the lake, I put my face under and saw nothing but bottomless water. The old sensation returned in miniature. I laughed and said, "Well, Mr. Terror, what do you think you can do to me?" It fled and I swam on. Yet I had residual doubts. At my first opportunity I hurried west, went up the Tieton to Conrad Meadows, up the Conrad Creek Trail to Meade Glacier, and camped in the high meadow by the side of Warm Lake. The next morning I stripped, dived into the lake, and swam across to the other shore and back—just as Doug Corpron used to do. I shouted with joy, and Gilbert Peak returned the echo. I had conquered my fear of water.

Focus

1. Explain how the author's fear of water developed.
2. Why did the author finally decide he had to overcome his fear of water?
3. List briefly the steps that the author followed to learn to swim.
4. What character qualities do you think were necessary for the author to overcome his fear?
5. How was Wilma Rudolph's victory over her handicap similar to William Douglas's victory over his fear?

In Writing

Imagine that you are faced with a creature from your worst nightmare. It accuses you of being afraid. In one paragraph, write a defense for yourself. Then, in a second paragraph, write about a plan to conquer the horrible creature and your fear.

Vocabulary

On a piece of paper, write the numbers 1 to 5. Then look at the words in the first column and find an antonym for each word in the second column. Next to each number on your paper, write the letter of the antonym for each word.

1. perpetual
2. tepid
3. subdued
4. oblivion
5. aversion

A. cold
B. ending
C. remembering
D. intellectual
E. liking
F. loud

LIFE SKILL: Reading and Using Road Maps

A special moment can happen when you least expect it. For example, consider a group of lost travelers. It could be your family. It could be your classmates on a school trip. You are the only person who knows how to read a road map accurately. After studying the map, you are able to direct the stranded vehicle onto the right road. Everyone on the trip reaches their destination safely. You are a highway hero!

Well-written maps are packed with useful information. They show:

• the most direct routes.
• where bridges and ferries cross waterways, and whether they carry cars.

• alternate routes, so detours and other road hazards don't trap the driver.
• mileage between major points, which helps you to determine how long the trip will take.

Road maps are also sources of ideas. They can be useful for walking tours or shopping in unfamiliar areas. Many times, maps list special places to visit. They also assist in locating campgrounds. Historical sites and tourist-information stations are sometimes shown. Other facts provided by road maps can include major airports and where to get help (hospitals, state police, traveler's aid, and rest areas).

471

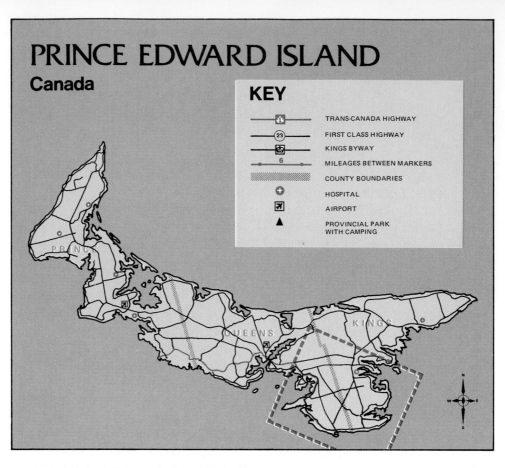

PRINCE EDWARD ISLAND
Canada

KEY

	TRANS-CANADA HIGHWAY
(23)	FIRST CLASS HIGHWAY
	KINGS BYWAY
6	MILEAGES BETWEEN MARKERS
	COUNTY BOUNDARIES
+	HOSPITAL
✈	AIRPORT
▲	PROVINCIAL PARK WITH CAMPING

MILEAGE CHART	Alberton	Borden	Brackley Beach	Cavendish	Charlottetown	Crapaud	Dalvay Beach	East Point	Georgetown	Hunter River	Kensington	Montague	Mount Carmel	Mount Stewart
Alberton		59	72	62	78	62	79	142	109	64	48	106	36	93
Borden	59		32	29	34	11	39	98	65	24	17	62	52	51
Brackley Beach	72	32		13	12	21	7	70	45	8	24	42	47	21
Cavendish	62	29	13		24	23	20	83	58	10	14	55	37	34
Charlottetown	78	34	12	24		23	15	64	31	14	30	28	53	17
Crapaud	62	11	21	23	23		28	87	54	13	19	51	35	40
Dalvay Beach	79	39	7	20	15	28		63	38	15	31	35	54	14
East Point	142	98	70	83	64	87	63		47	78	94	44	117	49
Georgetown	109	65	45	58	31	54	38	47		45	61	9	84	24
Hunter River	64	24	8	10	14	13	15	78	45		16	42	39	29
Kensington	48	17	24	14	30	19	31	94	61	16		58	23	45
Montague	106	62	42	55	28	51	35	44	9	42	58		81	20
Mount Carmel	36	52	47	37	53	35	54	117	84	39	23	81		68
Mount Stewart	93	51	21	34	17	40	14	49	24	29	45	20	68	

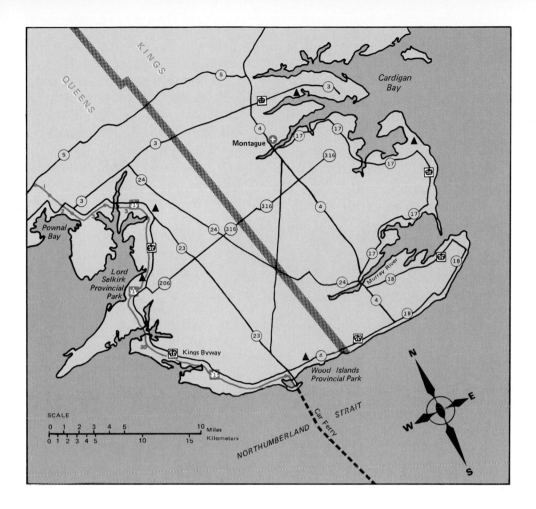

Look at the road map (left) of Prince Edward Island. Notice the "key" at the top. The key explains the map's symbols. It uses different colors to represent different highways. There are key marks all over the map. Try to match each symbol to an example on the map.

Another useful map symbol is the direction pointer. It tells North, South, East, and West. These compass points are shown on the lower right-hand section of the map.

Use the enlarged section of Prince Edward Island (above) to answer these questions.

1. You have just crossed Northumberland Strait on the car ferry. You have landed on the southeast corner of the Island. Where are you?
   a. Disneyland
   b. Cape Bear
   c. Wood Islands

2. If you turn west at Wood Islands, what numbered route will you be traveling? Check the key, and tell the name of this route.

3. There is another road running parallel with Route 1. It shows a symbol instead of a number. The symbol represents the highway name. What is it called?

4. Along Route 1, Lord Selkirk is mentioned. What is Lord Selkirk?
   a. a Provincial Park
   b. a knight of the round table
   c. a friend

5. Return to Wood Islands. You are now on Route 4 and approaching Murray River. If you continue north, what town will you reach that has a hospital?

The answer to 1 is c, Wood Islands. Route 1 is the first answer to 2; Trans-Canada Highway is the second answer. The symbol in 3 is a crown, and it is called Kings Byway. In 4, Lord Selkirk is a Provincial Park. The answer to 5 is Montague. This is the closest area with a hospital symbol.

The road map on the previous two pages shows three ways to find the distance from one place to another. It shows—

• a *scale of miles and kilometers* (located in the enlarged section); this measures straight routes.

• a *mileage chart* (located below the small map); this shows distances between major points.

• *red numbers* and *markers* along the roadways (review the key); these are useful for short distances. They also tell distances between places not shown on the mileage chart.

Look at the mileage chart, below the small map of the island. Place one index finger at "East Point" on the list at the left side of the chart. Place your other index finger at "Hunter River" on the list at the top of the chart. Run your fingers across and down from those titles. The number in the box where your fingers meet is the mileage between the two towns (78 miles).

Use the mileage chart to answer these questions.

6. What is the distance from Mount Stewart to Kensington?

7. How far is it from Cavendish to Charlottetown?

8. Is Montague closer to Mount Carmel or to Borden?

CASEY AT THE BAT

Ernest Lawrence Thayer

The outlook wasn't brilliant for the Mudville nine that day;
The score stood four to two, with but one inning more to play;
And so, when Cooney died at first, and Burrows did the same,
A sickly silence fell upon the patrons of the game.

A straggling few got up to go in deep despair. The rest
Clung to the hope which springs eternal in the human breast;
They thought, if only Casey could but get a whack, at that,
They'd put up even money now, with Casey at the bat.

But Flynn preceded Casey, as did also Jimmy Blake,
And the former was a pudding and the latter was a fake;
So upon that stricken multitude grim melancholy sat,
For there seemed but little chance of Casey's getting
  to the bat.

But Flynn let drive a single, to the wonderment of all,
And Blake, the much despisèd, tore the cover off the ball;
And when the dust had lifted, and they saw what had
    occurred,
There was Jimmy safe on second, and Flynn a-hugging third.

Then from the gladdened multitude went up a joyous yell,
It bounded from the mountain top, and rattled in the dell;
It struck upon the hillside, and recoiled upon the flat;
For Casey, mighty Casey, was advancing to the bat.

There was ease in Casey's manner as he stepped into
    his place,
There was pride in Casey's bearing, and a smile on
    Casey's face;
And when, responding to the cheers, he lightly doffed
    his hat,
No stranger in the crowd could doubt 'twas Casey at
    the bat.

Ten thousand eyes were on him as he rubbed his hands
    with dirt,
Five thousand tongues applauded when he wiped them
    on his shirt;
Then while the writhing pitcher ground the ball into his hip,
Defiance gleamed in Casey's eye, a sneer curled
    Casey's lip.

476

And now the leather-covered sphere came hurtling through the air,
And Casey stood a-watching it in haughty grandeur there;
Close by the sturdy batsman the ball unheeded sped.
"That ain't my style," said Casey. "Strike one," the umpire said.

From the benches, black with people, there went up a muffled roar,
Like the beating of the storm-waves on a stern and distant shore;
"Kill him! Kill the umpire!" shouted someone on the stand.
And it's likely they'd have killed him had not Casey raised his hand.

With a smile of honest charity great Casey's visage shone;
He stilled the rising tumult; he bade the game go on;
He signaled to the pitcher, and once more the spheroid flew,
But Casey still ignored it, and the umpire said, "Strike two."

"Fraud!" cried the maddened thousands, and the echo answered, "Fraud!"
But a scornful look from Casey, and the audience was awed;
They saw his face grow stern and cold, they saw his muscles strain,
And they knew that Casey wouldn't let that ball go by again.

The sneer is gone from Casey's lips, his teeth are clenched
   in hate,
He pounds with cruel violence his bat upon the plate;
And now the pitcher holds the ball, and now he lets it go,
And now the air is shattered by the force of Casey's blow.

Oh, somewhere in this favored land the sun is shining bright,
The band is playing somewhere, and somewhere hearts
   are light;
And somewhere men are laughing, and somewhere
   children shout,
But there is no joy in Mudville—Mighty Casey has struck out.

The Captive Outfielder

Leonard Wibberley

Like Casey in the poem, the boy in this story seems to keep striking out. What part does Mr. Olinsky play in the boy's "moment"? When is Mr. Olinsky's moment?

The boy was filled with anxiety which seemed to concentrate in his stomach, giving him a sense of tightness there, as if his stomach were all knotted up into a ball and would never come undone again. He had his violin under his chin and before him was the music stand and on the walls of the studio the pictures of the great musicians were frowning upon him in massive disapproval. Right behind him on the wall was a portrait of Paganini, and he positively glowered down at the boy, full of malevolence and impatience.

That, said the boy to himself, *is because he could really play the violin and I can't and never will be able to. And he knows it and thinks I'm a fool.*

Below Paganini was a portrait of Mozart, in profile. He had a white wig tied neatly at the back with a bow of black ribbon. Mozart should have been looking straight ahead, but his left eye, which was the only one visible, seemed to be turned a little watching the boy. The look was one of disapproval. When Mozart was the boy's age—that is, 13—he had already composed several pieces and could play the violin and the organ. Mozart didn't like the boy either.

On the other side of the Paganini portrait was the blocky face of Johann Sebastian Bach. It was a grim face, bleak with disappointment. Whenever the boy was playing it seemed to him that Johann Sebastian Bach was shaking his head in resigned disapproval of his efforts. There were other portraits around the studio— Beethoven, Brahms, Chopin. Not one of

them was smiling. They were all in agreement that this boy was certainly the poorest kind of musician and never would learn his instrument, and it was painful to them to have to listen to him while he had his lesson.

Of all these great men of music who surrounded him the boy hated Johann Sebastian Bach the most. This was because his teacher, Mr. Olinsky, kept talking about Bach as if without

Bach there never would have been any music. Bach was like a god to Mr. Olinsky, and he was a god the boy could never hope to please.

"All right," said Mr. Olinsky, who was at the grand piano. "The Arioso. And you will kindly remember the time. Without time no one can play the music of Johann Sebastian Bach." Mr. Olinsky exchanged glances with the portrait of Bach, and the two seemed in perfect agreement with each other. The boy was quite sure that the two of them carried on disheartened conversations about him after his lesson.

There was a chord from the piano. The boy put the bow to the string and started. But it was no good. At the end of the second bar Mr. Olinsky took his hands from the piano and covered his face with them and shook his head, bending over the keyboard. Bach shook his head too. In the awful silence all the portraits around the studio expressed their disapproval, and the boy felt more wretched than ever and not too far removed from tears.

"The *time*," said Mr. Olinsky eventually. "The time. Take that first bar. What is the value of the first note?"

"A quarter note," said the boy.

"And the next note?"

"A sixteenth."

"Good. So you have one quarter note and four sixteenth notes making a bar of two quarters. Not so?"

"Yes."

"But the first quarter note is tied to the first sixteenth note. They are the same note. So the first note, which is C sharp, is held for five sixteenths, and then the other three sixteenths follow. Not so?"

"Yes," said the boy.

"THEN WHY DON'T YOU PLAY IT THAT WAY?"

To this the boy made no reply. The reason he didn't play it that way was that he couldn't play it that way. It wasn't fair to have a quarter note and then tie it to a sixteenth note. It was just a dirty trick like Grasshopper Smith pulled when he was pitching in the Little League. Grasshopper Smith was on the Giants, and the boy was on the Yankees. The Grasshopper always retained the ball for just a second after he seemed to have thrown it and struck the boy out. Every time. Every single time. The boy got a hit every now and again from other pitchers. Once he got a two-base hit. The ball went joyously through the air, bounced and went over the center-field fence. A clear, good two-base hit. But it was a relief pitcher. And whenever Grasshopper Smith was in the box, the boy struck out. Him and Johann Sebastian Bach. They were full of dirty tricks. They were pretty stuck-up too. He hated them both.

Meanwhile he had not replied to Mr. Olinsky's question, and Mr. Olinsky got up from the piano and stood beside him, looking at him, and saw that the boy's eyes were bright with frustration and disappointment because he was no good at baseball and no good at music either.

"Come and sit down a minute, boy," said Mr. Olinsky, and led him over to a little wickerwork sofa.

Mr. Olinsky was in his sixties, and from the time he was this boy's age he had given all his life to music. He loved the boy, though he had known him for only a year. He was a good boy, and he had a good ear. He wanted him to get excited about music, and the boy was not excited about it. He didn't practice properly. He didn't apply himself. There was something lacking, and it was up to him, Mr. Olinsky, to supply whatever it was that was lacking so that the boy would really enter into the magic world of music.

How to get to him then? How to make a real contact with this American boy when he himself was, though a citizen, foreign-born?

He started to talk about his own youth. It had been a very grim youth in Petrograd. His parents were poor. His father had died when he was young, and his mother had, by a very great struggle, got him into the conservatory. She had enough money for his tuition only. Eating was a great problem. He could afford only one good meal a day at the conservatory cafeteria so that he was almost always hungry and cold. But he remembered how the great Glazunov had come to the cafeteria one day and had seen him with a bowl of soup and a piece of bread.

"This boy is thin," Glazunov had said. "From now on he is to have two bowls of soup, and they are to be big bowls. I will pay the cost."

There had been help like that for him—occasional help coming quite unexpectedly—in those long, grinding, lonely years at the conservatory. But there were other terrible times. There was the time when he had reached such an age that he could no longer be boarded at the conservatory. He had to give up his bed to a smaller boy and find lodgings somewhere in the city.

He had enough money for lodgings, but not enough for food. Always food. That was the great problem. To get money for food he had taken a room in a house where the family had consumption.[1] They rented him a room cheaply because nobody wanted to board with them. He would listen to the members of the family coughing at nighttime—the thin, shallow, persistent cough of the consumptive. He was terribly afraid—afraid that he would contract consumption himself, which was incurable in those days, and die. The thought of death frightened him. But he was equally frightened of disappointing his mother, for if he died he would not graduate and all her efforts to make him a musician would be wasted.

Then there was the time he had had to leave Russia after the revolution. And the awful months of standing in line to get a visa and then to get assigned to a train. It had taken seven months. And the train to Riga—what an ordeal that had been. Normally it took eighteen hours. But this train took three weeks. Three weeks in cattle cars in midwinter, jammed up against his fellow passengers, desperately trying to save his violin from being crushed. A baby had died in the cattle car, and the mother kept pretending it was only asleep. They had had to take it from her by force eventually and bury it beside the tracks out in the howling loneliness of the countryside.

And out of all this he had got music. He had become a musician. Not a concert violinist, but a great orchestral violinist, devoted to his art.

---

[1] consumption (kən səmp'shən): tuberculosis, a lung disease

He told the boy about this, hoping to get him to understand what he himself had gone through in order to become a musician. But when he was finished, he knew he had not reached the boy.

That is because he is an American boy, Mr. Olinsky thought. *He thinks all these things happened to me because I am a foreigner, and these things don't happen in America. And maybe they don't. But can't he understand that if I made all these efforts to achieve music—to be able to play the works of Johann Sebastian Bach as Bach wrote them—it is surely worth a little effort on his part?*

But it was no good. The boy, he knew, sympathized with him. But he had not made a real contact with him. He hadn't found the missing something that separated this boy from him and the boy from music. He tried again. "Tell me," he said, "what do you do with your day?"

"I go to school," said the boy flatly.

"But after that? Life is not all school."

"I play ball."

"What kind of ball?" asked Mr. Olinsky. "Bouncing a ball against a wall?"

"No," said the boy. "Baseball."

"Ah," said Mr. Olinsky. "Baseball." And he sighed. He had been more than thirty years in the United States and he didn't know anything about baseball. It was an activity beneath his notice. When he had any spare time, he went to a concert. Or sometimes he played chess. "And how do you do at baseball?" he said.

"Oh—not very good. That Grasshopper Smith. He always strikes me out."

"You have a big match coming up soon perhaps?"

"A game. Yes. Tomorrow. The Giants against the Yankees. I'm on the Yankees. It's the play-off. We are both tied for first place." For a moment he seemed excited, and then he caught a glimpse of the great musicians around the wall and the bleak stare of Johann Sebastian Bach, and his voice went dull again. "It doesn't matter," he said. "I'll be struck out."

"But that is not the way to think about it," said Mr. Olinsky.

"Is it inevitable that you be struck out? Surely that cannot be so. When I was a boy—" Then he stopped, because when he was a boy he had never played anything remotely approaching baseball, and so he had nothing to offer the boy to encourage him.

Here was the missing part then—the thing that was missing between him and the boy and the thing that was missing between the boy and Johann Sebastian Bach. Baseball. It was just something they didn't have in common, and so they couldn't communicate with each other.

"When is this game?" said Mr. Olinsky.

"Three in the afternoon," said the boy.

"And this Grasshopper Smith is your thorn in the side, huh?"

"Yeah," said the boy. "And he'll be pitching. They've been saving him for this game."

Mr. Olinsky sighed. This was a long way from the Arioso. "Well," he said, "we will consider the lesson over. Do your practice and we will try again next week."

The boy left, conscious that all the musicians were watching him. When he had gone, Mr. Olinsky stood before the portrait of Johann Sebastian Bach.

"Baseball, maestro,[2]" he said. "Baseball. That is what stands between him and you and him and me. You had twenty children and I had none. But I am positive that neither of us knows anything about baseball."

He thought about this for a moment. Then he said, "Twenty children. Is it possible, maestro—is it just possible that with twenty children . . . You will forgive the thought, but is it just possible that you may have played something like baseball with them sometimes? And perhaps one of them always being—what did he say?—struck out?"

He looked hard at the blocky features of Johann Sebastian Bach, and it seemed to him that in one corner of the grim mouth there was a touch of a smile.

Mr. Olinsky was late getting to the Clark Stadium Recreation Park in Hermosa Beach for the play-off between the Giants and the Yankees because he had spent the morning transposing the Arioso from A major into C major to make it simpler for the boy. Indeed, when he got there the game was in the sixth and last inning and the score was three to nothing in favor of the Giants.

The Yankees were at bat, and it seemed that a moment of crisis had been reached.

"What's happening?" Mr. Olinsky asked a man seated next to him who was eating a hot dog in ferocious bites.

"You blind or something?" asked the man. "Bases loaded, two away and if they don't get a hitter to bring those three home, it's good-by for the Yankees. And look who's coming up to bat. That dodo!"

Mr. Olinsky looked and saw the boy walking to the plate.

Outside the studio and in his baseball uniform he looked very small. He also looked frightened, and Mr. Olinsky looked savagely at the man who had called the boy a dodo and was eating the hot dog, and he said the only American expression of contempt he had learned in all his years in the United States. "You don't know nothing from nothing," Mr. Olinsky

---

[2]maestro (mī'strō): a master in an art

486

snapped.

"That so?" said the hot-dog man. "Well, you watch. Three straight pitches and the Grasshopper will have him out. I think I'll go home. I got a pain."

But he didn't go home. He stayed there while the Grasshopper looked carefully around the bases and then, leaning forward the ball clasped before him, glared intently at the boy. Then he pumped twice and threw the ball, and the boy swung at it and missed, and the umpire yelled, "Strike one."

"Two more like that, Grasshopper," yelled somebody. "Just two more and it's in the bag."

The boy turned around to look at the crowd and passed his tongue over his lips. He looked directly at where Mr. Olinsky was sitting, but the music teacher was sure the boy had not seen him. His face was white and his eyes glazed so that he didn't seem to be seeing anybody.

Mr. Olinsky knew that look. He had seen it often enough in the studio when the boy had made an error and knew that however much he tried he would make the same error over and over again. It was a look of pure misery—a fervent desire to get an ordeal over with.

The boy turned again, and the Grasshopper threw suddenly and savagely to third base. But the runner got back on the sack in time, and there was a sigh of relief from the crowd.

Again came the cool examination of the bases and the calculated stare at the boy at the plate. And again the pitch with the curious whip of the arm and the release of the ball one second later. Once more the boy swung and missed, and the umpire called, "Strike two." There was a groan from the crowd.

"Oh and two the count," said the scorekeeper, but Mr. Olinsky got up from the bench and, pushing his way between the people on the bleachers before him, he went to the backstop fence.

"You," he shouted to the umpire. "I want to talk to that boy there."

The boy heard his voice and turned and looked at him aghast. "Please, Mr. Olinsky," he said. "I can't talk to you now."

"Get away from the back fence," snapped the umpire.

"I insist on talking to that boy," said Mr. Olinsky. "It is very important. It is about Johann Sebastian Bach."

"Please go away," said the boy, and he was very close to tears. The umpire called for time out while he got rid of this madman, and the boy went to the netting of the backstop.

"You are forgetting about the Arioso!" said Mr. Olinsky urgently. "Now you listen to me, because I know what I am talking about. You are thinking of a quarter note, and it should be five sixteenths. It is a quarter note—C sharp—held for one sixteenth more. *Then* strike. You are too early. It must be exactly on time."

"What the heck's he talking about?" asked the coach, who had just come up.

The boy didn't answer right away. He was looking at Mr. Olinsky as if he had realized for the first time something very important which he had been told over and over again, but had not grasped previously.

"He's talking about Johann Sebastian Bach," he said to the coach. "Five sixteenths. Not a quarter note."

"Bach had twenty children," said Mr. Olinsky to the coach. "He would know about these things."

"For goodness' sakes, let's get on with the game," said the coach.

Mr. Olinsky did not go back to the bleachers. He remained behind the backstop and waited for the ceremony of the base inspection and the hard stare by the pitcher. He saw the Grasshopper pump twice, saw his hand go back behind his head, saw the curiously delayed flick of the ball, watched it speed to the boy and then he heard a sound which afterward he thought was among the most beautiful and satisfying he had heard in all music.

It was a clean, sharp "click," sweet as birdsong.

The ball soared higher and higher into the air in a graceful parabola. It was fifteen feet over the center fielder's head, and it cleared the fence by a good four feet.

Then pandemonium broke loose. People were running all over the field, and the boy was chased around the bases by half his teammates, and when he got to home plate he was thumped upon the back and his hair ruffled, and in all this Mr. Olinsky caught one glimpse of the boy's face, laughing and yet with tears pouring down his cheeks.

A week later the boy turned up at Mr. Olinsky's studio for his violin lesson. He looked around at all the great musicians on the wall, and they no longer seemed to be disapproving and disappointed in him.

Paganini was almost kindly. There was a suggestion of a chuckle on the noble profile of Mozart, and Beethoven no longer looked so forbidding. The boy looked at the portrait of Johann Sebastian Bach last.

He looked for a long time at the picture, and then he said two words out loud—words that brought lasting happiness to Mr. Olinsky. The words were: "Thanks, coach."

The Arioso went excellently from then on.

Focus

1. What skill, important in both baseball and music, did the boy have trouble acquiring? Explain how this skill is important in each activity.
2. Mr. Olinsky was a music teacher. Why would he want to help the boy with his baseball playing?
3. Do you think the boy's problems with music and baseball were caused by inability or by his attitude? Give reasons for your answer.
4. In what way did the musicians' portraits look different to the boy at the end of the story? Why do you think this happened?
5. Give evidence from the story to support this statement: Mr. Olinsky was an effective teacher.

In Writing

Teaching something simple can be difficult! Assume that you have to teach a being from outer space how to walk. Write a complete set of directions on what to do. Be careful—if you skip anything, the being could fall flat on its face. Test your directions by asking a friend to follow them exactly.

Vocabulary

On a piece of paper, write the numbers *1* to *5*. Then look at the words in the first column and find a synonym for each word in the second column. Next to each number on your paper, write the letter of the synonym for each word.

1. anxiety	A. evil
2. malevolence	B. certain
3. inevitable	C. chaos
4. transposing	D. worry
5. pandemonium	E. changing
	F. throwing

CHECKPOINT

Read the word list and paragraph below. Decide which word makes the best sense in each blank space. Then write the numbers *1* to *6* on a piece of paper and write the correct word next to each number.

Vocabulary:
Word
Identification

discordant   dingy   plummeted
lament   incessant   pandemonium
tepid   stammered

We reached the abandoned cabin just as the full force of the storm hit. The __(1)__ interior offered us shelter from the __(2)__ rain and wind. Sheets of water __(3)__ from the sky. __(4)__ crashes of thunder echoed through the valley as the __(5)__ nature had enacted grew more violent. The wind shook the walls of our frail building. I began to __(6)__ my decision to take the high trail across the mountain.

Comprehension:
Character

7. Reread the last four paragraphs on page 404 and all of page 405. What do Riley's actions suggest about his character?
8. Reread the conversation between Mathilde and her friends on page 414 and ending with the friends' exit on page 415. What do Mathilde's excuses tell you about her character?

Comprehension:
Fact/Opinion

For each sentence below, write *fact* or *opinion* on your paper.
9. The children missed school because they had the flu.
10. I finished the test seconds before the bell rang.
11. You should run three miles a day to improve your health.

Study Skills:
Outlines

12. Reread "Shadow of the Past," on pages 457-460. Make an outline on "Wilma Rudolph's Track Experiences." Divide your outline into two subtopics: "Tennessee State University" and "Olympics." Review the sample outline on page 450 to use as a model for your outline.

The Eyes of the Amaryllis

Natalie Babbitt

Many waters cannot quench love,
neither can the floods drown it.

Prologue

Seward's Warning

Listen, all you people lying lazy on the beach, is this what you imagine is the meaning of the sea? Oh, yes, it winks and sparkles as it sways beside you, spreading lacy foam along the sand, as dainty as a handkerchief. But can you really think that this is all it means? The foam, and these tender cowrie shells as pearly as a baby's toes? This purple featherweed floating up fine as the plume of an ostrich? That child in yellow, her face so grave beneath the brim of her linen hat? She sits there filling her bright tin bucket with those tiny shovelsful of sand, as cautious as a pharmacist measuring a dose, and watching her, you murmur to each other, "Sweet! How sweet!"

But listen. That is not the meaning of the sea. Less than a hundred and fifty years ago, on this very spot, out there where that row of rocky points thrusts up above the swells, a ship was lost. There, see? Where those herring gulls are wheeling down? It all looks much the same today: the rocks, and this beach that narrows to a pathway when the tide is in. But on that day at summer's end, the sky went dark, like twilight, with a shrieking wind, and the sea rose up tall as trees. Out there, where the gulls sit sunning now, it flung a ship against the rocks and swallowed her. It swallowed her whole, and every member of her crew. Captain, cargo, every inch of sail and rigging, gone in a single gulp, while the captain's wife stood helpless, watching. Up there, on that little bluff, that's where she stood, shrieking back at the wind, her son gone dumb with horror at her side. And there was nothing to bury afterwards. Nothing. The sea had taken it all, and gave back not one plank or shred of canvas.

That is part of the meaning. But there's more. A little later, three months or four, a young man broke his heart over a foolish girl. Nothing to remark about in that, you think. But he was an artist, that young man. He had carved a figurehead for the Amaryllis, *the ship that was swallowed, carved it in the likeness of the captain's wife—proud and handsome, with long red hair. Then he up and broke his heart over a foolish girl, and one morning very early, while the mist was still thick, he climbed into a dinghy and rowed himself straight out, out there well past the place where that sailboat skims along. He rowed out early in the morning, and he vanished. Oh, they found the dinghy later, just here, washed up, its oars stowed neat and dry inside. But he was not washed up, though they searched the shore for days. He was swallowed, they said at last, swallowed like the* Amaryllis.

But he was not quite swallowed. Listen. That is the rest of the meaning of the sea. You lie here so unthinking—have you forgotten that the surface of the earth is three-fourths water? Those gulls out there, they know it better than you. The sea can swallow ships, and it can spit out whales upon the beach like watermelon seeds. It will take what it wants, and it will keep what it has taken, and you may not take away from it what it does not wish to give. Listen. No matter how old you grow or how important on the land, no matter how powerful or beautiful or rich, the sea does not care a straw for you. That frail grip you keep on the wisp of life that holds you upright—the sea can turn it loose in an instant. For life came first from the sea and can be taken back. Listen. Your bodies, they are three-fourths water, like the surface of the earth. Ashes to ashes, the saying goes, and maybe so—but the ashes float on the water of you, like that purple featherweed floating on the tide. Even your tears are salt.

You do not listen. What if I told you that I was that carver of figureheads, the one they said was swallowed by the sea? The breeze in your ears, it carries my voice. But you only stretch on your fluffy towels and talk of present things, taking the sea for granted. So much the worse for you, then. My two Genevas listened, long ago, and understood.

 "Well, Mother," said the big man uneasily, turning his hat round and round in his hands.

"Well, George," the old woman returned. Her voice was strong and brisk, but, for him, a little critical. She looked up at him from her wing chair by the sunny window and saw—her son, yes, but also a stranger, well into middle age, tall but stooped, with the pale skin and scratchy-looking clothes of an inland man of business. And she saw in him also what he had been: a happy, wild-haired boy running barefoot on the beach. The two were one and the same, no doubt, but she loved the man because she had loved the boy. For her, the boy had been much easier to love.

"So you've broken your ankle," the man said.

"So it seems," she answered. She looked down impatiently at her foot propped up on a hassock. It was thick with bandages and wooden splints, and beside it on the floor a crutch lay waiting. "It's a nuisance, but there you are. Where's my granddaughter? Where's my namesake?"

"She's out on the beach. She's—well, she's never seen the sea before, you know. I suppose she's . . . interested in having a look."

"Interested! Yes, I should imagine so." The old woman smiled faintly.

The man took a deep breath. "Look here, Mother, you know we've always wanted you to come and live with us in Springfield. Now that you're laid up and can't take care of yourself, it's a good time to leave this godforsaken place and come inland where we can look after you."

The old woman shook her head. "It's good of you, George, of course. But when I wrote to you, that wasn't what I had in mind at all. You've brought Geneva down to stay with me, haven't you? That was the plan, wasn't it? My ankle will mend, and when it does, I'll go on the same as I always have."

"I just don't understand it," her son exploded then. "All by yourself here, year after year! The sea pounding, day and night, the dampness, this blasted sand everywhere. And the wind! It never stops! I can hardly bear it for five minutes, and you've been listening to it for thirty years!"

"Fifty, George. You've forgotten. Your father and I, we came here fifty years ago."

"No, but I meant . . ."

"I know what you meant," she said. "You're thinking it's thirty years since the day your father was drowned."

The man gripped his hat more firmly. "All right, Mother, never mind that. Be sensible for once and come back with me. There's plenty of room for three in the buggy, and we can send a wagon later for your things. Surely you can't be so all-fired stubborn about it now, when you can scarcely hobble."

His mother shook her head again. "I don't need you, George. Not yet. It's not time yet. I'll come to you at

Christmas, just as I've always done. But the rest of the year I belong right here. Geneva can take care of me till my ankle mends, and then you can come and fetch her."

"But, Mother!"

The old woman frowned at him and her eyes flashed. "George! Enough! We've had this argument a hundred times, and it bores me. You ran away from here a long time ago, and that's all right for you. But I will not budge an inch, not one inch, until . . . " She paused and looked away. Her anger seemed to leave her all at once, and she sighed. "George. Send Geneva in to me and then—go away, George. We only make each other cross."

At this the man seemed to sag a little. A look of pain crossed his face, and he turned half away from her, toward the door, though he watched her still. She was as handsome and vigorous as ever, her gray hair still streaked with red, her back straight as . . . a mast, he thought unwillingly, and then corrected it. Straight as a yardstick. A safer image.

She saw that he was watching her, and her face softened. "George. Dear boy, come and kiss me."

He went to her at once and knelt, and she put her arms around him and pulled him close. For a moment, the last long thirty years dissolved. They were mother and child again, she newly widowed, he newly fatherless, and they clung to each other. Then she loosened her hold and pushed him away gently. "Tell me," she said, smiling at him. "Geneva—what sort of child is she getting to be, do you think?"

"She's exactly like you," he said, sitting back on his heels.

The first Geneva Reade nodded and her eyes twinkled. "It's a judgment on you, George. Well, send her in. And then go home to Springfield and leave me in peace."

The big man kissed his mother's cheek and stood up, putting on his hat. Then, at the door, he said carefully, "I should have thought, though, that you'd want to come away from this spot. I couldn't stand it, looking out there every day, remembering. I'd have gone mad by now."

"Mad?" said his mother. "Well, perhaps I am a little mad."

"Mother," he blurted then, turning back to her, "for the love of heaven, watch out for Jenny. She's all we've got. Don't let her—"

"Hang your clothes on a hickory limb, and don't go near the water," the old woman chanted, bobbing her head from side to side. And then she said, scornfully, "Don't worry. I'll keep her out of the sea. You weren't such a faintheart before your father died."

The man's face closed. "I'll be back in three weeks," he told her flatly. "To fetch Jenny home. And if you're not mended by then, you'll come and stay with us till you are, whether you want to or not."

"Goodbye, George," said his mother, dismissing him. "Have a pleasant ride home. We'll see you in a month or two."

"Three weeks, Mother. Not a moment longer."

"*Goodbye,* George," said the first Geneva Reade.

 The journey that takes a traveler from inland places to the sea will follow roads that stay, in themselves, exactly the same, but they seem to change entirely. Carefree and busy, now leaf-shadowed, now blank and blinding in the summer sunshine, they stretch ahead importantly between green fields, and the air lies lightly on them. But by the time they have come within three miles, then two, then one, of their destination, they have turned submissive. The trees stand back and stand thin, and scrub pines appear, ragged as molting birds. The edges of the roads are lost now in drifts of sand, and the grass, thinner, like the trees, is rough and tall, rising, kneeling, rising, kneeling, as the breeze combs by.

There seems to be more sky here, a great deal more, so that the traveler is made aware, perhaps for the first time, that he moves along quite unprotected on the crust of the earth and might do well to move with caution, lest all at once he fall off, fall up, endlessly, and disappear. So he holds his gaze to the ground and finds that the air has grown heavy with new, wet smells, and the roads and everything around them look uncared-for. But this is not the case. They are cared for with the closest attention—by the sea.

498

The second Geneva Reade had observed all this on the way to Gran's house and was astonished by it in spite of the heavy presence beside her in the buggy. Her father had not spoken a word for miles, and he had allowed the horse to slow its pace to a clopping walk. His clenched hands, wrapped in the reins, were white at the knuckles. Jenny observed this, also, but she could not worry about it now. She was going to see the ocean for the first time in her life.

To be away from home—to stay with Gran and help her while her ankle mended—this seemed a very grownup thing to do, and Jenny had boasted about it to her friends. But in truth she was a little alarmed about that part, though her grandmother, whom she had seen before only for the two weeks of the yearly Christmas season, had long been a figure of romance to her. Gran was not like other grandmothers, smelling of starch or mothballs, depending on the time of year, and spending their time watering their plants. Gran stood straight and proud. Her face and arms were sunburned. And though she talked and listened, there always seemed to be something else on her mind, something far more absorbing than Christmas conversation.

But Jenny did not care for household chores, and was not at all sure that somewhere in her lay hidden the makings of a bedside nurse. So it wasn't that part of her adventure that excited her. No, the real enticement was the ocean. But this she could not admit. She was the only one of her friends who had never been to the shore. Preposterous, when it was only thirty miles from Springfield! But her father had never let her come, had always refused to discuss it. He hardly ever went, himself, to see Gran at her house.

But now, because of Gran's ankle, all that had changed. She was going to see the ocean, and she had all she could do to keep from bouncing on the buggy's padded seat. When would the water show itself? Over the next rise? Now! The buggy started up—and then she had gasped once and sat erect and very still.

For there it was, suddenly, the great Atlantic, so vast a thing that all of her imaginings could never have prepared her. It stretched away so far beyond the grassy plain that its sharp horizon curved to prove the roundness of the planet. In an instant she felt diminished, and with that new sensation came an unexpected sense of freedom. The breath she had caught and held slipped out in a long sigh, and she turned her head to see how her father was responding to the sight. But his face was rigid as a stone.

So she had turned back, and as the buggy rolled nearer, the coastline below them revealed itself slowly. A bay emerged and, far to the leftward tilt of its concavity, a tidy-looking town, with docks and the hulls of a few small ships. Then, as the buggy, reaching a fork, turned right, she saw that there were. houses scattered all along the shore. Far to the right, however, they sat fewer and farther between until at last there was only one house, quite by itself, on a low bluff at the farthest edge of the bay, where the land curved slowly in and down and sank a heavy arm into the water.

"Is that Gran's house?" she had asked, pointing.

"Yes," said her father.

"That's where you lived when you were little?"

"Yes," he said shortly.

Her head filled at once with a thousand questions, but it was clear that he didn't want to talk. "I can ask Gran," she had thought to herself. "Later."

When the buggy rolled down and stopped at last beside the house, Jenny had climbed out slowly, her eyes turned to the beach. "Can I go and look?" she pleaded. "Before I go in to see Gran?"

"All right, I guess so," her father said. "But, Jenny, remember what I told you. Stay back from the water. Don't ever forget that it's dangerous." And then, taking down her satchel, he had gone to the door of the house, knocked once, and stepped inside.

The sea did not look dangerous. Jenny saw the whole of its low-tide shore behavior in one long glance—how it tipped and slopped, sifting the wet sand, stroking the beach with sliding foam. Well up on this beach, a straggling fringe of seaweed, like a scratchy penline, lay drying where the last high tide had

500

stranded it, and here, too, intermingled, had been left abandoned pebbles by the million and broken bits of shell. Above
the seaweed the toast-colored sand was loose and warm, and
she longed to take off her shoes and stockings and dig her toes
into it. Not now. Later. After her father had gone. Gran had
promised her that if she, Jenny, were ever allowed to visit here,
there would be much to do on the beach, things that could only
be done correctly if one were barefoot.

Jenny took a cautious step over the seaweed line, down to
where the sand was hard and wet, and at once a sly finger of
foam slid up and curled around her ankle. She leapt back and
the foam slipped away with a sigh, to be lost beneath the curl of
the next small wave. Now new fingers of foam reached for her
up the sand, and she retreated behind the seaweed reluctantly.
Another wave, a soft thump, the slide of foam, repeated over
and over again. She watched it, amazed and faintly hypnotized, and the feeling of freedom that had come to her at first
grew deeper. Wisps of her dark red hair, tied back so neatly at
home by her mother, blew about her face as the breeze swept
past her, and suddenly it seemed as if she could hear it
speaking. *True to yo-o-o-ou*, it whispered, and the foam answered: *Yes-s-s* (thump) *yes-s-s* (thump) *yes-s-s*.

"Jenny!"

She heard her father's voice behind her and, turning,
plodded up across the sand to where he stood at the edge of
the swaying grass.

"Jenny, look at you. You've soaked one foot already," he
said despairingly. "Will you promise to stay safe, now? Will
you be careful? I've kept you away from this place as long as I
could, and—I know you're nearly grown, but still, it worries
me to death to leave you here."

"I'll be careful, Papa," she said.

He put his hands on her shoulders and peered into her face,
and then, dropping his hands, he shrugged. "Well, do your
best to be useful to your grandmother. It's remarkable how she
never seems to change, but still, she's getting on. You'll see.
She's waiting for you—better go on in. I'll be back in three
weeks."

"All right, Papa."

He left her, then, and climbed into the buggy, and as he urged the horse into the turn, she saw the stiffness of his shoulders ease, and he looked back at her almost cheerfully. "Goodbye!" he called.

She answered, "Goodbye," and added, to herself, "He's happy to be leaving." She watched him go and felt stranded and lonely, like the pebbles, but then she turned back for one more look at the sea and the lonely feeling fled away. For it seemed as if she had known this beach and loved it all her life, that she belonged here; that coming to this place, with its endless sky and water, was a kind of coming home.

 "Quick, child, come and tell me," said Gran from her chair when Jenny went inside. "What did you find on the beach? Anything unusual?" And then she caught herself. "Dear me, listen to the old lady, ranting on without even saying hello." She held out her arms and Jenny went to her and gave her a hug of greeting.

"Well!" said Gran. "So here you are at last! Let me look at you." She sat back, folding her arms, and tilted her head solemnly. "Your father says you're just like me, and I know he thinks I'm stubborn and unreasonable. Are you?"

"I don't know," said Jenny, laughing. "I guess so, sometimes."

"You've still got my red hair," Gran observed, "but otherwise you've changed a little since Christmas. How old are you now?"

"Twelve," said Jenny. "Last February."

"Yes, and now it's the middle of August," said Gran. "So you're halfway to thirteen. Not a child at all, really, though you mustn't expect me to stop calling you a child. I have a hard time remembering new things, sometimes. But I can remember the old things as if they happened yesterday. I met your grandfather for the first time when I was thirteen. Imagine that! He was twenty-one, and as handsome . . . well, as handsome as a walrus."

502

"A walrus!" said Jenny, laughing again. "Walruses aren't handsome."

"Well, now, that's a matter of taste," said Gran with a smile. "Your grandfather was a big man, heavyset, with a fine, big pair of mustaches. To me he was wonderfully handsome, and I fell in love with him at once."

"When you were thirteen?"

"Yes, indeed."

"I'm not in love with anyone," said Jenny, "and no one's in love with me."

"Someone will be, someday," said Gran.

"Oh, no," said Jenny. "I don't expect it. I'm much too ugly."

"Ugly!" Gran exclaimed, throwing up a hand in mock dismay. "But, child, how can you be ugly when you look so much like me? Your grandfather fell in love with me, remember."

"When you were thirteen?"

"Oh, no, certainly not," said Gran. "Years later. He was a sailor—well, you know that, of course—and when he wasn't on a voyage he would come to Springfield to visit his sister. Your Great-aunt Jane. It was ten years later, when I was twenty-three and he was thirty-one—that's when he noticed me. Two years after that he had his own ship, and we were married and came to live right here, in this house." She looked about her with satisfaction at the tidy, low-ceilinged room with its simple chairs and tables, and its mantel full of odd bits of china. "Then—let's see. Your father was born six years after that, in the spring of '36, and then when he was fourteen, that's when the *Amaryllis* was . . . lost. Out there on the rocks in a terrible storm." She said this calmly enough, tipping her head to indicate the stretch of sea outside the window behind her, but a look of intensity came to her face and she leaned forward and put a hand on Jenny's arm. "You went down to the beach just now?"

"Yes," said Jenny.

"Did you see anything? Anything at all?"

"Well," said Jenny, "I saw sand, and pebbles, and some long, stringy-looking weeds, and—the ocean, Gran! Oh, it's wonderful! It makes me feel . . . "

"Free!" said Gran triumphantly.

"Yes, that's it exactly," said Jenny, surprised. "How did you know?"

"How did I know?" said Gran. "What a question! It keeps me strong, that sense of freedom. And yet your father doesn't seem to feel it at all. Isn't that peculiar! But, child, was there nothing unusual on the beach? Nothing washed up?"

"What sort of thing?" asked Jenny, puzzled by the urgency in her grandmother's voice. "What are you looking for?"

"Never mind," said Gran, turning away from it. "Plenty of time for that later. Hand me the almanac on that table over there. I'll check the tides and then we'll have supper. Yes. Thank you, my dear. Now, let me see . . . here we are." She ran a fingertip down the page. "I thought so. High tide at 12:15 tonight. Good. Well! Now for supper."

"What shall I cook?" asked Jenny nervously. This was the part she had dreaded.

But Gran said, mercifully, "Cook? Why, nothing at all! What an idea!" She bent and picked up the crutch, and then, pulling herself up onto her good leg, she stood tall and straight and glared at her granddaughter. "I'm not an invalid, you know. And I don't intend to sit here and be fussed over. I shall do the cooking."

"But, Gran, I thought—"

"Never mind what you thought. Follow me. You can set the table, and fetch and carry now and then, but that's not why I sent for you."

Jenny tried hard to disguise her relief, but Gran, looking at her narrowly, recognized it anyway. "You don't like to cook?"

"No," said Jenny. "Not very much."

"Neither do I," said Gran. "We shall do as little of it as we possibly can without starving. Come along."

 In the dining room, over the mantel, hung a drawing of a ship. "That's the *Amaryllis*," said Gran as they sat down to eat. "A brig, she was, a big two-master. A beautiful thing to see.

Your grandfather owned her, and he was her captain, too. He
sailed her up and down the coast from Maine to the Caribbean."

"Did you ever go along?" asked Jenny.

"No, I never did. Women aren't welcome on trading ships,
you know, and anyway, I had your father to care for. No, I

stayed right here. And yet in a way I did go along. Look more closely there. Do you see the figurehead? Go and look."

Jenny got up from her chair and went to peer at the picture. "It's a woman," she reported, "and she's holding some kind of flower in her hands."

"It's a likeness of me," said Gran proudly. "That's an amaryllis I'm holding. A big red lily from the islands. Your grandfather thought they were very handsome, and he always said they reminded him of me. A romantic notion, but that's the way he was. So he named the ship after them, and put me on the prow. He tried time and again to bring me one—an amaryllis—but they always died on the way. Sometimes he'd be gone for months at a time, you see. It's a long way down to the islands."

"You couldn't have had much time with him," said Jenny, coming back to the table. "If he was gone so much. Weren't you lonely?"

"One gets used to it," said Gran. "But when the *Amaryllis* was due, I would go out to the bluff there and watch for it, and then we'd have such lovely parties when he was home again."

"My father comes home at the same time every day," said Jenny. "Five-thirty, when he's closed up the store."

"I know," said Gran, without interest. "It sounds very dull."

Jenny thought so, too, now. It seemed unbearably dull. But she added, in unconscious imitation, "Still, one gets used to it."

"I suppose so," said Gran.

Supper was nearly over when suddenly Gran put down her fork. She lifted her head, holding out a hand in a signal for silence. "Shh!" she whispered. "There! Do you hear it?"

Jenny listened. Nothing came to her ears but the breeze and the slap of waves. She looked at Gran questioningly. "What? What should I hear?"

"The tide," said Gran. "It's turned." She stared at Jenny and her eyes were blank, as if she'd forgotten for an instant that she was not alone. Then she was herself again, but with a difference. Something in her concentration had shifted, some inner curtain dropping while another opened. "Finish your supper," she said. "Then we'll clear away and go out to the beach."

 Leaning on her crutch, with Jenny at her other side to steady her, Gran stumped across the swaying grass to the little bluff that thrust out before the house. On three sides of it, the land dropped steeply four feet or so to the beach, so that it formed a small point, and here there was an old wooden bench. Gran eased herself down onto it and settled her bundled ankle out in front of her with a grimace of pain.

"You shouldn't go about on it so much," said Jenny.

"I have a doctor to tell me what to do," said Gran indifferently. "And if I don't pay attention to him, what makes you think I'll pay attention to you? Now, be a good child and sit here beside me. It will be dark soon. We've only an hour before bedtime, and I want to talk to you."

Jenny sat down and waited, but Gran was silent, leaning forward, staring out to sea. The sun, dropping rapidly behind them, seemed to be drawing the daylight with it like a veil, revealing behind the blue, as it slid away, the endlessness of space. A star appeared, and before them the green-brown waves took on an iridescence and spilled a sort of glow along the sand.

"At this time of day," said Gran at last, "it looks different. There almost seems to be a light . . . coming up from the bottom."

Jenny had to lean close to hear her grandmother's words, for the breeze had quickened and was whispering again in her ears. "The wind almost talks, doesn't it?" she said shyly.

Gran, at this, turned and looked at her closely. "So you hear it, too? Good. I was hoping for it. Give me your hand."

Gran's sun-browned hand was dry and strong, hard in spite of the rumpled skin at her wrist and knuckles. But her long fingers, holding Jenny's, were trembling slightly. Jenny looked down and saw how different this hand was from her mother's, so soft and padded and white. "It's important to look after your hands," her mother always said. "A lady doesn't go about with ragged fingernails, dear, and get her skin all chapped. You must learn to take more care. Your hands look so . . . *used*, Jenny. Like a boy's." Now Jenny saw that her hands were like Gran's, and for the first time she was proud of them. Oh, they were younger, to be sure. But very like.

"Pay close attention, Geneva," said Gran. "There's very little time. We must go to bed soon, and sleep, if we're to be fresh again by midnight."

"Midnight?" Jenny echoed.

"Certainly," said Gran. "We must be up again at midnight."

"But why?"

"High tide, child," said Gran, and then she stiffened. "Hist! Look there."

Jenny, startled, turned her head in the direction of Gran's gaze, and saw the figure of a man trudging slowly toward them along the shadowed beach. It was impossible to see his features, for his head was bowed, but Jenny could tell that he was rather small and hunched. He wore a dark, short coat of some heavy material, and his hands were plunged deep into his pockets. Then, as he came abreast of them, below the little bluff, he halted and looked up, and in the last gleam of daylight, Jenny saw a bearded face, ruined and rutted, with quiet but watchful eyes. "Good evening, Mrs. Reade," he said to Gran, and his voice had the same insistent rustle as the wind.

"Good evening, Seward," said Gran, and her fingers gave Jenny's a brief, unconscious squeeze.

The man stood looking at Gran for a moment, and then his gaze shifted to Jenny and his eyebrows lifted. But he said nothing more, and, dropping his head again, he moved off slowly down the beach, disappearing at last in the gloom.

"Who was that?" asked Jenny.

"Then you saw him, too," said Gran, and there was evident relief in her voice.

"Yes, of course I saw him," said Jenny. "What do you mean? How could I not have seen him?"

"Never mind," said Gran. "Now. There's very little time."

Her fingers tightened once more on her granddaughter's. "Geneva, listen carefully. Do you believe in things you can't explain?"

Jenny sat silent, considering. No one had ever asked her such a question before. At last she said, "Like things in fairy tales?"

"No, child," said Gran. "I mean—that all the daily things we do, and all the things we can touch and see in this world, are only one part of what's there, and that there's another world around us all the time that's mostly hidden from us. Do you ever think such things?"

"Well," said Jenny, confused and a little uncomfortable, but pleased, too, that Gran should speak to her this way. "Well, I think so. Yes, sometimes. Especially at night. But it's kind of scary."

"Ah!" said Gran. "Then you don't see quite what I mean. To me it's not 'scary' at all. Why should things we can't explain have to be frightening?"

"I don't know," said Jenny, "but they are. Sometimes, at night, I'm afraid to hang my hand down over the edge of the bed, because . . . well . . ."

"Because you're afraid something will grab it from under the bed!" said Gran, finishing the thought for her. "I know. Everyone has that notion sometimes. But that's our imagination, Geneva. I'm not talking about imagined things. I'm talking about . . . well, never mind. I'll just have to take a chance and hope you'll understand. You did see Seward just now, after all . . . " Her voice trailed off, but before Jenny could speak, she began again. "At high tide, child, I want you to come down here to the beach and search. I've done it by myself for thirty years, and then, last week, I stumbled in the sand and broke my silly ankle, and now, with that and this blasted crutch, I can't get about well enough. Not to do it properly. That's why I sent for you, Geneva. I'm depending on you to help me. You must come and search, and if you find anything, you must bring it back at once. You must get there first, before Seward."

"Seward? The man who just went by?" said Jenny.

"Yes. He goes for miles along the beach," said Gran, "and picks things up."

"But who is he?"

Gran ignored this question. "I'll give you a lantern at midnight. Then you must come out and search."

"But what am I to look for?" Jenny cried. "I don't understand at all."

Gran drew her hand away and laced her own fingers tightly together. There was a long pause, and then: "For thirty years," she said, "I've waited for a sign from my darling. It *will* come, it will, on the high tide someday. Any day now, surely. But someone must be here to find it. You must be my legs now, and my eyes, on the beach. To think of its coming, and my not even seeing it! No, Geneva, you must find it for me."

"A sign? From my grandfather? Oh, Gran!" said Jenny, dumfounded. "Gran, how?"

"When I tell you," said Gran, "you mustn't think I've gone mad." It was nearly dark, but Jenny could see that her grandmother's eyes burned brightly, her heavy brows drawn down into a furrow. "I've never talked of this to anyone before. But now it appears I must. Dear child, the *Amaryllis,* and all the swallowed ships . . . I know it seems impossible, and yet it's true. Seward told me. At first I didn't believe him, but then, when I saw how things were, I knew. He watches me. He has to, poor soul—he hasn't any choice. And he knows I'm waiting for a sign. Geneva, namesake, after the *Amaryllis* sank, I walked on the beach for weeks. I wanted something back—a button, a length of rope, anything to make the sinking real. Because it was so strange, Geneva, so strange to stand here and watch the ship go down in such a gulp, so near to shore, and then—for there to be nothing! Do you see how strange it was? It was as if there had never been a ship at all, and no beloved husband—as if my happy life with him had only been a dream that was over suddenly and I had waked from it to find that it had never even happened."

"But, Gran," said Jenny, "you had my father, didn't you? Why wasn't he a good reminder?"

"George?" said Gran, surprised. "Yes, yes, there was

George. But he was so . . . he didn't make the difference I needed. So I walked on the beach and waited for something, some sign to hold on to. But Nicholas Irving had been drowned, too, at almost the same time, and nothing had been found of him either. It seemed as if the sea was taking everything, and giving nothing back."

"Who was Nicholas Irving?" Jenny asked.

"Poor Nicholas!" said Gran. "So gifted. He carved the figurehead for the *Amaryllis*, and made that drawing in the dining room. He could do things with a pen or a bit of wood or plaster that were wonderful to see. He drowned himself, they said." Gran's voice turned careful for a moment. "I don't know. That's another story. But, Geneva, some time after that, one night, Seward came to me on the beach, and when he told me—when we walked and talked—he told me things, and at last I understood. And I knew that there *would* be a sign sent back to me and that I must wait and watch for it."

"Then you mean," said Jenny, "that my grandfather's ship is down there somewhere, and that something is bound to be washed ashore sometime?"

"No, Geneva," said Gran, and her eyes burned bright again. "I mean that there will be a *sign*. Not by accident, but on purpose. From him. Because the swallowed ships, it keeps them at the bottom to guard its treasures. And all the drowned sailors are there, Geneva, all the poor drowned sailors, sailing the ships forever at the bottom of the sea."

 Upstairs, in the room that had been her father's, Jenny leaned against the big four-poster bed and blinked. She hardly recognized herself against these strange new backgrounds. She had often thought of herself as a character in a story—a story where nothing ever happened. But now it was as if she had been lifted bodily into a new story—Gran's—where everything was different. Out there on the beach, Gran had talked to her as if they were two women, not a grandmother and a child, and Gran expected her to understand.

But what would her father say? He had told her that Gran

was getting on. He had said that Jenny would "see." Did he know, then, about this waiting for a sign? No, somehow Jenny knew he didn't. And all at once she feared that, if he were to know, he would decide that Gran *was* mad. He had not wanted Jenny to come here. And he might never have allowed it at all if he had known about the waiting. Would he have come, instead, by himself, and taken Gran away? But taken her where?

There was a building at home, a large, square building of yellow brick, standing in a barren, treeless yard inside an iron fence. There were rows and rows of narrow windows, blank and silent, and some of them were barred. Remembering that building, Jenny shuddered. They had passed it many times, she and her friends, passed it on purpose, taking the long way home from school to scare themselves with what they hoped and feared to see. Or hear. For the building was a madhouse. If her father thought that Gran was mad, would he put her there, behind those silent windows? No, he wouldn't do a thing like that. That was Springfield. Here, things were different.

Then, as she leaned against her father's bed, the music at the back of her thoughts—the music of the rising tide—pushed through and commanded her attention. She went to the window and looked down at the beach. The water was black now, much blacker than the star-strewn sky, and it looked thick, almost solid, like gelatin. But the foam still glowed with an inner light that made it seem a different substance from the spilling waves, like a magic kind of lace on a black satin skirt.

A skirt, with lace. People always talked about the sea as if it were a "she," while Father Neptune was a "he." But the sea was real, and Neptune only a made-up figure, silly, really, with his trident and his curly beard. Silly to think of a trident, a fork—for that was all it was—as a weapon for a ruler of the sea. You couldn't calm those waves, or stir them up, for that matter, with a fork. Gran had called the sea an "it." Yes, that was better. It was far too big to be a he or a she. It was beyond such small distinctions. And it did not have a ruler; it was a rule all by itself.

512

She opened the window, and the cool, wet breeze rushed in. Behind her, in a sconce above the bureau, the flames of the candles leaned and flickered, so that her shadow shifted. She sighed and, closing the window, wandered over to the washstand. There was a mirror there, with a bone frame and handle, and she picked it up and stared at her reflection. It, at least, looked just the same as always. "I'm ugly," she told herself, studying the heavy brows, too heavy; the narrow nose, too narrow; the pale white skin, too pale, with too many freckles. She had always gone along content with her face. It hadn't seemed important in the least. But lately she had begun to suspect, with sorrow, that a face might be very important. And hers, her face, was ugly. Would always be ugly. There was nothing to be done for it.

"Still, my hair is all right," she allowed herself. "It's the only nice thing about me." She had decided that she would never cut it. Not a single strand. Someday, when she was sixteen, she would be old enough to twist it up, away from her neck, and wear it in a heavy coil on the back of her head. Like her mother. Like Gran. Gran's hair must have looked like this when she was young. There was lots of red in it still. Red was unusual. Special. Like Gran herself.

From somewhere downstairs, a clock chimed ten. Jenny struggled out of her clothes—her rumpled dress, her stockings, her petticoat, her bloomers—and pulled a cotton nightgown over her head. "My father slept in this bed when he was little," she told herself, climbing in, but it was impossible to see him as someone her own size, so she gave it up and snuggled down under the covers. After all, he had always been a man to her, always old, always married to her mother. It was impossible to imagine him young, growing up, falling in love like someone in a play. Of course they loved each other, her father and mother. Of course they did. But they didn't talk about it, as Gran had. Gran had declared, "Your grandfather fell in love with *me*," and later, on the beach, she had said, in a different sort of voice, "For thirty years I've waited for a sign from my darling." My darling! Jenny's father and mother did not call each other "my darling." Jenny lay staring in the candlelight, and all at once decided that she would do anything for Gran. Whatever she was asked to do. And then, with the music of the sea in her ears, she fell asleep.

 It seemed as if she'd only dozed a moment before she woke to hear Gran calling her. "Geneva! Get up! High tide." Dazed, she stumbled out of bed, found her shoes, pulled them on without thinking, and shrugged into her dressing gown. Downstairs, Gran waited at the door, a lantern dangling from one hand, the other gripping her crutch. She was still dressed, and Jenny said, "Gran! You haven't been to bed!"

"I slept in my chair here," said Gran, "in the parlor. Come, quickly. You must get down to the beach."

Outside, the noise of the water was deafening, and Jenny could see in the dimness that the waves were high now, surging forward, tumbling over with a crash that flogged the beach, almost made it quake. The foam spilled up and slid away in a rapid rush of bubbles, spreading nearly to the foot of the little bluff, so that the beach was narrowed to a slender strip of damp, cold sand.

It had been gentle and playful before, this ocean, but now it was dark, magnificent, alarming. Jenny hesitated, apprehensive, but Gran did not seem to notice. Instead, she moved on firmly, out to the wooden bench. "Quick!" she urged, over the roar of the wind and water. "There! Along the tide line! Now, before Seward comes! Search all along the edges of the foam. Anything you find, *anything,* bring it to me at once."

Jenny took the lantern and slid down the bluff to the beach. She paused as the rolling water seized her feet and dragged at them, and for a moment she was filled with dread. But then, in her ears, the wind rose up distinct from the noise of the water. It called to her, and a strange new rising feeling of excitement filled her, driving out the fear. She plunged off through the foam, her shoes a sodden wreck at once, her nightgown and wrapper soaked and plastered to her legs. The lantern, swinging high from her lifted hand, rocked a golden arc of light

across the streaming sand, and she forgot to notice how cold the water was, how rasping when it flung its load of broken shell and seaweed round her ankles. She was aware only of freedom and exhilaration. Springfield—what was that? Buggies and school and being careful—what were they? Gran did not say, "Be careful," because Gran was not afraid. Here they were all one thing, she, and Gran, the wild, dark, rushing water, and the wind. Up and back she went along the beach, passing the bluff a dozen times, searching through the fringes of the tide. She wanted now, more than anything else, to believe in the sign and to find it. For Gran.

But there was nothing. And at last, spent and disappointed, she waded back to the bluff and stood below it, shivering now from cold. "There's nothing, Gran. Nothing at all."

"Yes," said Gran. "The tide is turning back. Might as well come in now, and go to bed."

Inside the house, Gran paused and looked at her and Jenny saw that her concentration had shifted back. Gran was her afternoon self, her usual self, again. "Why, bless me, child, you're soaked to the skin! And your shoes—why ever did you wear your shoes? But, of course. You didn't realize—how foolish of me. Go and towel off. Have you another nightgown? Put it on, and I'll go light the fire and make some tea."

Upstairs, Jenny piled her dripping clothes thoughtlessly into the basin on the washstand and rubbed herself dry. And then, warm again, wrapped in the towel, she picked up the bone-handled mirror once more and peered at her face. The pale white skin was rosy now, and the eyes that stared back at her under those heavy brows were shining. "Gran isn't mad," she reassured this new reflection. "She's just—well, she's got the sea in her, somehow. I can feel it, too. Everything feels different here. I'm different. Oh, I wish I could stay forever!"

When Jenny woke up in the morning, she climbed out of bed and went at once to the window. The beaming sea lay far out, at low tide, much as it had the afternoon before, and it sparkled in the early sunshine, flicking tiny, blinding flashes of light into the air. The horizon, impossibly far away, invited her. The soft breeze invited her. This was a mermaid morning—a morning for sitting on the rocks and combing your long red hair. She was enchanted by it, and found that the feeling of freedom was stronger than ever. Why, she had walked on the beach last night, when the sea was up and roaring, and no one had said, "You mustn't." No one had said, "It's dangerous." Imagine! Gran was taking it for granted that she could take care of herself. And all at once she felt stronger here, at the edge of this other world, than she ever had in Springfield.

But what about the *Amaryllis* and the sign? What about the man on the beach? All right. There were things she didn't understand. But this morning they didn't seem to matter. It was enough that Gran understood them. Gran needed her to do the searching now. Well, she would do it. In Springfield, to get up in the middle of the night on such an errand would be outrageous. But this was not Springfield. This was a different place. Gran's place.

And so, as the pattern of her days and nights took hold, Springfield receded to a distant blur. It began to seem that she had always lived here by the sea, had always watched for the turning of the tide. She had come to this house on a Saturday afternoon, and on Sunday she could run as free along the beach as her father had those long, long years before, shoeless, joyful, and at home. These first few days were bright and hot, the sea a wide green smile. She collected little shells and, once, a sturdy clam who lived for a day in a bucket of sand and sea water, spitting occasionally like a miniature geyser, before she put him back.

Each day the tide came in a little later, advancing slowly, so that by Thursday she was out with Gran long after midnight and again late in the afternoon. Sometimes, when the wind was up, the waves were tall, and sometimes they rolled in gently, like breathing, deep and slow. But there was never anything to find, nothing whatever washed up except the seaweed and the outcast pebbles. And soon the search began to seem to her to be a sort of game she played with the sea, she and Gran, twice every day, the way some people play at reading cards for prophecies, caught by belief and disbelief like a pin between two magnets. But believing didn't matter with games, and anyway, by Thursday, the night sky was turning to dawn when the time came for the search, and the high tides of the daylight hours were frothy and warm with sunshine. The sea was a good-humored presence, a playmate, and not at all mysterious.

In between, they talked, she and Gran. Gran took her through the house and showed her everything, opening drawers and chests and wardrobes. For the house was full of treasures: a fluffy boll of cotton from Antigua; a brittle red lobster's claw from Maine; a huge, rough, curling shell from Puerto Rico that had a flaring ear lined with shiny pink as delicate as china; a little pig from Haiti, carved from satinwood; a length of gaudy cloth from Trinidad; a snuff box from New York City with a picture on it of Martin Van Buren, an old campaign souvenir. And with each treasure came stories from Gran that filled Jenny's head with rich, exotic pictures of the color and slow heat of the Caribbean, the noise and bustle of the northern American ports.

In one of the trunks there was a miniature tin trumpet and a wooden cannon, toys that had been her father's when he was young. She lingered over them, delighted to find that the trumpet still gave out a reedy bleat when she blew it. But Gran had no stories to go with these treasures. She only said, "George was such an active child. How he loved the sea when he was little!"

"He doesn't love it now," said Jenny. "Why not, Gran?"

Gran's face took on a shadow. "He was there with me the day the *Amaryllis* sank. He adored his father, and I suppose he just never got over it. He went away to Springfield soon after, and didn't even try to understand." She put the trumpet and the cannon back into the trunk and took out an object wrapped in paper. "Here. Look at this. Isn't this remarkable?"

The object, unwrapped, turned out to be a plaster sea gull, its wings arched, ready for flight. But as Jenny turned it round in her hands, it looked like a wave, too, with dipping curls of foam. "Is it meant to be a bird," she asked, "or . . ."

"Good for you!" said Gran. "It's both. It's lots of things. Nicholas Irving made it. It was a model for a bigger piece, a statue he tried to carve once from marble. Poor Nicholas! Bring it downstairs if you like. I haven't looked at it for years. Anyway, it's time for lunch."

This had been Friday morning. The first week was coming to an end, and Jenny, stuffed with wind and sea, was sunburned and deeply contented. The days had been richer than any she had ever known, and except for occasional reminders of some old quarrel between Gran and her father, she was completely happy. But after lunch on this Friday, the sky turned heavy. It began to drizzle, and as so often happens when the weather changes, the mood changed, too, helped along by a visitor who soured the calm of Gran's house like a drop of vinegar in cream.

Jenny answered the knock at the door, and was surprised to find, instead of the egg man or the green-grocer, a woman dressed in the very height of fashion: a tailored suit of dark, ribbed silk, its skirt draped in rich folds over her hips, and ending in an underskirt of pleated yellow that just brushed the tops of smart black-leather boots. "And who have we here, I wonder?" said the woman, as if all outdoors belonged to her and Jenny had just knocked at *her* door to be let out into it.

"I'm Geneva Reade," said Jenny, suddenly aware of her own bare feet and untidy gingham pinafore. "Did you want to see my grandmother?"

"Grandmother!" exclaimed the woman. She laughed, tilting her head so that the yellow plume on her black felt hat bobbed and waved. Her face, though it was no longer young, was extremely pretty: a round face, dimpled, framed in becoming waves of gray-brown hair drawn back over small, neat ears. "A grandmother? But, of course. It *has* been that long."

"Who's there?" called Gran from the kitchen.

"Hello, Geneva," the woman called back, as she came in, furling her black umbrella. "You'll never guess! Come here at once and see!"

Gran came stumping into the parlor and stopped dead. "Isabel! Heaven help me, it's Isabel Cooper, isn't it?"

"Right and wrong," said the woman gaily. "Isabel Owen for a good long time now. What *have* you done to yourself, Geneva? Sprained your ankle?"

"Broke it," said Gran. "What in the world are you doing here?"

"We're on our way down to Greenville, my dear. But Harley had some tiresome business or other to do in town, so I said, 'Harley, I'll just go and see some of my old friends,' so he dropped me here. He'll only be a short time, but I did so want to see you, Geneva, before we went our way. Why, it's been ages and ages!"

"Sit down, Isabel," said Gran without enthusiasm, lowering herself into her own chair. "This is my namesake, George's daughter. Geneva, this is Mrs.—uh—Owen, did you say? I used to know her long ago, when she lived here in town."

"How do you do," said Jenny, bobbing a small curtsy in her best Springfield manner.

"George's child!" said the woman. "I declare! I can't imagine little George all grown up. Geneva, she's the image of you, the very image."

"Yes, she is," said Gran complacently. "She's here to help me while my ankle mends."

"I see," said Mrs. Owen, and instantly lost interest in Jenny, who sat down across the room to watch this fascinating visitor. "Geneva, you've hardly changed at all. I'd have known you anywhere. Why, it's amazing how well you've kept over the years."

"One foot in the grave," said Gran. "You've kept well yourself, I see."

"Yes, but, my dear, I *am* a ways behind you, after all. Twenty-five years younger, at least, if my memory serves."

"Twenty," said Gran, "but never mind. We're both past our prime."

The woman frowned briefly, and then turned sunny again. "Oh, well," she said carelessly, "whatever *that* may mean. I'm sure I don't think of myself as one whit different from what I used to be. Happy times, Geneva, the old days here!"

"Yes, you were quite a belle," said Gran dryly.

The woman dimpled. "I was, rather, wasn't I! But, Geneva, here you are still, while I've been out and doing. How ever have you kept yourself amused in this boring old place? I'm sure I couldn't wait to get away!"

"Why should I leave?" said Gran. "This is my home."

"Of course," said Mrs. Owen, turning solemn on the instant. "The Captain. Forgive me. You know, I was just sure you'd never marry again. Here you sit, and unless I'm mistaken, you haven't changed a thing in this room since the Captain . . . that is—"

"No," said Gran. "Nothing's been changed. Why should I change it? I like it this way."

The woman rose from her chair and wandered around the room, picking things up, looking at them, putting them down again. "I remember that teapot," she said, pointing to the china on the mantelpiece. "You let my mother borrow it once, and I came down to get it for her. Remember? It was the day of my sixteenth birthday party, and the hired girl had broken *our* teapot that very morning. Dear me! It seems like yesterday."

"Close to forty years ago," said Gran, "if it's a day."

"I'm sure I don't know why you keep harping on exact numbers of years, Geneva," said Mrs. Owen. "It's such a tiresome habit. Dear me, what's this?" She paused at a side table where, before lunch, Jenny had set down the plaster sea gull that looked like a wave. "Geneva, what in the world is this old thing?"

"Do you mean to tell me, Isabel," said Gran, her ironic enjoyment of this visitor drying up on the instant, "that you don't remember? Of course you do. I can't imagine why you bother to pretend you don't. That's Nicholas Irving's work, as you very well know—the model he made for the statue."

"Nicholas Irving? Oh. Dear me. Of course. Now I remember. What a funny duck he was. Yes, I do remember something about a statue."

"I should think you would," said Gran. "Don't try to play your little games with me, missy. You remember it perfectly well, and now that I come to think of it, I dare say that's why you came here today—to see if you'd been forgiven at last. A guilty conscience can be very troublesome, I've heard."

"Well, you're entirely wrong about that, Geneva," said the woman resentfully. "I don't in the least feel guilty. But I might have guessed you'd still be blaming me for what happened to Nicholas."

"He loved you, heaven help him," said Gran, "and you let him think you loved him back. He was making that statue for *you*, and then you laughed at it, Isabel. You laughed, and broke his heart."

"Well, I'm sure it wasn't *my* fault if he cared for me," said Mrs. Owen, her round face puckering a little. "*I* couldn't help it. Lots of boys cared for me, and *they* didn't go and drown themselves."

"Nicholas wasn't 'lots of boys,'" said Gran. "Nicholas was special."

"I'm sure you see it that way, Geneva," said the woman, "but I couldn't go and marry *everyone*, now, could I? Anyway, Nicholas was so . . . solemn. Oh, I liked him at first, but after a while he just got too . . . well, too solemn, as I say. About as much fun as an old sheep. And I never could see what that silly statue had to do with anything."

Gran started to speak, stopped, and turned to look at Jenny, who was sitting open-mouthed, listening. "Geneva," she said, "I'd very much appreciate it if you'd go up to your room for a while. I'll call you down later."

"But, Gran!" Jenny protested, and then, seeing the look in her grandmother's eye, she said, almost meekly, "All right." She went out into the hall and up the stairs, as slowly as she dared, but there was silence in the parlor, and once in her room, when the conversation started up again, she could hear nothing more than a murmur from the two women. After a time, however, their voices rose suddenly and the words were audible.

"Listen to the pot calling the kettle black!" cried the visitor. "You're a fine one, Geneva Reade, to talk about sparing a person's feelings! Everyone knows how you neglected that boy of yours after the Captain drowned. Why, you never cared a straw for George. It was just the Captain, the Captain, always the Captain, until—"

"Leave this house, Isabel Cooper," Gran thundered, "and never come back. I don't ever want to see you again."

Crisp footsteps in the hall, and then: "But, Geneva, it's

raining outside, and Harley isn't back yet. You can't expect me to—"

"Yes, I can," said Gran, and Jenny could imagine the grim expression on her grandmother's face. "Goodbye, Isabel."

The sound of the door opening and closing. A moment of silence. Next the thump as Gran's crutch swung her back to the parlor. Then nothing but the rain and the slosh of waves. But Jenny sat on her father's bed, and the visitor's words hung in her ears, so that she did not hear anything else. "You never cared a straw for George." Could it be true? And all at once the little tin trumpet seemed the saddest thing in the world to her. What chance had its thin sound ever had, trying to be heard above the tide?

 When Jenny came downstairs again, she found Gran standing at the window behind her chair, staring out at the sea. Searching for something to say, Jenny managed at last, "She's not very nice, that woman who was here."

"No," said Gran, without turning around. "She isn't, and wasn't. The face of an angel, even now, but in no way like an angel otherwise."

"Did Nicholas Irving really drown himself because of her?" asked Jenny.

"So they say," said Gran. She came away from the window and sat down in her chair. She looked exhausted. "Geneva, people do strange things for love sometimes. You're old enough to realize that."

A silence fell between them. Jenny fingered a fold of her pinafore, and then she said, with difficulty, "Gran, didn't you love my father?"

"You mustn't think such things," said Gran stiffly. "Forget you ever heard it. That woman—Isabel—she's a fool. She understands nothing at all. The only thing she cares about is what others think of her. To people like that, the rest of the world is there just to hold up a mirror for them to see their own reflection in. She never understood poor Nicholas, and she doesn't understand anything about your father and me. He's my son. Of course I love him. We don't agree on certain things, that's all. Put it out of your mind.'' She turned away and took up the almanac. "High tide at five o'clock. An hour from now,'' she announced, staring down at the page. Then she closed the almanac and laid it aside. "This rain is going to be with us for a while, Geneva,'' she said. "You'll need something to keep you dry. Go upstairs to the back bedroom and look in the bottom of that big trunk, the one where we found the sea gull. I think there's an old oilskin there somewhere that your father had when he was about your age. And a sou'wester, too.''

Upstairs, Jenny knelt before the trunk and lifted its great domed lid. The trumpet and the cannon were lying on top of the accumulation inside, but she did not pick them up again. Instead, she thrust a hand down under the layers of odds and ends, searching for the slick feel of the oilskin. At last she found it and, as carefully as she could, began to pull it up and out, trying not to disturb the things resting on top of it. But this appeared to be impossible, and as she gave the oilskin a final yank to free it, it brought up with it, caught in the stiffness of a too-long-folded sleeve, a small, square leather box which tumbled out onto the floor.

She left the oilskin dangling from the trunk and, picking up the box, tried to open it. There was a little metal knob sticking out of its front side and this she pressed firmly. At first nothing happened, but a stronger jab released an inner catch, and the lid sprang open. The box was lined with purple velvet, and there, resting in a depression that fit it exactly, lay a wafer-thin gold pocket watch. It was a handsome thing, much more handsome than the watches for sale in her father's store, the kind he carried himself: of some metal that was silver-colored but not silver, and thick as a thumb. Jenny eased the gold watch out of its nest and turned it over. The back was engraved with curling vines and leaves, and in the center a small square, left plain, was marked with the single initial R.

Jenny had often opened the back of her father's watch to look at the works, so intricate, fitted so precisely into their round, neat skull. She pried this one open now with a fingernail, and peered in. And then her eye fell on the inside of the lifted back, and she saw that it, too, was engraved:

MORGAN READE 1818
GEORGE MORGAN READE 1857

George Morgan Reade. That was her father! She stood up, tucking the stiff, creased oilskin under her arm, and went downstairs, the watch cupped carefully in one palm. "Gran," she said, going into the parlor, "look what I found! It's got my father's name in it."

Gran had been studying the almanac again, and looked up from it vaguely, as if it were an effort to bring herself out of her thoughts. But when Jenny put the watch into her hand, her eyes cleared. "Dear heaven!" she exclaimed. "It's your grandfather's watch."

"But it has Papa's name in it, too," said Jenny. "Look—it's on the inside of the lid."

Gran opened the back and stared at the names engraved there. "Yes. I remember now. Your grandfather got this watch on his twenty-first birthday, from *his* father. But he never carried it with him when he went to sea. He used to say it was too special, that it might get lost or stolen, and that he wanted to save it for . . . George. For George's twenty-first birthday. He had the name and date put in long before, to be ready."

"But, Gran! Papa's way past twenty-one by now. Why didn't you ever give it to him?"

"I forgot," said Gran. "I clean forgot all about it. When the time came, your father had been a long time in Springfield. I remember sending him a letter, to wish him a happy birthday, but I just plain forgot about this."

"It would've meant a lot to Papa, I expect, to have it," said Jenny disapprovingly. "You should've remembered."

"Now you're angry," said Gran, and the tired look came back into her face.

"Well, I just don't understand it," said Jenny. "What's the trouble with you and Papa, anyway?"

"Geneva, dear child," said Gran, "I don't know how to explain it to you, or even if I should try. But—well—your father, he's a fine man, but he just doesn't see. After the

Amaryllis went down, he kept saying to me, 'It's over.' And he wanted me to move back to Springfield and start a new life. But I didn't want a new life. I wanted this one, and I didn't believe it was over. I wanted to stay here where I could be close to . . . the ship, where I could wait. Your grandfather and I—what we felt for each other doesn't just stop. Remember what we talked about the first night you were here? There's another world around us, Geneva, around us all the time, and here I can be closer to it. But your father—he doesn't sense the other world around him; he doesn't see that things don't end. If he did, he wouldn't be so frightened. Ever since his father drowned, he's been terrified of endings. He thinks of the sea the way other people think of graveyards, and he can't stand this place because it keeps reminding him. That's why he ran away—to run away from endings. He was very young, and some people thought I was wrong to allow the separation. But what could I have done? He couldn't stay here, and I couldn't leave."

She paused and ran a fingertip over the names engraved inside the lid of the gold watch. And then she said, "This watch, now—it's like a sign in itself, isn't it? A sign from father to son. The numbers stand on the face in an endless circle, and the hands will keep going round and round when we wind it up. But George wouldn't have seen it like that. He'd only have seen an old watch that had stopped—time come to an end—and he wouldn't have wanted to have it. Do you understand?"

Jenny stood staring at Gran, and could feel herself pulled between them, her father and her grandmother. "I don't know," she said.

Gran stared back at her and then she pulled herself up out of her chair and stood tall. "Enough," she said. "Come. High tide."

And so, another useless search, another supper. But things felt very different. The rain continued, filling in the chinks of silence that *would* fall between them, Gran and Jenny, no matter how hard they tried to keep a conversation going.

Bedtime came as a welcome relief, and Jenny, protected by an earnest wish not to think about the watch, and the little tin trumpet, and the ugly words of the pretty Mrs. Owen, went to sleep almost at once.

When Gran next called her, Jenny woke to find that the windows of her room were touched faintly with light, the pale beginnings of dawn. There was scarcely a breath of wind. She went to the window and saw that the sea had been transformed. It was hung with a thin fog, against which the rain still fell, straight down, with a whispering sound, hushed and dim. Downstairs, Gran was waiting with the oilskin and Jenny put it on obediently, but they both moved quietly, as if there were someone or something near that must not be awakened or disturbed. "We won't need the lantern," said Gran in a low voice. "It's almost light, Geneva, I have a feeling that perhaps, this time . . . Come, let's go out and begin."

The beach was ghostly, muffled, in the silvery half-light. The warm rain was so fine that it was almost a mist, but it raised tiny knobs of the surface of the swelling water, water that rolled so gently it did not crest, but merely flattened, sighing, on the sand, sliding far up to the bottom of the bluff with only the barest film of bubbles. The far horizon had vanished in the fog, and the swells seemed to be coming in from nowhere, only to this place and nowhere else, glinting with that same pale silver light that was part dawn, part fog, part rain. Jenny started off along the dark strip of sand with her hands deep in the pockets of the oilskin, feeling as if she were still asleep and dreaming, carrying the dream along around her.

For the fog gave way ahead and closed behind her as she went, and the now-familiar landmarks, as they swam into focus, looked strange: the boulder, gleaming now with rain; the withered scrub-pine stump decked with moisture-beaded spiderwebs; the rotted dock, its far end faint in fog out over the water; and finally another bluff that marked the limit of that arm of the search, soft now, its rough grass leaning and heavy with raindrops. She paused here, blinking, her checks wet under the brim of the old sou'wester. She could feel the silence and the waiting everywhere. And then she turned and started back.

She had reached the scrub-pine stump again when she saw it: a dark something floating just within her sight, where the sea faded into the fog. It rose and fell on the soundless, shifting water, and with each swell it was brought a little closer to shore, a little closer to where she stood. "Driftwood," she suggested to herself, but it did not look like driftwood. Its shape seemed too regular, too smooth. As she stood there, her eyes wide, straining to see more clearly, the wind lifted and the rain began to fall a little harder, digging tiny pockmarks in the sand. Riding a taller swell, the object rolled, submerged, bobbed up again, and Jenny saw a touch of color on its surface. "It isn't driftwood," she said aloud. "It's—something else."

The object, floating now in sight, now lost between the swells, came nearer and nearer. Suddenly Jenny could wait no longer. She waded out, deeper and deeper, until at last she stood in water to her waist. Heaves of sea lifted the oilskin up around her and dragged at her, but her eyes were fixed on the object, and at last it washed into her reaching arms. Clutching it, she struggled back to shore, and stood there in the rain, holding the thing, staring down at it.

It was made of wood and it was heavy with years of seeping water, but she saw at once what it was, in spite of its softened planes and curves, its barely visible residue of paint. She was holding in her arms the carved head of a woman, split at an angle across the lower face so that only a portion of the mouth remained. But the eyes, under heavy brows, were lidded and calm, the nose long and narrow, the section of mouth curved upward in a smile. And the hair, swept down from the brow in deep-carved strands, still held bright fragments of dark red color.

Staring at the head, Jenny swallowed hard. And then she began to run down the beach, clumsy in the flapping oilskin, her heels thudding over the firm, wet sand, holding the wooden head tight against her chest. "Gran!" she cried. "Gran! I've got something!" The fog opened out ahead of her, and at

last she could see her grandmother standing on the little bluff, a dim shape under a big umbrella. "Gran!" she cried again.

"Quick!" came Gran's voice. "Quick! Oh, Lord, it's come! Yes, *yes*, child, bring it to me!"

Jenny arrived breathless at the bottom of the bluff and struggled up, and Gran, dropping her crutch, flinging aside the umbrella, reached out and seized the wooden head. She took one look at it and sank down on the old bench, clasping the head to her bosom, rocking back and forth. "Geneva," she cried, "do you know what this is? Do you see? It's my head, from the ship! Heaven be praised, he's sent me a sign at last!" Her voice broke and she began to weep, her words coming slow between deep, gasping breaths. "It's the figurehead, Geneva—from my darling—from the *Amaryllis*—sent up from the bottom of the sea."

And the wind, rising, whispered around them: *True to yo-o-o-ou.*

The rest of that day, and the next and the next, were as confused and cloudy as the first days had been calm and bright. Outside, the sky hung low, clouds drifting over clouds, and the rain fell softly, continuously, turning the sea and beach into a blur. Inside, Gran was feverish. She would talk, excitedly, and then lapse into silence, drop off to sleep for a moment, and wake to talk again. Jenny did not know what to do with her, and a vague alarm moved in to tremble in her stomach. The head from the *Amaryllis* lay on the table beside Gran's chair in the parlor, and the calm smile on its carved face was more like the Gran Jenny knew than this agitated woman who sat, stood, stumped about, sat again, dozed exhausted, doing none of these for more than five minutes at a time, it seemed.

Jenny took over the cooking, producing from Gran's unfamiliar stores peculiar meals whose inharmonious parts were never ready at the same moment, never ready to the same degree of doneness; and she carried them in to the parlor on a tray, but Gran would scarcely touch them. "Geneva," she would say, "did I ever tell you the story of how—" and would begin a tale told once so far that hour and twice the hour before, of her life in the old days with the Captain. For she called him "the Captain" now, not "your grandfather," and she talked of nothing, no one, else, putting out her hand again and again to touch the wooden head. And then, in the middle of the story, her voice would fade and she would fall asleep, her head bowed down on her chest.

It was clear from the brightness of her eyes and the flush on her cheeks that she was ill. But Jenny did not know how to find the doctor and was in any case afraid to leave her grandmother alone while she went out to look, for she feared that now, in addition to the fever, Gran might really be going mad. The building in Springfield, the one with the dark, barred windows, was never far from her thoughts. "If the doctor comes," she worried, "he'll see how it is with her. He'll send for my father and they'll take her away." And so she waited, helplessly.

530

But at the end of the third day, late in the afternoon, she tiptoed into the parlor from the kitchen and found that Gran was truly asleep at last, her breathing deep and regular. The flush was gone from her face, and her hands lay relaxed in her lap. The fever, at least, had passed. Weak with relief, Jenny smoothed the quilt over her grandmother's knees, tucking it under, and sank down on a footstool near the window. Outside, the rain still fell, the swells still spilled across the sodden beach, and Jenny realized that she had not left the house since the day of the discovery. There had been no watching for the tides, no searching up and back along the sand. There was, of course, no need for searching now.

Then, for the first time, she turned and looked—really looked—at the wooden head lying on the table next to her. Reaching out a hand, she ran her fingertips over its water-softened cheek. The surface, drying a little in the warmth of the lamp beside it, felt fuzzy, and the fragments of red paint in the deep-carved strands of hair were curling here and there, turning up their edges as they, too, dried in the lamplight. The head was real. There could be no doubt about that. The place where it had split from the rest of the body was lighter in color, and rougher, as if the break were recent: the wood was raw, not mellowed yet by the constant caress of salt water.

Yes, the head was real. It had been a part of the *Amaryllis*, and now it was here. It had come—here. A queer coincidence. Perhaps. But it was here. Gran stirred in her sleep and her mouth curved into a smile, and Jenny saw how much her grandmother's face still looked like this younger, wooden face carved so long ago—strong, handsome, a very good face. And all at once she remembered something the terrible and pretty Mrs. Owen had said to Gran: "She's the image of you, Geneva—the very image."

The very image? Did she, too, then, have a very good face? After all? Not ugly? Would someone, some shadowy someone, love her someday the way her grandfather had loved Gran? Or perhaps still loved Gran from . . . wherever he was? Unexpectedly, she found that she was blushing. "That's silly," she said aloud, and stood up, moved about the room, plumping pillows, bustling, embarrassed. But her heart had a new lightness, and the trembling in her stomach had disappeared.

Gran woke in the morning, after the third long night in her chair, pale but refreshed. "What are we doing down here in the parlor?" she demanded as Jenny, sitting up from her own sleep on the sofa, greeted her. "Good grief, I'm stiff as a board."

"You've been sick, Gran," said Jenny. "I was so worried—how do you feel?"

"Well, now, let's see," said Gran doubtfully, patting herself here and there. "I seem to be all right, but I'm hungry as a bear. Yes, I remember now. Foolish old woman, to stand so long outside in the rain. And yet"—she turned to gaze at the wooden head—"it wasn't entirely foolish."

They were quiet then. Jenny came to stand by Gran, and they both looked at the head, which smiled back serenely. "I knew it would happen," said Gran, "and it did." She put a gentle hand on her granddaughter's arm. "Geneva," she said, "remember this: nothing is impossible."

There followed three lighthearted days, in spite of the steady rain cocooning them, lighthearted for Jenny because Gran was all right again, better, in fact, than she had been before; lighthearted for Gran because her dearest wish had been granted. All of her old intensity, her obsession with the tides, was gone, to uncover, by its absence, a great capacity for pleasure.

She taught Jenny how to play German whist; they read aloud; they made salt-water taffy. A new trunk was opened, revealing hats and dresses in the opulent style of the 1830's and 40's, and for hours they played at dressing up. Gran pulled out one tall-brimmed bonnet with plumes and ribbons and ruffled white lace, and, clapping it on her head, went to see herself in a mirror. "Well, it looked all right in its heyday," she said, laughing at her reflection. "Or in *my* heyday, I should say. Wait. I know. Come with me." She stumped to the parlor and, picking up the wooden head, placed the bonnet over the carved hair lovingly. "That's the way it looked, more or less." The head smiled indulgently. "No," said Gran, removing the bonnet and laying the head back, gently, in its place. "What's the matter with me? Blasphemy, almost. But your grandfather gave me this bonnet. How he would laugh to see the figurehead wearing it! He was a great laugher, that man. Everything amused him."

Jenny remembered, then, her father's sober face. "Gran," she said slowly, "if Papa could see the head, would it make him feel better? Would it make him love the sea again, and not be so afraid?"

Gran turned and looked at her. "When he comes for you, the end of next week," she said thoughtfully, "we'll show it to him. And give him the watch. And see."

And so it came to a Friday again, and still the rain fell. The beach had a drowned, abandoned look, and in the afternoon Jenny, growing restless, put on the old oilskin and ventured out to look around. She had entirely lost track of the tides, but the sea seemed to her to have sunk beyond even its farthest point, slapping sullenly at the hard, ridged sand. Below the line of soggy seaweed, she found a sharp trail of new clawprints, like little forks, etched cleanly in the sand, and following them she spotted at last the sea gull responsible, waddling discontentedly some distance ahead. His feathers looked bedraggled and askew, like an old shirt, ragged and none too clean. But when he heard her approaching, he opened perfect wings and, transformed, lifted into the air, beating off above the water, powerful and sure. Somehow his flight from her made her feel alien and wistful. She hung her head and started back along the empty beach, higher up, above the tide line. It seemed, now, to be a kind of trespassing to mark the smoother sand, where the gull had walked, with feet that did not belong there.

It was because of this higher route home that she noticed the deep prints of a man's heavy boots, stretching ahead of her near the edge of the sand where the wet grass leaned. The rims of the prints were softened from the rain, no longer crisp, as the gull's prints had been, so Jenny knew that the man who had made them had come along some time before. But still she felt queer to see them there. Abruptly, she lost the sense that she was the intruder here. Instead, it now began to feel as if she herself—and Gran—had been intruded upon, on this sand that was theirs alone. She hurried back to the house and said to Gran, "There's been a man walking on our beach."

And Gran, putting down her mending, frowned and said, "Seward."

 At supper Gran said musingly, "I wonder if Seward knows the head has come."

"But how could he?" Jenny asked, surprised. "And, Gran, I don't see why he should care about it, anyway. Unless," she added quickly, "if he's your friend and would be glad to see you happy."

"He's not exactly . . . a friend," said Gran.

"Oh," said Jenny. A vague apprehension filled her and she asked, a little timidly, "Is he a bad person?"

Gran looked hard at her, as if she were trying to see inside her head. "Geneva," she said, "it's not a question of good or bad. It's a question of whether he's . . ." She paused.

"Whether he's what?" asked Jenny, frowning, fearful of what the answer would be.

"Finish your supper," said Gran. "We'll talk in the parlor afterwards. I can see I'd better tell you the whole story."

The parlor, with the lamps turned up and a fresh fire popping in the grate, should have been cozy and secure, but Jenny sat nervously on the sofa, opposite Gran's chair, and folded her hands. "I feel the way I do at home when we tell ghost stories," she said as her grandmother eased herself down and laid the crutch on the floor.

"Well," said Gran, lifting her eyebrows, "in a way that's what we're going to do."

"I don't believe in ghosts, though," said Jenny. "Do you?"

"I don't know," said Gran. "I didn't when I was your age, but now . . . Geneva, you see that the sign has come, don't you?"

"Yes," said Jenny, "but . . . "

"I know," said Gran. "You believe it's accidental. Well, perhaps you're right, perhaps not. Nevertheless, the head from the *Amaryllis* has come home after thirty years, and it lies here on this table, in plain sight. And there's something more about it you didn't notice, being unfamiliar with such things. It's got no barnacles on it, and no signs of rotting. Keep that in mind, Geneva, while I talk."

She settled her ankle more comfortably on the hassock and leaned back. "Do you remember that I told you about Nicholas Irving, and how he drowned himself not long after the *Amaryllis* sank?"

"Yes," said Jenny. "Because of that woman who was here."

"Isabel Cooper," said Gran. "Yes. Because at first she pretended to be fond of him, but then, later, she laughed at him to his face, laughed at his work and at his love for her. We thought at first, when he disappeared, that he'd gone away— inland, perhaps, or down the coast. It wasn't until two days later that his dinghy was found, washed up. Without him in it. Still, some people thought it had drifted loose by itself and that Nicholas was holed up somewhere, licking his wounds. But he didn't come back, and at last some of his friends went to his workshop to see if he'd left any messages or clues. They found all his tools lying about, and another figurehead for some other ship, only half finished. His clothes were there, food stores, everything. And the marble statue he'd been working on, it was still there, too, but it looked as if he'd tried to smash it. It was all chipped and scarred with chisel marks." She sighed. "He was . . . temperamental. Another man might have squared his shoulders and gone ahead with his life in spite of being unlucky in love, but not Nicholas. He was completely addled over Isabel."

"Well," said Jenny, "I guess she was very pretty."

"Yes, she was," Gran returned, "but Nicholas should have known that wasn't much all by itself. 'Pretty' doesn't mean 'good,' you know, Geneva. Real life isn't like fairy tales. 'Pretty' simply means that by accident you've got things arranged on your outside in an extra-pleasing manner. It doesn't tell a thing about your inside. Still, Nicholas was temperamental, as I said, notional, the way they say all artists are, and beauty was important to him. But we were very fond of him. He came here often. He was almost ten years older than your father, but he was rather like a son to us, and sometimes when your grandfather was off on a voyage, he'd come and read to George and me, or take a hand of whist. He was a good boy, and very, very gifted." She sighed again, remembering, and shook her head. "His friends found a note in his workshop. It said, 'I can't go on. Look for me in the sea.'"

"That's sad!" said Jenny, much moved by this romantic tale.

"It's absurd," Gran contradicted severely. "A terrible, terrible waste, and all for nothing."

"Still," said Jenny dreamily, liking the story anyway, "I feel sorry for him."

"It's not a happy story, certainly," said Gran, the hardness of her tone melting away. "A month or two after his disappearance—his drowning—whatever—one night when I was walking on the beach—remember, I was newly widowed then, and half crazy with it, heaven help me—I was walking on the beach, it was one of those nights when the moon is very bright, and I was wandering along, worried about George, who'd gone away to Springfield to live with your Great-aunt Jane, and I was longing for something from the *Amaryllis*, thinking about the sinking, trying to figure it out, when all at once I noticed a man coming toward me. He looked familiar, somehow, his clothes and his way of walking, and I cried out, 'Nicholas!' And it *was* Nicholas, but he was different."

"Different how?" asked Jenny, fearful again of the reply.

"It was his eyes, mostly. They didn't have that fiery light in them any more," said Gran. "They were quiet. And he had a beard, too. He tried to ignore me, to go on past me, but I spoke to him again, and he stopped and said, as if he were a stranger, 'Not Nicholas, ma'am. My name is Seward.'"

"Seward!" Jenny exclaimed.

"Yes," said Gran. "And for a moment I thought I'd made a mistake. But he raised his hand up to his beard and I saw the scar on his thumb where his chisel had slipped once long before when he was working. No, it was Nicholas, all right, and I said so. So we walked together and he told me . . ."

"What?" Jenny urged.

"Geneva, you may believe it or not, just as you choose. *I* believed it, and I'll tell you why in a minute. He told me he'd rowed the dinghy out, far out to sea, the night of the day that Isabel laughed at him. And he stowed the oars, stood up, and flung himself overboard. He was so determined to drown that when he sank he opened his mouth and tried to breathe the water into his lungs, but in the next moment he came to the surface again and began to choke. In that moment he forgot about Isabel and wanted to stay alive after all, so he looked around for the dinghy, but it was gone."

"Gone?" said Jenny, breathless. "You mean, disappeared?"

"So he told me," said Gran. "He began trying to swim, but found that he couldn't, somehow, and instead he sank again and kept on sinking, in spite of kicking and trying to come back up. He described the water to me as voices, talking to him, pulling him down and down. And all he could think of was how much he didn't want to drown. He tried to speak to the voices, and found that he could, and he argued with them all the way to the bottom. Yes. He went all the way to the bottom. And he told me, Geneva, that when he got to the bottom, he saw the *Amaryllis*."

"Oh, Gran!" said Jenny, forgetting for the moment that she was supposed to be making up her mind about all this.

"Yes," said Gran. "It was the *Amaryllis*, and it was moving over the sea bottom. Its lamps were lit and there were men working on the deck, though he told me he was too far away to see who they were."

"But how did he know it was the *Amaryllis*, if he was so far away?" asked Jenny.

"Why," said Gran, "he recognized the figurehead. There was light, he told me, coming from the face, from the eyes, and he recognized it, even through the blur of water. And all the time the voices kept talking to him and he kept arguing, saying he didn't want to stay down there, and at last it seemed as if a

bargain had been struck, and the next thing he knew, he was lying on the beach in the dark, and he was completely dry. As if he'd never been in the water at all. And he told me that he knew he wasn't Nicholas Irving any more, but someone—something—else; that he would be called Seward now because it meant 'guardian of the sea.' And he realized that he'd promised, in exchange for being returned, to walk along the beaches and give back to the sea anything that it valued—that was the word, 'valued'—that had somehow been washed ashore. And that if he didn't keep his promise, he'd be brought back down to the bottom of the sea again and kept there."

"Drowned after all," said Jenny.

"Yes," said Gran. "Drowned after all. And then he told me that he knew, as clearly as if he'd been told—in fact, he believed that he had been told—that your grandfather wanted more than anything else to send a sign to me—that his desire was very strong—and that he, Seward, would have to watch and make sure that, if a sign was sent, it was something I'd be allowed to keep."

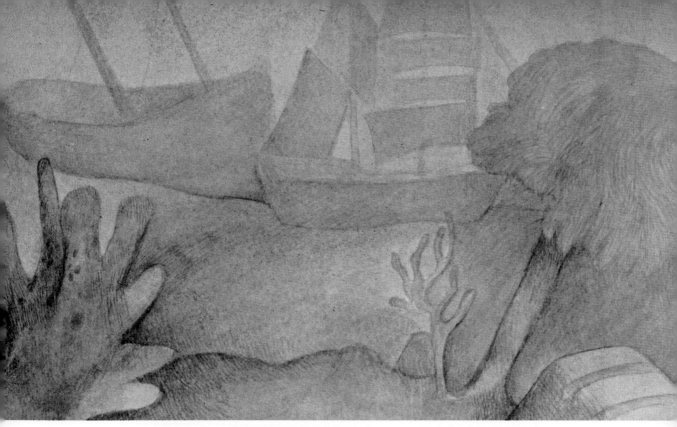

Jenny frowned, trying to picture the scene underwater. "He really saw the ship on the bottom," she said.

"Yes," said Gran. "Sailing. Keeping watch. The sea bottom was covered with treasure, he told me, and there were lots of wrecked ships, too, great ruined hulls, lying down there forsaken, full of holes and rotting away. But the *Amaryllis*, and all the ships with figureheads, are kept whole and clean, he said, to sail on the bottom and guard the treasure."

All at once Jenny could not accept the story. Springfield asserted itself, and she said, "I don't believe it."

"You don't?"

"No. It's crazy. That man—Seward, or whoever he is—he must have dreamed it."

"Very well," said Gran calmly. "There's one last piece to the story. As we stood there on the sand in the moonlight, talking, two of your grandfather's friends came down from the grass above us. One of them took my arm and said, 'Geneva, come back with us. We've been looking for you. You know the Captain wouldn't want you to wander out here night after night all by yourself.' And I turned around to them and I said, 'But I'm not by myself,' and they said, in this pitying sort of way, 'Come with us now. You must try to get hold of yourself.' I turned back, and Seward had walked away, on down the beach. 'No,' I said, 'I want to stay here and talk to Nicholas,' and I called to him to come back. And one of the men said, 'Geneva, please, there's no one there.'"

"You mean they didn't see him?" said Jenny.

"No," said Gran, "they didn't see him. But I couldn't see him, either, very well, by that time, he'd gone so far. So I thought, well, perhaps they just hadn't noticed him, so I pointed to the row of footprints he'd made as he walked away. They were very clear in the moonlight. And I said, 'Look. See the footprints? I haven't been alone. It was Nicholas, and we've been walking.' And then one of the men put his arm around me and said, 'Geneva, you're exhausted and you're making yourself sick. There aren't any footprints there.'"

"But, Gran!" Jenny began, eyes wide.

"Wait," Gran interrupted. "Seward—or Nicholas—has been walking this beach for thirty years, and no one's ever seen him but me. Him *or* his footprints. Not then, on that night, or at any time thereafter."

They sat staring at each other in silence. At last Jenny said, "But, Gran, *I* saw him—and I saw his footprints, too."

"Yes, child," said Gran. "You did."

 Later Jenny lay in bed, eyes wide and staring into the dark. She kept thinking about Seward, but she did not want to think about him. If the rain would only stop, if the sun would shine tomorrow, everything would seem a great deal more reasonable. This place, this house—she saw more clearly than ever, now, that it stood at the edge of another world, at the edge where the things she understood and the things beyond her understanding began to merge and blur. That other world—it brought on transformations, and its blurring edge was marked by the hemline of the sea.

540

Still, even the sea seemed simple in the sunshine. Funny how clear, bright daylight made you laugh at phantoms. They vanished, fled away like smoke, under the sun's round, candid eye. Yes, that was the thing: sunshine to light the corners.

But there was no sunshine next morning. The rain had stopped at last, but the sky still hung with gray, against which new humps of vapor hurried by, changing their shapes and rolling as they went. After breakfast, Gran turned the pages of the almanac and read, aloud:

Final days of August
  Usher in September.
Autumn equinox ahead—
  Stormy seas. Remember.

"Stormy seas!" said Jenny, discouraged. "Does that mean it's going to rain again?"

"It's coming into that time of year, Geneva," said Gran. "Always bad weather at the equinox. Is it getting on your nerves?"

"A little," said Jenny.

"I know," said Gran. "Moss in the bones. Still, I like it, somehow."

"Better than when the sun is out?"

"Yes, I really do. It's much more interesting, I've always thought. Come, let's bake a cake. That should cheer you up."

Jenny cracked the eggs—twelve of them, a whole dozen days of labor for some unknown, dedicated hen—and beat their slippery whites into a rigid cloud of foam. She had beaten egg whites often before, but now she saw the process as yet another transformation. She sifted the flour, measured the sugar, watched as Gran folded everything into a batter smooth and pale as thickened cream. Transformations again. And the humble dailiness of these activities only increased the knowledge that, at some undetermined point, her world had slid away a final barrier and allowed that other world to merge with it at last, like the fog moving in from nowhere, into the air she breathed, changing its flavor, giving it a richness it had not had before. Like the scent of the angel-food cake drifting out from the oven to fill the house with promises. Like the head on the parlor table.

While the cake was baking, she found herself wandering again and again to the dining room to look at the drawing of the *Amaryllis,* with its wind-belled sails and thrusting prow, the figurehead tilting unafraid over a frill of splitting waves, chin lifted to the wide and blank horizon. She tried to picture the ship sailing like this on the sea bottom, and found that she *could* picture it—could easily imagine the heavy silence of the deep, deep water, the schools of little fish flitting soundlessly before the prow, the dim green wavering light surrounding it. And she could see, too, rotting chests and boxes, lids askew, the rocks and sandy bottom glinting here and there with scattered treasures. She could picture all this, and more: the shadowy figures on the deck, one of them surely the grandfather she had never seen, striding effortlessly up and down. Phantoms. But real. And wonderful. Why not?

Why not. There was no answer for "why not," except to say "why not, indeed." And so, at last, accepting everything, she said to Gran at lunch, "Will Seward want you to give back the head?"

"I don't know," said Gran. "I've been asking myself that very question. But if he doesn't know I have it . . . Geneva, perhaps I should put it away somewhere for a while. Just in case." And the deed was done at once, the head nested deep in a drawer of the lowboy in the dining room, the drawer locked, the key dropped into the china teapot on the parlor mantelpiece. "Now," said Gran, "if he should come here—which is very unlikely—he won't discover it. I think we shall be safe. Have another piece of cake. Why, bless my soul, look there! The sun's come out!"

It was true. The house brimmed suddenly with light—hard, yellow light—as if a curtain had been swept aside. From the parlor window after lunch, Jenny saw a sky wiped clean, and polished to a glittering blue. The tide was in, the sea still seemed sullen, thumping fretfully no more than halfway up the sand as the breeze puffed, dropped, puffed again. She craned her neck to look both ways along the beach, and that was when she saw him—Seward, plodding along, still some distance away, headed in their direction.

Her first thought was: He walks here even when the sun shines! And then: "Gran!" she called. "Come look. He's on the beach again."

Gran came in from the kitchen, where she'd been setting a pot of beans to soak, and stumped up to the window. By this time, Seward had made his way a great deal closer and his face was lifted. He was looking toward the house.

"Speak of the Devil, and he'll appear," said Gran.

Jenny understood for the first time what this expression really meant, and she shivered a little. "Do you think he's coming to the house?" she whispered, as if she feared he'd hear her through the glass.

"He never has before," said Gran. "He'll pass on by, no doubt."

But he did not pass on by. When he arrived at the bluff, he turned and, coming up the sand beside it, paused, pulling at his beard.

"Stand back," Gran murmured. "He'll see us. He's coming in." She moved away from the window, and Jenny, turning too, saw that she stood very straight beside her chair, her chin up. "We'll tell him nothing, Geneva," she said. "Whatever he asks, we'll tell him nothing. There. There's his knock. Let him in, child."

If Seward was a ghost, he was a very solid one, a rather short man, only a few inches taller than Jenny, but stocky, wearing the same coat she had seen him in before. His tousled hair and beard were damp and beaded with sea spray, and the rough-skinned folds and pouches of his face made him look as if he'd spent a dozen lifetimes on the beach. He wiped his sandy boots carefully before he came in, and he stood in the parlor a little awkwardly, keeping his hands in his pockets. He looked about the room, and when his quiet eyes found the plaster sea gull, they flickered briefly and then were quiet once more. "I'm sorry to intrude on you this way, Mrs. Reade," he said, and Jenny thought again how much his low voice sounded like the breeze.

"You're welcome here," said Gran stiffly.

"Something had come," he said.

Gran's fingers tightened on her crutch. "I don't know what you mean," she said.

"It's valued," he said, ignoring her words. He spoke without severity, without any emotion at all. "You must give it back at once."

"I don't know what you mean," Gran repeated. "Nothing has come."

There was a pause, and then his gaze moved to Jenny. "She must give it back, miss," he said.

Jenny found herself unable to speak. She could only stand there clutching the skirt of her pinafore, staring at him.

At last he said, "I'll come again." He turned and stood at the door, waiting. Jenny went and opened it, and he stepped over the sill into the wind, his hair lifting and fluttering. Jenny noticed, then, that much of it was white. "Goodbye, Mrs. Reade," he said without looking back.

"Goodbye, Seward," said Gran with the same stiffness in her voice.

Jenny shut the door behind him and went to the window to watch him move away. Gran said, "He shan't have it." And all the easy calm of the last few days was gone. "I've waited too long. I'll never give it up."

"How did he know?" asked Jenny, feeling again a trembling in her stomach. "What will he do?"

"I don't know," said Gran, "but he shan't have it. If he comes back, Geneva, you're not to let him in."

Early in the evening, after supper, Gran said, "I want to go out and have a look around. Let's go sit on the bench for a while."

"But what if Seward comes back?" Jenny asked her nervously. "What if he's out there now?"

"If he is, he is," said Gran defiantly. "I'm not going to shut myself up in this house because of him. I haven't been out for a week, and I need a breath of air. Get the oilskin, Geneva. The bench will still be damp and we'll need something to sit on."

Outside, settled on the bench, the two sat for a long time without speaking. Gran kept her back straight, standing the crutch upright against her knees, gazing up and down the beach, but there was no one to be seen walking there. Waves came rolling in smoothly, in even rows that smacked the whole length of the beach at once till the sand seemed to ring with them. There was no wind at all.

"Gran," Jenny said at last, "doesn't the sky look funny!" She had been studying it, and had thought at first that it was promising another sunny day tomorrow, but now she was not so sure. From far to the south, high feathers of cloud were fanning up and out from what appeared to be a single point on the horizon, and behind the house they were stained to brilliant orange and scarlet as the sun dropped. "Gran," said Jenny, "look! The clouds are coming in a great big V."

Gran looked up, and her eyes narrowed. After a pause, she said, "Yes. I've seen it like that before. There's a storm somewhere out to sea. Maybe even a hurricane. It's the time of year for it."

"A hurricane!" Jenny exclaimed, and all at once she was dismayed. They heard of such things in Springfield from time to time, and had even felt the fringes of the worst ones in the form of lashing rains and wind. Her father—how pale and quiet he would be until the storm was over! She remembered standing beside him at a window when she was much smaller, watching the raindrops drive against the pane, and he had said, not really to her, "It's a terrible way to go, out at sea in such a storm." And she had thought at the time that by "go" he had meant, simply, "travel," and could not understand the dread she sensed in him. Now she understood it very well, and felt the dread herself. The *Amaryllis* had been lost in a hurricane, and he had stood here, right here where she was sitting now, and watched it all happen. And couldn't do a thing to stop it. "A hurricane!" she repeated. "Will it come here?"

"Perhaps," said Gran, "but I don't think so. They very rarely do. We might get the edges, if there is one, but that's all." Her manner was casual, but there was something behind it that Jenny couldn't read—something hard.

"The air is so quiet," said Jenny uneasily. "There isn't any wind at all."

"Not now," said Gran, "but it may pick up. You mustn't let it frighten you, Geneva. Weather is only weather. It comes and goes."

Jenny was amazed by this response. She stared at Gran, and then she said, "But, Gran, how can you say that when you know what the sea can do?"

"*What* can it do, Geneva?" Gran asked, and her voice was harsh. "Rise up? Swallow ships? Wash away a town? Yes, it can do all that. It can take your life, your love, everything you have that you care for. So. What should *you* do? Run away from it, as your father did? Run to Springfield and hide in a closet so you don't have to hear it or see it, or even think of it? That doesn't make it go away. It's still here, doing what it pleases. So you stay and try to keep what's left to you. You wait it out. You fight it and survive it. Lots of storms have blown across this bay, blown and gone, and I'm still here. Strong as ever. I'm not afraid of it, and never was." She sat breathing hard for a moment and then she said, in a cooler voice, "You mustn't be afraid of it, either."

Jenny was silent, her grandmother's scorn for her father burning deep inside her. Gran seemed like a rock there next to her. Invincible. And unforgiving. There was something fine in her defiance, but something heartless, too. Jenny wondered if she herself could be a rock, but looking out at the water, she doubted it. The sea was full of transformations. It was very wide, and very deep. And she was very small.

"Come," said Gran at last, pulling herself up. "We'll go inside now."

546

In the time that remained till bedtime, as they sat in the parlor, each with her own book open in her lap, the breeze came back gradually, first in little puffs and gusts, and then in longer sweeps that whined at the corners of the house. Gran looked up, listened, and laid her book aside. "Geneva," she said, "we've left the oilskin out on the bench. I can hear it flapping. Go out and get it, child, before it blows away."

"Yes, Gran," said Jenny. She went outside and stood in front of the house for a moment. It was growing dark very rapidly, and the sea, though it had been lying far out before, was rising, in those long smooth swells, at a pace that seemed unusual even to Jenny's inexperienced eye. She hurried to the bench and took up the oilskin, and then, turning, she stopped short and gasped. Seward was standing on the grass between her and the house.

"Good evening, miss," he said.

"G-good evening," Jenny stammered.

"I said I'd come again," he reminded her. "I didn't mean to startle you."

Jenny stared at him, not knowing what to say. Gran had told her she mustn't let him into the house, but what if he insisted?

"Tell her for me," he said, as if he could read her thought, "that she must give it back at once."

"She won't, though," Jenny blurted, forgetting that she was to tell him nothing. "She said so."

"She must," said Seward. "It's valued. The ship can't find its way along the bottom without its eyes. Explain to her. She must give it back now, before it's too late."

Jenny's breath caught. "Oh, please," she begged, "what do you mean? What will happen?"

"If she doesn't give it back," said Seward in that voice without emotion, "the sea will come and take it." He turned away. "Tell her," he said over his shoulder, and then he disappeared into the dark.

But, inside, Gran set her jaw and said, "Never. No matter what. Does he think I waited half a lifetime just to give up now? Don't be afraid, Geneva. Go to bed." She sat up straight in her chair, her eyes bright and hard, gripping the crutch across her knees like a weapon. "I shall stay down here tonight," she said, "and wait."

  All night the hurricane—for there was a hurricane—wheeled slowly north. Its eye rode far offshore, but its sweeping arms of wind and rain clawed at the nearest beaches, and the sea rose up before it in great, spreading welts that raced for miles ahead, rolling in to land in the measured waves Jenny had seen at evening.

It had begun a week before, this hurricane, on the very day of the arrival of the sign, begun as a petulance deep in the Caribbean. But as it swung in an upward arc to the west and north, its indignation grew, the speed of its winds increased, until at last, arriving in mid-coastal waters, it had spun itself into a rage. It was small, no more than forty miles across, but deadly: round its eye the winds were whirling ninety miles an hour. It paused at dawn and hung for an hour, and then, as if its orders had been heard, its target sighted, it veered abruptly westward toward the coast, and the sea ran on ahead in a frenzy of excitement.

All night Jenny had slept in fits and starts, aware of the booming rhythm of the waves. Then, after hours of tossing, she was brought bolt upright by a sudden Niagara of rain. At the same moment a blast of wind slammed at the house, a wind that did not pass off but kept on coming, its voice rising steadily. The light was so dim that she could barely see, and could not guess what time it was. Alarmed, she slipped out of bed, pulled on her clothes, and crept downstairs, holding tight to the banister. The clock in the lower hall said eight o'clock. Morning! But it seemed more like the onset of the night.

She peered into the parlor and saw that Gran was sitting rigid in her chair, wide awake, still gripping the crutch across her knees. "Gran," Jenny quavered, "is this it? Has the hurricane come?"

"Yes," said Gran. "It's here. It's just beginning."

"Oh, Gran, what shall we do?" wailed Jenny.

"We shall wait!" Gran rapped out. "It's only a storm. Only a storm, Geneva! We shall sit here and wait it out."

Jenny was drawn almost against her will to the window, and what she saw there dizzied her. Under the darkened sky, the sea was white, running sidewise, exploding in sheets of spray against the long arm of land that formed their end of the little bay. Clots of foam fled by through the air like rushing phantoms, and the water was so high that the beach had vanished. Rain was flung past the window horizontally, so that it was hard to tell the place where it ended and the sea began. Everything was water. And noise. For the voice of the wind kept rising steadily. Jenny shrank back from the window. "Oh, Gran!" she whispered.

"It's only a storm, I tell you," Gran insisted. Her face was stony. "Go put the kettle on for tea."

Jenny went to the kitchen and took up the kettle. She was trembling so much that it rattled in her hand, and she could not get the pump to work. She leaned against the metal sink and worked the handle up and down, up and down, but nothing came. Helplessly, she went back to the parlor. "There's no water!" she exclaimed.

Gran laughed at this, a harsh, unnatural laugh. "No water!" she echoed. "Milk, then. And bread. We must keep up our strength."

They sat in the parlor with their bread and milk, but Jenny could scarcely swallow. She wanted to cover her ears, to run away, but there was nowhere to run. That other world she had accepted, that world that lay beyond the edges of the sea, had loomed up now and was blotting out, shouldering out, drowning out the real world altogether. The parlor, the house, and everything in it seemed altered—thin and unfamiliar—as if the order she depended on had warped and might collapse at any moment. She wanted to cry, but Gran's fierce expression kept her from it. Her grandmother sat with narrowed eyes and ate slowly, refusing to acknowledge the rising bellow of the wind, ignoring the spray dashed in around the windows, down the complaining chimney, under the bolted door. The house trembled, Jenny trembled, the whole world trembled. Gran alone was firm.

Outside, the wind increased. Impossible, and yet its voice grew stronger, till the roaring was almost intolerable. Jenny doubled over on the sofa, her arms around her head, but still she dared not cry. And then, after a time, Gran seemed to notice her and said, "Geneva. Sit up." Her voice was steely. "Take away the plates and glasses. Now."

Jenny got to her feet somehow, and did as she was told. "I *won't* cry," she told herself over and over. "I won't let her see me cry."

When she came back to the parlor, Gran said to her, "Bring me the head." Without a word, Jenny took the key from the china teapot, opened the drawer in the dining room, lifted out the wooden head, brought it to Gran. Gran took it and settled it in her lap, pushing the crutch off onto the floor. "Now," she said, "go and sit down. And wait."

Perched again on the sofa, Jenny wrung her hands and fought back tears. There was nothing else to do but sit and wait, while the storm shrieked on, all around the house. Outside, the sea rose higher and came searching almost to the top of the little bluff. Sit and wait—it can't go on forever—there isn't that much wind and water in the world. Jenny's thoughts presented these alternatives to nightmare, but other thoughts rejected them: sit and wait for the sea to come and take us—take the wooden head and me and Gran and everything.

And then, after a screaming eternity, the clock in the hall began to strike, a faint, feeble sound against the wind—bong, bong, bong, all the way up to ten. And as if the tenth stroke were a signal, the storm stopped. Suddenly. The rain stopped, the wind stopped, the room was full of dazzling sunlight. Jenny thought, "We're dead. We've gone to heaven." Her ears rang with the silence. She looked at Gran, but her grandmother sat as stiffly upright as before. "Gran!" she cried. "Is it over? How can it be over all at once like that?"

"It's *half* over," said Gran. "We're in the eye. It will only last a few minutes." She did not take her hands from the wooden head in her lap. She did not stir at all.

Jenny got up from the sofa and ventured again to the window. The sea had risen just over the top of the bluff and now, instead of rushing sidewise to the arm of land beside them, it raged like boiling water in a great pot, tumbling, churning, rushing in every direction at once, smashing against itself and casting up bursts of glittering spray. The sky overhead was a brilliant blue, with only a few loose clouds to mottle it.

But Jenny saw with horror that before them and encircling them was a towering wall of thick, black clouds, closing them in, rising from the water like the sides of a chasm, miles into the air—a chasm from which there could be no escape. She could see the top-most edges of the wall, folded back smoothly against the sky. And she could see that it was moving, its far arc gliding toward them across the furious sea.

Gran did not get up to look. She stayed where she was, her hands on the wooden head, and she said, "It will start again soon."

Jenny stood hypnotized at the window, watching as the wall of black came onward. Gradually, the room grew dimmer, the dazzling patch of sky was curtained out. And then the clouds engulfed them. Instantly, the wind began again, shrieking louder than ever, and the world outside was lost in new sheets of rain that swept in the opposite direction now, northward toward the town at the other end of the bay.

This shift seemed to catch the house off-guard. There was a crash high over their heads, and a sluice of water spread into the parlor from the fireplace, like blood streaming from a wound. "Why, the chimney's gone!" Gran exclaimed. She sounded shocked, surprised. The sudden breaching of her fortress seemed to jar her own determination; she bent a little in her chair, gripping the wooden head, and her voice had lost a fraction of its metal.

Jenny sensed the loss and it chilled her, for she had been drawing her own slim courage from Gran. She moved backward from the window and stood distracted in the middle of the room, her hands tight over her ears now to cut the screeching wind. She had no notion what to do. Her mind was numb, her bones like jelly, and it seemed as if only the locking of her muscles could hold her upright. From the kitchen came another crash, a sound of shattering glass, and at once the house was full of wind. A lamp toppled, the curtains rose up like banners. And with a noise like a cork popping from a bottle the front door burst its bolt and was flung wide open. It hung flapping from one twisted hinge, and in the next moment the sea came over the sill.

It purled into the parlor silently, a foam-flecked, spreading puddle, soaking the braided rug, reaching across the floor. It looked harmless, a simple spill from a pitcher, easy to mop away. But Gran shrank back in her chair. She lifted the wooden head from her lap and held it close in her arms while the water rippled toward her. A low wave rushed at the doorsill and the puddle deepened, spreading rapidly, sliding around her feet, and Jenny's feet, until an inch stood on the floor, from wall to wall, and still Gran sat transfixed. The wind screamed round and round the house and rushed in through the breaches in a triumph, bringing with it salty flakes of spray. The water on the floor rose slowly, with little currents of its own that beckoned backward toward the gaping doorway even while it rippled in.

Jenny could stand it no longer. "Give the head back, Gran!" she shrilled. "Give it back!" But she could hardly hear her own voice against the wind, and she began to sob, explosively, all efforts to control her tears gone flying.

Then Gran was pushing up from her chair. Her crutch had drifted out of reach, but she stood erect without it. "All *right!*" she cried, but she was not speaking to Jenny. Her face was dark, her jaw thrust out. "All *right!*" she cried again. "All *right!*" She began to wade across the room, moving firmly in spite of her bundled foot.

Jenny's sobs caught in her throat. "Gran!" she gasped. "What are you doing?"

But Gran did not hear her, did not reply. She moved forward, the drenched hem of her skirt trailing out behind her. She came to the doorway and without a pause went out into the storm.

Jenny splashed after her. At the battered door, she shouted,

"Gran! Be careful! Just drop it into the water, Gran, and then come . . ." But the shout died in her throat, for all at once it was clear that Gran did not mean to come back. She was pushing forward, leaning against the wind, out toward the flooded bluff, and she showed no signs of dropping the wooden head. Her hair tore loose from its pins and twists and streamed out sidewise. "Gran!" shrieked Jenny. "Gran, no. Come back!"

But Gran could not have heard, for the wind shrieked louder, and the waves were dragging at her knees. She staggered, her arms flew out, and the head, released at last, fell free. And as it fell, the sea rose up and swallowed it. She paused. And then she found her balance once again and struggled on, nearer to the margin of the bluff. Jenny, near fainting, floundered over the doorsill. "Gran!" she shouted. "Wait!"

Then: a miracle. A hand grasped her shoulder from behind, a voice boomed out above the wind: "Jenny! Go back." It was her father—drenched, his hair wild, his jaw thrust out like Gran's. He lifted her and set her back inside the doorway. And then he plunged out into the wind and water, and seized Gran in the final instant, just as she sagged and was dropping into the sea.

 Tea. Strong, hot, with lots of sugar. It warmed away the cold of Jenny's heart as the blankets wrapped around her warmed away the shivers in her legs. She sat upstairs, in Gran's room, sipping, and watched as her father ministered to his mother. He had cut away the sodden bandages and splints from her ankle, stripped away her dripping dress and petticoats, and bundled her into bed. Then he had gone downstairs, sloshed to the kitchen, coaxed water from the balky pump. He had managed somehow to kindle a fire in the stove, had boiled water in the kettle. He was amazing. And now he was spooning tea into Gran as if he were feeding a little child, except that her cup had been sharpened with brandy. She lay quietly, accepting it. She had not said a word.

The hurricane was gone. It had whirled directly over them, moved inland, and was breaking up against the hills and trees. "Just another rainstorm by now," said Jenny's father when she asked him. "Noisy and wet, but mostly harmless. You had the worst of it here."

"But, Papa," she said, "how did you know to come?"

"I sat there in the store," he told her, "and I watched the barometers go down and down and down. Finally I couldn't stand it any longer. I hitched up the buggy and I came."

Jenny held her hand over her tea and felt the rising steam turn to dew against her palm. She was thinking about her father—coming out in the storm, coming to the sea. "Papa," she asked him, "where's the buggy now? Where's the horse?"

"I haven't any idea," he said. "After a while the wind got so bad that limbs were cracking and there were twigs flying everywhere. The horse kept shying, and at last he reared and broke the traces. He ran off, and there I was, sitting like a dummy in the buggy all alone, with rain blowing in my face. So I just climbed out and came the rest of the way on foot." He seemed, himself, amazed at this, even while he told about it.

"On foot!" Jenny exclaimed. "How far?"

"I really don't know," he answered. "A few miles."

"That must have been terrible!" said Jenny, her eyes round. "When Gran went out, I thought the wind would blow her over!"

"I didn't really think about it much," he said. "All I wanted to do was come to the two of you. Why, for all I knew, the house had flooded and you might be . . . well, never mind. It didn't happen. I got here in time."

They were quiet then. He set aside Gran's spoon and teacup, and smoothed a red-gray strand of hair away from her cheek. She sighed and closed her eyes, and he murmured to Jenny, "Come, we'll let her sleep a little now."

In her bedroom, in *his* bedroom, they sat together on the edge of the bed, and he took her hand and held it. Jenny thought about the sign—the wooden head—and wondered if he'd understand when he knew.

"You've had a bad time," he said at last.

"Oh, no!" she protested. "Not until today! Before the storm, it was—fine, mostly. Papa, do you remember a woman named Isabel Cooper?"

"Hmmm," he said. "No, I don't think so. Why?"

"Well, but do you remember a man named Nicholas?"

"Yes," he said, "if you mean Nicholas Irving, the one who carved the figurehead for the *Amaryllis*. He was like a big brother to me there for a while. Why, he taught me how to swim! But that was a long time ago, Jenny. Has Gran been talking about him?"

"Yes," said Jenny. "She's talked a lot about the old days. Nicholas Irving was in love with Isabel Cooper, but she didn't like him. That's why he tried to drown himself."

"Ah!" said her father. "Yes, I remember now. A terrible thing. Isn't it amazing what people will do for love!" He paused, and his serious expression turned into a smile. "Why, some people will even go out in a buggy in the worst storm of the age!"

"And come to the sea, even if they don't like it," Jenny added wisely.

"Yes," he said. "And come to the sea."

After a moment, she asked, "Were you scared, Papa?"

He lifted her hand and moved her fingers about, as if he was amazed at how well they worked. "You know," he said, "I didn't even stop to think about it. I just . . . got into the buggy and came."

"You were brave, the way you went and rescued Gran," said Jenny admiringly. "Maybe you won't be scared ever again after this."

There was a pause, and then he said, "Maybe not."

Jenny hopped down off the bed. "Wait here, Papa," she said. "I want to show you something." She hurried into the back bedroom and returned with the little tin trumpet and the wooden cannon. "Look, Papa. Look what we found in the trunk!"

Her father took the toys and stared at them in astonishment. "Good Lord. Why, I remember these. Imagine her saving them all this time!" He sat there thinking, and then he said, "Jenny, what was Gran doing, out there in the storm like that?"

Jenny looked at him soberly. "It's hard to explain, Papa. Wait. I've got one more thing to show you." She hurried out again and went to Gran's room. Gran was dozing, her face slack against the pillow. Jenny tiptoed in, went to the highboy in the corner, and took the gold watch from the drawer where Gran had told her to put it for safekeeping. Back in her father's room, she laid it gently in his hand. "It's for you," she said. "Grandfather had it all engraved and everything. For your twenty-first birthday. But Gran forgot." Then she added quickly, "But she's very sorry. Look inside the lid, Papa. Open it."

Her father lifted the thin back carefully and stared at the engraving. "Oh!" he whispered. Then, in a steadier voice: "Jenny, how incredible! Why, it's almost like a message, isn't it? After all these years!"

Jenny drew a deep breath. "Papa," she said, "do you believe in things you can't explain?"

He looked at her, puzzled, and then he said slowly, "Yes, I guess I do. Sometimes. Here, especially."

And so she told him everything.

Later, when the story was done, Jenny leaned her head against her father's shoulder and sighed. "But, you know, Papa, she waited so long—and now she doesn't have anything."

"But she does!" said her father. "She has us, just as she always did. Maybe she'll see that now." He picked up the little tin trumpet and blew into it. The thin bleat sounded loud in the quiet, and he put it down quickly, but it was too late. From the next room a voice called.

"George?"

They went to the door of Gran's room and saw that she was sitting up in bed. "Well, George," she said. She sounded very tired.

"Well, Mother," he returned.

"Dear boy," she said to him, "come and kiss me."

They ate their supper upstairs in Gran's room, a supper thrown together, by Jenny and her father, any old way in the ruined kitchen. But Gran had very little appetite. She sat propped up with pillows, and she kept moving her foot under the covers.

"How does it feel?" Jenny asked.

"Light without all those bandages," she said. "But whether it's mended or not, I really can't tell."

"Well," said Jenny's father, "either way, you'd better come back to Springfield, at least until we can get someone to clean up the mess downstairs."

"Is it very bad?" she asked him.

"I'm afraid so," he said. "The wind smashed the kitchen window and blew everything all around, the front door's almost off, the chimney's gone entirely. And the floor—some of the boards are bound to warp. It may take weeks to dry."

"It's been a good house," said Gran. "It just couldn't quite hold out. I couldn't hold out, either, George. We're old, this house and I."

"And yet," he said, "you can mend, both of you."

"No," said Gran. "We can be patched up, stuck back together one way or another, perhaps, but it wouldn't last for long. You've been urging me to come and stay in Springfield for years, George. I think the time has come for me to do it now."

"We've always wanted you," he said, "but only if you really wanted to come."

She shrugged. "I'm tired," she said. "I think I'll go to sleep now."

"I'll find a horse and buggy first thing in the morning," he told her, spreading up her covers. "We'll get an early start."

"All right," she said, and closed her eyes.

Jenny went up to the bed and leaned down to kiss her grandmother's cheek. "Good night, Gran," she said.

And Gran said, "Good night . . . Jenny."

 In the morning, Jenny woke to soft sunshine. She climbed

out of bed and crossed to the window. Below, the beach was clean and smooth, and the sea lay smiling and slopping contentedly far down the sand. Just offshore, a gull was wheeling against the bright blue sky. "Yesterday," Jenny reminded herself, "there was a hurricane!" But it was hard to remember now. Until she remembered Gran. "We're all going home today," she murmured, and in spite of the warm sunlight, she was filled with sadness.

She was pulling on her clothes, when her father appeared in the doorway. "Well, lazybones," he said, "it's about time you were up. I've been to town already and brought back a first-rate horse and buggy. Pack your things. We'll be leaving soon."

"How's Gran?" she asked him.

"She's ready," he said. "We've both had breakfast. There's milk and bread and an orange for you downstairs. Come along. I'm anxious to get started. Your mother will be worried to death."

"I'll be ready in a minute," she said.

Downstairs, it would have been impossible to forget the storm. The parlor had a dismal look and a damp, unnatural smell. Water stood in the corners, and there was wet sand crusted everywhere. From the blown-in kitchen window a light breeze stirred the limp curtains and passed on out through the space where the front door had been propped against a side of the gaping doorframe. The clock in the hall had stopped. Jenny took up her orange and, peeling it as she went, wandered sadly through the rooms. The life had gone from the house. It looked defeated.

She paused in the dining room and, sucking her orange, looked at the picture of the ship. It hung a little crooked now, but here, there was spirit still. The ship was so beautiful, a crisp, strong, winged thing, the figurehead intact and calm, with the big red blossom cradled in its hands. It had a presence, an unshakable intent; it seemed almost, this morning, to leap from the frame and sail into the room. Jenny could feel its force. She lowered the orange from her mouth and stood puzzled, staring.

"Jenny!" her father called. "We're ready. Come along."

She backed away from the picture reluctantly and, turning, went through the parlor to the door. Her father was carrying Gran in his arms, crossing the strip of grass to the rented buggy. Gran's face was quiet, closed. The horse stood waiting, jingling his harness. Jenny went out across the doorsill and hesitated for a moment. The air was warm and soft and the sea sparkled, tossing up tiny whitecaps. It was very still, and yet—somewhere there was an urgency. "Just a minute," Jenny said to her father. She felt drawn strongly to the beach. She ran down across the sand, down to the water's edge, and looked out.

The flashes of sunlight reflected from the sea were blinding. She rubbed her eyes to free them of the dancing red spots that filled them and made them water. And then she began to walk along the edges of the low, ruffling waves, down the empty beach in a final tracing of the searches of the week before, still responding to the urgency that seemed to be drawing her.

Coming at last to the scrub-pine stump, she stopped and looked out again. And caught her breath. No more than ten yards out, a small, bright object floated on the swells. No, it was only the flashing of the sun in her eyes again. But something seemed to stay beyond her blinking, something reddish-orange, a vibrant spot of color that rode forward on the water. The breeze increased and the object took on dimensions, sailing nearer and nearer, and then, with a final lift of wave, it was slipped across the foam to her feet.

It was a blossom, not made of wood, but real, with six wide, curling petals, and a long white fragile stamen arching out from its cone-shaped heart. A lily, just like the one in the picture. A big red lily from the islands—an amaryllis.

Jenny bent and lifted it up, cupping it in her hands. And then she turned. "Gran!" she cried. "Oh, *Gran!*" She ran back along the beach to the bluff and crossed, up the sand, holding the blossom out before her. "Gran!" she cried again.

As she ran, Gran rose up in the buggy—rose up and then climbed down and went to meet her, striding with long, strong steps. They came together and Gran seized the blossom. Color seemed to flood from it up into her face. And as she stood there, tears running down her cheeks, the breeze came up and whispered once more: *True to yo-o-o-ou.*

Later, as the buggy rolled away, Gran said briskly to her son, "We may have to lay a new floor, George, but that shouldn't be too difficult. And the chimney can be built back up with the same old bricks."

"I can do a lot of the work myself," he said. "We'll rest up at home for a day or two and then bring everybody back and get started. I need a vacation, anyway. Exercise. Do you know I haven't been swimming in years?"

"I know," said Gran. "You're white as a clam."

As their talk went on, Jenny sat looking backward at the battered house dropping away behind them. And then she saw a short, dark figure standing on the beach. He was looking after them, and on an impulse Jenny lifted an arm and waved. He stood motionless, and then he turned and walked away down the beach, but his step seemed lighter to her, now, than it had before. As he disappeared, the sea flashed its wide green smile and answered her wave with a careless toss of foam. She leaned far out of the buggy and shouted to it, "We're coming back!" And then she settled herself in her seat and put a hand into the pocket of her pinafore. There was sand in the pocket, and she chased it around the thready inside seam with her fingertips, humming under her breath.

The buggy topped the rise and rolled on under a stand of trees, and after a while came to a fence along the road, behind which a few cows were grazing peacefully. There was a boy at work in the grass, picking up the litter of twigs and small branches scattered by the vanished storm, and as the buggy passed him, he straightened and stared at Jenny with wide-eyed admiration. She ignored him, holding her chin high, and said to herself, "That's silly." But she retied the ribbon that held back her hair, settling its bow more carefully, and smiled all the way to Springfield.

Glossary

Pronunciation Key* The pronunciation of each word is shown just after the word, in this way: **ab·bre·vi·ate** (ə brē′vē āt).

The letters and signs used are pronounced as in the words below.

The mark ′ is placed after a syllable with primary or heavy accent, as in the example above.

The mark ′ after a syllable shows a secondary or lighter accent, as in

ab·bre·vi·a·tion (ə brē′vē ā′shən).

a	hat, cap	l	land, coal	u	cup, butter
ā	age, face	m	me, am	u̇	full, put
ä	father, far	n	no, in	ü	rule, move
b	bad, rob	ng	long, bring	v	very, save
ch	child, much	o	hot, rock	w	will, woman
d	did, red	ō	open, go	y	young, yet
e	let, best	ô	order, all	z	zero, breeze
ē	equal, be	oi	oil, voice	zh	measure, seizure
ėr	term, learn	ou	house, out	ə	represents:
f	fat, if	p	paper, cup		a in about
g	go, bag	r	run, try		e in taken
h	he, how	s	say, yes		i in pencil
i	it, pin	sh	she, rush		o in lemon
ī	ice, five	t	tell, it		u in circus
j	jam, enjoy	th	thin, both		
k	kind, seek	ᵺ	then, smooth		

*The Pronunciation Key, respellings, and dictionary entries are from *Scott, Foresman Intermediate Dictionary* by E. L. Thorndike and Clarence L. Barnhart. Copyright © 1979 by Scott, Foresman and Company. Reprinted by permission.

A

ab·hor·rent (ab hôr′ənt) *adjective.* Causing horror; disgusting; hateful.

a·bide (ə bīd′) *verb.* 1. To put up with; endure. 2. To stay, remain. 3. To dwell, reside. **abided, abiding.**

a·buse (ə byüz′) *verb.* 1. To make wrong or bad use of; misuse. 2. To treat roughly or cruelly; mistreat. 3. To use harsh and insulting language about or to; scold severely. **abused, abusing.** (ə byüs′) *noun.* 1. A wrong or bad use; misuse. 2. Rough or cruel treatment. 3. A bad practice or custom. 4. Harsh and insulting language; severe scolding.

ac·cel·e·rate (ak sel′ə rāt′) *verb.* 1. To go or cause to go faster; increase in speed; speed up. 2. To cause to happen sooner; hasten: Rest often *accelerates* recovery from sickness. **accelerated, accelerating.**

ac·quaint (ə kwānt′) *verb.* To make aware; let know; inform. **acquainted, acquainting.**

ac·quire (ə kwīr′) *verb.* To come to have; get on one's own; obtain. **acquired, acquiring.**

a·cute (ə kyüt′) *adjective.* 1. Sharp and severe. 2. Brief and severe. 3. Threatening, critical. 4. Quick in perceiving and responding to impressions; keen. 5. Having a sharp point.

ad·junct (aj′ungkt) *noun.* Something that is less important or not necessary, but helpful.

ad·just·ment (ə just′mənt) *noun.* 1. Act or process of adjusting: The *adjustment* of the seats to the right height was necessary for the children's comfort. 2. Settlement of a dispute, a claim, etc.

a·do·be (ə dō′bē) *noun.* 1. Brick made of clay baked in the sun. 2. A building made of adobe.—*adjective.* Built or made of adobe.

af·ter·math (af′tər math) *noun.* A result or consequence: The *aftermath* of war is hunger and disease.

a·gen·da (ə jen′də) *noun.* List of things to be dealt with or done.

al·i·bi (al′ə bī) *noun.* 1. The statement that an accused person was somewhere else when an offense was committed. 2. (informal) An excuse—*verb.* (informal) To make an excuse.

al·ien (ā′lyən) *noun.* Person who is not a citizen of the country in which he or she lives.—*adjective.* 1. Of another country; foreign. 2. Entirely different; not in agreement; strange.

a·lign·ment (ə līn′mənt) *noun.* 1. Arrangement in a straight line: The pictures were in perfect *alignment*. 2. A joining with others for or against a cause.

al·lay (ə lā′) *verb.* 1. To put at rest; quiet: His fears were *allayed* by the news of their safety. 2. To make less, weaken or relieve: Her fever was *allayed* by the medicine. **allayed, allaying.**

an·guish (ang′gwish) *noun.* Very great pain or grief; great distress: He was in *anguish* until the doctor set his broken leg.

an·gu·lar (ang′gyə lər) *adjective.* 1. Having angles; having sharp corners: an *angular* piece of rock. 2. Somewhat thin and bony; not plump: Many basketball players have tall, *angular* bodies.

an·o·nym·i·ty (an′ə nim′ə tē) *noun.* Condition of being anonymous, or not known.

an·tag·o·nism (an tag′ə niz′əm) *noun.* Active opposition; hostility.

an·ti·so·cial (an′ti sō′shəl) *adjective.* 1. Opposed to the principles upon which society is based: Stealing is an *antisocial* act. 2. Opposed to friendly relationship and normal companionship with others.

anx·i·e·ty (ang zī′ə tē) *noun.* 1. Uneasy thoughts or fears about what may happen; troubled, worried, or uneasy feeling. 2. Eager desire.

ap·pease (ə pēz′) *verb.* 1. To make calm or quiet; pacify. 2. To give in to the demands of: The girl *appeased* her parents and returned to finish school. **appeased, appeasing.**

ap·pre·hen·sion (ap′ri hen′shən) *noun.* 1. Fear, dread. 2. A seizing or being seized; arrest. 3. A grasping by the mind; understanding.

arch·en·e·my (ärch′en′ə mē) *noun.* A principal enemy.

ar·rest (ə rest′) *verb.* 1. To seize by authority of the law; take to jail or court. 2. To stop; check: Filling a tooth *arrests* decay. 3. To catch and hold: Our attention was *arrested* by the unusual sound. **arrested, arresting.**—*noun.* 1. A seizing of a person by authority of the law; a taking

to jail or court. 2. A stopping; checking.

ar·ti·san (är′tə zən) *noun.* Person skilled in some industry or trade; craftsperson.

a·skance (ə skans′) *adverb.* 1. With suspicion or disapproval. 2. To one side; sideways.

as·sault (ə sôlt′) *noun.* A sudden, vigorous attack. —*verb.* To make an assault on. **assaulted, assaulting.**

as·sent (ə sent′) *verb.* To express agreement; consent; agree: Everyone *assented* to the plan. **assented, assenting.**—*noun.* Acceptance of a proposal, statement, etc; agreement: She gave her *assent* to the plan.

a·stray (ə strā′) *adjective* or *adverb.* Out of the right way; off.

at·ta·ché (at′ə shā′) *noun.* Person on the official staff of an ambassador or minister to a foreign country: a naval *attaché*.

at·test (ə test′) *verb.* 1. To give proof of; certify: Your good work *attests* to the care you have taken. 2. To bear witness; testify. **attested, attesting.**

at·trib·ute (ə trib′yüt) *verb.* 1. To regard as an effect of: She *attributes* her good health to a carefully planned diet. 2. To think of as belonging to or appropriate to: We *attribute* courage to the lion and cunning to the fox. **attributed, attributing.** —(at′rə byüt) *noun.* 1. A quality considered as belonging to a person or thing; characteristic.

au·dit (ô′dit) *verb.* To examine or check. **audited, auditing.**—*noun.* 1. An examination and check of business accounts. 2. Statement of an account that has been examined and checked.

a·ver·sion (ə vėr′zhən) *noun.* 1. A strong or fixed dislike. 2. Thing or person disliked.

av·id (av′id) *adjective.* Extremely eager: She is an *avid* golfer.—**avidly** *adverb.*

B

bal·ance (bal′əns) *noun.* 1. Instrument for weighing. 2. Condition of being equal in weight, amount, etc. 3. Steady condition or position. 4. Difference between the amount one owes or has withdrawn from an account and the amount one is owed or deposits in an account: I have a *balance* of $20.00 in the bank. 5. Part that is left over; remainder.—*verb.* 1. To weigh two things against each other. 2. To put or keep in a steady condition or position. 3. To be equal or equivalent in weight, amount, force, effect, etc. 4. To make the amount one owes and the amount one is owed equal. **balanced, balancing.**

balk (bôk) *verb.* To stop short and stubbornly refuse to go on. 2. To prevent from going on; hinder. **balked, balking.**—*noun.* 1. Hindrance. 2. In baseball, an illegal motion made by a pitcher, especially one in which a throw that has been started is not completed.

ban·dan·na (ban dan′ə) *noun.* A large handkerchief, often worn on the head or neck.

ban·quet (bang′kwit) *noun.* 1. A large meal with many courses, prepared for a special occasion or for many people. 2. A formal dinner with speeches.

bard (bärd) *noun.* 1. Poet and singer of long ago. 2. Any poet.

bar·ra·cu·da (bar′ə kü′də) *noun.* A saltwater fish with a long, narrow body, sharp teeth, and a jutting lower jaw.—*plural* **barracudas** or **barracuda.**

bar·rage (bə räzh′) *noun.* 1. Barrier of artillery fire to check the enemy or to protect one's own soldiers when advancing or retreating, 2. A large number of words, blows, etc. coming quickly one after the other.

beck·on (bek′ən) *verb.* To signal by motion of the head or hand: He *beckoned* me to follow him. **beckoned, beckoning.**

bed·lam (bed′ləm) *noun.* Noisy confusion; uproar.

be·fud·dle (bi fud′l) *verb.* To confuse; bewilder. **befuddled, befuddling.**

be·grudge (bi gruj′) *verb.* 1. To give or allow something unwillingly; grudge. 2. To envy. **begrudged, begrudging.**

blight (blīt) *noun.* 1. Disease that causes plants or parts of plants to wither and die. 2. Bacterium, fungus, or virus that causes such a disease. 3. Anything that causes destruction or ruin.

blitz (blits) *noun.* 1. A sudden violent attack using many airplanes and tanks. 2. Any sudden, violent attack.—*verb.* To attack or overcome by a blitz. **blitzed, blitzing.**

bob·ble (bob′əl) *verb.* To fumble. **bobbled, bobbling.**

bois·ter·ous (boi′stər əs) *adjective.* 1. Noisily cheerful: The room was filled with *boisterous* laughter. 2. Violent;

rough.—**boisterously** *adverb.*

brace (brās) *noun.* 1. Thing that holds parts together or in place. 2. **braces,** *plural.* Metal wires used to straighten crooked teeth. 3. A pair; couple: a *brace* of ducks.—*verb.* 1. To give strength or firmness to; support. 2. To prepare oneself.

broach (brōch) *verb.* To begin to talk about: She *broached* the subject of a raise in her allowance. **broached, broaching.**

C

ca·pac·i·ty (kə pas′ə tē) *noun.* 1. Amount of room or space inside; largest amount that can be held by a container. 2. Ability to receive and hold.

ca·pri·cious (kə prish′əs) *adjective.* Likely to change suddenly without reason; changeable; fickle. —**capriciously** *adverb.*

ca·reen (kə rēn′) *verb.* To lean to one side or sway sharply; to tilt; tip. **careened, careening.**

car·ri·on (kar′ē ən) *noun.* Dead and decaying flesh.

cas·u·al (kazh′ü əl) *adjective.* 1. Happening by chance; not planned or expected; accidental. 2. Without plan or method; careless. 3. Informal in manner; offhand. 4. Designed for informal wear.—**casually** *adverb.*

cat·a·pult (kat′ə pult) *noun.* 1. Weapon used in ancient times for shooting stones, arrows, etc. 2. Slingshot. 3. Device for launching an airplane from the deck of a ship.—*verb.* 1. To throw, hurl. 2. To shoot up suddenly, spring. **catapulted, catapulting.**

ca·tas·tro·phe (kə tas′trə fē) *noun.* A sudden, widespread, or extraordinary disaster; great calamity or misfortune.

ca·vort (kə vôrt′) *verb.* To prance about; jump around. **cavorted, cavorting.**

ce·leb·ri·ty (sə leb′rə tē) *noun.* 1. A famous person; person who is well known or much talked about. 2. A being well known or much talked about; fame.

cen·sor·ship (sen′sər ship) *noun.* Act or system of examining, changing, or taking out part of (news reports, books, letters, motion pictures, etc.).

chaff (chaf) *noun.* 1. The tough, outer skin of wheat, oats, rye, etc., especially when separated from grain

by threshing. 2. Worthless stuff; rubbish. 3. Good-natured joking about a person to his face.—*verb.* To make fun of in a good-natured way to one's face. **chaffed, chaffing.**

chain gang (chān gang) *noun.* A group of people chained together and set to outdoor labor.

cha·os (kā′os) *noun.* Very great confusion; complete disorder: The tornado left the town in *chaos.*

clam·ber (klam′bər) *verb.* To climb, using both hands and feet; to climb awkwardly or with difficulty; scramble. **clambered, clambering.**

clime (klīm) *noun.* 1. Region. 2. Climate.

clo·ven (klō′vən) *adjective.* Split; divided: Cows and sheep have *cloven* hoofs.

com·mem·o·rate (kə mem′ə rāt′) *verb.* To preserve or honor the memory of: a stamp *commemorating* the landing of the Pilgrims. **commemorated, commemorating.**

com·par·a·ble (kom′pər ə bəl) *adjective.* 1. Able to be compared. 2. Fit to be compared.

com·pen·sate (kom′pən sāt) *verb.* 1. To make an equal return to; give an equivalent to. 2. To balance by equal weight or power; make up. 3. To pay. **compensated, compensating.**

com·pet·i·tive (kəm pet′ə tiv) *adjective.* Decided by competition; using competition.

com·po·sure (kəm pō′zhər) *noun.* Calmness, quietness, self-control.

com·press (kəm pres′) *verb.* To squeeze together; make smaller by pressure: Cotton is *compressed* into bales. **compressed, compressing.**— (kom′pres) *noun.* Pad or cloth applied to some part of the body to prevent bleeding, lessen inflammation, etc: I put a cold *compress* on my forehead to relieve my headache.

con·ceal·ment (kən sēl′mənt) *noun.* 1. A concealing or keeping secret. 2. Means or place for concealing.

con·de·scend (kon′di send′) *verb.* 1. To appear gracious to people considered lower in rank or status. 2. To grant a favor with a haughty or patronizing attitude. **condescended, condescending.**

con·fines (kon′fīnz) *noun.* Boundary, border, limit.

con·front (kən frunt′) *verb.* 1. To meet face to face; stand facing. 2. To face boldly; oppose: We crept downstairs with baseball bats in hand to *confront* the prowler. 3. To bring face to face; place before. **confronted, confronting.**

con·se·quence (kon′sə kwens) *noun.* 1. A result or effect. 2. Importance: The loss of her ring is a matter of great *consequence* to her.

con·serv·a·to·ry (kən sėr′və tôr′ē) *noun.* 1. School for instruction in music. 2. Greenhouse for growing and displaying plants and flowers.

con·ster·na·tion (kon′stər nā′shən) *noun.* Great dismay; paralyzing terror.

con·tem·pla·tion (kon′təm plā′shən) *noun.* 1. A looking at or thinking about something for a long time; deep thought: I was sunk in *contemplation* and didn't hear the doorbell. 2. Expectation or intention.

con·tempt (kən tempt′) *noun.* The feeling that a person, act or thing is mean, low, or worthless; despising; scorn.—**contemptuously** *adverb.*

con·tract (kən trakt′) *verb.* 1. To draw together; make shorter. 2. To become shorter or smaller; shrink. 3. To shorten (a word, phrase, etc.) by omitting some of the letters or sounds. 4. To bring on oneself; get; form: She *contracted* a cold. **contracted, contracting.**—(kon′trakt) *noun.* 1. Agreement: In a *contract,* two or more people agree to do or not to do certain things. 2. A written agreement that can be enforced by law.

con·verge (kən vėrj′) *verb.* 1. To tend to meet in a point. 2. To turn toward each other. 3. To come together; center. **converged, converging.**

con·vey (kən vā′) *verb.* 1. To take from one place to another; carry. 2. To transmit; conduct. 3. To make known; communicate. 4. To transfer ownership of; hand over; give: *convey* property by a will. **conveyed, conveying.**

con·vic·tion (kən vik′shən) *noun.* 1. Act of proving or declaring guilty. 2. Condition of being proved or declared guilty. 3. Firm belief.

cor·dial (kôr′jəl) *adjective.* Warm and friendly in manner; hearty: Her friends gave her a *cordial* welcome.—**cordially** *adverb.*

coun·cil (koun′səl) *noun.* Group of people called together to give advice and to discuss or settle questions.

cow·er (kou′ər) *verb.* To crouch or draw

back in fear or shame. **cowered, cowering.**

cred·it (kred′it) *noun.* 1. Belief in the truth of something; faith; trust. 2. A trust in a person's ability and intention to pay. 3. Amount of money in a person's account. 4. Reputation in money matters.—*verb.* 1. To believe in the truth of something; have faith in; trust. 2. To add to one's credit in a bank account, business record, etc. **credited, crediting.**

creep·er (krē′pər) *noun.* 1. Person or thing that creeps. 2. Any plant that grows along a surface, sending out rootlets from the stem, such as ivy.

cres·cent (kres′ənt) *noun.* 1. Shape of the moon in its first or last quarter. 2. Anything that curves in a similar way.—*adjective.* Shaped like the moon in its first or last quarter.

crest·fall·en (krest′fô′lən) *adjective.* In low spirits; discouraged.

cul·ti·vate (kul′tə vāt) *verb.* 1. To prepare and use land to raise crops by plowing it, planting seeds, and taking care of the growing plants. 2. To help plants grow by labor and care. 3. To improve or develop by study or training. **cultivated, cultivating.**

cum·ber·some (kum′bər səm) *adjective.* Hard to manage; clumsy, unwieldy, or burdensome.—**cumbersomely** *adverb.*

cu·ra·tor (kyu̇ rā′tər) *noun.* Person in charge of all or part of a museum, library, art gallery, zoo, etc.

D

da·is (dā′is) *noun.* A raised platform at one end of a hall or large room.

daze (dāz) *verb.* 1. To make unable to think clearly; bewilder, stun. 2. To hurt (one's eyes) with light; dazzle. **dazed, dazing.**—*noun.* A dazed condition.—**dazedly** *adverb.*

de·but (dā′byü) *noun.* A first public appearance.

de·cep·tive (di sep′tiv) *adjective.* 1. Deceiving or misleading. 2. Meant to deceive.—**deceptively** *adverb.*

de·com·pose (dē′kəm pōz′) *verb.* 1. To separate a substance into what it is made of. 2. To rot or become rotten; decay. **decomposed, decomposing.**

de·crep·it (di krep′it) *adjective.* Broken down or weakened by old age; old and feeble.—**decrepitly** *adverb.*

deed (dēd) *noun.* 1. Thing done; act;

action. 2. A written or printed statement of ownership. The buyer of real estate receives a *deed* to the property from the former owner.

de·fect (dē′fekt) *noun.* 1. A shortcoming or failing; fault or blemish. 2. Lack of something necessary for completeness.

de·fen·sive (di fen′siv) *adjective.* Of or for defense; intended to defend.—**defensively** *adverb.*—*noun.* Position or attitude of defense.

de·fer (di fėr′) *verb.* To put off; delay. **deferred, deferring.**

deft (deft) *adjective.* Quick and skillful in action; nimble: The fingers of a violinist must be *deft.*—**deftly** *adverb.*

de·lib·er·ate (di lib′ər it) *adjective.* 1. Carefully thought out beforehand; made or done on purpose; intended. 2. Slow and careful in deciding what to do. 3. Not hurried; slow.—**deliberately** *adverb.*—(di lib′ə rāt) *verb.* 1. To think over carefully; consider. 2. To talk over reasons for and against; discuss, debate. **deliberated, deliberating.**

de·lin·quent (di ling′kwənt) *adjective.* 1. Failing in a duty; neglecting an obligation: He was *delinquent* in paying his overdue taxes. 2. Guilty of a fault or an offense: The *delinquent* children had to pay for the windows they broke. 3. Due and unpaid; overdue.—**delinquently** *adverb.*—*noun.* 1. A delinquent person; offender. 2. Juvenile delinquent.

de·lir·i·um (di lir′ē əm) *noun.* A temporary disorder of the mind that occurs during fevers and characterized by restlessness, wild talk, and hallucinations.

der·e·lict (der′ə likt) *adjective.* 1. Abandoned by its crew or owner; forsaken. 2. Failing in one's duty; negligent.—*noun.* 1. Ship abandoned at sea. 2. A penniless person who is homeless, jobless, and abandoned by others.

de·ri·sion (di rizh′ən) *noun.* Laughter, ridicule.

des·ig·nate (dez′ig nāt) *verb.* 1. To mark out; point out; indicate definitely; show: Red lines *designate* main roads on this map. 2. To name: Historians *designate* the period A.D. 400 to A.D. 1000 the Dark Ages. **designated, designating.**

des·o·la·tion (des′ə lā′shən) *noun.* 1. A ruined, lonely, or deserted condition: After the fire, the forest was in complete *desolation.* 2. Lonely sorrow; sadness: *desolation* at the loss of loved ones.

de·spond·ent (di spon′dənt) *adjective.* Having lost heart, courage, or hope; discouraged; dejected:—**despondently** *adverb.*

de·tain (di tān′) *verb.* 1. To keep from going ahead; hold back; delay. 2. To keep from going away; hold as a prisoner. **detained, detaining.**

de·vise (di vīz′) *verb.* To think out; plan or contrive; invent. **devised, devising.**

dil·i·gence (dil′ə jəns) *noun.* Working hard; careful and steady effort; industry.

din·gy (din′jē) *adjective.* Lacking brightness or freshness; dirty-looking; dull.

dis·ar·ray (dis′ə rā′) *noun.* Lack of order; disorder; confusion.

dis·con·so·late (dis kon′sə lit) *adjective.* Without hope; forlorn, unhappy, cheerless.—**disconsolately** *adverb.*

dis·dain (dis dān′) *verb.* To look down on; consider beneath oneself; scorn: Now that they are rich, they *disdain* to speak to their old friends. **disdained, disdaining.**—*noun.* A looking down on an act beneath one; scorn.

dis·heart·en (dis härt′n) *verb.* Cause to lose hope; discourage; depress. **disheartened, disheartening.**

dis·in·clined (dis′in klīnd′) *adjective.* Unwilling: I was watching TV and was *disinclined* to clean up my room.

dis·lo·cate (dis′lō kāt) *verb.* To put out of joint: She *dislocated* her shoulder when she fell down the stairs. **dislocated, dislocating.**

dis·pense (dis pens′) *verb.* 1. To give out; distribute. 2. To carry out; put in force; apply. 3. To prepare and give out. **dispensed, dispensing.**

dis·place·ment (dis plās′mənt) *noun.* 1. A displacing or a being displaced. 2. Weight of the volume of water displaced by a ship or other floating object. This weight is equal to that of the floating object.

dis·re·gard (dis′ri gärd′) *verb.* To pay no attention to; take no notice of: *Disregarding* the cold weather, we played outside all day. **disregarded, disregarding.**—*noun.* Lack of attention; neglect: The reckless driver was arrested for *disregard* of the traffic laws.

dis·traught (dis trôt′) *adjective.* 1. In a

state of mental conflict and confusion. 2. Crazed.

di ur nal (dī ėr′nl) *adjective.* 1. Occurring every day; daily. 2. Of or belonging to the daytime. 3. Active in the daytime.

di·vine (də vīn′) *verb.* 1. To foresee or foretell by inspiration, by magic, or by signs and omens; predict. 2. To find out without actually knowing; guess correctly. **divined, divining.**

doc·ile (dos′əl) *adjective.* Easily trained or managed; obedient.—**docility** *noun.*

dole (dōl) *verb.* To give in small portions: The teacher *doled* out a dab of paste to each student. **doled, doling.**

dor·mant (dôr′mənt) *adjective.* 1. Sleeping; seeming to sleep; not moving or feeling. 2. Without activity; inactive: Many volcanoes are *dormant.*

draught·y (draf′tē) *variant* of DRAFTY. *adjective.* 1. In a current of air. 2. Having many currents of air.—**draughtily** *adverb.*

E

ec·cen·tric (ek sen′trik) *adjective.* Out of the ordinary; not usual; odd; peculiar: People stared at the artist's *eccentric* clothes.—*noun.* Person who behaves in an unusual manner: The behavior of an *eccentric* is hard to predict.

ed·dy (ed′ē) *noun.* Water, air, smoke, etc. moving against the main current, especially when having a whirling motion; small whirlpool or whirlwind.—*verb.* To move against the main current in a whirling motion; whirl. **eddied, eddying.**

ec·stat·ic (ek stat′ik) *adjective.* 1. very joyful and thrilling; full of ecstasy. 2. Caused by ecstasy.—**ecstatically** *adverb.*

ed·i·ble (ed′ə bəl) *adjective.* Fit to eat.

e·lec·tri·fy (i lek′trə fī), *verb.* 1. To charge with electricity. 2. To equip for the use of electric power. 3. To give an electric shock to. 4. To excite, thrill. **electrified, electrifying.**

e·lim·i·nate (i lim′ə nāt) *verb.* 1. To get rid of; remove. 2. To leave out; omit. **eliminated, eliminating.**

em·broi·der (em broi′dər) *verb.* 1. To ornament with a raised design or pattern of stitches. 2. To make an ornamental design or pattern on cloth, leather, etc., with stitches. 3. To add

imaginary details to; exaggerate. **embroidered, embroidering.**

em·broil·ment (em broil′mənt) *noun.* Involvement in a quarrel.

em·er·ald (em′ər əld) *noun.* 1. A clear, hard deep-green precious gem. 2. A bright green.—*adjective.* Bright-green.

e·mit (i mit′) *verb.* To give off; send out. **emitted, emitting.**

en·coun·ter (en koun′tər) *verb.* 1. To meet unexpectedly. 2. To be faced with: She *encountered* many difficulties before the job was done. 3. To meet as an enemy; to meet in a fight or battle. **encountered, encountering.**—*noun.* 1. An unexpected meeting. 2. A meeting of enemies; fight.

en·cum·ber (en kum′bər) *verb.* 1. To hold back; hinder, hamper. 2. To block up; fill. 3. To burden with weight, difficulties, cares, debt, etc. **encumbered, encumbering.**

en·er·get·i·cal·ly (en′ər jet′ik lē) *adverb.* With energy; vigorously.

en·ig·mat·ic (en′ig mat′ik) *adjective.* Like a riddle, baffling; puzzling.

en·thu·si·as·tic (en thü′zē as′tik) *adjective.* Full of enthusiasm; eagerly interested.

en·tice (en tīs′) *verb.* To attract by arousing hopes or desires; tempt. **enticed, enticing.**

ep·i·thet (ep′ə thet) *noun.* A descriptive expression; word or phrase expressing some quality or attribute: In "Honest Abe" and "Richard the Lion-Hearted" the *epithets* are "Honest" and "the Lion-Hearted."

e·qui·lib·ri·um (ē′kwə lib′rē əm) *noun.* 1. Balance. 2. Mental poise.

er·ro·ne·ous (ə rō′nē əs) *adjective.* Not correct; wrong; mistaken: Years ago many people held the *erroneous* belief that the earth was flat.—**erroneously** *adverb.*

e·rupt (i rupt′) *verb.* 1. To burst forth. 2. To throw forth. 3. To break out in a rash. **erupted, erupting.**

es·thet·ic (es thet′ik) *adjective.* 1. Having to do with the artistic or beautiful rather than the useful or practical. 2. Having an appreciation of beauty in nature or art. 3. Showing good taste; artistic.

eth·ics (eth′iks) *noun.* 1. *plural in form, singular in use.* The study of standards of right and wrong; the part of philosophy dealing with moral conduct, duty, and judgment. 2. *plural in form* *and use.* Formal or professional rules of right and wrong.

e·vac·u·ate (i vak′yü āt) *verb.* 1. To leave empty; withdraw from. 2. To withdraw, remove. 3. To make empty. **evacuated, evacuating.**

ex·act·ing (eg zak′ting) *adjective.* 1. Requiring much; hard to please. 2. Requiring effort, care, or attention.

ex·as·pe·ra·tion (eg zas′pə ra′shən) *noun.* Extreme annoyance; irritation, anger.

ex·cur·sion (ek skėr′zhən) *noun.* 1. A short trip taken for interest or pleasure, often by a number of people together. 2. Trip on a train, ship, or aircraft, at fares lower than those usually charged.

ex·hil·a·rate (eg zil′ə rāt′) *verb.* To make merry; make lively; cheer. **exhilarated, exhilarating.**

ex·o·dus (ek′sə dəs) *noun.* A movement away; a departure, usually a large number of people.

ex·ot·ic (eg zot′ik) *adjective.* Foreign; strange; not native: We saw many *exotic* plants at the flower show.**—exotically** *adverb.*

ex·panse (ek spans′) *noun.* Open or unbroken stretch; wide, spreading surface: *The Pacific Ocean is a vast expanse* of water.

ex·port (ek spôrt′) *verb.* To send (goods) out of one country for sale and use in another: *The United States exports* many kinds of machinery. **exported, exporting.**—(ek′spôrt) *noun.* 1. Article exported. 2. Act or fact of exporting.

ex·pul·sion (ek spul′shən) *noun.* 1. A forcing out. 2. A being forced out: *Expulsion* from school is a punishment for bad behavior.

ex·qui·site (ek′skwi zit) *adjective.* 1. Very lovely; delicate. 2. Sharp, intense. 3. Of highest excellence; most admirable.

ex·u·ber·a·tion (eg zü′bə rā′shən) *noun.* Condition of being exuberant, feeling exhilarated.

ex·ude (eg züd′) *verb.* 1. To come or send out in drops; ooze. 2. To give forth. **exuded, exuding.**

F

fac·sim·i·le (fak sim′ə lē) *noun.* An exact copy or likeness.

fac·tion (fak′shən) *noun.* 1. Group of persons who stand up for their side or act together for some common purpose against the rest of a larger group. 2. Strife among the members of a political party, church, club, or neighborhood.

fam·ished (fam′isht) *adjective.* Very hungry; starving.

fa·tigue (fə tēg′) *noun.* Weariness caused by hard work or effort—*verb.* To make weary or tired; cause fatigue in. **fatigued, fatiguing.**

fa·vor·it·ism (fā′vər ə tiz′əm) *noun.* A favoring of a certain one or some more than others; having favorites.

feath·er (feth′ər) *noun.* One of the light, thin growths that cover a bird's skin.—*verb.* 1. To change the angle of (airplane propeller blades) so that the chords become approximately parallel to the line of flight. 2. To turn (an oar blade) almost horizontal when lifting from the water at the end of a stroke to reduce air resistance. **feathered, feathering.**

fe·roc·i·ty (fe ros′ə tē) *noun.* Great cruelty; savageness; fierceness.

fe·ver·ish (fē′vər ish) *adjective.* 1. Having fever. 2. Excited, restless.**—feverishly** *adverb.*

flail (flāl) *noun.* Instrument for threshing grain by hand.—*verb.* 1. To strike with a flail. 2. To beat, thrash. **flailed, flailing.**

flank (flangk) *noun.* 1. Side of an animal or person between the ribs and the hip. 2. Piece of beef cut from this part. 3. Side of a mountain, building, etc. 4. The far right or the far left side of an army, fort, or fleet.—*verb.* 1. To be at the side of. 2. To get around the far right or the far left side of. 3. To attack from or on the side. **flanked, flanking.**

flay (flā) *verb.* 1. To strip off the skin or outer covering of. 2. To scold severely; criticize without pity or mercy. **flayed, flaying.**

floun·der (floun′der) *verb.* 1. To struggle awkwardly without making much progress; plunge about. 2. To be clumsy or confused and make mistakes. **floundered, floundering.**

fod·der (fod′ər) *noun.* Coarse food for horses, cattle, etc. Hay and corn stalks with their leaves are *fodder.*

foil (foil) *verb.* To prevent from carrying out plans; get the better of; outwit. **foiled, foiling.**—*noun.* 1. Metal beaten, hammered, or rolled into a very thin sheet. 2. Anything that makes something else look or seem better by contrast. 3. A long, narrow sword with a knob or button on the point to prevent injury, used in fencing.

ford (fôrd) *noun.* Place where a river, stream, etc, is not too deep to cross by walking or driving through the water.—*verb.* To cross a river, etc. by walking or driving through the water. **forded, fording.**

for·feit (fôr′fit) *verb.* To lose or have to give up by one's own act, neglect, or fault: Careless drivers *forfeit* their lives. **forfeited, forfeiting.**—*noun.* Thing lost or given up because of some act, neglect, or fault; penalty; fine.

for·ti·fy (fôr′tə fī) *verb.* 1. To build forts, walls, etc.; protect a place against attack; strengthen against attack. 2. To give support to; strengthen. 3. To enrich with vitamins and minerals: *fortify* bread. **fortified, fortifying.**

foun·der (foun′dər) *verb.* 1. To fill with water and sink. 2. To fall down; stumble. **foundered, foundering.**

fra·cas (frā′kəs) *noun.* A noisy quarrel or fight; disorderly noise; uproar; brawl.

frag·ile (fraj′əl) *adjective.* Easily broken, damaged, or destroyed; delicate; frail.

fray (frā) *noun.* A noisy quarrel; fight.

fren·zied (fren′zēd) *adjective.* Very much excited; frantic; wild.**—frenziedly** *adverb.*

fre·quen·cy (frē′kwən sē) *noun.* 1. Rate of occurrence. 2. A frequent occurrence. 3. Number of complete cycles per second of an alternating current or other electric wave.

fruit·less (früt′lis) *adjective.* 1. Having no results; useless, unsuccessful. 2. Producing no fruit; barren.

fu·gi·tive (fyü′jə tiv) *noun.* Person who is running away or who has run away.—*adjective.* Running away; having run away.

fur·row (fėr′ō) *noun.* 1. A long, narrow groove or track cut in the earth by a plow. 2. Any long, narrow grooves or tracks: Heavy trucks made deep *furrows* in the muddy road. 3. A wrinkle.—*verb.* 1. To make furrows in. 2. To make wrinkles in. **furrowed, furrowing.**

fu·tile (fyü′tl) *adjective.* 1. Not successful, useless. 2. Not important; trifling.

G

gall (gôl) *noun.* 1. Anything very bitter or harsh. 2. Bitterness, hate. 3. (Informal.) Too great boldness; impudence.

gal·va·nize (gal′və nīz) *verb.* 1. To apply an electric current produced by chemical action. 2. To arouse suddenly; startle. 3. To cover iron or steel with a thin coating of zinc to prevent rust. **galvanized, galvanizing.**

gar·ret (gar′it) *noun.* Space in a house just below a sloping roof; attic.

ga·zelle (gə zel′) *noun.* A small, swift, and graceful antelope of Africa and Asia, having soft, lustrous eyes.

gild (gild) *verb.* 1. To cover with a thin layer of gold or similar material; make golden. 2. To make (something) look bright and pleasing. 3. To make (something) seem better than it is. **gilded, gilding.**

glance (glans) *noun.* 1. A quick look. 2. A flash of light; gleam.—*verb.* 1. To look quickly. 2. To flash with light, gleam. 3. To hit and go off at a slant. **glanced, glancing.**

glen (glen) *noun.* A small, narrow valley.

glow·er (glou′ər) *verb.* To stare angrily; scowl fiercely. **glowered, glowering.**

goad (gōd) *noun.* 1. A sharp-pointed stick for driving cattle. 2. Anything which drives or urges one on.—*verb.* To drive or urge on; act as a goad to. **goaded, goading.**

grat·i·fy (grat′ə fī) *verb.* 1. To give pleasure to; please. 2. To give satisfaction to; satisfy, indulge. **gratified, gratifying.**

grave (grāv) *noun.* Hole dug in the ground where a dead body is to be buried.—*adjective.* 1. Serious, threatening, critical. 2. Sober, dignified, solemn.—**gravely** *adverb.*

gri·mace (grim′is) *noun.* A twisting of the face; ugly or funny smile.—*verb.* To make faces. **grimaced, grimacing.**

grope (grōp) *verb.* 1. To feel about with the hands. 2. To search blindly and uncertainly. 3. To find by feeling about with the hands; feel one's way slowly. **groped, groping.**

gro·tesque (grō tesk′) *adjective.* 1. Odd or unnatural in shape, appearance, manner, etc.; fantastic, odd. 2. Ridiculous, absurd.—**grotesquely** *adverb.*

gy·ra·tion (jī rā′shən) *noun.* Circular or spiral motion; whirling, rotation.

H

half·heart·ed (haf′här′tid) *adjective.* Lacking courage, interest, or enthusiasm; not earnest. —**halfheartedly** *adverb.*

hal·lu·ci·nate (hə lü′sən āt) *verb.* To see or hear things that exist only in a person's imagination. **hallucinated, hallucinating.**

hand·bill (hand′bil′) *noun.* Notice or advertisement, usually printed on one page, that is to be handed out to people.

han·dling charge (han′dling chärj) *noun.* Additional cost added to the price of an item to pay for postage, packaging, etc.

har·bin·ger (här′bən jər) *noun.* One that goes ahead to announce another's coming; forerunner.

har·ry (har′ē) *verb.* 1. To raid and rob with violence. 2. To keep troubling; worry; torment. **harried, harrying.**

har·row·ing (har′ō ing) *adjective.* Very painful or distressing.

haugh·ty (hô′tē) *adjective.* 1. Too proud of oneself and too scornful of others. 2. Showing too great pride of oneself and scorn for others.—**haughtily** *adverb.*

haunt (hônt) *noun.* Place often gone to or visited.—*verb.* 1. To go often to; visit frequently. 2. To be often with; come often to. **haunted, haunting.**

heif·er (hef′ər) *noun.* A young cow that has not had a calf.

heir (er) *noun.* Person who has the right to somebody's property or title after the death of its owner.

hos·pi·ta·ble (hos′pi tə bəl) *adjective.* 1. Giving or liking to give a welcome, food and shelter, and friendly treatment to guests or strangers. 2. With the mind open or receptive.

host (hōst) *noun.* 1. A person who received another person as a guest. 2. A living plant or animal in or on which a parasite lives. 3. A large number; multitude.

hub (hub) *noun.* 1. The central part of a wheel. 2. Center of interest, activity, etc.

hu·mil·i·ty (hyü mil′ə tē) *noun.* Humbleness of mind; lack of pride; meekness.

I

ig·no·ble (ig nō′bəl) *adjective.* 1. Without honor; disgraceful; base: To betray a friend is *ignoble*. 2. Not of noble birth or position; humble.—**ignobly** *adverb.*

il·lit·er·ate (i lit′ər it) *noun.* 1. Person who does not know how to read and write. 2. An uneducated person.—*adjective.* 1. Not knowing how to read and write. 2. Showing a lack of education.

im·mi·nent (im′ə nənt) *adjective.* Likely to happen soon; about to occur.—**imminently** *adverb.*

im·pas·sive (im pas′iv) *adjective.* 1. Without feeling or emotion; unmoved. 2. Not feeling pain or injury; insensible.—**impassively** *adverb.*

im·per·cep·ti·ble (im′pər sep′tə bəl) *adjective.* Not able to be perceived or felt; very slight; gradual. —**imperceptibly** *adverb.*

im·pe·ri·ous (im pir′ē əs) *adjective.* 1. Haughty or arrogant; domineering; overbearing. 2. Not to be avoided; necessary; urgent.—**imperiously** *adverb.*

im·pet·u·ous (im pech′ü əs) *adjective.* 1. Acting or done with sudden or rash energy; haste. 2. Rushing with force and violence.—**impetuously** *adverb.*

im·pli·ca·tion (im′plə kā′shən) *noun.* 1. An implying or a being implied. 2. Something implied; indirect suggestion; hint: She did not actually refuse, but the way that she frowned was an *implication* of her unwillingness. 3. An implicating or a being implicated.

im·pound (im pound′) *verb.* 1. To shut up in a pen or pound. 2. To enclose or confine within limits. 3. To put in the custody of a court of law. **impounded, impounding.**

im·pro·vise (im′prə vīz) *verb.* 1. To make up (music poetry, etc.) on the spur of the moment; sing, recite, speak, etc. 2. To make for the occasion. **improvised, improvising.**

in·cal·cu·la·ble (in kal′kyə lə bəl) *adjective.* 1. Too great in number to be calculated; innumerable: The sands of the sea are *incalculable*. 2. Impossible to foretell or reckon beforehand. —**incalculably** *adverb.*

in·ces·sant (in ses′nt) *adjective.* Never stopping; continual.

in·con·se·quen·tial (in′kon sə kwen′shəl) *adjective.* Not important, trifling.

in·con·sol·a·ble (in′kən sō′lə bəl) *adjective.* Not to be comforted; broken-hearted.

in·con·tro·vert·i·ble (in kän′trə vert′ə bel) *adjective.* Not open to question; indisputable.

in·de·struct·i·ble (in di struk′tə bəl) *adjective.* Not able to be destroyed.—**indestructibility** *noun.*

in·dif·fer·ence (in dif′ər əns) *noun.* 1. Lack of interest or attention; not caring. 2. Lack of importance.

in·dis·crim·i·nate (in′dis krim′ə nit) *adjective.* 1. Mixed up; confused. 2. Without discrimination; not distinguishing carefully between persons, things, etc.—**indiscriminately** *adverb.*

in·di·vid·u·al·ize (in′də vij′ü ə līz) *verb.* 1. To make individual in character. 2. To treat or notice individually. 3. To adapt to the needs or special circumstances of an individual. **individualized, individualizing.**

in·dus·tri·al (in dus′trē əl) *adjective.* 1. Of or resulting from industry. 2. Engaged in or connected with industry. 3. For use in industry.

in·ef·fec·tu·al (in′ə fek′chü əl) *adjective.* 1. Without effect, failing to have the effect wanted; useless. 2. Not able to produce the effect wanted; powerless.

in·ev·i·ta·ble (in ev′ə tə bel) *adjective.* Not to be avoided; sure to happen; certain to come.

in·ex·plic·a·ble (in′ik splik′ə bəl) *adjective.* Not able to be explained; mysterious.

in·flame (in flām′) *verb.* 1. To make more violent; excite. 2. To become excited with strong feeling. 3. To make or become unnaturally hot, red, sore, or swollen. **inflamed, inflaming.**

in·gra·ti·ate (in grā′shē āt) *verb.* To bring oneself into favor; make oneself acceptable. **ingratiated, ingratiating.**—**ingratiatingly** *adverb.*

in·junc·tion (in jungk′shən) *noun.* 1. A formal order from a court of law requiring a person or group to do or not to do something. 2. Command; order.

in·sa·tia·ble (in sā′shə bəl) *adjective.* Not able to be satisfied; extremely greedy.—**insatiably** *adverb.*

in·stall (in stôl′) *verb.* 1. To put (a person) in office with ceremonies. 2. To put in a place or position; settle. 3. To put in place for use. **installed, installing.**

in·su·late (in′sə lāt) *verb.* 1. To keep from losing or transferring electricity, heat, sound, etc., especially by covering, packing, or surrounding with a material that does not conduct electricity, heat, etc. 2. To set apart; separate from others; isolate. **insulated, insulating.**

in·ter·mi·na·ble (in tėr′mə nə bəl) *adjective.* 1. Never stopping; unceasing, endless. 2. So long as to seem endless; very long and tiring.—**interminable** *adverb.*

in·tern (in′tėrn′) *noun.* Doctor acting as an assistant and undergoing training in a hospital.

in·ter·pose (in′tėr pōz′) *verb.* 1. To put between; insert. 2. To come or be between other things. 3. To put forward; break in with; interrupt: I'd like to *interpose* an objection at this point. **interposed, interposing.**

in·ter·val (in′tėr vel) *noun.* 1. Time or space between: There is an *interval* of two days between Friday and Monday. 2. (in music) The difference in pitch between two tones.

in·ter·vene (in′tėr vēn′) *verb.* 1. To come between; be between. 2. To come between persons or groups to help settle a dispute. **intervened, intervening.**

in·tu·i·tion (in′tü ish′ən) *noun.* Immediate perception or understanding of truths, facts, etc., without reasoning.

in·var·i·a·bly (in ver′ē ə blē) *adverb.* In an invariable manner; without change; without exception.

in·vert (in vert′) *verb.* 1. To turn upside down. 2. To turn the other way; change to the opposite; reverse in position, direction, order, etc. **inverted, inverting.**

ir·re·sist·i·ble (ir′i zis′tə bel) *adjective.* Not able to be resisted; too great to be withstood; overwhelming.

ir·rup·tion (i rup′shən) *noun.* A forcible or violent rushing in; breaking in or bursting in.

joust (joust) *noun.* Combat between two knights on horseback, armed with lances.—*verb.* To fight with lances on horseback. **jousted, jousting.**

jowl (joul) *noun.* 1. Jaw, especially the lower jaw. 2. Cheek. 3. Fold of flesh hanging from the jaw.

ju·di·cious (jü dish′əs) *adjective.* Having, using, or showing good judgment; wise; sensible: *Judicious* parents encourage their children to make their own decisions. —**judiciously** *adverb.*

jur·is·dic·tion (jür′is dik′shən) *noun.* 1. Right or power to give out justice. 2. Authority; power; control. 3. The things over which authority extends.

ka·lei·do·scope (kə lī′də skōp) *noun.* 1. Tube containing bits of colored glass and two mirrors. As it is turned, it reflects continually changing patterns. 2. A continually changing pattern.

la·bo·ri·ous (lə bôr′ē əs) *adjective.* 1. Needing or taking much effort; requiring hard work: Climbing a mountain is *laborious.* 2. Showing signs of effort; labored. 3. Willing to work hard; industrious.—**laboriously** *adverb.*

lac·e·ra·tion (las′ə rā′shən) *noun.* 1. A rough tearing or mangling. 2. A rough tear; mangled place: A torn, jagged wound is a *laceration.*

lack·a·dai·si·cal (lak′ə dā′zə kəl) *adjective.* Lacking interest or enthusiasm; languid; listless. —**lackadaisically** *adverb.*

le·git·i·mate (lə jit′ə mit) *adjective.* 1. Allowed or admitted by law; rightful; lawful. 2. Valid; logical; acceptable. —**legitimately** *adverb.*

lei·sure·ly (lē′zhər lē) *adjective* and *adverb.* Without hurry; taking plenty of time.

lin·guist (ling′gwist) *noun.* 1. An expert in languages or linguistics. 2. Person skilled in a number of languages.

list·less (list′lis) *adjective.* Seeming too tired to care about anything; not interested in things; not caring to be active.—**listlessly** *adverb.*

lit·e·rar·y (lit′ə rer′ē) *adjective.* 1. Having to do with literature. 2. Knowing much about literature. 3. Engaged in literature as a profession.

liv·er·y (liv′ər ē) *noun.* 1. Any uniform provided for servants, or adopted by any group or profession. 2. The feeding, stabling, and care of horses for pay. 3. The hiring out of horses and carriages. 4. The keeping of cars, boats, bicycles, etc., for hire.

lux·u·ri·ous (lug zhŭr′ē əs) *adjective.* 1. Fond of luxury; tending toward luxury; self-indulgent. 2. Giving luxury; very comfortable and beautiful. —**luxuriously** *adverb.*

M

mag·nif·i·cence (mag nif′ə səns) *noun.* Richness of material, color, and ornament; grand beauty; splendor.

ma·jes·tic (mə jes′tik) *adjective.* Of or having majesty; grand, noble, dignified, stately.

ma·lev·o·lence (mə lev′ə ləns) *noun.* The wish that evil may happen to others; ill will; spite.

ma·lign (mə līn′) *verb.* To speak evil of; slander. **maligned, maligning.** —*adjective.* 1. Evil; injurious. 2. Hateful; malicious.

man·da·to·ry (man′də tôr′ē) *adjective.* Of or containing a command; commanded, required.

man·i·fest (man′ə fest) *verb.* To show plainly; reveal, display. **manifested, manifesting.**—*noun.* A list of passengers for a ship or plane.

mar·a·thon (mar′ə thon) *noun.* 1. A foot race of 26 miles 385 yards (42.2 kilometers), named after Marathon. 2. Any long race or contest. 3. Marathon, plain in Greece about 25 miles (40 kilometers) northeast of Athens. After the Athenians defeated the Persians there in 490 B.C., a runner ran all the way to Athens with the news of the victory.

maul (môl) *noun.* A very heavy hammer or mallet.—*verb.* To beat and pull about; handle roughly. **mauled, mauling.**

may·hem (mā′hem) *noun.* 1. Crime of intentionally maiming or injuring a person. 2. Needless or intentional damage.

mem·o·ran·dum (mem′ə ran′dəm) *noun.* 1. A short written statement for future use; note to aid one's memory. 2. An informal letter, note, or report.

mes·mer·ize (mez′mə rīz′) *verb.* To hypnotize. **mesmerized, mesmerizing.**

mi·cro·film (mī′krō film′) *noun.* Film for making very small photographs of pages of a book, newspapers, records, etc., to preserve them in a very small space.

mi·li·tia (mə lish′ə) *noun.* Army of citizens who are not regular soldiers but who undergo training for emergency duty or national defense.

mill (mil) *verb.* 1. To grind (grain) into flour or meal. 2. To move in a confused way: The frightened cattle began to *mill* around. **milled, milling.**

min·i·mize (min′ə mīz) *verb.* 1. To reduce to the least possible amount or degree. 2. To state at the lowest possible estimate; make the least of. **minimized, minimizing.**

mi·rage (mə räzh′) *noun.* An optical illusion, usually in the desert, at sea, or on a paved road, in which some distant scene appears to be much closer than it actually is. Often what is reflected is seen upside down or as something other than it is: Travelers on the desert may see a *mirage* of palm trees and water.

mis·giv·ing (mis giv′ing) *noun.* A feeling of doubt, suspicion, or anxiety.

mod·est (mod′ist) *adjective.* 1. Not thinking too highly of oneself; not vain; humble. 2. Not too great; not asking too much. 3. Not expensive or showy.

mon·o·syl·la·ble (mon′ə sil′ə bəl) *noun.* Word of one syllable.

mo·not·o·nous (mə not′n əs) *adjective.* 1. Continuing in the same tone. 2. Not varying; without change: *monotonous* food. 3. Wearying because of its sameness.

mon·ster·ma·ni·a (mon′stər mān′nē ə) *noun.* Excessive or unreasonable enthusiasm for or about imaginary creatures.

mort·gage (môr′gij) *noun.* 1. A claim on property, given to a person, bank, or firm that has loaned money in case the money is not repaid when due. 2. Document that gives such a claim.

mus·tang (mus′tang) *noun.* A small, wild horse of the North American plain.—*verb.* To capture mustangs. **mustanged, mustanging.**

mut·ton (mut′n) *noun.* Meat from a sheep.

mys·ti·fy (mis′tə fī) *verb.* 1. To bewilder purposely; puzzle; perplex. 2. To make mysterious. **mystified, mystifying.**

N

ne·go·ti·a·tion (ni gō shē ā′shən) *noun.* A negotiating; arrangement.

non·plus (non plus′) *verb.* To put at a loss; baffle. **nonplussed, nonplussing.**

no·to·ri·ous (nō tôr′ē əs) *adjective.* Well-known or commonly known, especially because of something bad.—**notoriously** *adverb.*

nov·ice (nov′is) *noun.* One who is new to something; beginner.

nu·tri·ent (nü′trē ənt *or* nyü′trē ənt) *noun.* A nourishing substance; food.—*adjective.* Nourishing.

O

o·be·di·ent (ō bē′dē ənt) *adjective.* Doing what one is told; willing to obey.—**obediently** *adverb.*

o·blig·ing (ə blī′jing) *adjective.* Helpful; willing to do favors.

o·blique (ə blēk′) *adjective.* 1. Not straight up and down; not straight across; slanting. 2. Not straightforward; indirect.

o·bliv·i·on (ə bliv′ē ən) *noun.* 1. Condition of being entirely forgotten. 2. Forgetfulness.

o·bliv·i·ous (ə bliv′ē əs) *adjective.* Forgetful, not mindful.

o·cean·ar·i·um (ō′shə nar′ē əm) *noun.* A large marine aquarium.

out·stand·ing (out stan′ding) *adjective.* 1. Standing out from others; well-known; important. 2. Unpaid: *outstanding* debts. 3. Standing out; projecting.

o·ver·se·er (ō′vər sē′ər) *noun.* Person who oversees others or their work.

P

pal·i·sade (pal′ə sād′) *noun.* 1. A long, strong, wooden stake pointed at the top end. 2. A fence of stakes set firmly in the ground to enclose or defend.

pan·de·mo·ni·um (pan′də mō′nē əm) *noun.* 1. Wild uproar or confusion. 2. Place of wild disorder or lawless confusion.

pa·rab·o·la (pə rab′ə lə) *noun.* 1. A plane curve formed by the intersection of a cone with a plane parallel to a side of the cone. 2. Something bowl-shaped.

par·a·noid (par′ə noid) *adjective.* 1. Like

570

or tending toward feelings of persecution. 2. Having the characteristics of paranoia.—*noun.* A person suffering from feelings of persecution.

pa·ri·ah (pə rī′ə) *noun.* An outcast.

par·ox·ysm (par′ək siz′əm) *noun.* 1. A sudden, severe attack of the symptoms of a disease, usually recurring periodically. 2. A sudden outburst of emotion or activity.

pe·cu·li·ar·i·ty (pi kyü′lē ar′ə tē) *noun.* 1. A being peculiar; strangeness; oddness; unusualness. 2. Some little thing that is strange or odd.

pen·e·trate (pen′ə trāt) *verb.* 1. To get into or through. 2. To pierce through; make a way. 3. To soak through; spread through. 4. To see into; understand: I could not *penetrate* the mystery. **penetrated, penetrating.**

pen·sion (pen′shən) *noun.* A regular payment to a person which is not wages: A *pension* is paid by an employer to a person who is retired or disabled.

per·cep·ti·ble (pər sep′tə bəl) *adjective.* Able to be seen or heard; able to understand.—**perceptibility** *noun.*

per·fect (pėr′fikt) *adjective.* 1. Without defect; not spoiled at any point; faultless. 2. Completely skilled; expert. 3. Having all its parts; whole; complete.—(pər fekt′) *verb.* 1. To remove all faults from; to make perfect; add the finishing touches to. 2. To carry through; complete. **perfected, perfecting.**

per·me·ate (pėr′mē āt) *verb.* 1. To spread through the whole of; pass through: Smoke *permeated* the house. 2. To penetrate: Water will easily *permeate* cotton. **permeated, permeating.**

per·pet·u·al (pər pech′ü əl) *adjective.* 1. Lasting forever; eternal. 2. Lasting throughout life. 3. Never ceasing; continuous.

per·plex·i·ty (pər plek′sə tē) *noun.* 1. Perplexed condition; being puzzled; a not knowing what to do or how to act; confusion. 2. Something that perplexes.

pil·grim (pil′grəm) *noun.* 1. Person who goes on a journey to a sacred or holy place. 2. Traveler, wanderer.

pin·ion (pin′yən) *noun.* 1. The last joint of a bird's wing. 2. A wing.—*verb.* 1. To cut off or tie the pinions of (a

bird) to prevent flying. 2. To bind the arms of; bind: The bank robbers *pinioned* the guard's arms. **pinioned, pinioning.**

pin·to (pin′tō) *adjective.* Spotted in two or more colors.—*noun.* A spotted, white and black or white and brown horse.

pith (pith) *noun.* 1. The central, spongy tissue in the stems of certain plants. 2. The soft inner substance of a bone, feather, etc. 3. The important or essential part.

piv·ot (piv′ət) *noun.* Shaft, pin, or point on which something turns.—*verb.* 1. To mount on, attach by, or provide with a pivot. 2. To turn on a pivot. **pivoted, pivoting.**

piv·ot·al (piv′ə təl) *adjective.* 1. Of, having to do with, or serving as a point on which something turns. 2. Being that on which something turns, hinges, or depends; very important.

plain·tive (plān′tive) *adjective.* Mournful, sad—**plaintively** *adverb.*

plan·ta·tion (plan tā′shən) *noun.* A large farm or estate, especially in a tropical or semitropical region, on which cotton, tobacco, sugar cane, rubber trees, etc., are grown.

plaque (plak) *noun.* 1. An ornamental tablet of metal, porcelain, etc. 2. A platelike ornament or badge.

plau·si·ble (plô′zə bəl) *adjective.* 1. Appearing true, reasonable, or fair. 2. Apparently worthy of confidence but often not really so.

plum·met (plum′it) *verb.* To plunge, drop. **plummeted, plummeting.**

pock·marked (pok′märkt′) *adjective.* Marked with pocks, pimples, or pits on the skin caused by smallpox and certain other diseases.

pom·pous (pom′pəs) *adjective.* 1. Trying to seem magnificent; fond of display; acting proudly; self-important. 2. Characterized by pomp; splendid; magnificent; stately.

po·rous (pôr′əs) *adjective.* Full of pores or tiny holes through which water, air, etc., can pass: Cloth is *porous.*

po·tent (pōt′nt) *adjective.* Having great power; powerful; strong: a *potent* remedy for a disease.

prac·ti·tion·er (prak tish′ə nər) *noun.* Person engaged in the practice of a profession.

pre·con·ceived (prē′kən sēvd′) *adjective.* Formed beforehand: The

beauty of the scenery surpassed all our *preconceived* notions.

pre·dic·a·ment (pri dik′ə mənt) *noun.* An unpleasant, difficult, or bad situation.

pre·lim·i·nar·y (pri lim′ə ner′ē) *adjective.* Coming before the main business; leading to something more important.—*noun.* A preliminary step; something preparatory.

pre·mo·ni·tion (prē′mə nish′ən) *noun.* A forewarning.

pre·oc·cu·pied (prē ok′yə pīd) *adjective.* Absorbed, engrossed.

pre·side (pri zīd′) *verb.* 1. To hold the place of authority; have charge of a meeting. 2. To have authority; have control. **presided, presiding.**

prime (prīm) *adjective.* 1. First in rank; chief. 2. First in time or order; primary. 3. First in quality; first-rate; excellent.

pry (prī) *verb.* 1. To look with curiosity; peep. 2. To raise or move by force. 3. To get with much effort. **pried, prying.**

prob·a·bil·i·ty (prob′ə bil′ə tē) *noun.* 1. Quality or fact of being likely or probable; good chance. 2. Something likely to happen.

pro·duce (prō′düs) *noun.* Farm products, especially fruits and vegetables.—(prə düs′) *verb.* 1. To bring into existence; make. 2. To bring about; cause. **produced, producing.**

pro·fi·cient (prə fish′ənt) *adjective.* Advanced in any art, science, or subject; skilled; expert.—**proficiently** *adverb.*

pro·gram·mer (prō′gram′ər) *noun.* 1. Person who plans what is to be done. 2. Person who prepares a set of instructions for an electronic computer or other automatic machine outlining the steps to be performed by the machine in a specific operation.

prop·o·si·tion (prop′ə zish′ən) *noun.* 1. What is offered to be considered; proposal. 2. Statement. 3. Statement that is to be proved true.

pro·tract (prō trakt′) *verb.* To draw out; lengthen in time. **protracted, protracting.**

pro·trude (prō trüd′) *verb.* 1. To thrust forth; stick out: The turtle *protruded* its head. 2. To be thrust forth; project. **protruded, protruding.**

pro·tu·ber·ance (prō tü′bər əns) *noun.* Part that sticks out; bulge, swelling.

prov·erb (prov′ėrb′) *noun.* A short wise

, saying used for a long time by many people.

pro·voke (prə vōk′) *verb.* 1. To make angry; vex. 2. To stir up; excite. 3. To start into action; cause. **provoked, provoking.**

pru·dence (prüd′ns) *noun.* 1. Wise thought before acting; good judgment. 2. Good management; economy.

prune (prün) *noun.* Kind of sweet plum that is dried.—*verb.* 1. To cut out useless or undesirable parts from. 2. To cut unnecessary or undesirable twigs or branches from (a bush, tree, etc.) **pruned, pruning.**

psy·chi·at·ric (sī′kē at′rik) *adjective.* Of the treatment of mental and emotional disorders.

psy·chic (sī′kik) *adjective.* 1. Of the mind; mental. 2. Outside the known laws of physics; supernatural. —**psychically** *adverb.*

Q

quad·ru·ped (kwod′rə ped) *noun.* Animal that has four feet.

quaint (kwānt) *adjective.* Unusual in an interesting and pleasing way.

quar·ry (kwôr′ē) *noun.* 1. Place where stone is dug, cut or blasted out for use in building. 2. Animal chased in a hunt; game; prey.

qua·ver (kwā′vər) *verb.* 1. To shake tremulously; tremble. 2. To sing or say in trembling tones. **quavered, quavering.**

quip (kwip) *noun.* A clever or witty saying.—*verb.* To make a clever or witty saying. **quipped, quipping.**

quiv·er (kwiv′ər) *noun.* A case to hold arrows.

R

rack (rak) *noun.* A frame with bars, shelves, or pegs to hold, arrange, or keep things on.—*verb.* 1. To hurt very much. 2. To stretch; strain. **racked, racking.**

ra·di·ate (rā′dē āt) *verb.* 1. To give out rays of. 2. To issue in rays. 3. To give out; send forth. 4. To spread out from a center. **radiated, radiating.**

ram·page (ram′pāj) *noun.* Fit of rushing wildly about; spell of violent behavior; wild outbreak.

rav·age (rav′ij) *noun.* Violence; destruction; great damage.—*verb.* To damage greatly; lay waste; destroy. **ravaged, ravaging.**

re·cede (ri sēd′) *verb.* 1. To go backward; move backward; withdraw. 2. To slope backward. **receded, receding.**

rec·i·ta·tion (res′ə tā′shən) *noun.* 1. A telling of facts in detail. 2. A reciting of a prepared lesson by pupils before a teacher. 3. A repeating of something from memory.

re·coil (ri koil′) *verb.* 1. To draw back; shrink back: Most people would *recoil* at seeing a snake in the path. 2. To spring back. —(ri koil′ *or* rē′koil) *noun.* A drawing or springing back.

re·dou·ble (rē dub′əl) *verb.* 1. To double again. 2. To increase greatly; double. **redoubled, redoubling.**

re·fine (ri fīn′) *verb.* 1. To make or become pure: Sugar, oil, and metals are *refined* before being used. 2. To make or become fine, polished, or cultivated: *refine* one's way of speaking. **refined, refining.**

re·flec·tive (ri flek′tiv) *adjective.* 1. Able to reflect; reflecting. 2. Thoughtful.—**reflectively** *adverb.*

reg·i·men·ta·tion (rej′ə men tā′shən) *noun.* 1. Formation into organized or uniform groups. 2. A making uniform.

re·lapse (ri laps′) *noun.* A falling or slipping back into a former state or way of acting.—*verb.* To fall or slip back into a former state or way of acting. **relapsed, relapsing.**

rel·ish (rel′ish) *noun.* 1. A pleasant taste; good flavor. 2. Something to add flavor to food. 3. Liking, appetite, enjoyment.—*verb.* To like the taste of; like, enjoy. **relished, relishing.**

re·mit (ri mit′) *verb.* 1. To send money to a person or place. 2. To refrain from carrying out; cancel. 3. To pardon; forgive. **remitted, remitting.**

rep·e·ti·tious (rep′ə tish′əs) *adjective.* Full of repetitions; repeating in a tiring way.—**repetitiously** *adverb.*

rep·re·sent·a·tive (rep′ri zen′tə tiv) *noun.* 1. Person appointed or elected to act or speak for others. 2. A typical example; type.

re·press (ri pres′) *verb.* 1. To prevent from acting; check. 2. To keep down; put down; suppress. **repressed, repressing.**

re·served (ri zėrvd′) *adjective.* 1. Kept in reserve; kept by special arrangement. 2. Self-restrained in action or speech.

3. Disposed to keep to oneself: A *reserved* person does not make friends easily.

re·sid·u·al (ri zij′ü əl) *adjective.* Of or forming a residue; remaining, left over.

re·sound·ing (ri zound′ing) *adjective.* Emphatic, much talked about.

res·tive (res′tiv) *adjective.* 1. Restless; uneasy. 2. Hard to manage: a *restive* child. 3. Refusing to go ahead; balky.

res·ur·rect (rez′ə rekt′) *verb.* 1. To raise from the dead; bring back to life. 2. To bring back to sight, use, etc. **resurrected, resurrecting.**

rev·e·la·tion (rev′ə lā′shən) *noun.* 1. Act of making known. 2. The thing made known.

re·ver·ber·ate (ri vėr′bə rāt′) *verb.* To echo back. **reverberated, reverberating.**

ric·o·chet (rik′ə shā′) *noun.* The skipping or jumping motion of an object as it goes along a flat surface.—*verb.* To move with a skipping or jumping motion. **ricocheted, ricocheting.**

rit·u·al (rich′ü əl) *noun.* 1. A form or system of rites. 2. Any regularly followed routine.—*adjective.* Of rites; done as a rite.

riv·et (riv′it) *noun.* A metal bolt with a head at one end, the other end being hammered into a head after insertion: *Rivets* fasten heavy steel beams together.—*verb.* 1. To fasten with a rivet or rivets. 2. To fasten firmly; fix firmly: Their eyes were *riveted* on the speaker. **riveted, riveting.**

riv·u·let (riv′yə lit) *noun.* A very small stream.

rou·tine (rü tēn′) *noun.* A fixed, regular method of doing things; habitual doing of the same things in the same way.—*adjective.* 1. Using routine. 2. Average or ordinary; run-of-the-mill.

ruf·fi·an (ruf′ē ən) *noun.* A rough, brutal, or cruel person; bully; hoodlum.

rum·mage (rum′ij) *verb.* 1. To search thoroughly by moving things about. 2. To search in a disorderly way. **rummaged, rummaging.**

S

sar·don·ic (sär don′ik) *adjective.* Bitterly sarcastic, scornful, or mocking: a *sardonic* laugh.

sa·teen (sa tēn′) *noun.* A cotton cloth made to imitate satin.

scan (skan) *verb.* 1. To look at closely;

examine with care. 2. To glance at; look over hastily. **scanned, scanning.**

scav·enge (skav′ənj) verb. To pick over (discarded objects) for things to use or sell. **scavenged, scavenging.**

schol·ar·ship (skol′ər ship) noun. 1. Possession of knowledge gained by study; quality of learning and knowledge. 2. Money or other aid given to help a student continue his or her studies.

scor·pi·on (skôr′pē ən) noun. A small animal belonging to the same group as the spider and having a poisonous sting at the end of its tail.

scowl (skoul) verb. To look angry or sullen by lowering the eyebrows; frown.—noun. An angry, sullen look; frown. **scowled, scowling.**

sear (sir) verb. 1. To burn or char the surface of: The hot iron seared my hand. 2. To dry up; wither: The hot sun seared the grain. **seared, searing.**

self-cen·tered (self′sen′tərd) adjective. 1. Occupied with one's own interests and affairs. 2. Selfish.

sem·i·cir·cle (sem′i sėr′kəl) noun. Half a circle.

sen·ti·nel (sen′tə nəl) noun. Person stationed to keep watch and guard against surprise attacks.

sev·er (sev′ər) verb. 1. To cut apart; cut off. 2. To part; divide; separate. **severed, severing.**

shame faced (shām′fāst′) adjective. 1. Showing shame and embarrassment. 2. Bashful, shy.

shift·y (shif′tē) adjective. Not straightforward; tricky: shifty eyes, a shifty person.

shrewd (shrüd) adjective. Having a sharp mind; showing a keen wit; clever; keen, sharp.

shy (shī) verb. 1. To start back or aside suddenly: The horse shied at the newspaper blowing along the ground. 2. To throw; fling: The boy shied a stone at the tree. **shied, shying.**

sil·hou·ette (sil′ü et′) noun. A dark image outlined against a lighter background.—verb. To show in outline. **silhouetted, silhouetting.**

sing song (sing′sông′) noun. 1. A monotonous, up-and-down rhythm. 2. A monotonous tone or sound in speaking.—adjective. Monotonous in rhythm.

slith·er (slith′ər) verb. 1. To slide down or along a surface, especially

unsteadily. 2. To go with a sliding motion. **slithered, slithering.**

sock·et (sok′it) noun. A hollow part or piece for receiving and holding something.

sol·der (sod′ər) verb. To fasten, mend, or join with a melted metal or alloy. **soldered, soldering.**

so·lic·i·tude (sə lis′ə tüd) noun. Anxious care; anxiety; concern.

sor·rel (sôr′əl) noun. 1. A reddish brown. 2. A horse having this color. 3. Any of several plants with sour leaves.

spec·ter (spek′tər) noun. 1. Ghost. 2. Thing causing terror or dread.

spin·dle (spin′dl) noun. 1. The rod or pin used in spinning to twist, wind, and hold thread. 2. Any rod or pin that turns around, on which something turns.—verb. To grow very long and thin. **spindled, spindling.**

spon·ta·ne·ous (spon tā′nē əs) adjective. 1. Caused by natural impulse or desire; not forced or compelled; not planned beforehand. 2. Taking place without external cause or help; caused entirely by inner forces.—**spontaneously** adverb.

spree (sprē) noun. A short period of excessively engaging in a particular activity.

sprint·er (sprint′ər) noun. A person who runs at full speed, especially for a short distance.

spurn (spėrn) verb. 1. To refuse with scorn; scorn. 2. To strike with the foot; kick away. **spurned, spurning.**

stag·nant (stag′nənt) adjective. 1. Not running or flowing. 2. Foul from standing still. 3. Not active; sluggish; dull.

stam·i·na (stam′ə nə) noun. Strength; endurance: physical or moral stamina.

stand (stand) noun. A group of growing trees or plants.

start (start) verb. 1. To begin to move, go, or act. 2. To move suddenly. **started, starting.**

sta·tus (stā′təs) noun. 1. Social or professional standing; position; rank. 2. State; condition.

sti·fle (stī′fəl) verb. 1. To stop the breath of; smother. 2. To be unable to breathe freely; stop. 3. To keep back; suppress, stop. **stifled, stifling.**

stig·ma (stig′mə) noun. 1. A mark of disgrace or shame; stain or reproach on one's reputation. 2. Spot in the skin which bleeds or turns red.

stitch (stich) noun. 1. One complete movement of a threaded needle through cloth in sewing, or through skin, flesh, etc. in surgery. 2. Piece of cloth or clothing. 3. A sudden, sharp pain.

strat·e·gy (strat′ə jē) noun. 1. Science or art of war; planning and directing of large-scale military movements and operations. 2. The skillful planning and management of anything. 3. Plan based on strategy.

stren·u·ous (stren′yü əs) adjective. 1. Very active. 2. Full of energy. 3. Requiring much strength. —**strenuously** adverb.

stri·dent (strīd′nt) adjective. Making or having a harsh sound; creaking; grating; shrill.

sub·con·scious (sub kon′shəs) adjective. Not wholly conscious; existing in the mind but not fully perceived or recognized.—noun. Thoughts, feelings, etc., that are present in the mind but not fully perceived or recognized.

sub·due (səb dü′) verb. 1. To overcome by superior force; conquer. 2. To keep down; hold back; suppress. 3. To tone down; soften. **subdued, subduing.**

sub·mit (səb mit′) verb. 1. To yield to the power, control, or authority of some person or group; surrender, yield. 2. To refer to the consideration or judgment of some person or group. 3. To suggest or urge respectfully. **submitted, submitting.**

suf·fo·cate (suf′ə kāt) verb. 1. To kill by stopping the breath. 2. To keep from breathing; hinder in breathing. 3. To gasp for breath; choke. **suffocated, suffocating.**

suf·fuse (sə fyüz′) verb. To overspread. **suffused, suffusing.**

sul·try (sul′trē) adjective. 1. Hot, close, and moist. 2. Hot or fiery.

su·per·cil·i·ous (sü′pər sil′ē əs) adjective. Proud, haughty, and contemptuous; disdainful; showing scorn or indifference because of a feeling of superiority.—**superciliously** adverb.

sus·pi·cious (sə spish′əs) adjective. 1. Causing one to suspect. 2. Feeling suspicion; suspecting. 3. Showing suspicion.—**suspiciously** adverb.

sus·tain (sə stān′) verb. 1. To keep up keep going: Hope sustains her in her misery. 2. To supply with food, provisions, etc. 3. To hold up; support: Arches *sustain* the weight of the roof. 4. To bear; endure. 5. To suffer; experience. 6. To allow; admit; favor: The court *sustained* his suit.

swag·ger (swag′ər) *verb.* 1. To walk with a bold, rude, or superior air; strut about or show off in a vain or bragging way. 2. To boast or brag noisily. **swaggered, swaggering.**

switch (swich) *noun.* 1. A slender stick used in whipping. 2. A stroke or lash. 3. Device for making or breaking a connection in an electric circuit.

sym·pa·thet·ic (sim′pə thet′ik) *adjective.* 1. Having or showing kind feelings toward others; sympathizing. 2. Approving; agreeing. 3. Enjoying the same things and getting along well together. 4. Harmonious; agreeable. 5. Given to, marked by, or arising from sympathy, compassion, friendliness, and sensitivity to others' emotions.

T

taint (tānt) *noun.* 1. A stain or spot; trace of decay, corruption, or disgrace: No *taint* of scandal ever touched the mayor. 2. A cause of any such condition.—*verb.* 1. To give a taint to; spoil: Flies sometimes *taint* what they touch. 2. To become tainted; decay. **tainted, tainting.**

tan·dem (tan′dəm) *adjective.* Arranged one behind the other.—*noun.* 1. Two horses harnessed tandem. 2. Bicycle with two seats, one behind the other.

ten·ta·tive (ten′tə tiv) *adjective.* 1. Done as a trial or experiment; experimental: a *tentative* plan. 2. Hesitating: a *tentative* laugh.—**tentatively** *adverb.*

ten·u·ous (ten′yü əs) *adjective.* 1. Thin or slight; slender. 2. Not dense. 3. Having slight importance; not substantial.—**tenuously** *adverb.*

tep·id (tep′id) *adjective.* Slightly warm; lukewarm.

thatch (thach) *noun.* Straw, rushes, palm leaves, etc., used as a roof or covering.—*verb.* To roof or cover with thatch. **thatched, thatching.**

the·o·ry (thē′ə rē) *noun.* 1. An explanation based on observation and reasoning. 2. The principles or methods of a science or art rather than its practice. 3. Idea or opinion about something.

tor·tu·ous (tôr′chü əs) *adjective.* 1. Full

of twists, turns, or bends; twisting; winding; crooked. 2. Mentally or morally crooked; not straightforward.

tour·na·ment (tėr′nə mənt) *noun.* Series of contests testing the skill of many persons in some sport.

tou·sle (tou′zəl) *verb.* To put into disorder; make untidy; muss. **tousled, tousling.**

trac·tion (trak′shən) *noun.* 1. A drawing or pulling or a being drawn. 2. The drawing or pulling of loads along a road, track, etc. 3. Friction between a body and the surface on which it moves, enabling the body to move without slipping. 4. A pulling force exerted on a skeletal structure by means of a special device; a state of tension created by such a pulling force.

tra·di·tion·al (trə dish′ə nəl) *adjective.* 1. Of tradition. 2. Handed down by tradition. 3. Customary.

tran·sient (tran′shənt) *adjective.* 1. Passing soon; fleeting; not lasting. 2. Passing through and not staying long.—*noun.* Visitor or boarder who stays for a short time.

trans·la·tion (tran slā′shən) *noun.* 1. A translating or a being translated. 2. Result of translating; version.

trans·mit·ter (tran smit′ər) *noun.* 1. Person or thing that transmits something. 2. That part of a telegraph or telephone by which sound waves are converted to electrical impulses and sent to a receiver. 3. Device that sends out signals by means of electromagnetic waves.

trans·port (tran spôrt′) *verb.* 1. To carry from one place to another. 2. To carry away by strong feeling. **transported, transporting.**—(tran′spôrt) *noun.* 1. A carrying from one place to another. 2. Ship used to carry troops and supplies. 3. Aircraft that transports passengers, mail, freight, etc.

trans·pose (tran spōz′) *verb.* 1. To change the position or order of; interchange. 2. (in music) To change the key of. **transposed, transposing.**

trel·lis (trel′is) *noun.* Frame of light strips of wood or metal crossing one another with open spaces in between, especially one supporting growing vines.

tuft (tuft) *noun.* 1. Bunch of feathers, hair, grass, etc., held together at one end. 2. Clump of bushes, trees, etc. 3. Cluster of threads sewn tightly

through a mattress, comforter, etc., so as to keep the padding in place.

tur·bu·lence (tėr′byə ləns) *noun.* 1. Turbulent condition; disorder, tumult, commotion. 2. Irregular atmospheric motion especially when characterized by up and down currents; departure in a fluid from a smooth flow.

U

un·ceas·ing (un sēs′ing) *adjective.* Never ceasing; continuous; incessant. —**unceasingly** *adverb.*

un·com·pre·hend·ing (un kom′pri hend′ing) *adjective.* Not understanding the meaning of.—**uncomprehendingly** *adverb.*

un·daunt·ed (un dôn′tid) *adjective.* Not afraid; not discouraged; fearless.

un·der·es·ti·mate (un′dər es′tə māt) *verb.* To estimate at too low a value, amount, rate, etc. **underestimated, underestimating.** —(un′dər es′tə mit or un′dər es′tə māt) *noun.* An estimate that is too low.

un·furl (un fėrl′) *verb.* To spread out; shake out; unfold. **unfurled, unfurling.**

un·or·tho·dox (un ôr′thə doks) *adjective.* 1. Not generally accepted, especially in religion. 2. Not having generally accepted views or opinions, especially in religion; not adhering to established customs and traditions. 3. Not approved by convention; not usual; not customary.

un·pic·tur·esque (un pik′chə resk′) *adjective.* Not pleasing to the eye, not pretty.

un·prec·e·dent·ed (un pres′ə den′tid) *adjective.* Having no precedent; never done before; never known before.

un·yield·ing (un yēl′ding) *adjective.* Not yielding; not giving way; firm.

up·right (up′rīt′) *noun.* 1. Something standing erect; vertical part or piece. 2. An upright piano.

u·sur·er (yü′zhər ər) *noun.* A person who lends money at an extremely high or unlawful rate of interest.

V

vague (vāg) *adjective.* Not definite; not clear; not distinct.—**vaguely** *adverb.*

va·lid·i·ty (və lid′ə tē) *noun.* 1. Truth or soundness. 2. Legal soundness or force.

va·lise (və lēs′) *noun.* A traveling bag to

hold clothes.

vein (vān) *verb.* To cover with veins; mark with veins. **veined, veining.**

veld (velt) *noun.* Open country in South Africa, having grass or bushes but few trees.

ven·om·ous (ven′ə məs) *adjective.* 1. Poisonous: a *venomous* snake. 2. Spiteful; malicious.

ve·ran·da (və ran′də) *noun.* A large porch along one or more sides of a house.

verge (vėrj) *noun.* The point at which something begins or happens; brink.—*verb.* To be on the verge; border. **verged, verging.**

ver·min (vėr′mən) *noun.* 1. Small animals that are troublesome or destructive. 2. Very unpleasant or vile person or persons.

ver·sa·tile (vėr′sə təl) *adjective.* Able to do many things well.

ves·tige (ves′tij) *noun.* A slight remnant; trace, mark.

vile (vīl) *adjective.* 1. Very bad; wretched. 2. Foul, disgusting. 3. Evil, immoral.

vis·i·bil·i·ty (viz′ə bil′ə tē) *noun.* 1. Condition or quality of being seen;

visible. 2. Distance at which things are visible.

vi·tals (vī′tlz) *noun.* 1. Parts or organs necessary to life. 2. Essential parts or features.

viv·id (viv′id) *adjective.* 1. Strikingly bright; strong and clear; brilliant. 2. Full of life; lively. 3. Strong and distinct. 4. Very active or intense.—**vividly** *adverb.*

vo·cif·er·ous (vō sif′ər əs) *adjective.* Loud and noisy; shouting; clamoring: a *vociferous* person.

vul·gar (vul′gər) *adjective.* Showing a lack of good breeding, manners, taste, etc.; not refined; coarse; low.

vul·ner·a·ble (vul′nər ə bəl) *adjective.* 1. Capable of being wounded or injured; open to attack. 2. Sensitive to criticism; temptations, influences, etc.

W

wal·low (wol′ō) *verb.* 1. To roll about; flounder. 2. To live contentedly in filth, wickedness, etc. **wallowed, wallowing.**

wan·ton (won′tən) *adjective.* 1. Done in a reckless, heartless, or malicious way; done without reason or excuse. 2. Not restrained; frolicsome; playful. —**wantonly** *adverb.*

wa·ter·logged (wô′tər logd′) *adjective.* 1. So full of water that it will barely float. 2. So filled or soaked with water as to be heavy or hard to manage.

whim·sy (hwim′zē) *noun.* 1. An odd or fanciful notion. 2. Odd or fanciful humor; quaintness.

whirl·pool (hwėrl′pül′) *noun.* Current of water whirling round and round rapidly and violently.

wind·fall (wind′fôl′) *noun.* 1. Fruit blown down by the wind. 2. An unexpected piece of good luck.

X, Y, Z

zeal (zēl) *noun.* Eager desire or effort; earnest enthusiasm: work with *zeal*.